Ethics and Christology in John's Gospel

Biblical Hermeneutics Rediscovered

The Series as the name suggests will focus on Biblical Hermeneutics, i.e., literary works concerned with methods of interpreting the Old and New Testaments of Bible via different stream of topics like Literature & Poetry, Indigenous Philosophizing, Ethical response towards Ecology, Health & Healing, Science & Technology, Feminist Theology, Sociological approach towards Human Rights, Law & Politics, Arts, History of Ideas, Ancient Civilizations, Cultural Contiguity, Religious Cosmologies & Mysticism, Appraisal of various Theologians, World Peace & Harmony, Global Capitalism, Network Marketing, Cybertheology, Population & Demographics, Epigraphic Studies, Contextualized Education, and many others. We welcome a Mss. on any topic/s mentioned, whether they are original works, scholarly monographs, collections of conference papers, revised dissertations, or translations of historical documents. Through the Series we, the Publishers, are striving to put forward published works that may help Institutions, Academic Bodies, Researchers, Scholars and the World at large in furthering their respective knowledge and understanding on the concerned subject. We welcome your comments on our efforts and further suggestions on how we can enshrine new ray of analysing & explaining the written Texts through our upcoming books.

Biblical Hermeneutics Rediscovered - 36

Ethics and Christology in John's Gospel

Huten Donhring Anal

Christian World Imprints

First Published in 2020 by

Christian World Imprints
Christian Publishing & Books from India
C-3, Wazirpur Industrial Area
Delhi-110052
cwidelhi2017@gmail.com
www.ChristianWorldImprints.com
Phone: +91 11 41526079

ISBN: 978-93-5148-490-5

Printed in India.

Contents

This book in its original form is the thesis submitted to the Senate of Serampore College, towards the D.Th degree and is published with written permission. The candidate is responsible for the title, contents and opinions expressed in it. The title of the dissertation has been reframed to the present title for the purpose of publication. The candidate is accountable for framing the topic, methodology applied, arguments in place to support the propositions, the materials consulted and the conclusions arrived at.

Acknowledgement

I am thrilled and obliged to express my deepest gratitude to a host of people who have stood and supported me in various aspects: Intellectually, morally, financially and in much prayer. Had it not been for these people, this dissertation would not have taken this present form. First of all, I stand in awe before the Holy presence of our living almighty God with immense feeling of gratitude for putting in my heart to undertake this research work. His constant guidance by the power of the Holy Spirit has provided, guided and sustained me throughout these years of my research project.

Rev. ST Colling Anal my dear husband who has allowed me to pursue my doctoral study and for his constant support in all matters of financial assistances in spite of so many challenges that were cropping up in between. My three little angels, Seltun Kolhring, Seltun Warriihring and Seltun Unsahman who made my motherhood experience worth. They brought me enough challenges to make me realize how awesome and difficult it is to undertake study in such a time when my presence was badly needed to cater their early childhood needs. I am profoundly thankful to my sister-in-law (esp. Seltun Hmanna) for taking care of my two older children in my absence.

The Rev. Janet Roberts Echols and family who have instilled in me the initial courage to look forward to this research study. Their timely financial support has bolstered my appetite for academic career during the time of my financial struggles. My mother and elder sisters Dr. HT. Julhlung, HT. Shanti, HT. Shangshung, Dr. HT. Rozy Veronica and HT. Joyni, my only brother HT. David and brother-in-laws (esp. Rev. SR. Onesima and PS. Tanghring) without whose moral, prayer and generous financial supports I would not have been able to complete my dissertation. And not to forget my niece Sumpi Christani Anal who volunteered to bear my up-down airfares for my D.Th convocation at Senate of Serampore College.

Fr. Dr. Reji Mathew, my supervisor, has been a compassionate mentor throughout the years of my research endeavor. He diligently mentored me through his comments, suggestions and corrections. He patiently went through my research work for which I cannot thank him enough. I will always be indebted to him for his intellectual contribution towards my research work.

I extend my gratitude to Dr. Johnson Thomaskutty who helped me to get the soft copy material required for my research work.

I owe thanks to Dr. Feba Christopher, Maisuangdibou, Christy Abraham, Minchong, Igumpeule, Kigolui Rangkau, Pancilia Thawmuit and others whom I cannot mention them all for their timely help in their respective capacities.

Not the least, I am also very grateful to the MTTS Principal, Rev. Dr. Prakash K. George for accommodating me in the Ladies hostel during my extension period (2017) at MTTS, Kottayam.

Preface

The Church since its inception has turned to the Bible, particularly the New Testament for moral guidance and has embraced the Canonical Scripture as the normative part of her moral tradition. The moral teachings of the New Testament have been considered relevant and essential to illuminate and guide the church's moral and ethical decisions. Eventually, for Christians, the Bible has been the primary guiding yardstick for their faith in Christ Jesus and as a matter of fact, the New Testament has significantly occupied a vital and immense place in the hearts of Christian community. As a consequence, the ethical contents of the New Testament are continually employed for preaching, teaching, nurturing, and edifying the Christian community. The Scripture for years continues to be an authoritative ethical source for believing Christians communities.

Christians in the past and even now have been profoundly influenced by the narratives of the life and ministry, death and resurrection of Jesus of Nazareth as recorded in the Gospel(s). Especially the Gospel of John[1] has spoken to our experience as a Christian in a very significant way over the centuries. Behind the Gospel narrative stands the perennial ethical challenge of the life and teaching of Jesus, who is the logos incarnate later identified as the Son of God, the Son of Man, and who is the promised Christ comes from the Father God, into the world to offer us life eternal. The salvific divine revelation of God in Jesus of Nazareth is seen through his life, activities (or say 'signs' (*semeia*) in Johannine terminology), death and resurrection. John's Gospel has delivered a clear and concise meaning of ethics for his first century readers and the subsequent future readers. His artistry showcases that while his central focus is on the consciousness of who Jesus is, he has definitely brought ethical significance in harmony with Christology. The Fourth Gospel narrates to us the story of Jesus (who He is, for what and why He came) in a very unique and certain way that catches our attention so deeply. The evangelist of the Fourth Gospel who wrote Jesus' story to the circle of his intended

1 The phrase 'the Gospel of John (or simply John's Gospel)' and 'the Fourth Gospel' will be interchangeably used in this book, and all Scripture references refer to the New Revised Standard Version of the Bible.

readers, the so-called Johannine Community must have definitely spoken to their experience as they might have believed and accepted it as their story. The legacy that the intended readers of the Gospel of Jesus of the first century passed it on to the next generation of believers continues to be applicable and relevant for us today (implied readers). Likewise as believers in Jesus Christ we have the moral responsibility to pass on the same legacy to our immediate generation(s).

This work primarily concentrates on the writings of John's Gospel, and prefer to call the author of the Gospel as 'John' for convenience sake without discussing the question of who he might have been. Nevertheless with the acceptance of the fact that in all probabilities John seems to have been a disciple very close to Jesus, 'the beloved disciple' who is highly responsible to pass the heritage from Palestine and from Jesus (Jn. 19:26, 35; 21:20, 24). It is obvious at the first glance of reading that the Fourth Gospel lacks specific and precise rules for the direction of every circumstance of behavior. But this has to be answered by stating the nature of the Gospel that it is not written as an ethical treatise. As such, method that seriously considers the literary and rhetoric aspects will be of great significance in unfolding the narrative of the Fourth Gospel how it persuaded its intended reader/s then, and continues to persuade us now as modern readers to live a moral and ethical life. Precisely speaking, attention will be given to the narrative structure and the manner in which the narrative communicates its ethical implications. So, the absence of specific ethical directives however do not stop us from further exploration of the possibility to unveil what might have been there (*in the text*) besides the conventional understanding of ethical directives (example, as is in the case of the Sermon on the Mount).

This work proceeds with an assumption that there is much more to what has often been thought of ethics in the Gospel of John. The journey is dedicated to establish the inter-connection that may have existed between ethics and Christology in the Gospel of John as we have it before us today (*in front of the text*). Congruently, detailed attention is given to the ethical pointers or indicators in order to draw the ethical significance within the body of the Gospel of John. The approach is largely governed by the acceptance that Johannine Gospel has a wealth of ethical importance. So, respecting the social context of the Johannine community facing its own particular problem of faith and conduct, we allow the individuality and integrity of the uniqueness of the Gospel in addressing the concrete situation of his time and then giving concrete moral exhortations. This attention however is approached by means of narrative study which considers both the spatial and temporal flow of the text. The narrative reading evolves in particular space and time. Close attention is given to the narrative reading of the text, as an implied reader and attempt to discover the importance of the ethical message encoded in the narrative literary style of the Gospel of John, which unfolds in the course of reading the text *behind*, *in* and *in front*. So, the focus is to read the Gospel of John as a unified narrative and not decompartmentalizing or dissecting narrative blocks as though they are independent[2] but read the references of the passages of the text as qualifying and complementing to one another rather than taking them as in tension. Francis J. Moloney rightly asserts that,

> What the real author of the Fourth Gospel desired to communicate can be rediscovered only through a careful investigation of the story as a finished and carefully constructed whole. Thus, attention must be given to a particular shape of its narrative unit within the Fourth Gospel and to an explanation of that unit, both in terms of its own internal message and in terms of the shape and message of the Fourth Gospel as whole.[3]

Repetitions may occur to emphasize the crux of the essential message. The present work is primarily dedicated to navigate into the relationship between ethics and Christology in the Gospel of John. Besides, it is committed to identify its core characteristics and then understand its implications, relevance and to contribute to our contemporary Christian ethical discernment to remain faithful, obedience and loyal to our Lord Jesus Christ who continues to guide us by the Spirit-*Paraclete* in our everyday living.

'To believe' (and its noun form 'faith') and 'love' are two fundamental ethical components of ethics in John's Gospel. They are supreme ethics of faith and love combined to understand the essence of ethics as presented by the Fourth Gospel. Faith and love are two essential ethical virtues that are pulled together to explicate what entails ethics in the Gospel of John. Faith is human which evolves from a believing heart in response to the revelation of Jesus by His words and deeds as coming from the bosom of the Father (Jn.1:18) entering into the reality of this world (became flesh Jn. 1:14) and revealed the glory of God and his (17:6, 26, etc) by the *semeia* he performed (Jn. 10:24, 37, 38; 20:31). These *semeia* was a purposeful selection to call upon faith on the part of those who witnessed them (and also to the readers). Faith, however, is rooted in response to the *semeia* of

2 The Gospel of John reflects a literary process that may have involved several successive authors and subsequent redactors (eg. John 20:31 indicates that the literary written work of the Gospel ended here. But it is commonly acknowledged that the epilogue (ch. 21) in the Gospel was added to an earlier form of the Gospel).

3 Francis J. Moloney, *Belief in the Word* (Minneapolis: Fortress Press, 1993), 5-6. He puts forward some of the important attention that needs to be considered in the identification of narrative units and an understanding of their relationship to one another in the Gospel as a whole. That is the use of the rhetoric by the author such as relationship between incidents, inclusions, the use of key words, direct and indirect speech, foreshadowing and retrospection, double-meaning words, the deliberate use of misunderstanding and irony. Besides, attention also must be devoted to the details of time, scenes, space, and character in determining to understand the relationship that exists within the Gospel as a whole. For similar idea, see Richard B. Hays, *The Moral Vision of the New Testament: A Contemporary Introduction to New Testament Ethics* (New York: Harper Collins, 1996), 140.

Jesus. The performances of these *semeia* are of paramount importance in more than one aspect – it serves as a vehicle to reveal God's glory through Jesus – reveals the true identity of Jesus – so reveals the underlying motivational purpose that which is divine love – intention to evoke faith to the viewers (here faith is seen as a demand on human beings to commit themselves to faith in Jesus the Christ) – that may eventually lead to eternal life – the ultimate goal of eternity. So, we can assume the multi-purpose significance of *semeia* in John's Gospel. Behind the performance of 'signs' lies the divine love mission of God. As such, to delineate ethical principles in the Fourth Gospel, faith and love together takes complementary importance in defining the true essence of ethics.

This work is dedicated to all believers in Jesus Christ and to anyone who is committed to virtuous living in this world where there is a huge gap or a mismatch between one's faith and his/her ethical conduct. May the footprints that the community of believers leave before us in telling and retelling *of* and *about* the life and ministry, death and resurrection , and the second coming of Jesus Christ make sense so much so that we continue the tradition of passing on this ethical legacy to our subsequent generations. And most importantly, the ethical challenge to remain in our faith in Jesus as sent by God, earnestly obey the commandment Jesus gave to 'love one another' as he has loved us and to continue the work of testifying about the salvific works of God accomplished in and through Jesus be the portion of our everyday living as disciples of Jesus Christ. May every believer in Christ Jesus affirm the enduring power of the Gospel of Jesus Christ as narrated in the Fourth Gospel. May the impinging empowering work of the Holy Spirit of God be affirmed in our lives and society always.

List of Abbreviations

Alphabetical order

Ant.	=	Jewish Antiquities
ANTC	=	Abington New Testament Commentaries
B.C. E.	=	Before the Common Era
BTB	=	Biblical Theology Bulletin
ca./c	=	*circa* (about), used to indicate an appropriate date
C.E.	=	Common Era
cf.	=	*confer* (compare)
ch.	=	Chapter
Chron.	=	Chronicles
chs.	=	Chapters
Cor.	=	Corinthian
Dan.	=	Daniel
Deut.	=	Deuteronomy
DSSE	=	Dead Sea Scrolls in English
e.g.	=	*exempli gratia* (for example)
E.N.	=	*Ethica Nicomachea* (*Nicomachean Ethics*)
Eccls.	=	Eclesiastus
Ecclus.	=	Ecclesiasticus
EDNT	=	Exegetical Dictionary of the New Testament
Esd.	=	Esdras
Esp.	=	especially
Exod.	=	Exodus
f.	=	following, used after a page, verse, or paragraph number to mean 'also the next.'
Gal.	=	Galatians
Gen.	=	Genesis
Heb.	=	Hebrews
Hos	=	Hosea

HTR	=	Harvard Theological Review
i.e.	=	*id est* (that is)
ibid.	=	the same, used as an footnote to mean ' the same work as the one just cited.'
IDB	=	The Interpreter's Dictionary of the Bible
Isa.	=	Isaiah
ISPCK	=	Indian Society for the Promotion of Christian Knowledge
JBL	=	*Journal of Biblical Literature.*
JETS	=	Journal of the Evangelical Theological Society
Jn.	=	John
JSNTSS	=	Journal for the Study of New Testament Supplement Series
Kgs.	=	Kings
Lev	=	Leviticus
Lk	=	Luke
Macc.	=	Maccabees
Matt.	=	Matthew
Mk.	=	Mark
MTTS	=	Mar Thoma Theological Seminary
Neh	=	Nehemiah
NIB	=	New Interpreter's Bible
NIV	=	New International Version
NovTsup	=	Novum Testamentum, Supplements
NTS	=	New Testament Studies
NT	=	New Testament
Num.	=	Numbers
Pet.	=	Peter
Phipp.	=	Philippians
Ps	=	Psalm
QS	=	Rule of the Community from Qumran
RevQ	=	Quarterly Review
Rom.	=	Romans
Sam.	=	Samuel
SPCK	=	Society for the Promotion of Christian Knowledge
TDNT	=	Theological Dictionary of the New Testament
Tim.	=	Timothy
vol.	=	volume
WBC	=	Word Biblical Commentary
WUNT	=	Wissenschaftliche Untersuchungen zum Nuen Testament
ZNW	=	*Zeitschrift fur die Neutestamentliche Wissenschaft*

Introduction

1.1. Background of the Research

There is a lack of scholarly attention given to the ethical thrust in John's Gospel and to understand the distinct presentation of what entails ethics in the Fourth Gospel. This consequently, fails to see the interconnectedness between Christology and ethics in the Gospel of John. Hence, the distinct embodiment and development of Johannine ethics within Christological articulation (in John's Gospel) deserves attention which has for centuries been missed out by most scholars.

1.2. An Elaboration

The theme of ethics is very central to human behavior. Surprisingly, there has been no serious study undertaken to analyze the ethical emphasis in the Fourth Gospel. There is therefore lack of scholarly attention to the pertinent ethical thrust in John's Gospel. The modern Johannine studies projects a misunderstood impression that John's Gospel has little or no ethical importance. For the past many centuries in the academic exercise of the New Testament studies on ethics, scholars who devote themselves in this particular study find no place/reason or if at least a very insignificant place for the Fourth Gospel to contribute to the understanding of the New Testament studies. It has been assumed that John's Gospel indicates no ethical interest. As an effect, there is certainly a failure to see how John's Christological articulation may inform the ethical teachings embedded in it. Most scholars have advocated that John's Gospel contributes nothing useful in determining issues related to New Testament ethics. For instance, J. L. Houlden commented that the Fourth Gospel "accords a minimal role to autonomous ethics."[1] Consequently, in the general investigations of the New Testament, John's Gospel is either sided insignificant or given a very little space. This surfaced the issue signifying the noticeable lack of interest given to Johannine ethics. There are considerably fewer explicit references on the teaching of ethics in John's Gospel, as compared to the synoptic and other New Testament documents (especially that

1 J. L. Houlden, *Ethics and the New Testament* (London: T&T Clark, 1992), 35.

of Pauline writings) and a few scholars have even dismissed the necessity to talk about the ethics in John's Gospel.[2] But, this however is not to sideline the studies done in this respect of Johannine ethics because there are few recent articles though no monographs thus far.[3] There is no full-scale treatment of Johannine ethics. The lack of present biblical scholarship suggests that there is a need for further exploration in the area of Johannine ethical dimensions. The Gospel as unique as it stands is characterized by its distinctive literary style in driving home the intended religious message to his/her[4] intended audience. Lack of vice and virtues do not suggest lack of ethical concerns but one should be open to accept John's liberty to express in a rather distinctive way – the ethical concern. John,[5] a good interpreter and a good narrator, immensely impressed the readers of his time and later generations to go behind the text for a deeper message which is figuratively or dramatically presented. There are significant ethical indicators/ pointers embedded within Christological articulation which demand a critical analysis of the text.

---

2 W. A. Meeks, "The Ethics of the Fourth Evangelist," *Exploring the Gospel of John: Essays in Honor of D. Moody Smith*, edited by R. Alan Culpepper & C. Clifton Black (Louisville, Kentucky: Westminster John Knox Press, 1996), 317-326.

3 Jan G. van der Watt, "Ethics Alive in Imagery," *Imagery in the Gospel of John: Terms, Forms, Themes, and Theology of Johannine Figurative Language,* edited by Jorg Frey, Jan G. van der Watt and Ruben Zimmermann (Tubingen: Mohr Siebeck, 2006), 421-448; *idem*, "Radical Social Redefinition and Radical Love: Ethics and Ethos in the Gospel According to John," *Identity, Ethics, and Ethos in the New Testament,* edited by Jan G. van der Watt (Berlin: De Gruyter, 2006), 107-134; Janos Bolyki, "Ethics in the Gospel of John," *Communio Viatorum*, 45 (2003): 63-80; D. Moody Smith, "Ethics and the Interpretation of the Fourth Gospel of John," *Word, Theology, and Community in John,* edited by John Painter, R. Alan Culpepper, and Fernando F. Segovia (St. Louis, Miss.: Chalice Press, 2002), 109-122; Jey J. Kanagaraj, "The Implied Ethics of the Fourth Gospel: A Reinterpretation of the Decalogue," *Tyndale Bulletin* 52/1 (2001): 33-60; Johannes Nissen, "Community and Ethics in the Gospel of John," *New Readings in John: Literary and Theological Perspectives*, edited by Johannes Nissen and Sigfred Pederson (Sheffield: Sheffield Academic Press, 1999), 194-212; Meeks, "The Ethics of the Fourth Evangelist," 317-326.

4 The grammatical usage of the pronouns (he/she) is in respect to some scholars who have argued that the author of the Fourth Gospel could probably be a woman. Of course I am not much inclined to this contention though. Compare, Robert Tomson Fortna, *The Fourth Gospel and Its Predecessor* (Philadelphia: Fortress Press, 1988), 7-8.

5 As early as the second century the Fourth Gospel was traditionally titled "the Gospel according to John." But who is John or who is the "Beloved Disciple" (19:26-35; 20:2; 13:23) is debated. There are different proposals for who is the Beloved Disciple. For details see R. Alan Culpepper, *John, the Son of Zebedee: The Life of a Legend* (Minneapolis: Fortress Press, 2000), 72-83. Keeping aside, the debated issue of authorship, John 19:35 and 21:24 attest the Gospel to be written by someone who was an eyewitness of the events of Jesus' life. However, without assuming John, son of Zebedee as the author of the Gospel, the researcher would use the name John for convenience sake.

This work will address such understanding which proposes that there are little or minimal significant ethical teachings of Jesus in the Gospel of John.[6] For more instances, Meeks states that "one cannot and should not speak of ethics in John's Gospel."[7] So, also, Sanders commented on the Johannine ethics as one which is weak and morally bankrupted.[8] Wolfgang Schrage sees an almost total absence of specific injunctions or detailed paraenetic passages for a discussion of ethics in John's Gospel and therefore poses a question if at all "Johannine writings even belongs in a book on the ethics of the New Testament" and better "limit ourselves to evaluating the place of John within the theology of the New Testament."[9] Birger Gerhardson contends that the Love commandment becomes the *only* significant ethical theme in Johannine writings[10] and Houlden went even further stating that John's primary concern is not ethical at all.[11] Scholars who have worked on the ethics of the New Testament devoted little space to the discussion of Johannine ethics with very few comments.[12] However, this is to downplay the author's distinctively framed concept with underlying implication, which, however is not laid vibrantly on the surface. Lack of explicit ethical teachings does not guarantee any denial for ethical concerns expressed in the Fourth Gospel. Fewer or no explicit references to ethics do not therefore imply the total lack of ethical elements in the Gospel of John. In fact, ethics in John's Gospel is dramatized through narrative discourse rather than simply communicated through didactic teachings. It is acted out by Jesus himself as an ideal pattern and as an essential quality to be emulated for the believing community. Therefore, this work will argue for the important pointers within Christological articulation to identify ethics in John's Gospel.

Johannine ethics is intrinsically Christo-centric in nature and as such ethics in John's Gospel depicts a chief significance that demands intensive study. Johannine Christology being one of the dominant themes that controls the other aspects of theology (for instance, eschatology, ecclesiology, Holy spirit, etc)

---

6 Donald Guthrie, *New Testament Theology* (Illinois: Inter-Varsity Press, 1981), 907.

7 Meeks, "The Ethics of the Fourth Evangelist," 317-326.

8 Jack T. Sanders, *Ethics in the New Testament: Change and Development* (London: SCM Press Ltd, 1975), 34.

9 Wolfgang Schrage, *The Ethics of the New Testament*, translated by David E. Green (Philadelphia: Fortress Press, 1988), 297.

10 Birger Gerhardsson, *Ethos of the Bible*, translated by Stephen Westerholm (Eugene: Wipf & Stock Publishers, 1981), 98.

11 Houlden, *Ethics and the New Testament*, 35-41.

12 For instance, Richard A. Burridge, *Imitating Jesus: An Inclusive Approach to New Testament Ethics* (Michigan: Wm. B. Eerdmanns Publishing Company, 2007), 285-346; Richard B. Hays, *The Moral Vision of the New Testament: A Contemporary Introduction to New Testament Ethics* (Edinburgh: T&T Clark, 1997), 138-157; Frank J. Matera, *New Testament Ethics: The Legacies of Jesus and Paul* (Louisville, Kentucky: Westminster John Knox Pres, 1996), 92-117; Schrage, *Ethics of the New Testament*, 297-319.

is highly intertwined with the concept of ethics in the Gospel of John. Matera had contended that, "the gospel exemplifies à Christological implosion so that ethics becomes Christology."[13] Likewise, ethics, which is theologically related, is essentially the offshoot of God's character himself. And most interestingly, Johannine Jesus is said to be the ultimate reflection of God's own character. For that reason, Johannine ethics which is highly Christological resonates the broader aspect of Johannine theology and it is essentially relational which demands a human response. This suggests that ethics springs from the right understanding of who God is in and through Jesus and His dealings with the humankind. To reiterate, Johannine ethics is Christologically stanched and therefore has a high Christological significance for understanding Christian ethics in our world today.

Contrast to the subscription of the view that there are no significant ethical teachings in John's Gospel, the present work is an attempt to state that there are significant ethical dimensions embedded within Christological articulation which henceforth requires to explore the connection that exist between ethics and Christology in the Fourth Gospel. So, as far as the researcher reading and observation is concerned, there has been no (extensive) investigation carried out to see the connection of ethics and Christology content in the Gospel i.e., a close connection that exists between Christology and ethics is not distinctively established yet. The inter-connection of Johannine ethics and Johannine Christology is so pertinent and are indispensably linked which is profoundly central to the thought of the author of the gospel in presenting the ethical obligation for the believing community. The Johannine Christology which is the pertinent inbuilt of the Gospel content serves as veritable model on how to behave in and outside the community. Johannine ethics and Christology are inseparably intertwined in as much as the contained of the Fourth Gospel is concerned in explicating the ethical obligation of the community. So, the main purpose of the work is to investigate the connection between ethics and Christology in the Gospel. Where Jesus' identity illuminated by his very deeds generates the motivation for the believers to realize the ethical obligation about the correct ethical response to the circumstances and challenges in which they live. The validity of Johannine Christology that pertinently impacts the ethical behavior of the Johannine community is well supported by several pieces of the material, language and thought contained in the Gospel. Christology becomes the interpretive and defining key to right ethical living in the Johannine community and which is still binding for our contemporary society today. Congruently, it is an attempt to draw how ethics and Christology are inter-connected that is basically the relationship that exists between these two aspects and delineate some significant characteristics of Johannine ethics from the Gospel of John. Though some scholars would still say Johannine community is esoteric and eventually the ethical implication was restricted to the core Johannine community, the

13 Matera, *New Testament Ethics*, 93.

researcher would however endorse that Johannine ethics has a wider implication for all humanity that includes today's 21st century society.

1.3. Previous Research

It is clear from the previous section of the paragraph that there is no definite denial that John's Gospel lacks ethical contents. Though the Gospel may relatively contain less ethical teachings as compared to the rest of the New Testament documents, it is nevertheless not an option to rebuff some of the prime ethical contents contained in the Gospel. Interestingly at the very recent year in May 2010, there was a conference on Ethics in the Johannine Literature at Nijmegen, which upholds the significant presence of ethical teaching at various levels in the Johannine literature. This indeed is a new interest and a shift from the old consensus to a new interest that has provoked scholars to dig out unattended ethical teachings embedded in the literature. Ruben Zimmermann has vibrantly worked and presented a paper on the Nijmegen Conference, entitled - *What is "Ethics in John"? Challenging an outdated Consensus*. It is a very stimulating paper as the sub-title suggested - *Challenging an outdated consensus* (No ethics in John). It is fairly a well work work which gives a telling concluding remark on John's Gospel as enabling "different readers in various situations to act concretely."[14] This sufficiently indicates an enriching ethical aspect of John's Gospel from the past and continuing to reach into the 21st century of our everyday lives. Some Biblical scholars have talked of John's presentation of the Gospel being undergirded by Jewish ethics which is embodied in the phrase 'keep my commandments' in the Gospel.[15] So, also William Loader has addressed the significance of the Law (Torah) in relation to the understanding of Johannine ethics.[16] In line with the contention that John's Gospel affirms the ongoing validity of the Law, it signifies then that John's Gospel has much to say about ethics in spite of the absence of rich ethical teachings that are present in the Synoptic such as, the Sermon on the Mount and ethical elements like virtues and vices found in Pauline letters.[17] Culpepper further acknowledges that there however is a distinctive Johannine theological ethic which is clear: "a dualistic worldview, the new commandment to love one

14 Zimmermann taking up Meeks' main argument that John's Gospel does not serve as a vehicle of moral instruction and is therefore inappropriate to talk of ethics in the Fourth Gospel, challenges this consensus by setting up four objections from – phenomenological, methodological, form critical, and tradition-historical perspectives.

15 Kanagaraj, "The Implied Ethics of the Fourth Gospel: A Reinterpretation of the Decalogue," 33- 60.

16 A paper presented at the Nijmegen conference on Ethics in the Johannine Literature (May, 2010).

17 R. Allan Culpepper, "Anti-Judaism in the Fourth Gospel as a Theological Problem for Christian Interpreters," *Anti- Judaism and the Fourth Gospel*, edited by R. Bieringer, D. Pollefeyt, and F. Vandecastelle-Vanneuville (Louisville: Westminster John Knox Press, 2001), 61-82.

another, and the model of Jesus."[18] John's Gospel has a distinctive Christological ethic in its nature and character. Jan G. van der Watt's article, "Ethics Alive in Imagery," speaks clear enough to find ethical contents in the Gospel. In this article, Watt illustrates the ethical dimensions of the Gospel by John's animated usage of imageries.[19] Such precedent work prompts us toward further exploration for Johannine ethics from a new perspective[20] to find the integral connection and establish the relation between ethics and Christology.

It may lead to an over sweeping remark to content the absence of ethics in John's Gospel except for the *only* explicit ethical content in John 13:34; 15:12, where Jesus commands to love one another as he has loved[21] and this passage has also been viewed as restricting only within the Johannine community (by Houlden). Lack of explicit ethical language (as normally understood) does not rule out the fact that John's gospel lacks ethical concerns. Though relatively less explicit ethical teaching is to be found in John's gospel, one must be very careful to infer minimal importance to Johannine ethics within the broad spectrum of the New Testament ethics. Jesus "a man from heaven' is laden with ethical implications for the community that accepts the message and finds itself rejected by the world."[22] John's Gospel standing out uniquely from the rest of the Gospels is characterized by a very profound theological message. The idea of ethics is expressed in a way that is different from its presentation in the other New Testament documents. Anyone who reads the Gospel material very intuitively is possibly taken on a higher plane this is because of the profundity of the Gospel. The Fourth Gospel has been popularly described as a pool in which a child can wade and an elephant can swim. One cannot simply understand the depth and width of the ethical message conveyed just at the face value. It demands an inquisitive heart and mind to dive deep and get oneself transposed to a step further to grasp what is said beyond words. In addition, one cannot therefore be limiting him/herself to find the same ethical language/issues found in the rest of the New Testament. The ethical language and thought takes a different height in the Gospel of John which demands a more careful and critical observation than that meets the eye at the first sight. So, the nature of the Gospel demands a closer look and move a further step "beyond explicit ethical commands and turn to the actions of figures in John's narrative to determine" about appropriate ethical conduct.[23] The identity

---

18 Culpepper, "Anti-Judaism in the Fourth Gospel," 61-82.

19 van der Watt, "Ethics Alive in Imagery," 421-448.

20 Here a new perspective might mean to *expand* the horizon of the understanding of ethics more than a mere collection of moral laws and their interpretation.

21 Schrage, *The Ethics of the New Testament*, 297; Matera, *New Testament Ethics*, 92; Nissen, "Community and Ethics in the Gospel of John," 194.

22 Nissen, "Community and Ethics in the Gospel of John," 199.

23 Andrew T. Glicksman, "Light, Truth, and Time: Ethical Connections between Old Testament Wisdom Literature and John's Gospel" *A Paper Presented During Conference: Ethics in the*

of Jesus as the truth and light exerts important ethical implications, because he reveals and exemplifies what constitutes an appropriate behavior (Jn. 8:12). Jesus models a pattern of conduct for his disciples (Jn. 13:1-12) and for those who will believe in Him because of the testimony of his disciples. Especially in the second half of the Fourth Gospel, that is, in the farewell discourse, there are considerable moral exhortations. We shall come to realize how Johannine Christology has influenced, established and shaped the perception of the Johannine community in their eschatological existence (living in the eschatological age but yet to be fully realized in the future *aeon*).

1.4. Significance of the Work

The purpose of this work is to bring to the forefront the Christological significance in understanding Johannine ethics and thereby contribute to the scholarship of Johannine literature. The work also looks forward to venturing into a new look (ethical aspects) at the Johannine writings and thereby laying this interest as a foundational work and pave the way for other aspiring Johannine scholars to explore from other variant angles. Subsequently, this work will contribute to the expansion of Johannine theme studies and might also be conducive for more intellectual, logical, and practical implications for the Christian community at large. The research, thereby, aspires to strengthen and sensitize the ethical dimension of John's Gospel which certifies a close connection between ethics and Christology as contained in the Gospel of John.

On the other side, the importance of this work is that it is inter-disciplinary in nature. Congruently, it endorses the strong relationship that exists between theology and ethics. This is also to suggest the integral and indispensible characteristic in the understanding of Christology and ethics. The present work is an attempt to investigate and respect the underlying significance of how ethics and Christology confluence in John's Gospel. Here in due allowance for ethics in John's Gospel will be given and thus receive its due attention. John embraces and brings to articulation the essence of ethics with Christology which is distinctive from the rest of the New Testament. And elucidate how the Johannine Christian community's behavior has been formed resulting from the emergence of Johannine Christology. Thus, John's Gospel can be perceived as contributing to the greater understanding of the New Testament ethics.

1.5. Working Hypothesis

The work will proceed on the hypothesis that the Johannine Christology and ethics are integrally intertwined forming a coherent whole in the presentation of the religious message by the author. The Johannine ethics finds its primary basis in Christ. As a reader proceeds to read in between the lines, the narrative unfolds the ethical implications that are implied in the text. The ethical messages

---

Johannine Literature (Nijmegen, May 2010), 3.

in the Gospel of John are differently integrated into the story that is narrated. The literary style of the Fourth gospel is unique in the ways that it incurs the reader's deeper knowledge to comprehend the intended meaning which points beyond the face value of what has been stated often. There is, therefore a need to see things at a higher level of reality. There is a vibrant and yet hidden ethical dimension in Johannine Gospel and that Jesus himself is the co-author[24] (with God, the Father) of the brilliant interpretation/explication (which is enacted in his ministry) of what constitutes a right ethical conduct. Therefore, the main objective of this work is to dive deep investigating the close relatedness between ethics and Christology and endeavors to see the Christological significance of Johannine ethics and to understand the depth of Johannine ethical aspects.

1.6. Method of Work

The historical circumstance/s has/have certainly occasioned the writing of the Gospel of John. The Gospel undeniably reflects the point in history of a community of believers and so any pressing issue prevalent at that point of time does not take place in a vacuum. A community's ethical behavior is unquestionably guided by the community's perception of its role model. To this effect, an investigation is to be carried out in the line how the community's ethics have (/been) informed the (/by the) understanding of Johannine Christology in a given Johannine social milieu. Having acknowledged that the society informs the ethical identity of any community under study, the approach of the work goes along the sociological approaches, i.e., the Johannine understanding of ethics is occasioned by and product of a particular social setting.[25] All New Testament writers have produced their respective documents with the sociologically conditioned language and experience of their worlds.[26] So, no New Testament document comes from a vacuum but springs from a sociologically conditioned milieu. The first attempt to understand the early Christians by employing a social description was by Edwin Judge in 1960. The explicit use of sociological method to the study of New Testament surfaced the theological circle from the mid 1970s. Gerd Theissen,

---

24 Here the word *author* signifies the sense of origin.

25 James F. McGrath, *John's Apologetic Christology: Legitimation and development in Johannine Christology* (Cambridge: Cambridge University Press, 2001), 5; idem, "Change in Christology: New Testament Models and the Contemporary Task," *Irish Theological Quarterly* 63/1 (1998): 42-49; Wayne A. Meeks, "The Divine Agent and His Counterfeit in Philo and the Fourth Gospel," *Aspects of Religions Propaganda in Judaism and Early Christianity,* edited by Elizabeth Schussler Fiorenza (Notre Dame: University of Notre Dame Press, 1976), 43-67; Idem, "The Man from Heaven in Johannine Sectarianism," *The Interpretation of John,* edited by John Ashton (London: SPCK, 1986), 141-173; Jerome H. Neyrey, *An Ideology of Revolt: John's Christology in Social-Science Perspective* (Philadelphia: Fortress Press, 1988).

26 M. Robert Mulholland, "Sociological Criticism," *Interpreting The New Testament: Essays on Methods and Issues,* edited by David Alan Black & David S. Dockery (Nashville: Broadmann & Holman Publishers, 2001), 171.

one of the pioneers in social analysis employed the sociological approach to understand aspects of the early Palestinian Christians. He studied the charismatic role of the leadership in the faith community with an emphasis on the character Jesus as one charismatic model.[27] When sociological criticism is applied to the present research, it is an attempt to understand the Johannine ethics from the social dimension of the Johannine community. This is viable because Johannine community is understood as living in a specific and historic sociological milieu. As such the sociological criticism when applied to the Johannine community is to understand the community and their community relations within them in a disciplined way.[28] In other words it is to lay bare the Johannine community in its socio-cultural setting wherein the community ethos and ethics find their expression and how it functioned socially both internally and externally at a given point in time.

The written text (i.e. Scripture) implicitly or explicitly contains traditions shaped by people based on social institutional structures (like family, economy and government, religious beliefs, etc). These social units/structures serve as the basis for biblical interpretation.[29] Congruently, it is vital to acknowledge that the Johannine Gospel conveys meanings derived through a specific Johannine culture and its social arrangements[30] and thereby its social behavior can be deduced from the text. Ethics is so closely connected with the social life of a community that one cannot isolate the study of the ethical values without considering the social world of the given community. To unveil the profound meaning of the text, then, one has to "hold together social and narrative worlds" because of the fact that the Gospel "speaks in a rich and distinctive voice" that any interpreter cannot fully grasped in "one-sided studies of either social history or narratology."[31] This eventually requires an approach whereby the written text serves as a mapping route to the study of the Johannine community's behavior in relation to the Johannine Christological presentation. The socio-historical context is considered so as to be able to draw insights from the socio-cultural context of John's Gospel. The work goes in line with the view that the finished form of the Gospel functions as a mirror to Johannine community in their particular circumstances (this somewhat has an inclination towards the so-called narrative criticism as well which is a tool

---

27 Gerd Theissen, *Sociology of Early Palestinian Christianity* (Philadelphia: Fortress Press, 1978), 10.

28 Derek Tidball, *An Introduction to the Sociology of the New Testament* (Exeter: The Paternoster Press, 1983), 12. He defines sociology as an attempt to understand society and social relations within society in disciplined way.

29 Norman Gottwald, *The Hebrew Bible: A Socio-Literary Introduction* (Minneapolis: Fortress Press, 1979), 26.

30 K. C. Hanson and Douglas E. Oakman, *Palestine in the Time of Jesus: Social Structures and Social Conflicts* (Minneapolis: Fortress Press, 1998), 4.

31 Gail R. O'Day, "Toward a Narrative Study of John," *Interpretation* 49 (1995): 345.

to be employed alongside the mentioned approach). The Gospel is not written as an ethical treatise. As such method that seriously considers the literary and rhetoric aspects will also be of great significance in unfolding the narrative of the Fourth Gospel, how it persuaded its intended reader/s then, and continues to persuade us now as modern readers to live a moral and ethical life. Precisely speaking, alongside the sociological approach attention will also be given to the narrative structure and the manner in which the narrative style of John's Gospel reflects and communicates its ethical significances and implications.

As such, the Gospel is read as a "window" to Johannine community concerning its particular history and circumstances. But, the gospel could be more than a window because it is in the finished form of the text that the fact is embedded or encoded for any imaginative reconstruction of the history of any given community under study. The reconstruction of any history must therefore find its impetus and its foundation and certainly its confirmation in the evidence provided by the text-the extant, finished form of that text.[32] Having affirmed the nature of John's Gospel as a narrative text and that the Gospel narrative being considered as a literature,[33] the development of the thought will side by side follow the thematic approach in conformity with the literary-narrative and exegetical analyses of the contents of the Gospel. John's Gospel contains the basic and elementary rhetorical literary devices (such as irony, symbolism, misunderstanding, double meanings, dualism, etc.) of a narrative criticism in trying to understand the intended meaning of the text. From the literary and narrative point of view the Gospel is reckoned as a complete whole[34] wherein the text serves as an imminent interpretative key. The Gospel of John is henceforth considered as an artistry work that knits together each literary part to present a complete and a beautiful tapestry of the whole story. And this coherent story of the Gospel is conditioned by the social life setting of the Johannine community which then is embedded in the finished form of the text. This text in it embodies and expresses the symbolic world of the community's 'orientation and identity.'[35] The supposition that Johannine Gospel is a story that distinctively narrates about God's love towards human kind is manifested in the social structures and practices of its community. This is to assert the ethical concerns thus contained in the Johannine text are embedded in

---

32 M. C. de Boer, "Narrative Criticism, Historical Criticism, and the Gospel of John," *The Interpretation of John*, 2nd edition, edited by John Ashton (Edinburgh: T&T Clark, 1997), 306. Historical-critical method attempts for further confirmation beyond the text (outside the text) from both documentary and archeological sources that are (roughly) contemporaneous with the gospel under study.

33 James L. Resseguie, *Narrative Criticism of the New Testament: An Introduction* (Michigan: Baker Academic, 2005), 18-19.

34 Mark Allan Powell, *What is Narrative Criticism?* (Minneapolis: Fortress Press, 1990), 2.

35 Richard B. Hays, "Mapping the Field: Approaches to New Testament Ethics," *Identity, Ethics and Ethos in the New Testament*, edited by Jan G. van der watt (Berlin: Walter de Gruyter, 2006), 16.

the stories that are narrated. Therefore, considering the literary-narrative of the Gospel will shed light for the understanding of the Johannine significant ethical teachings embedded within the Johannine Christological articulation.

1.7. Scope and Limitation

The work work will remain focused on the ethical contents of the Fourth Gospel. It is an adventure to find what it means and takes to be an ethically oriented community according to John's Gospel. By nature of the content of the Gospel, it demands a careful reading beneath the surface of the text where the text serves as an impetus to the finding of ethics in the finished form of the Gospel. Selected ethical indicators (such as belief, doing the will of God, signs (σημεῖα), etc) and narrative passages (For instance John chapter 2, 6, 9, 13, 15-16, 17 will be considered for the discussion of the ethics of the Gospel of John). So, considering such terms (e.g., 'belief,' 'work' '*ergon*,' 'sign') that serve as ethical pointers, we will closely examine the ethical dimension embedded in them through selected passages where one can draw insights about Johannine ethics. So, the study will be confined to explore the ethical aspects by analyzing the narrative content of John's Gospel. The theologically inherent and embedded relational ethics of John's Gospel will primarily be investigated to find the inter-connectedness between ethics and Christology and how either has influenced and shaped the other. References will also be inferred from other New Testament writings whenever it substantiates the point under discussion for advancing the theme.

Why did the Fourth Evangelist not explicitly talk on ethics? Does this mean that the Evangelist was not concerned about ethics? What is the author trying to emphasize to his first hand reader in regard to a Christian conduct? How do Johannine ethics contribute to our understanding of who God is in Jesus? How are we to evaluate the place of Johannine ethics within the Johannine Christological articulation? In particular, do Johannine ethics fit in the author's overall purpose of the Gospel? What implications and relevance do Johannine ethics has for the Indian Christians today?

1.8. Outline of the Work

The work work is divided into five chapters. The first chapter will exclusively be on introduction to the literary survey of Johannine ethics. The second chapter will concentrate on the socio-cultural and religious milieu of the Johannine Community. The third chapter will deliberate on curving out the major ethical indicators/pointers by closely examining the selected passages for the ethical evidences in John's Gospel. The fourth chapter will deal with the Christology of John and its ethical significances. And in the fifth chapter we will discuss the Johannine ethics and its divine and communitarian parameters and bring out some of the major important ethical features of John's Gospel. The work comes to a close with the implications and relevance of the study undertaken.

Chapter 1

Literature Survey in Johannine Ethics

Introduction

The word 'ethics' is used in three different but related ways. These three main ways signify (i) a general pattern or 'way of life,' (2) a set of rules of conduct or 'moral code,' and (3) inquiry *about* ways of life and rules of conduct.[1] Concisely 'ethics' is a science of morals. Etymologically the word 'ethics' shares a common root with 'ethos.' Both come from the Greek word ἦθος meaning character. It was a cliché in Greek moral writing in antiquity, found already in Plato and Aristotle, that ethos led to ἦθος; that is, 'habit' (practicing the virtues until they become second nature) would eventually build 'character.'[2] Ethics is primarily the philosophical study of moral values and rules and the motivation on which

---

1 Raziel Abelson and Kai Nielsen, "History of Ethics," *The Encyclopedia of Philosophy*, vols. 3 & 4, edited by Paul Edwards *et al.*, (New York/ London: Macmillan Publishing Company & The Free Press/Coller Macmillan Publishers, 1967), 81. Also see R. M. Hare, "Ethics," *A Dictionary of Christian* Ethics, edited by John Macquarrie (London: SCM Press, 1967), 114-116. The first term of ethics may be spoken of Buddhist or Christian ethics, second of professional ethics and of unethical behavior and in the third sense philosophical ethics (which was invented by the Greeks in the fifth century B.C.E, with the appearance of Socrates, a secular prophet whose self-appointed mission to awaken his fellow men to the need for rational criticism of their beliefs and practices). The first and second senses include practices and codification of practices which are basically the threads out of which all human culture is woven. Philosophical ethics is often understood in a broad way as including all essential thought about human beings' conduct.

2 M. E. Glasswell, "ἦθος ους τό", *Exegetical Dictionary of the New Testament*, vol. 1, edited by Horst Balz and Gerhard Schneider (Michigan: Wm. B. Eerdmans Publishing Company, 1980), 384.

ideas of right and wrong are based.[3] It is also commonly understood as a set of rules or principles that govern an individual's concrete conduct or a group's behavior. Ethics[4] in more comprehensible words might be known as a system of moral values and duties concerning with ideal human character, action, and ends.[5] Ethics therefore concerns the "systematic study of the nature of value concepts."[6] Subsequently, ethics in general can be defined as the critical study of morality[7] systematically examining the right and good[8] of human's behavior. It is a science of morals and concisely of human duties which precisely is concerned with human actions. As such, ethics is concerned with all of human's decisions and choices and evaluations, implying more on element of reflection upon the right and good conduct.

The Bible has been received and accepted as the normative part of moral tradition by the believing community. Then what constitutes the New Testament ethics? The New Testament ethics basically refers to the ethical teachings that are presented in the canonical twenty seven books of the New Testament (Matthew-Revelation). The New Testament ethics is distinctive because of its appeal to the person and teachings, death and resurrection of Jesus of Nazareth, and his continuing influence and presence through the Holy Spirit.[9] The New Testament as a whole is more of religious oriented documents. Its ethical teaching is embedded in a context which consists of an account of "historical facts and an explanation of their religious significance."[10] Nonetheless, no New Testament book is "written in the genre of ethical treatise"[11] by nature. And so one must not expect nor look,

---

3 E. Clinton Gardner, *Biblical Faith and Social Ethics* (New York: Harper & Row Publishers, 1960), 3-5.

4 Ethics is inclined much towards a reflective study while morality is more of a descriptive term. So ethics is reflection on the basis of moral action that is ethics as a reflective process reaches its completion in action. In the words of K. C. Abraham: "Ethics is the action or fruit of a mature human life" in his book *Transforming Vision: Theological-Methodological Paradigm Shifts* (Tiruvalla: Christian Sahitya Samithi, 2006), 75.

5 Robertson McQuilkin, *An Introduction to Biblical Ethics*, 2nd edition (Secunderabad: OM Books, 2002), ix.

6 M. Stephen, *Christian Ethics: Issues and Social Ethics* (New Delhi: Concept Publishing Company, 2007), 9.

7 Gardner, *Biblical Faith and Social Ethics*, 3.

8 Gardner, *Biblical Faith and Social Ethics*, 5. The concept of right entails the notion of duty, of moral law, and of imperatives wherein the ideal life for human is envisaged as obedience to law while the concept of good involves the idea of goods or ends to be aimed at where satisfaction of desire and the achievement of ends for an ideal human becomes a primary concern.

9 Daniel J. Harrinton and James F. Keenan, *Jesus and Virtue Ethics: Building Bridges between New Testament Studies and Moral Theology* (New York: Rowman & Littlefield Publishers, 2002), 8.

10 C. H. Dodd, *Gospel and Law* (Cambridge: Cambridge University Press, 1951), 8.

11 Richard A. Burridge, *Imitating Jesus: An Inclusive Approach to New Testament Ethics* (Michigan: Wm. B. Eerdmans Publishing Company, 2007), 347.

in the New Testament, for set of systematically designed rules and principles for a moral conduct. Nonetheless there are variable ethical instructions either in the form of a series of imperatives or admonitions or even encouragements. And so, one cannot run the risk of sidelining the important ethical obligations present in every New Testament document though with varying emphases. It is necessary, therefore to first set in place the meaning and nature of the New Testament ethics to which the ethics of John's Gospel comes within this fold.

1.1. Meaning and Nature of the New Testament Ethics

The New Testament is a religious book basically recounting the salvific plan and event of God in and through the person of Jesus, for the wellbeing of the human race. It showcases the divine intervention where human race has a moral responsibility to ethically respond to the divine saving act of God in and through the person of Jesus. Congruently, the New Testament on the whole contains an account of how the proclaimed Kingdom of God (Jesus' ethical horizon)[12] and the saving justice of God (Paul's ethical horizon) prompt the ethical conduct of an individual in a community. The New Testament books however do not classify itself into a systematic arrangement of ethics but rather gives principles for ethical behavior through its presentation of role models (especially Jesus), narratives, and doctrines.[13] So, the New Testament ethics "does not contain philosophic teaching about norms or virtues, or definitions and legitimations deriving from some kind of natural law governing justice and property, labor and society"[14] but in the various documents of the New Testament we hear an oft-repeated call to an appropriate conduct on the part of the individual morality in the private sphere[15] and to the community of believers in a larger circle. As such, the ethics of the New Testament is distinct from the philosophical tradition wherein the former appeals to the "shape of Jesus' life, to what happened through it, as well as to what happened to those who believed that this was the salvific work of God."[16] So, the ethics of the New Testament is seen as a "normative theological discipline"[17] that contributes to the shaping of the life of the members of the Church.

The theme of ethics is very central to Biblical thought and to human behavior as well. In the words of C. H. Dodd, "Christian religion, like Judaism (to take

12 Frank J. Matera, *New Testament Ethics: The Legacies of Jesus and Paul* (Louisville: Westminster John Knox Press, 1996), 6.

13 Walter C. Kaiser, "New Approaches to Old Testament Ethics," *JETS*, vol. 35/3 (Sept., 1992): 289.

14 Wolfgang Schrage, *The Ethics of the New Testament*, translated by David E. Green (Philadelphia: Fortress Press, 1988), 2-3.

15 Schrage, *The Ethics of the New Testament*, 2-3.

16 Leander E. Keck, "Rethinking "New Testament Ethics," *JBL* 115/1 (1996): 10.

17 Richard B. Hays, *The Moral Vision of the New Testament: A Contemporary Introduction to New Testament Ethics* (New York: HarperCollins, 1996), 3.

another example), is an ethical religion in a specific sense that it recognizes no ultimate separation between the service of God and social behavior."[18] The present work is thereby dedicated to explore the inter connection between ethics and Christology in John's Gospel. The Gospel as unique as it stands is characterized by its distinctive literary style in driving home the intended religious message to his intended audience. Lack of vice and virtues do not suggest lack of ethical concerns but one should be open to accept John's liberty to express his ethical concern in a distinctive way. John, a good interpreter and a good narrator, immensely impressed the readers of his time and later generations to go behind the text for a deeper message which is figuratively or dramatically presented. There is a significant ethical teachings embedded within Christological articulation which demand a critical analysis of the text. The New Testament writings being the literary records containing the distinctive theological orientation of each author, record the moral teachings of its writings and to which the New Testament ethics can be spoken of. New Testament ethics can thereby be understood as the critical reflection on the biblical principles as a guide to a moral conduct wherein Scripture is reckoned as the final authority for any moral guidance. Hays' assertion of the fundamental authority of the Scriptures is encouraging. He said, "Tradition shapes and orders our reading in deeply significant ways, but there remains a persistent creative tension between the text and the tradition; Scripture has its own voice, and the responsibility of the faithful interpreter is to listen for that voice both through and apart from the community's interpretative traditions."[19] Subsequently, New Testament ethics in general can be understood as the "Christian way of being in the world"[20] guided by the belief in the Lord Jesus and his continuing guidance through the Holy Spirit.

The New Testament ethics is significantly oriented towards the Christ-event which thereby exerts a Christological appeal to the community of believers that resulted because of the event of Jesus' life and ministry. The New Testament ethics is fundamentally religious ethic "oriented towards encountering God and doing God's will in the light of the Christ event."[21] It is an ethic of building relationship with God (vertical relationship) in and through Jesus of Nazareth and with fellow human beings (horizontal social relationship) in the light of that vertical relationship. This is to suggest that the New Testament ethics is Christocentric or theocentric in its orientation and content. Therefore, New Testament ethics can be spoken of as primarily Christological or theological in nature wherein its criterion and basis is God's saving act in and through his Son Jesus Christ.[22] Subsequently,

---

18 Dodd, *Gospel and Law*, 3.

19 Hays, *The Moral Vision of the New Testament*, 8.

20 Jack T. Sanders, *Ethics in the New Testament: Change and Development* (London: SCM Press Ltd., 1975), 34.

21 Harrington, *Jesus and Virtue Ethics*, 8.

22 Schrage, *The Ethics of the New Testament*, 8.

in the understanding of the New Testament ethics, the historical Jesus of Nazareth has been understood to have taught the ideal life of men and women of his time.[23] Jesus' ethical teaching comprises of *what* and *how* one ought to relate to God and to his/her fellow beings especially within the formed disciples' community. So, we can assert the ethics of the New Testament as an ethics of relationship with God in and through Jesus Christ, and also with fellow human beings.[24] It thereby exerts two principle relational dimensions: vertical and horizontal effects. One's relation to God in and through Jesus the Son must be reflected in loving fellowship within and around the members of the believing community (social context).

As such, New Testament ethics cannot be rightly understood without the proper understanding of who God is *in* Jesus. Rightly, Dodd asserted that the New Testament Christians "approach to ethics sharply distinguished from that of the contemporary Greek moralists, who from the time of Aristotle had set out to provide a self-contained and self-justifying system of ethics. For Christianity, ethics is not self-contained or self-justifying; they arise out of a response to the Gospel."[25] It therefore has a distinctive appeal having oriented toward encountering God in and through the person of Jesus which further prompts and necessitates a believing heart to do the will of God in the light of Christ-event.[26] The incarnation in the person of Christ of the character of God becomes a determinative concept for all generations of Christian disciples for the practical implicate of the moral imitation of God as revealed in Jesus, the Christ.[27] Appropriately, Stephen C. Barton sees ethics of the New Testament "as reflecting the lives of a particular people seeking to display in their attitudes and actions the glory of God,"[28] whose emphasizes above all, is on the glorified Christ. For that reason, New Testament ethics must be understood in the light of the historical and sociological context of the New Testament writers who were confronted by specific occasions and situations.[29]

New Testament ethics is contextual[30] in a sense that revolves in the context of specific occasions and situations. As such New Testament ethics is an ethics

23 C. A. Anderson Scott, *New Testament Ethics: An Introduction* (Cambridge: Cambridge University Press, 1948), 3.

24 Harrington, *Jesus and Virtue Ethics*, 8.

25 Dodd, *Gospel and Law*, 10.

26 Harrington, *Jesus and Virtue Ethics*, 8.

27 R. E. O. White, *Biblical Ethics: The Changing Continuity of Christian Ethics*, vol. 1 (Exeter: The Paternoster Press, 1979), 112.

28 Stephen C. Barton, "The Epistles and Christian Ethics," *The Cambridge Companion to Christian Ethics*, edited by Robin Gill (Cambridge: Cambridge University Press, 2001), 64.

29 Cf. James F. McGrath, *John's Apologetic Christology: Legitimation and Development in Johannine Christology* (Cambridge: Cambridge University Press, 2001), 5-6.

30 Schrage, *The Ethics of the New Testament*, 5.

of the New Testament texts and period[31] that inform the moral teaching of the twenty seven canonical books of the New Testament texts. And the vital message conveyed by these canonical texts revolves around the salvific plan of God in and through Jesus which consequently demands believers of moral responsibility. The Christ-event itself is moral instruction because his life incarnates the moral and religious message he had proclaimed.[32] In a way, there is no single self-standing ethical treatise in the twenty seven books of the New Testament. Any ethical directives found in the Bible (e.g. Sermon on the Mount in Matthew's Gospel) are all part of Jesus' story (especially in the Gospels). As a result, what Jesus said and did provide an ideal pattern of life to be followed. And so Jesus Christ is the central figure of the New Testament ethics. His life serves as the pivotal figure for any pattern of an individual's moral and ethical behavior in a given community.

1.2. Ethics of the Gospel of John: A Literature Survey

In the light of the briefly described ethical nature of the New Testament, the present focus is to make an attempt to take a quick survey of some literary works done on Johannine ethics. Few of the scholars' and commentators' work on Johannine ethics are considered to carry out the required literature survey. We begin by stating the fact scenario of the Johannine ethics, that, the Gospel of John has not received due attention and thereby given a minimal attestation with regards to ethical materials that may be present implicitly. There has been relatively little effort at exploring the ethical contents in the Fourth gospel. However, there are a handful of articles that call for a quick overview of each of them to put the present research in its perspective. This survey contains very few of the literature that focuses on Johannine writings (limited to the Gospel of John).

It deems necessary to, at the outset, present the general outlook to the ethical content of the Gospel of John. It appears that scholars who have worked on the ethics of the New Testament, devoted little space in the discussion of Johannine ethics with very few comments.[33] This shows that less attention or otherwise a minimal importance is given to the ethical elements contained in the Gospel. We shall now consider few of the scholars who have discussed the ethical content of the Gospel of John, chronologically (i.e., as per date of publication).

---

31 Keck, "Rethinking New Testament Ethics," 14.

32 Matera, *New Testament Ethics*, 252.

33 For instance, Birger Gerhardsson, *The Ethos of the Bible* (Philadelphia: Westminster Press, 1981); Donald Guthrie, *New Testament Theology* (Leicester : Inter Varsity Press, 1985), 907. Willi Marxsen, *New Testament Foundations for Christian Ethics* (Edinburgh: T&T Clark, 1989); Emmanuel E. James, *Ethics: A Biblical Perspective* (Bangalore: Theological Book Trust, 1992); Burridge, *Imitating Jesus*, 37; Hays, *The Moral Vision of the New Testament* (1996); Matera, *New Testament Ethics* (1996); Schrage, *Ethics of the New Testament*, 92-117; Wayne A. Meeks, "The Ethics of the Fourth Evangelist," *Exploring the Gospel of John: Essays in Honor of D. Moody Smith* (Lousiville: Westminster John Knox Press, 1996).

T. B. Matson's[34] work in analyzing the ethical content of the New Testament has probed into the Biblical content for ethical insights. On analyzing the ethical content of the Johannine literature he first made an attempt to give some preliminary observations on the Gospel of John and the synoptic and then with Paul. He affirms that though John's Gospel contains less ethical emphasis as compared to the Synoptic, nevertheless it has its own priori containing considerable ethical content which is of major importance. Considering John and Paul, he pointed out certain basic point of contact especially in their ethical approach which is largely theological and inner. That is, the outer conduct is a natural expression of an inner relationship with Christ. Matson considers the theme of 'Eternal life,' 'the fruitful life,' 'A new commandment,' and 'The will of God' as having important ethical significances in the Gospel. Eternal life is a present reality which evolves from a union with the Eternal Person. The indwelling of the Eternal Person in him/her must be reflected in his/her day to day living and also extending fellowship with God's children.

Ethical behavior is the result of union with the Eternal Person. Eventually a person who has possessed eternal life has been chosen by Jesus for a mission to bear fruit (Jn. 15:16). This bearing of fruit is living a life of discipleship that is characterized by loving one another as he/she has been loved and living a fruitful life as lived by the Master Jesus. Living a fruitful life is determined by their relatedness to Jesus, as branches to the vine. Their constant union with Jesus is the route to fruitful life. Jesus prior to his crucifixion (which is a state of exaltation for John) gave a new commandment to his disciples. This commandment is new in its origin (comes from Jesus himself), in its motive (as loved by Jesus), in its nature (obedience that spontaneously sprang from a new relationship), and in its dimensions (love within the community; a new depth which evolves from the quality of life Christ lived and the life laid down for the sake of another's life). In a subsequent treatment of the theme 'the will of God,' Jesus is portrayed as having come into the world to do the will of the One who sent Him (Jn. 6:38; 4:34; 19:30). In a like manner, disciples are sent into the world to carry on the mission legacy of Jesus (Jn. 17:23; 20:21). Jesus sends out his disciples to do what the Father had sent him to do. On one occasion of unprecedented work Jesus said that 'we must work the works of the One who sent me while it is day' (Jn. 9:4). This indicates that there is a chain of continuity in the sending motif and the subsequent mission to be carried out. Matson has beautifully brought out significant ethical aspects of John's Gospel but what the researcher sees lacking is that he has not substantially established the interconnection between ethics and Christology of the Gospel. Besides, intensive and exhaustive study on the ethical aspects of the Gospel of John is not exclusively dealt.

34 T. B. Matson, *Biblical Ethics: A Guide to the Ethical Message of the Scriptures from Genesis to Revelation* (Georgia: Mercer University Press, 1969), 211-244.

R. E. O White's[35] assessment on *Biblical Ethics* has devoted a little space to discuss on the Johannine ethics. Drawing ethical insights from the Gospel he commenced by citing the purpose of the Gospel wherein one is called to have faith in Jesus because there is life in his name (Jn. 20:23). He insists that possessing a divine life is a priori to what is to be performed because the latter will automatically result in well-doing. He substantiates his point by pointing that character determines conduct. There is a definite moral dualism in the Gospel. There is no midway position. That means, you are in the light or darkness, truth or false, life or death, faith or unbelief. And one cannot be on both the sides. He remarks 'love' as John's basic ethical theme patterned after the historic example of Jesus Christ which in return also demands a Christian response in obedience to keep the commandment to love one another (Jn. 15:10,13). Love is not a mere abstract word but is an ethically oriented word to take a concrete act of faith and obedience. And according to John's Gospel, love has to be performed initially within the fellowship and extend to the wider context. White has dealt very little with ethical aspects of the Gospel this suggests he finds less important aspect of the ethical concerns of the Gospel. While White sees the historic Jesus as the standard on which Christian response is based, he fails to explain the inter-connection between ethics and Christology of the Gospel of John.

Allan Verhey's[36] analysis on the Ethics of the New Testament devotes a little space to discuss on the content of ethics in John's Gospel. He begins by acknowledging the distinctive feature of the Gospel and the crisis John addresses within Judaism. The crisis was of the Jewish response to Jesus, the Christ. Some believed and some did not. And for those of the Jews who believed, choose light over darkness, truth over against falsehood and life over death. The Jews then were making "the choice in their response to their Messiah."[37] It is against this Jewish backdrop that the ethics of the Gospel has to be understood. The Law came through Moses as a preliminary to the 'grace and truth' fully revealed in the person of Jesus, the Christ (Jn. 1:17). The Mosaic Law still stands valid. The law was never discarded nor discredited by Johannine Jesus. In fact the Scripture bears witness to Jesus and Moses too wrote about him (Jn. 5:39-47; 7:19). The validity of the law that came through Moses is of importance in pointing towards Jesus, the perfect bearer of the Law. Verhey points out that "the law was to guide conduct in ways that were familiar to the Synagogues and to the Christian conventicles within them."[38] Having passed comments on the validity and the significant place that the Law of Moses holds for the ethics of the Johannine community Verhey nevertheless states that John's moral concern was not focused on the law nor its

35 White, *Biblical Ethics*, vol. I, 196-203.

36 Allen Verhey, *The Great Reversal: Ethics and the New Testament* (Michigan: Wm. B. Eerdmans Publishing Company, 1984), 142-153.

37 Verhey, *The Great Reversal*, 143.

38 Verhey, *The Great Reversal,* 143.

Messianic interpretation but to Christ and the "life in his name" (Jn. 20:31; 10:10; 12:50).[39]

And this life is a life formed and informed by love. This love is the Father's love in Christ (Jn. 3:35; 5:20) and the love of Christ in his own (Jn. 13:1). Christ Jesus brings God's love for and to the world so that world and its inhabitants may be saved and have life (Jn. 3:16). Jesus then instructs the disciples to abide in his love (Jn. 15:9) and keep his commandments (15:10) by loving one another as "I have loved you" (Jn. 15:12, 17). The Father acts in love in Christ who in turn makes the Father's love known by manifesting through his deeds by serving the disciples in love (washing of feet). Johannine Jesus' example of humble service and instructions to love one another are set in the context of his glorification (that is the Cross). The disciples are, then, obliged to love as they have been loved and commanded to do so. Jesus brings home a new commandment resting on a new reality that he himself has brought. Jesus' commandment is new because of the new situation he has inaugurated. The new imperative is based on a new indicative. It is thereby ethically right to continue to love as believers in Jesus, the Christ. Verhey seems to narrow down John's ethics to the love of God through the Son, Jesus which I see is fair but he has aborted the fact that 'life' in the Gospel of John is significantly ethical. In addition, Verhay has not also dealt with the valuable connection that exist between ethics and Christology of John' Gospel.

In treatment of the New Testament ethics Wolfgang Schrage[40] describes the Johannine ethics (Johannine literature as a whole) with reservation that there is "an almost total absence of specific injunctions or paraenetic passages."[41] And yet, wherever there are possible references to ethics it is exclusively christological in a way not encountered elsewhere. He takes up very pertinent theme of Johannine ethics: Separation from the world and freedom from sin and the command of brotherly love. Both these themes are closely connected with Christology. The ethics of the Johannine literature solely has its ethical basis and foundation on Christology. He stresses that the Johannine writings succinctly presents ethics solely related to the person of Jesus. And so Johannine Christology is of fundamental importance for its community and its subsequent act of behavior.

In his discussion on the subject of ethics, Schrage treats the discourse of Jesus about the true vine and its branches (John 15) as one major significant passage that projects the influence of Christology on ethics. Jesus is the one true vine without which no Christians will bear fruit unless taking abode in Jesus. But, abiding in Jesus to bear fruit is itself rooted on Jesus' abiding in those who belong to him. But, belonging to Jesus is preceded by a requisite fact of belief because unless one believes in Jesus he/she cannot be belonging to him. All those who belong to Jesus derive their growth and fruitfulness exclusively from their enduring union with

39 Verhey, *The Great Reversal,* 143.

40 Schrage, *The Ethics of the New Testament*, 295-319.

41 Schrage, *The Ethics of the New Testament*, 297.

him. No Christian can bring forth fruit in his/her own initiative. Schrage rightly espouses that "all that a Christian is and does can be realized and understood only in connection with Jesus."[42] Jesus as exemplar and model of the law of love also demands response to keep his commandments as an act of ethical conduct within the community (Jn. 15:12; 13:34). He advocates that Johannine ethics which is basically grounded in Christology has its reflex in the substance of the Christological imperatives. People are called to believe, love, hear, know, come, receive, serve, abide and follow and to continue to live in the actual spoken word of Christ which has bearing on being the true disciple of Jesus Christ. He also discussed 'separation from the world' as a fundamental theme of Johannine ethics. The world is identified as being evil ruled by sin (Jn. 16:8) or Satan (Jn. 12:37) and it is darkness (Jn. 1:9; 8:12). It is to this darkness that Jesus has come to bring light. And on the other end of his treatment, Schrage commented that "Jesus, too, resists entanglement with the world, but he also resists separation from the world."[43] To be on the closer side of Jesus is to remain between these two extremes. What Schrage puts it is that earthly things are transitory, worthless, irrelevant and inauthentic when compared to heavenly reality.

So, one cannot fully deny the earthly existence as long as he/she remains in the world but the fact that heavenly reality takes precedence over the worldly matters must be taken note. One cannot therefore do away with the world as long as one remains in the realm of this world. Having pointed this out, the Johannine ethics of love which often is perceived as restricted within the community is different from the Qumran community. He pointed out that the members of the Johannine community did not explicitly exclude others from being loved. He also cites Judas Iscariot who betrayed Jesus got his feet being washed. Further the disciples are sent into the world to carry the missionary message of the love of God. Thus, the phrase "one another" potentially is inclusive rather than being exclusive where the term includes everyone. He also subscribed that Johannine love is living for others and is communicative and reciprocal in nature and not just "a mere turning inward"[44] for the Father loves the Son and the world as well. Schrage has beautifully described ethics of the Gospel as rooted on Christology which is very telling but he has not pin pointed out the important ethical themes of the gospel that are integral part of Christology.

Willi Marxsen[45] while discussing on ethics in the Johannine circle describes love as the only one single ethical term present in the Gospel according to John. How this love has to be carried out is not stated except in the washing of the disciples' feet. This demonstrated love in action of Jesus serves as an exemplary act to carry out this legacy by the disciples so that the action can be publicly seen.

42 Schrage, *The Ethics of the New Testament*, 300.

43 Schrage, *The Ethics of the New Testament*, 312.

44 Schrage, *The Ethics of the New Testament,* 318.

45 Marxsen, *New Testament Foundations for Christian Ethics*, 285-299.

The disciples ought to reflect what and how their master Jesus had lived by loving one another in the public eye. The disciples are thereby to give form to love by loving one another as loved by Jesus. Since Jesus has set an example by washing his disciples' feet, so what and how to live is basically base on Christology. He further states that John's love is a reciprocal love which also is "used theologically and Christologically in a way that is especially characteristic of John in order to specify a mutual relationship."[46] Christology becomes the only standard for the ethical conduct of the disciples. So, the search for John's ethic proves to be a pursuit for his Christology. Marxsen has pinned down the Johannine ethical concern only to the term 'love.' This is to sideline the other ethical aspects present in the Gospel of John.

Richard B. Hays[47] started off with a negative comment stating that the Gospel according to St. John is a "puzzling text" because it contains no specific moral teaching. Nevertheless he does not stop with this comment but made further comment on the ethical elements present in the Gospel. He begins his articulation with an account of the text's Christology (the Man from Heaven), then turns to discuss on the concept and composite of the Johannine picture of a Church within which loving one another becomes the focal requirement of the Church. This has to be further concretized in abiding in Jesus and thus loving one another in a community. One's ethical behavior is determined or is directly affected by his/her relationship with Jesus. Congruently "the bond between Jesus and believers is determinative for the community's ethical norms."[48] A good number of scholars have asserted the 'love command' as exoteric but considering the historical situation of the Gospel, it justifies contending that the exhortation for love within the community comes as a response to a communal crisis of identity and whereby its exhortation comes alive "more like an urgent appeal for unity within an oppressed minority community."[49] Hays then, moves to the discussion of the text's eschatological and ethical implications and finally makes summary remarks on John's symbolic world wherein John's narrative world served as a context for establishing a framework for moral discernment and action. Nowhere did Hays establish or expound exhaustively the relationship that exists between ethics and Christology in John's Gospel.

Comparatively, Frank J. Matera's[50] work on the *New Testament Ethics* gives more elaborate discussion on the ethical instruction of Jesus as recorded in the Gospel according to John which he entitled "Ethics Becomes Christology." This subtitle is very catchy and impressive to an enthusiastic reader of the Gospel. He beautifully endorsed that "the gospel of John exemplifies a Christological

46 Marxsen, *New Testament Foundations for Christian Ethics*, 287.

47 Hays, *The Moral Vision of the New Testament*, 138-156.

48 Hays, *The Moral Vision of the New Testament*, 143.

49 Hays, *The Moral Vision of the New Testament*, 147.

50 Matera, *New Testament Ethics*, 92-117.

implosion so that ethics becomes Christology." Of course, at the start of his arguments on the subject he acknowledged that John's Gospel is a major challenge when one has to study the New Testament ethics and yet on the other side of the coin he contends that the Gospel according to John contains some of the most "sublime statements about love" within the whole range of the New Testament writings. He articulates that the Gospel according to John comparatively lacks ethical instructions as and when compared to the Synoptic Gospels but it presents in a "new and transformed way."

The Gospel according to John presents the most distinctive ethical teaching of all the Gospels. Almost every ethical requirement collapsed into Christology and most importantly the ethical behavior is related to the very person of Jesus Christ. And on the other end of the coin, Matera pointed out some common themes like: The Kingdom of God, Repentance, Faith, Love, Discipleship, and Judgment, that occurs both in the Synoptic and the Gospel according to John. Matera articulates that Faith and Love are the ethical poles in John's Gospel. The world remains in darkness which thereby needs to be redeemed. Faith is the human's responsibility to experience the divine intervention which is love in the Gospel according to John. This faith is the faith in Jesus as having come from the Father. He has come as the light to illumine the world that lives in darkness. He is altogether the Light, Truth and Life to those who will believe and receive him as one sent by the Father from above. The Father's love is expressed by sending his only begotten Son so that whoever believes in His sent Son might have life eternal (3:16; 5:24).

So, believing in the one God sent into the world is one ethical challenge depicted in the Gospel of John. There is a closed group that forms a new community characterized by love for one another. This group is Jesus' disciples who have adhered to believe in him and have thereby passed from darkness to light. These individuals who formed Jesus' disciples are left with certain directives that they must continue to believe in him even while he is not physically with them. They must love one another as he had loved them and manifest their love for the Master by keeping his commandment. They should not be grieved but rejoice for the Lord and their Master is returning to the Father who is greater than the Son Jesus. Now the disciples' moral lives are not possible without abiding in Jesus. Apart from Jesus there is no morality. Jesus is the source and foundation of the disciples' moral life but this does not exempt the disciples of moral responsibilities as long as they live in the world. So, the moral life is a life of grace which is rooted in and related to Jesus and a life of grace which is patterned after Jesus' redeeming love. Towards the close, Matera, gives a summary statement of Jesus' moral teaching in two important phrases. First, people are summoned to believe in the One the Father has sent into the world. Secondly, love for one another as Jesus has loved stands out as a dominant characterization for discipleship in the understanding of the Johannine community. Overall, Matera's conclusive remark

"Ethics becomes Christology" is remarkably appealing and intriguing. Matera gives the impression that ethics is reduced to Christology. His subscription is questionable because even when ethics is deeply rooted in Christology the former (ethics) has its own distinctive characteristic to stand as a significant theme. In short, Matera is lopsided to reduce ethics to Christology. Ethics and Christology are integrally linked but are not identical.

Jey J. Kanagaraj[51] investigates the ethics of the Fourth gospel against the backdrop of the Old Testament Decalogue and concludes to find the ethical aspects present throughout the gospel. His work appears to be more of a reinterpretation of the phrase "keep my commandments" in the light of the Ten Commandment of the Old Testament, Decalogue. He explains that the Jewish ethics that is embodied in the Decalogue is reflected in John's Gospel which is implied in the words 'keep my commandment.' The contention of his article is to bring into light the validity and the continuity of the Law of the Old Testament finding which however culminates in the very being of Jesus. John's Gospel does not, therefore, discredit the law but validates as a pointer to the person of Jesus, who is a model to moral guidance. Where the Jewish law serves as a guide to the moral life style, for John's Gospel, Jesus is a guide to one's moral conduct. Kanagaraj has established the authenticity that the Gospel of John validates the moral values contained in the Decalogue of the Old Testament. He further succinctly subscribed that as the Decalogue served as the standard of moral guidance so is Jesus of the Gospel of John to which the Law of the Old Testament points to and so Jesus is the very model to moral guidance. While Kanagaraj stand is to authenticate the validity of the Old Testament Law in the very life and ministry of Jesus, he has not touched on the inter-connection sandwiched between ethics and Christology in John's Gospel.

In line with the contention that John's Gospel affirms the ongoing validity of the Law it signifies then that John's Gospel has much to say about ethics in spite of the absence of rich ethical teachings that are present in the synoptic such as, the Sermon on the Mount and ethical elements like virtues and vices found in Pauline letters. R. Alan Culpepper further acknowledges that there however is a distinctive Johannine theological ethic which is clear: "a dualistic worldview, the new commandment to love one another, and the model of Jesus."[52] John's gospel has a distinctive Christological ethic in its nature and character. Culpepper's comment on the distinctive Christological ethic of the Gospel of John is impressive and yet he fails to vibrantly espouse the integral link that is present between ethics and Christology.

---

51 Jey J. Kanagaraj, "The Implied Ethics of the Fourth Gospel of John: A Reinterpretation of the Decalogue," *Tyndale Bulletin*, 52/1 (2001): 33-60.

52 R. Alan Culpepper, "Anti-Judaism as a Theological Problem for Christian Interpreters," *Anti-Judaism and the Fourth Gospel* (Louisville: Westminster John Knox Press, 2001), 61-82.

Jan G. van der Watt[53] proves the inseparable links that exist between identity, ethics and ethos in the Gospel of John. He confers that doing the works of God becomes the major ethical decision in the gospel according to John. This ethical action is to believe in Jesus and thereby faith in Jesus becomes the foremost crucial action required of a person to exercise his/her moral obligation in performing the works of God. There is a strong implication that a person's behavior is to be determined by his/her relationship to Jesus (Jn. 15). As a result, one's total moral behavior will stem from the exemplary act of the Father and His Son (Jn. 8:38-41; 13:15; 14:10-11). After a brief commendation on the major ethical decision as doing the works of God is to believe in Jesus, he discusses the love commandment in detail, which is patterned after the love of the Father and the Son. He then moves on to discuss the habitual action of the Johannine community which comprises of sharing meals, washing feet, and continuing the mission work of Jesus.

In another article, Watt did a study on Johannine ethics with special emphasis on chapter 8 focusing on the relationship and interaction between ethics and language and has shown the ethical dynamics of the narrative (where ethically related words and concepts are to be found).[54] The Gospel integrates a wide variety of language features and techniques to achieve his purpose and goal (to bring home the ethical message). Watt also discusses pertinently the ethical values coming alive in the imagery of Light and Life. He contends that the ethical system of John's Gospel is relational and grounded in Christology. And so, materials making a reference to the acceptance of Jesus have been considered to bring out the ethical elements in the Gospel. The major thrust of the Gospel's ethical injunction is to drive people to faith in Jesus as the Son of God and that they will enjoy the subsequent result of having life eternal (cf. 20:30-31). Watt's article is very telling and has affirmed the strong ethical presence which is very objective – to have faith in Jesus. And yet he has neither established the major ethical themes of John's Gospel nor the inter-connection between ethics and Christology vibrantly.

Richard A. Burridge[55] had a section on law and love command with a concluding remark that John's Christology brings along with it an ethic of the divine love, and to reflect the love of Jesus by loving others with the reason that Jesus has loved us. He further contends that John's Gospel shows a wider concern for the world and not just confined to the Johannine community alone

53 Jan G. van der Watt, "Radical Social Redefinition and Radical Love: Ethics and Ethos in the Gospel According to John," *Identity, Ethics, and Ethos in the New Testament*, edited by Jan G. van der Watt (Berlin: Walter de Gruyter, 2006), 107-134.

54 Jan G. van der Watt, "Ethics through the Power of Language," *Moral language in the New Testament*, edited by Ruben Zimmermann and Jan G. van der Watt in cooperation with Susanne Luther (Tubingen: Mohr Siebeck, 2010), 139-167.

55 Burridge, *Imitating Jesus*, 322-345.

and for which the Johannine approach to ethics has to apply the understanding of divine love brought about by Jesus to any individual moral issues guided by the exemplary gesture of Jesus who befriends a sinner (s), sets an example to be emulated, and creates a conducive environment for discipleship in a mixed community. Burridge speaks on universal principle of God's divine love which has a strong ethical implication and sees Jesus as the perfect model to understand God's love and so is Jesus a model for moral guidance where as he has not brought out the link between ethics and Christology that potentially impact the life of a community of believers. Russell Pregeant's[56] analysis of the ethics of the Johannine writings limits to the ethic of love. He argues that for the Johannine community, to do good correspond to loving one another in concrete ways which results from knowing the truth about Christ and thereby the Christological understanding becomes the foundation of ethics. This is an indication that Johannine ethical action flows from the true knowledge about Christ. Ethics is basically grounded in Christology in the Gospel according to John. However, this fact is not expressively dealt in his arguments. He also deals only with 'the Johannine ethic of love' which gives an impression to a probable proposition that ethics is limited only to the love commandment which however may not be an appropriate examination of the entire text (Gospel).

Recently, in May 2010, there was a conference on Ethics in the Johannine Literature at Nijmegen, which upheld the significant presence of ethical teaching at various levels in the Johannine literature. This indeed is a new trend and a shift from the old consensus to a new interest that has provoked scholars to bring out unattended ethical teachings embedded in the literature. In fact this said conference has broken the ground by evoking the need to pay serious attention to the ethical contents of the Johannine writings. Since then works on ethical contents of the Johannine writings seem to be gaining popularity in Johannine scholarship.

Ruben Zimmermann has vibrantly worked and presented a paper on the Nijmegen Conference, entitled - *What is "Ethics in John"? Challenging an outdated Consensus.* It is a very stimulating paper as the sub-title suggested – *Challenging an outdated consensus* (No ethics in John). It is fairly a well research work which gives a telling remark on John's Gospel as enabling "different readers in various situations to act concretely."[57] This sufficiently indicates an enriching ethical aspect of John's Gospel from the past and continuing to reach into the twenty-first century of our everyday lives. Earlier, some Biblical scholars have talked of John's presentation of the Gospel being undergirded by Jewish ethics which is embodied

56 Russell Pregeant, *Knowing Truth, Doing Good: Engaging New Testament Ethics* (Minneapolis: Fortress Press, 2008), 190-215.

57 The Nijmegen Conference 2010 papers are now published in *Rethinking the Ethics of John: "Implicit Ethics" in the Johannine Writings,* edited by Jan G. van der Watt and Ruben Zimmermann (WUNT 1/291; Tubingen, Germany: Mohr Siebeck, 2012).

in the phrase 'keep my commandments.'[58] So, also William Loader has addressed the significance of the Law (Torah) in relation to the understanding of Johannine ethics. He points out that putting Christ as the basis of ethics rather than the Torah in John is not a matter of "abandoning the God of Torah, but rather truly following where they allege it led."[59] The Gospel still reflects values of the Torah where it truly directs believers to have faith in Jesus as the Christ.

Conclusion

It becomes obvious, from the cursory survey, which eminent Johannine commentators and scholars have prescribed to the ethical elements of the Gospel. Expositions of Johannine ethical contents in the Gospel have opened a new horizon to which to look at, at the ethical aspects of the Gospel. This brief survey of the analyses of some of the scholars has shown the Christological importance in understanding Johannine ethics. Such precedent works prompt for further exploration for Johannine ethics from a new perspective to find the integral connection between ethics and Christology. Though it is not laid vibrantly on the surface the author (of the Gospel) nevertheless has a distinctive way of framing the ethical pointers and concepts with underlying implication in its own right.

John's Gospel always fascinates a reader who finds him/herself being taken to a deeper level than it appears in the first place. Ethics in John's Gospel is dramatized through narrative discourse rather than simply communicated through didactic teaching. It is acted out by Jesus himself as an ideal pattern and as an essential quality to be emulated for the believing community. Christology in fact becomes the way to dive into the understanding of ethics in John's Gospel because it is in Christology that ethics is articulated. And so this research will argue for the important pointers within Christological articulation to identify ethical elements in John's Gospel. John's Gospel standing out uniquely from the rest of the gospels is characterized by a very profound theological message. The idea of ethics is expressed in a way that is different from its presentation in the other New Testament documents. Anyone who reads the gospel material very intuitively is possibly taken on a higher plane. One cannot simply understand the depth and width of the ethical message conveyed just at the face value. It demands an inquisitive heart and mind to dive deep and get oneself transposed to a step further to grasp what is said beyond words.

In addition, one cannot therefore be limiting him/herself to find the same ethical language/issues found in the rest of the New Testament. The ethical language and thought takes a different height in the Gospel of John which demands a more careful and critical observation than that meets the eye at

58 For instance Kanagaraj, "The Implied Ethics of the Fourth Gospel of John:" 33-60.

59 William R. G. Loader, "The Law and Ethics in John's Gospel," *Rethinking the Ethics of John: "Implicit Ethics" in the Johannine Writings*, edited by Jan G. van der Watt and Ruben Zimmermann (WUNT 1/291; Tubingen, Germany: Mohr Siebeck, 2012), 143-158.

the first sight. So, the nature of the gospel demands a closer look and moves a further step and turn to the actions of figures in John's narrative to find out about appropriate ethical conduct. The identity of Jesus as the truth and light exerts an important ethical implication, because he reveals and exemplifies what constitutes an appropriate behavior (Jn. 8:12). Jesus models a pattern of conduct for His disciples (Jn. 13: 1-12) and for those who will believe in him because of the testimony of his disciples. We shall come to realize how Johannine Christology has influenced and shaped the perception of the Johannine community.

Johannine ethics is intrinsically Christo-centric in nature and as such ethics in John's Gospel depicts a chief significance that demands intensive study. Johannine Christology being one of the dominant themes that controls the other aspects of theology (for instance, eschatology, ecclesiology, Holy spirit, etc.) is highly intertwined with the concept of ethics in the Gospel. Wayne Meeks had contended that, "the gospel exemplifies a Christological implosion so that ethics becomes Christology." Likewise, ethics, which is theologically related, is essentially the offshoot of God's character himself. And most interestingly, Johannine Jesus is said to be the ultimate reflection of God's own character. For that reason, Johannine ethics which is highly Christological resonates the broader aspect of Johannine theology and it is essentially relational which demands response from human beings. This suggests that ethics springs from the right understanding of who God is in and through Jesus and his dealings with the humankind. To reiterate, Johannine ethics is Christologically stanched and therefore has a high Christological significance in understanding Christian ethics in our world today. The punch of the Johannine ethics is a call to ethics of faith/belief. Faith comes before action. According to John's Gospel, believing in Jesus will spontaneously lead to the right and basic ethical conduct.

The brief literary survey on Johannine ethics has become clear that there are scholars who have worked on Johannine ethics, examining the ethical contents critically and have thereby highlighted either the tacit or explicit ethical elements in the Gospel. And yet, as far as the present reader is concerned, there has been no intensive and exhaustive study done on the inter-connection between ethics and Christology in John's Gospel. The present work, therefore, is to venture into the relationship that might have existed between them. Having said this the present work will build upon the scholars' arguments referred and advance the field of research by establishing out rightly the interconnection between ethics and Christology limiting to John's Gospel. This present work, as such, is prompted by the need for doing a detailed study on the interconnection between the two very important aspects of the Johannine Gospel. One may, at the outset, find not convincing to accept ethics as one important aspect in Johannine themes because unlike many other New Testament documents, John does not present a set of rules at the face value. And it is this point that intrigues one to further explore and find out the implicit ethics that is implicitly indicated in the narrative of John's

Gospel and this is where the interest lies, to investigate the relation between ethics and Christology. The analysis for the ethical exploration in the Gospel will be taken up through the close readings of the narrative world of the Gospel of John in the third chapter. The immediate concern is to look into the social world of the Johannine community which might shed light to the better understanding of the intended research endeavor.

Chapter 2

Socio-Cultural and Religious Milieu of the Johannine Community

Introduction

It goes without saying that the New Testament documents by and large were written for particular and distinctive early Christian communities and so they speak to us from that distant particular social worlds.[1] The manuscripts of the New Testament presuppose and encode information regarding the social humanity in which they were produced.[2] This is essentially true also for the Fourth Gospel that it was written within a particular social world occasioned by the social dimensions of a particular community's life experiences. Thus, the trend in recent years has been to find the Fourth Gospel as the product of a particular Christian community (specifically the Johannine community) facing its own definite and particular pressures and tensions in its own situation.[3] And for which one has to carefully navigate into the social dimensions[4] of the community's experiences for better comprehension of the particular community which is under study.

---

1 From the social point of view these early Christians communities can be considered as social worlds.

2 Timothy J. M. Ling, *The Judean Poor and the Fourth Gospel* (Cambridge: Cambridge University Press, 2006), 2.

3 Christopher Tuckett, *Christology and the New Testament: Jesus and His Earliest Followers* (Edinburgh: Edinburgh University Press, 2001), 153.

4 Often the social dimensions/aspects include the social, economic, religious, cultural and political contexts without which a reliable understanding of the Biblical text may be far from adequate determination/investigation of the original meaning imbedded in it.

Respectively, social science (sociology) is being adopted as the most appropriate methodology to understand the social sides of the Johannine community in this research endeavor. "Social sciences as a discipline to approach the social world of the text are best seen as a necessary adjunct to established forms of criticism."[5] Social science as a discipline cannot overlook the significant place of historiography and so "in dealing with the past they must inevitably collaborate with history,"[6] for having considered the social science approach as the most appropriate methodology to understand the socio-historical milieu of the Fourth Gospel. Accordingly, the present chapter will focus on the aspects of the life experiences of the Johannine community which will provide a significant insight into the nature of the community's social identity and its subsequent historical situation.[7]

2.1. Nature and Composition of Johannine Community

The Johannine literature is the product of faith community or group of communities that evidently persisted with some consistent identity over a considerable span of time[8] reflecting its own historical perspectives and cultural patterns.[9] But, where does one locate the milieu of the Johannine writing (Gospel) initially? – Was it Palestinian Judaism[10] or Diaspora Judaism?[11] - Some suggest the former and some the latter. There are advocates for each of them.

The nature and composition of the community is predominantly the Jewish Christians and other Gentile and Samaritan Christians. It is rational to admit that the writing has its final shape in the non-Palestinian context though the context in its initial formation of the Johannine community would have been possibly

5 Philip F. Esler, *The First Christians in their Social Worlds: Social-Scientific Approaches to New Testament Interpretation* (London and New York: Routledge, 1994), 2.

6 Esler, *The First Christians in their Social Worlds*, 2. He rightly amended that the social scientific method is specifically developed to comprehend the social dimensions of human experience. So for the social interpretation of the New Testament documents social scientific approach is seen as most appropriate methodology for dealing with the social sides of the early Christian communities.

7 W. Randolph Tate, *Biblical Interpretation: An Integrated Approach*, 3rd edition (Grand Rapids, Michigan: Baker Academic, 2008), 78-81. For the social interpretation of the Fourth Gospel the social-scientific perspectives such as sociology of Knowledge (which encapsulates the insight that all knowledge has a social beginnings and that human consciousness is determined by its social setting) and sociology of sectarianism are taken valid for the present study.

8 Wayne A. Meeks, "The Man from Heaven in Johannine Sectarianism," *The Interpretation of John*, 2nd edition, edited by John Ashton (Edinburgh: T&T Clark, 1997), 173. The same article was first published in *JBL* 91 (1972): 44-72.

9 Tate, *Biblical Interpretation*, 80.

10 John Painter, *John: Witness & Theologian* (London: SPCK, 1974), 6.

11 Craig S. Keener, *The Gospel of John: A Commentary*, vol. 1 (Peabody, Massachusetts: Hendrickson Publishers, 2003), 175.

Palestinian Judaism. Considering the fact that the community was primarily Jewish in nature, the study henceforth is focused against its own Jewish backdrop. Palestine was a Jewish populated area and was therefore a geographical abode for the Jews (homeland of/for the people of the Jews).[12] And those of the Jews living outside Palestine were technically designated as Diaspora. It is against this non-Palestinian social set up that the socio-religious milieu of the community is to be looked upon. Judaism as a whole serves as the background of the Gospel. The Judaism of Jesus' time was subject to the political supremacy of the Romans. The whole of the Near West was brought under the Roman domination in the middle of the first century B.C.E.[13] and the Jews as a result were under the Roman rule politically.

One cannot bypass the social milieu of the Johannine community which has contributed significantly to the overall purpose of the writing of the Gospel in its extant and finished layout. The Gospel is not merely theological product and expression but it also bears and signifies the circumstances which the community as a group of believing people had experienced. Belief in Jesus as the expected Messiah and Son of God constitutes the Johannine community of faith as a discrete religious group in the religious environment of their time.[14] The Johannine community is a new community of God's children established by faith in Jesus (Jn. 1:12) filling the void created by Israel's rejection of the *logos*.[15] There

---

12 The Hebrew people traditionally composed of twelve tribes after the name of the sons of Jacob. These twelve tribes then called themselves and the land they inhabited as "Israel." They had their own kingdom of Israel. Saul (approx. 1020-1004 BCE) was appointed the first King of Israel. King David (1000-961 BCE i.e., 10th -9th century BCE) succeeded King Saul, and reign for almost 40 years. Then his son Solomon (965-928 BCE) took over the kingship. The kingdom reached its peak during the reign of King Solomon and it was a significant reign because there was peace and prosperity during which King Solomon (the final king of Israel before the split of the monarchic) built Temple for Yahweh in the capital city of Israel called Jerusalem. In 928 BCE, shortly after King Solomon died the kingdom of Israel was divided into two - (i) The 10 tribes of Israel formed the Northern Kingdom retaining the name "Israel" and had its capital at Samaria. It continued in existence until 722 BCE, when the Assyrian empire conquered it and deported many of its people. Till then the northern kingdom never existed as an independent state. (ii) The Southern kingdom consisted primarily of the tribe of Judah and Benjamin and had its capital at Jerusalem. The Southern state of Judea, after the fall of Israel, maintained its independence until 587 BCE, when Nebuchadnezzar, king of Babylonian empire, capture Jerusalem, destroyed Solomon's Temple, and exiled many prominent members of the Jewish people. The land of Judah or "Judea" gave its inhabitant the name "Judeans" from which came the term "Jews." So, technically, the term "Jews" embraces those belonging to the tribe of Judah. Delbert Burkett, *An Introduction to the New Testament and the Origins of Christianity* (Cambridge: Cambridge University Press, 2002), 15-16.

13 Eduard Lohse, *The First Christians: Their Beginnings, Writings, and Belief,* translated by M. Eugene Boring (Philadelphia: Fortress Press, 1983), 11.

14 Larry W. Hurtado, *Lord Jesus Christ: Devotion to Jesus in Earliest Christianity* (Michigan: Wm. B. Eerdmans Publishing Company, 2003), 351.

15 John W. Pryor, *John: Evangelist of the Covenant People* (Illinois: InterVarsity Press, 1992), 115.

was an ongoing tension over "who Jesus is?" and to absorb the truth about the identity of Jesus was crucial and defining moment for the Johannine Christians.[16] Thus, the Johannine Jewish Christian's controversies with the Johannine Judaism probably sharpened and refined their views concerning Jesus.

The Johannine faith community underwent alienation and hostility from which it had first stemmed from (Judaism) and as a result suffered "social ostracism and then the loss of relationship with family."[17] From whence do we get the information then? The material from which the historical situation of the community is to be deduced is from within the body of the text itself.[18] As such clues to the historical circumstances of the Johannine community can be delineated within the Gospel wherefore the historical content of the Gospel needs to be recognized and considered that has significantly contributed to the overall understanding of the Gospel itself. It is therefore essential *not* to view the Fourth Gospel simply as a reflection of a developed/developing theology.[19] The Gospel definitely lays bare the interpretation of the events and so the profound interpretation of the Gospel events corresponds to the events that had taken place in a specific time of history in the life of the Johannine community of the Fourth Gospel.

The present chapter dives into the study of the socio-religious circumstances of the Johannine community with a supposition that the socio-religious situation conditions the community's life experiences. And these existential experiences consequently contributed much to the ethical values of the so called Johannine community as much as it might have affected their beliefs in and about Jesus. Belief in Jesus was central to the formation of the Johannine community of faith over against those fellow Jews who rejected Jesus as the Messiah. Belief in Jesus therefore was significant in the "subsequent struggles among Johannine Christians over their continuing identity, directions of development, and religious integrity."[20] The social nature of the community inevitably has informed the content of ethics. Congruently, the historical experiences of the Johannine community must be taken into consideration to unmask the ethical aspects found in the Gospel. But, before we proceed further to the socio-cultural and religious experience of the Johannine community we will have a cursory look at the Greek and Jewish ethics consecutively.

---

16 David A. DeSilva, *An Introduction to the New Testament: Contexts, Methods & Ministry Formation* (Illinois: InterVarsity Press, 2004), 401.

17 David K. Rensberger, *Johannine Faith and Liberating Community* (Philadelphia: Westminster, 1988), 26.

18 Bart D. Ehrman, *The New Testament: A Historical Introduction to the Early Christian Writings*, second edition (Oxford: Oxford University Press, 2000), 166.

19 Painter, *John: Witness & Theologian*, 7.

20 Hurtado, *Lord Jesus Christ*, 350-351.

2.2. A Cursory Sketch of Greek and Jewish Ethics: Background Study

The Johannine community for sure did not live in isolation and so had lived in a specific socio-cultural historical context. It is considered that the Gospel of John was written sometime in the late first century C.E. and it is also believed that the author of the Gospel is a Palestinian[21] Jew. This Jewish homeland called the Palestine belonged to the Greco-Roman world i.e., a world governed politically by the Roman Empire but united by Greek language and culture.[22] The community as such has not escaped outside influence from its neighboring environment. As a result the community's moral development and formation has to be understood in the larger Mediterranean world. This so called 'Roman world' also lived in them: in their thinking, language, and their relationships.[23] It is said that "the first Christians paid careful attention both to the sayings and instructions offered to them by the Jewish and those which had been developed by the Greek philosophers."[24] The Johannine community however being a religious oriented community had its inclination more towards the Jewish in terms of moral values. The origin of the Gospel must thereby be sought in the world of the first - century Judaism.

The present sub-heading is an attempt to unravel the socio-ethical concerns in the first century among the Greeks and the Jews. However, there will be no discussion in length about the Greek ethics. It is beyond the scope of this present work that every detail of the socio-ethical discourses of the ancient Greek ethics be reduplicated at great length. And yet a sketchy portrait will only be discussed with an understanding that it may shed partial light to the present work undertaken. Keeping with the date of composition of the Gospel in the late first century, this period was an age of syncretism.[25] There probably was a fusion of Hebrew and Greek religious and philosophical thoughts in the first century.[26] As such, the period was occasioned by a wide spread of Greek religious and philosophical ideas that seem to converge in the Jewish thought world.[27]

---

21 Palestine geographically touches the Mediterranean Sea on the West, The Arabian desert on the East, Syria on the North, and Egypt on the South. It is said that the Roman government and Greek culture prevailed in the lands surrounding the Mediterranean in the first century to which almost every document of the NT books were written.

22 Burkett, *An Introduction to the New Testament*, 15; John Drane, *Introducing the New Testament*, revised edition (Oxford: A Lion Book, 1999[1986]), 15; Ehrman, *The New Testament*, 19.

23 Wayne A. Meeks, *The Moral World of the First Christians* (London: SPCK, 1986), 13.

24 Lohse, *The First Christians*, 88.

25 C. K. Barrett, *The Gospel According to St. John*, 2nd edition (Philadelphia: The Westminster Press, 1978), 27.

26 Jey J. Kanagaraj and Ian S. Kemp, *Gospel of John* (Bangalore: Asia Theological Association, 2000), 54.

27 For instance, Philo of Alexandria, a Jewish philosopher, contemporary of Jesus and of John the Baptist, in dispersion who was so influenced by Hellenism (a syncretism of Greek religious and

The Gospel was composed in such a time when political catastrophe, insecurity, poverty, persecution and religious pluralism were part of life experiences of the people in the late first century C.E.[28] The Jewish religion was merged with the Greek religious ideas and culture. Thus the materials we have to work are the fragments (/and texts) of the ethical discourse that informed us about the ethical characters of the Greek and Jewish ethics. It is assumed that the Johannine community has assimilated in them the socio-cultural aspects of the larger family within which it grew and that the community's life style was affected in its fundamental relationships, in its values, perceptions of reality, and to certain extent even the structures of the self. This is why it is vital to know ethical aspects of the Greeks and the Jews with which the Johannine community must have shared certain socially learned world views which further have consciously or unconsciously affected the individual's and eventually the community's way of conduct. So, we try to understand the symbolic, social, and the moral discourse of the Johannine community shared with Greeks and the Jewish people.

2.2.1. Ancient Greek Ethics

Among the Greeks, ethics began with an intellectual awareness of the need to put precise questions and look for answers with a conscious technique.[29] ἀρετή 'arete' or virtue was the main ethical category for ancient Greeks. Where *arete* or virtue would mean an impulse, certain strength or even a force, or an ability to do good with a view to attain the highest good. The Greeks invented the *polis* which is often translated as city or state and this polis served as the context for Greek ethics. This is to admit that the focus of the moral life, in the Greek society, was the city-state. The ancient Greek speculation was that an individual has no notion of good or evil apart from the law of his/her country or the creed of the church. This notion of the individual and the state, of ethics and politics pervaded the

---

philosophical thoughts) attempted to express the Hebrew faith and religious experience in the Greek philosophical and religious thought.

28 Jey J. Kanagaraj, *The Gospel of John: A Commentary* (Secunderabad: OM Books, 2005), 25.

29 T. E. Jessop, "History of Ethics," *A Dictionary of Christian Ethics*, edited by John Macquarrie (London: SCM Press, 1967), 116. Moral expression took philosophical form in Socrates. He search into the meaning of such ethical concepts/ terms as good, just and temperate, and practiced a method of suggested definitions, for instance comparing each with the kind of instances it claimed to cover, to make sure that it did cover instances of that kind and no others. Plato sketched out the first outline of the moral life in particular the realization of the four cardinal virtues (justness, courage, moderation of desire and practical insights) and in general a movement from the sensory and the sensual towards a perfection eternally there behind our only half-real world. He reserved the highest virtue of pure contemplation of the eternal to philosophers. Aristotle (on *Ethica Nicomachea* '*Nicomachean Ethics*') considered human life more concretely. Its raw stuff of appetites and emotions are not in us to be degraded or mortified but to be humanized by reason. He worked out moral scheme of fourteen virtues, and out of which, like Plato, reserved the highest virtue of pure contemplation of the eternal to philosophers.

genuine character of the ancient Greek thought.[30] So, the most obvious social context in shaping the major visible traditions of ancient Greek ethics is the life in the Greek *polis*.[31] The city-state is considered the highest form of community, where every state aims at the highest good (*Politic* i.i cf. *Republic* iv. 420b)[32] and wherein every moral life of an individual may be rightly appraised. The ethical end of an individual's life in ancient Greece was to be measured by the perfection of the State and the perfection of the State likewise determines the moral life of each individual (*Republic* iv. 434c; 433a, b; 443c; 442d; 420b).[33]

We shall consider three prominent ancient Greek philosophers consecutively who have laid the foundation of Greek ethics. Firstly, Socrates who was born in 469 and lived till 399 B.C.E.).[34] He is a great Athenian figure who is considered as a milestone in the history of ethics in Ancient Greece. He regarded *arete* for the first time as the rational part of human soul/mind (psyche).[35] For Socrates, virtue is knowledge through concept. It is the chief business of life (*Laws* 7. 807c) and the greatest good (*Laws* 2.661b). He maintains that morality is the knowledge of the Good through concepts (*Phaedrus* 247c).[36] Moral laws are based on rational thought, according to him, and not on feeling and desires as his immediate predecessors and contemporaries, namely, the Sophists believed. Socrates acknowledged the role of *reason* which plays in the formation of knowledge and morality, for *reason* is one and the same in all people, which alone can give to us what is universal and valid for all persons.[37] As such morality is

---

30 *The Dialogues of Plato*, vol. 2, translated into English with Analyses and Introductions by B. Jowett (Oxford: Clarendon Press, 1953), 27.

31 Meeks, *The Moral World of the First Christians*, 20-38.

32 *The Basic Works of Aristotle,* translated by J. W. Ross, edited and with Introduction by Richard Mckeon (New York: Random House, 1941), 1127.

33 *The Basic Works of Aristotle,* 1127.

34 Y. Masih, *A Critical History of Western Philosophy,* 5th revised & enlarged edition (Delhi: Motilal Banarsidass, 1994), 37. Earlier edition printed as *"A Critical History of Modern Philosophy."* Socrates completely gave himself to philosophical enquiry and yet has not written anything. However three accounts about him has been left by his followers - Plato, Xenophon (*Apology*), and Aristophanes (*The clouds*). Plato, among them, is the chief exponent of his master's life and teachings in his dialogues.

35 Giovanni Reale, *History of Ancient Philosophy IV, A: The Schools of the Imperial Age,* edited and translated by John R. Catan (New York: State University of New York Press, 1990), 200.

36 *The Dialogues of Plato*, vol. 3, translated into English with Analyses and Introduction by B. Jowett (Oxford: Clarendon Press, 1953), 153-154.

37 Masih, *A Critical History of Western Philosophy,* 39, 40, 46, 47. The Sophists held that the laws of the state are made in the interest of the ruling party, implying the idea that "might is right" but Socrates disagreed with their conclusion. Socrates appears that he was committed to know the inner man. So he was concerned to find the truth involved about the universal validity of moral laws, which was connected with the chief problem his maxim, "Man! Know thyself." So Socrates main inquiry is to discover and know one's own self (see *Phaedrus* 230 a in *The Dialogues of Plato,* vol. 3, by B. Jowett).

universal knowledge of the Good. The Good is advantageous for humankind and advances to his/her happiness. Socrates holds the view that there is one Idea of the Good which is the cause for all things of all that is right and beautiful (*Republic* vii. 517c).[38] The Idea of the Good, therefore, is one single reality which underlies all that is called virtue or good (*Republic* vii. 517c; *Protagoras* 349a).That means for Socrates virtue or goodness is one and where the idea of the good controls all other ideas and eventually "guides the whole man, his will and feelings too, and necessarily issues into good acts."[39]

Plato of Athens (429-347/8 B.C.E.) like his master Socrates took the Idea of the Good as the crowing of his thought: virtue as knowledge through the concept of Good. He holds that the Idea of the Good alone rules and regulates the order of all Ideas (which he deems as something *real* "ideal" but that cannot be seen (sensed) but that which can be thought (*Republic* vi. 507b).[40] The Idea of the Good then is the highest reality and is the cause of truth and knowledge (*Republic* vi. 509b)[41] for it is in the contemplation on the Idea of the Good that causes an upward urge towards sojourn to the higher region of the intelligible world in men [sic] and in all things (*Republic* vii. 517b,c, 518c). As such Plato's main goal in his ethical philosophy is to lead the way toward a vision of the 'good.'[42] Note that the good is good for its own sake and not a means to attain happiness (*Gorgias* 499c). Good is the end of all actions and that everything else must be done for its sake, not the good for the sake of everything else (*Gorgias* 449e). He contended that the soul perceives the highest good under certain situations in which the soul is no longer bounded to the particularity of sense experience.[43]

38 *The Dialogues of Plato*, vol. 2, 379.

39 Masih, *A Critical History of Western Philosophy*, 48.

40 *The Dialogues of Plato*, vol. 2, 369.

41 *The Dialogues of Plato*, vol. 2, 371-372.

42 Raziel Abelson and Kai Nielsen, "History of Ethics," *The Encyclopedia of Philosophy*, vols. 3 & 4, edited by Paul Edwards *et al.*, (New York/ London: Macmillan Publishing Company & The Free Press/Collier Macmillan Publishers, 1967), 83.

43 *The Dialogues of Plato*, vol. 2. Plato constructed a systematic view of nature, God and man from which he derived his ethical principles. He propounded the theory of Forms (see *Republic* book V esp. toward the end). He divided the objects of knowledge into two main categories and each into two subcategories. The main division is between the realm of changing, sensible objects and that of the unchanging, abstract forms. Knowledge of sensible objects acquired by sense perception is inaccurate and uncertain because the object of sense is in continual flux. Knowledge of timeless forms, in contrast, is precise and rigorously provable. The realm of sensible objects is subdivided into shadows and images, in the lower section, and natural objections in the upper section. The realm of forms is subdivided into mathematical and ethical forms. At the apex of this ascending line is the Form of the Good, in relation to which all other objects of knowledge must be defined if they are to be understood. Thus, ethics is the supreme and most rigorous kind of knowledge, surpassing even mathematics, but at the same time the most difficult to attain. Mathematics leads us away from reliance on visual images and sense perception, and ethical philosophy demands an even greater effort of abstraction.

Every individual is expected to do his/her own work because the happiness resides not in this or that class (e.g., cobbler, peasant, sculptor, artisan, etc.) but in the State as a whole (*Republic* iv. 441-442; *Gorgias* 504d).[44] Plato enlarges the picture of an individual ethics into that of the working of the State. He tried to inquire the individual's moral justice in its magnified form called the State/city (*Republic* iv. 434c). Plato identifies goodness with reality and reality with intelligible form and thus concludes that the search for value must lead away from sense perception and bodily pleasure.[45] When a person is under the guidance of reason, then soul becomes the author of good (*Phaedrus* 253c) which suggests that the soul is held responsible for moral good and evil (*Republic* iv. 439-442). He believed that the human reason is competent to know the necessity and sufficient insight to know the true content of human obligation (*Phaedo* 84a). His contention is practically and universally not applicable to all humanbeings because not every individual gets to attain the full and complete knowledge of the good. And most significantly, what is the 'good' is lacking a universally accepted specific definition and so is left undefined (Socrates himself gave no definite explanation about the Good).[46] What is understood as good may not necessarily be a universally accepted entity as good because what is good to one may not be the same to another fellow in a different social set-up.

Another founder of ancient Greek ethics worth mentioning is Aristotle of Macedonia (384-322 B.C.E.). For Aristotle *arete* or virtue implies intention and consistency of purpose (*E.N.* vi.4). Virtues are concerned with actions (*E.N.* ii.3).[47] He identifies the supreme/highest good with happiness which he defines

---

The objects of ethical knowledge are concepts and principles ultimately unified under all-encompassing concept of the Good.

44 Cf. Socrates who considers virtue as one and also equalizes with goodness. For instance, Cowness is one but many cows (with many particulars has some common qualities called essential (i.e., cowness is an essential quality of the whole class of cows, for without the quality of cowness, no animal can be called a cow) and some others as accidental (its color, shape, size, etc) poorly imitate it. Similarly, wisdom, temperance, justice and holiness are five kinds of virtue, there is but one single reality which underlies them all (*Protagoras* 349 a cf. *Republic* 7. 517c). Reasoning, temper and desires are three parts of the soul according to Socrates. And where the function of reasoning is wisdom, of temper is courage, and of desire is soberness or temperance. Wisdom commands, temper assists in the execution of these commands, and, desires (appetites) furnishes the material basis of action. All kinds of virtue follow from the health of the soul (where the soul is believed to have different functions corresponding to its basic component parts) which follows from the discipline among these parts. See *The Dialogues of Plato*, vol. 2, 295-297, and 602.

45 Abelson and Kai Nielsen, "History of Ethics," 83.

46 See remarks on various interpretations about the good in Masih, *A Critical History of Western Philosophy* , 51.

47 *The Basic Works of Aristotle*, 954. *Nicomachean Ethics* is a transliteration from the Greek "*Ethica Nicomachea.*" Aristotle on *Nicomachean Ethics* opens with the recognition that all knowledge

as the exercise of natural human faculties in accordance with virtue.[48] Happiness is the final end.[49] The concept of happiness, according to Aristotle, is something final and self sufficient good and is the end of action (*E.N.* i. 4). And so for him happiness is consisted in "cultivating the virtues and avoiding the vices at their extremes, so as to insure a life with the greatest possible happiness."[50] Analyzing the rational inquiry to the function of humankind, Edward LeRoy Long asserts that one can truly attain well being when he/she comes to understand what is truly excellent.[51] But, what is that true excellence also needs proper definition for `wider application and acceptance. Aristotle's discussions on certain account of ethics such as - of goods as the ends of human practices, of the human good as that end to which all other goods are ordered, and of the rules of justice required for a community of ordered practices, are some very essential features of human practice within the Greek polis.[52] Especially the assembly and the law courts were common public forum where a successful social career begins to flourish/establish.[53] For Aristotle, ethics is the determination of behavior in relation to an end. He defined the highest good of man [*sic*] in terms of happiness, happiness that which is understood in relation to the whole function and purpose of man [*sic*]. Moral life, for Aristotle, was then singularly governed by the human logic based on strict justice and not the logic unmerited love, mercy and forgiveness that are found in Jesus Christ.[54] Aristotle's final investigation result is the definition of happiness or good life as activity in accordance with virtue, and thus as the harmonious fulfillment of humankind's natural demand/tendencies.[55] So, for him happiness is the chief goal and good that every human must strive for.

---

and action aim at some good by inquiry into the nature of the good and, in particular, of the highest good.

48 Abelson and Kai Nielsen, "History of Ethics," 85.

49 Alasdair Maclntyre, *A Short History of Ethics*, special Indian edition (London and New York: Routledge, 1998), 60.

50 Daniel J. Harrington and James Keenan, *Jesus and Virtue Ethics* (Lanham: Rowman & Littlefield Publishers, 2002), 43.

51 Edward LeRoy Long, *A Survey of Christian Ethics* (New York: Oxford University Press, 1967), 4.

52 Maclntyre, *A Short History of Ethics*, xvii.

53 Maclntyre, *A Short History of Ethics*, 14.

54 Harrington and James Keenan, *Jesus and Virtue Ethics*, 43.

55 Aristotle's ethical writing *Nicomachean Ethics* is followed by the *politics* which is an extension of his ethical principles to social regulation. He begins his inquiry searching for the common feature of all things said to be good and concludes that there are many different senses of 'good' each of which must be defined separately for the limited area in which it applies (in contrast to Plato who held that there is a Form of Good in which all good things 'participate'). Each such 'good' is pursued by a specific practical art of science, such as economics, military strategy, medicine, shipbuilding. But the ends of these particular disciplines can be grouped in order of importance, so that the highest good can be identified with the goal of the most general

Ancient Greek ethics teaches "the good life as a whole without being confined either to justifying moral principles and values."[56] As such the traditional approach to ethics has been an attempt to answer questions such as: what values are most worthwhile? Why does one act better than the other? In simple terms, ethics basically is a study of human values, attempting to stimulate the moral sense, to discover the true values of life, and to inspire humans to join in the quest for these values. No person can live a satisfactory life unless he/she has not set up some scale of values.[57] Virtue gives happiness where happiness is the consequence of the harmonious working of all the faculties of the soul (i.e., the working of desires and appetites under the reason of the soul). This is an implication that true happiness is reached when the will has been under the control of 'reason.'[58] There was a belief and an interest in the traditional philosophical ethics, in the power of reason to guide human to the good of life where the good must be something final and self-sufficient (*E.N* i.7).[59] Thus, 'reason'[60] has been regarded as providing human a sufficient guidance for the conduct of life though the understanding of how reason functions differs among the exponents of the traditional approach to moral philosophy.

And so the Greek moralist(s) seem to "set out to provide a self-contained and self-justifying system of ethics."[61] That is a life dedicated to virtue that alone yields the good life and the ultimate end in happiness without much pain and trouble. The ethical system of Greek philosophy is concerned with abstract definitions which further seek to define various virtues like courage, generosity, or justice,

---

practical science to which the others are subordinate. On an individual level, this all-inclusive science is ethics; on a social level, it is politics. The end of ethics is personal happiness and that of politics is the general welfare, and since the good of the whole ranks above that of the part, personal ethics is subordinate to politics (*E.N.* Book 1 chapters 1-3).

56 Burkhard Reis (ed.), *The Virtuous Life in Greek Ethics* (Cambridge: Cambridge University Press, 2006), 1.

57 Harold H. Titus, *Ethics for Today*, 3rd edition (New York: American Book, 1957), 11, cited by Edward LeRoy Long, *A Survey of Christian Ethics* (New York: Oxford University Press, 1967), 4.

58 Masih, *A Critical History of Western Philosophy*, 62.

59 *The Basic Works of Aristotle*, 941-942.

60 Early Greek philosophers began to search for reasons for established modes of conduct and, where no reason were found, to suggest that action could be directed toward individual goals of defiance of tradition. Socrates and Sophists (the professional teachers) demanded reasons for rules of conduct, rejecting the self-justifying claim of tradition. Socrates (esp.) believed that by the use of reason man could arrive at a set of ethical principles that would reconcile self-interest with the common good and would apply to all men at all times. For more details on Greek ethics see, Abelson and Kai Nielsen, "History of Ethics," 82-85.

61 C. H. Dodd, *Gospel and Law* (Cambridge: Cambridge University Press, 1951), 10.

etc. and seeks out after the ethical perfection of an individual.[62] Greek ethics then is inclined much towards intellectualism where philosophers are considered the prime inhabitant of the highest intellect and thereby the most privileged because they are capable of pure contemplation of the eternal (*Republic* v. 474; vi. 484).[63] So, ancient Greek ethics is inclined much towards philosophical ethics in which ethics is the highest and greatest study for the Philosopher (*Republic* vi. 504, 505, 509a, 509b cf. v. 473d; viii.540d contrast viii.544e). But, this is not so as compared to the ethical teachings found in the New Testament documents. New Testament ethical teachings are religiously and theologically oriented more towards the Christ-event as compared to Greek ethics. If the Greek philosophers talked of an Ideal, it is Jesus Christ, for the Gospel narratives and for the Pauline corpuses, because Jesus is the Truth, the Way and the Life (esp. John's Gospel). If the ethics of Greek philosophers is based on rational will (that which they called virtue as knowledge) the Johannine ethics is based not on rational will but on the fact of the purpose and reason of the person and work of Jesus, the *logos* who became flesh and lived amongst us who is the Christ, the Son of God and the Son of Man (this christological aspect of Johannine ethics will be treated in chapter 4). There is therefore no abstract or comprehensive concept in the Fourth Gospel which parallels the ancient Greek ethics. By and large for the New Testament, ethics rather arises out of a response to the Gospel that was proclaimed, especially for the community of the Fourth Gospel, their fundamental conviction of the faith in the person of Jesus Christ is the core of their approach to ethics which nonetheless is founded upon the love of God in and through Jesus. This is to attest that the Johannine ethics is a theologically oriented ethics where Jesus is both the relative and absolute standard for the ethics of the Johannine Christian community.

2.2.2. Jewish Ethics

Jewish ethics is the moral philosophy of the Jewish religion and its people.[64] The ethics of the Jewish people is said to have originated with the Hebrew Bible,[65]

---

62 Jacob Licht and Andre Neher, "Ethics," *Jewish Values* (Jerusalem: Keter Publishing House Jerusalem Ltd., 1974), 133. This book is a compilation from the material originally published in the *Encyclopaedia Judaica.*

63 Jessop, "History of Ethics," 116.

64 David A. Teutsch, "Ethical Theories in the Reconstructionist Movement," *The Oxford Handbook of Jewish Ethics and Morality,* edited by Elliot N. Dorff and Jonathan K. Crane (Oxford: Oxford University Press, 2013), 264.

65 The Hebrew Bible is divided into three major divisions. Namely - (i) the Law (*Torah*) consisting of the first five books of the OT. Traditionally it is considered to be the works of Moses, so books of Moses (Genesis through Deuteronomy). It is also called the Pentateuch by Protestants; (ii) the Prophets (*Nebiim*), which consists the Former Prophets (Joshua, Judges, I & II Samuel, I & II Kings), Latter Prophets (Isaiah, Jeremiah, Ezekiel), and the Twelve minor Prophets (Hosea, Joel, Amos, Obadiah, Jonah, Micah, Nahum, Habakkuk, Zephaniah,

and is thereby believed as the source of all law. Importantly, the Hebrew Bible is considered God-given with moral code and examples of just law and religious behavior. As such the ethical element of the Hebrew Bible is central to the Jewish religion, both in principle (means) and as goal (end).[66] The law of the Bible with its broad legal injunctions, advisory narratives and prophecies are deemed as divine demands and revelations.[67] In effect the divine intervention of God is deemed as the root of the moral codes for the Jewish people. The Jewish people agreed that the laws of the Bible were of vital importance, and, as the Word of God, was binding on all Jews, at and for all times. To the Jews, Torah was the word of God, revealed and dictated on Mount Sinai and written down by Moses. The prophetic books were written by prophet themselves interpreting, if not repeating verbatim, the words of God, except the third major division of the Bible i.e., the Writings, was considered to have been written by human beings (notably kings, scribes like Ezra, Nehemiah). Having said this, most Jewish ethical claims are understood to be found in the themes and teachings of the written law (Torah) consisting of 613 commandments including the Ten Commandments.[68] These three major groups of the Hebrew Scriptures were regarded as inspired and sacred and yet all were not considered as of equal authority. They stood on three terraces -Torah is attributed the highest importance, then the Prophets and followed by the Writings.[69]

Haggai, Zechariah, Malachi) ;(iii) the Writings or Hagiographa (*Ketubim*) consist of the eleven books (Psalms, Proverbs, Job, Song of Songs (or Canticles), Ruth, Lamentations, Qoheleth (or Ecclesiastes), Esther, Daniel, Ezra-Nehemiah (as one book), and I & II Chronicles (as one book). For further categorization of the Hebrew Bible among Christian Churches (e.g., Protestant, Roman Catholic, Greek Orthodox, Eastern Christians like Ethiopian Church). See John J. Collins, *Introduction to the Hebrew Bible* (Minneapolis: Fortress Press, 2004), 2-5.

66 At least two principle trends can be distinguished i.e., we can see two facets of Jewish ethics - (i) Jewish ethics with moderation (middle way), set down in Proverbs and various Psalms. It condemns excess, both in the sense of evil and good, equally condemns greed and waste, debauchery and abstinence, pleasure and asceticism, impiety and bigotry. (ii) the second Jewish ethics insists on the extreme demands of an absolute. The middle way is rejected or strongly criticized especially in the biblical books of Job and Ecclesiastes. In the rabbinical writing, the attitude of moderation is placed on par with the attitude of Sodom (*Pierke Avot/ Aboth* 5:13). However, it is quite right to acknowledge that both the attitudes (moderate and absolute) are equally typical of Jewish ethics. Licht and Andre Neher, "Ethics," 141-146.

67 Robert A. Morey, *The Bible, Natural Theology and Natural Law: Conflict or Compromise?* (Millerstone: Christian Scholars Press, 2010), 2.

68 It was traditionally believed that the laws amounting to 613 commandments were revealed to Moses at Mount Sinai. Out of these 613, 365 are prohibitions i.e., those stipulations that the children of Israel must not do. And the remaining 248 commandments are mandates, or positive commands which constitute a variety of things children of Israel as Jews are obligated to do. See Emily Taizt, *Introduction to the World's Major Religions*: *Judaism,* vol. I, edited by Lee W. Bailey (London: Greenwood Press, 2006), 17, 24.

69 D. S. Russell, *Between the Testaments* (Philadelphia: Fortress Press, 1960, 1965), 59.

The Jewish religion stood on a concept that there is a single incorporeal God who gives commandments which constitutes a moral law for all humanity. As stated earlier, this divine moral law is said to have been embodied in the codes set out in the Torah.[70] The Torah is then attributed as the written expression of the covenant between God and the 'People of Israel,' to be kept by the latter, by which they must live the right way to an end which would be peace (e.g. Ps. 37:11).[71] Russell commented that the Jewish zeal for the Torah was "for the covenant to which the Book testified, a covenant made by God in which he had set the Jewish nation apart to be his peculiar people. To despise the Torah was to betray the covenant which God had made with their fathers."[72] The Torah, as such is placed at the heart of the Jewish life, belief and practices. Consequently, the Torah is acknowledged as the basis for ethics. It is at the center of the Jewish faith. It is said that even Artaxersas, the Persian king made the Torah the basis of communal and private life.[73] Nehemiah chapter 8 records the great gathering of the children of Israel in which Ezra the Scribe empowered by the Persian King read the Law for the first time (Neh. 8:8). Torah was held as a God-given moral and religious order for the children of Israel.[74] The Torah was a sort of a constitution for the Jewish people. There is an instruction to pursue justice and practice communal responsibility. Justice is one of the religious obligations of Judaism. True justice balances the needs of the community and not just the individual. So, for the Israelites, justice and fairness in their dealings with their fellow Jews in the society was of prime importance (Deut. 16:20). In Judaism, giving to those in need is an act of justice and the right thing to do.[75] It is the performance of a duty prescribed in the Torah: "Since there will never cease to some in need on the earth, I therefore command you, "Open your hand to the poor and needy neighbor in your land" (Deut. 15:11 cf. Jn. 12:8).

There is a general tendency to emphasize the aspiration of justice as the basis for every law.[76] So, the ideal of justice is depicted much in the Torah (Deut. 16: 18-20 cf. Deut 4:8; 5:14-15; 15:12; Exod. 21:2) and also in the books of Kings and the prophets. For instance, there is a call of God to the children of Israel to return to Him, and to maintain love and justice (Hos. 12:6; also Amos 5:15). We can say, that the God who gave the law on Mount Sinai by which the people of Israel must abide by and live, demands obedience. Obedience is a virtue

70 http://ijs.org.au/The-Ethical-Teachings-of-Judaism/default.aspx. Accessed on 11-08-2017.

71 J. Hempel, "Ethics in the OT," *The Interpreters Dictionary of the Bible*, edited by George Arthur Buttrick *et al.*, (Nashville: Abington Press, 1962), 161.

72 Russell, *Between the Testaments*, 47.

73 Nahum N. Glatzer (ed.), *The Rest is Commentary: A Source Book of Judaic Antiquity* (Boston: Boston Press, 1961), 2.

74 Glatzer, *The Rest is Commentary*, 7.

75 http://ijs.org.au/The-Ethical-Teachings-of-Judaism/default.aspx. Accessed on 11-08-2017.

76 Licht and Andre Neher, "Ethics," 140.

required on the part of human as a response to the divine revelation, deliverance, instructions and demands from God. As a result, obedience is ethically rooted in the God-given law of the Old Testament.

As a result, the study of the Torah was very crucial to the life of the people of Israel. It renewed their past experience and of the revelation at Mount Sinai which was more or less designed to the perfection of the individual and to moral action.[77] Simeon the Just said, "By three things is the world sustained: by the Law, by the [Temple-] service, and by deeds of loving-kindness" (*Pirke Aboth* 1:2 cf. Rabbi Meir 6: 6-7). The need to study the Torah was probably intensified following the destruction of the Second Temple in 70 C.E., specifically by the Jewish religious leaders.[78] Rabbi Shammai (*ca.* 30 B.C.E. - 10 C.E.) said, "Make thy [study of the] Law a fixed habit; say little and do much, and receive all men with a cheerful countenance" (*Pirke Aboth* 1:15). Subsequently, the term Torah, as used by the Jewish scholars/rabbis (post-70 C.E.) is a wider term than the Pentateuch or the Law. It came to embrace all the teaching contained in, or elicited from the sacred writings. That is, it covers all oral and fluid additions to or interpretations of the Pentateuchal Code of the Hebrew Bible. Torah is made the possession of the people, "discovering and interpreting its meaning so that men could apply it to their daily lives."[79] It was considered "a living oracle through which the word of God could come to generation after generation. Its word was not static but dynamic, capable of fresh interpretations for each succeeding age and capable of renewed application to every aspect of human life."[80] The Jewish rabbis propounded that the best antidote against evil was the study of Torah (Rabban Gamaliel (the third) (*Pirke Aboth* 2:2; Rabbi Meir in *Pirke Aboth* 6: 2).[81] For instance, Rabbi Hillel said, "the more study of the Law the more life; ...If a man has gained a good name he has gained [somewhat] for himself; if he has gained for himself words of Torah he has gained for himself life in the world

77 Glazter, *The Rest is Commentary*, 12.

78 Known by names *Soferim/Sopherim* 'Scribes' and *Tannaim* (Lit. 'repeaters,' teachers of the Law). They are the rabbis of the first two centuries A.D. who were engaged in the process of the study, the repetition of the written Torah with its oral tradition. As such their main task was to study the written Torah with its oral tradition and to transmit it to others. So, known by the name *Tannaim* taught the religious system of the Pharisees as opposed to that of the Sadducees. Pharisees believed in the supremacy of the Written Torah and equally acknowledge its binding authority of the oral law. While for the Sadducees, they hold the authority of the written Torah over against that of the oral tradition. That is the Pharisees were staunch supporters of the authority of the oral tradition but opposed by the Sadducees who regarded the written Torah as alone authoritative. See Russell, *Between the Testaments*, 67-68.

79 Russell, *Between the Testaments*, 64.

80 Russell, *Between the Testaments*, 64.

81 Taitz, *Judaism*, vol.1, 28.

to come" (*Pirke Aboth* 2:7).[82] This signifies that for the Jewish people Torah is a matter of life.

To the centrality of the Torah stands out a question – who gives the Torah? It is believed that it is Yahweh[83] the only God. The Torah provided the covenant boundary-maker to maintain Israel's distinctiveness[84] where the entirety of the Jewish life was under the divine law (Torah).[85] Yahweh is the God of the covenant who established the covenant of his love for Israel and the fathers (cf. e.g., Deut. 4:36; 7:8). The Jewish faith is centered on monotheism and their hope rests on the fact that they are the covenant People of God. So, for the Jewish ethics, *faith* in Yahweh is the deciding force. It is therefore appropriate to see Jewish ethics under the domain of their monotheistic belief, a belief in one God. The concept of the covenantal God of Abraham, Isaac and Jacob and of Moses is the God of their ethical standards (Exod. 3:6; 15: 25b, 26; 19:5-6; 20-30). That is, the Jewish ethics which originated with the Hebrew Bible (Old Testament), within the covenant, was governed by faith in the power of Yahweh in the creation of the world and no less in the historical circumstances of the People of Israel. So, the Jewish thought of ethics is not based on speculative principles or of reason but in terms of their human experience[86] under the covenantal God, who demands obedience.

God is above all gods in sphere of both the power and knowledge. And no human faculty can comprehend this truth (Isa. 40:7) but by the Spirit of Yahweh the Messiah would have them both (Isa. 11:2). The covenant, thereby, was for the Israelite faith a historical fact connected in all traditions with Moses and the deliverance from Egyptian bondage.[87] Hence, for the people of the Israelites or the

---

82 The law here encompasses the wider meaning of the term Torah. That is the written text of the first five books of the OT (Moses) and the exposition of that text given by later sages of the Jewish community.

83 The Jews believed that their God revealed his name to Moses as "YHWH" and only the high priests in the Temple were illegible to pronounce it while it was substituted by a circumlocution such as "the Lord" or "the Holy one" for others. See Burkett, *An Introduction to the New Testament and the Origins of Christianity*, 33.

84 N. T. Wright, *The New Testament and the People of God* (Minneapolis: Fortress Press, 1992), 238.

85 E. P. Sanders, *Judaism Practice and Belief 63 BCE-66 CE* (London/Philadelphia: SCM Press/ Trinity Press International, 1992), 50.

86 Licht and Andre Neher, "Ethics," 142.

87 Hempel, "Ethics in the OT," 157. It is said that the Covenant between God and the Israelite is modeled after the suzerainty treatise of the ancient Near West which were contracted between a mightier King (e.g., the Hittite Great king) and his vassals. It is the King who ordained the conditions under which his subjects might live in peace and friendship with him. The former was free to make or not to make the covenant. In case the king makes the covenant, he was bound to fulfill what he promised. The obligations of both the parties might greatly differ, but the sanctity of the covenant was the same for them under the guarantee of the gods. The Old Testament biblical covenant was employed to state the relation of the supreme God to his

Jews the covenantal phrase 'People of God' serves as the basic Jewish fundamental ethical context. So, it is quite appropriate to look back to the ethical context of the Jews as a nation chosen by God. Subsequently for the Jews the fundamental context of its ethical reflection was neither the polis nor the individual but Israel as a unified community "with variable set of institutions, rituals, stories,"[88] and ordinances.

The ethics of the Jews was more manifested in the religious sphere of their lives as 'People of God' than anything else. It is appropriate to deduce that the Jewish criteria of ethics are to fear God, remain obedient, and to take a stand in favor of doing good[89] which is justice. It is within this concept of community aspect that the Jewish ethics has to be understood and in the grander context provided by the concept of covenant.[90] So, we can articulate that the Jewish ethical concept is strongly connected with its theological concept. In fact its ethical perspectives are drawn from the theological perception of God, the original source of the law giver. For the Jewish people, every ethical behavior was determined by divine law (unlike the ancient Greeks where ethics were discussed by philosophers) for all of life was under God and regulated by divine law.[91] In short, the Jewish ethics is thought to have divine sanction, which is binding for every human's life affairs in relation to God and to their neighbors and strangers even (Lev. 19:2-34).

The Jewish ethics finds its vibrant expression in the term 'People of God.' In keeping with the notion that the community of the Fourth Gospel finds herself as a community of Messianic believers it is fairly right to surmise that there is a close conceptual link between 'People of God' and the Johannine community. Congruently, it is not a mistake to acknowledge the depth of John's indebtedness to Judaism or Jewish tradition. And most of all doubtless to say that majority of them that is, the author, the disciples of Jesus, and the very object of the written

chosen people tracing its beginning when God led them out of Egypt and promising them a land of Israel flowing with milk and honey.

88 Dodd, *Gospel and Law*, 65.

89 Licht and Andre Neher, "Ethics," 142.

90 The Old Testament biblical term 'Covenant' was used to express Yahweh's relationship with the people of Israel as chosen people. This covenant begins in the act of Yahweh who delivered the Israelites from the Egyptian bondage. Consequently, the ethics of the OT took on a strong *historical* character, as far as it was governed by the prescriptions of the law. This law was considered as given by Yahweh the God of the Covenant in the legislation on Sinai or in the land of Moab. Subsequently the people of Israel take on certain obligations to be carried out in response to Yahweh God as their covenant Lord. And so in the covenant context, the divine commandments are distributed throughout the Torah which becomes a way of responding to the prior revelation of God's saving power and of fulfilling His will by the people of Israel (who became the 'people of God' by God's choice and the circumstances of the people of the Israelites). The tradition knew that Israel had accepted the stipulations of the covenant (Exod. 19:8; 24:3; Josh. 24:21 ff) voluntarily and had been informed about its risk if they will deviate from fulfilling the obligation as covenantal people.

91 Sanders, *Judaism Practice and Belief*, 50-51.

Gospel who is Jesus and many other mentioned in the Gospel were Jews. John's audience was predominantly Jewish (this is however not to rule out the Gentiles (Greeks) and the Samaritans who are part of John's audience composition) and thereby probably continued to maintain and inherit the Jewish tradition in many significant areas (especially Jewish festivals and biblical citations). The Jewishness of the Fourth Gospel can be seen more clearly from the significant place he has put for the Scripture. The Gospel of John used Scripture in ways of references or allusions, the Old Testament to bring into light the intended message of the Scripture (which technically can be called as 'biblical interpretation').

2.3. The Socio-Religious Circumstances of the Johannine Community

Having discussed a short historical background of the ancient Greek and the Jewish ethics it deems necessary now to have a look at the socio-religious circumstances of the Johannine community. The socio-religious setting will definitely help one to avoid any misleading and sweeping uncritical conclusion/s. But, how are we to understand the social world of John? What is the source for the investigation into the social world of the Gospel? The answer at hand would be the text (literary) as we have now. It is often assumed that the literary text speaks volume and reflects about the social world and the historical circumstances of the author or of the community who directly or indirectly act as an impetus for the production of the study text. Besides, central to the sociology of knowledge is the assumption that ideas can be related to the social structures and that theological and ethical ideas may be influenced by society and the society may in turn be influenced by the theological and ethical ideas is well taken.[92] On a careful reading of the text, we get the impression that the Gospel is not a homogenous text[93] but a production that consisted of various layers of composition. It is believed that behind the Fourth Gospel were probably many authors of the traditions. These traditions believed to be mostly of oral traditions were then copied into the whole literary unit which we call it as the Gospel of John or simply the Fourth Gospel, by a real author.[94] In other words, the Gospel of John is understood as a multilayered work where the texts are seen to reflect the various stages of the community's history which have been preserved alongside one another.

One prime factor that undergirded the situation of the Johannine community is the tension between Johannine Judaism and Johannine Jewish Christianity. It

92 Robin Gill, *A Textbook of Christian Ethics*, 2nd edition (London: T&T Clark, 1995), 23-24.

93 John Ashton, *Understanding the Fourth Gospel*, 2nd edition (Oxford: Oxford University Press, 2007), 27.

94 Francis J. Moloney, *Belief in the Word* (Minneapolis: Fortress Press, 1993), 7. The real author is traditionally considered a historical person who is often identified as John or the fourth Evangelist. Interestingly the supposed 'real author' informs the intended reader that he is bearing personal and authentic witness to Jesus from whose pierced side flowed blood and water (19:35). For further information on authorship please see Kanagaraj, *The Gospel of John*, 21-23.

is significant to see that the Fourth Gospel draws a great deal of attention to the themes of conflict, opposition and persecution. The early record of Jesus' public ministry predominantly relates the crisis between Jesus and 'the Jews,'[95] and their following opposition to and persecution of Jesus. Early on in the Gospel account, we learn that Jesus' claim to be the Christ or Messiah is considered to be a serious offense to the Jewish authorities (esp. Jn. 5 -12).[96] The same conflict, opposition and persecution are inevitable part of the lives of those who follow Jesus. So, John informs the reader/s not to lose heart when they face the same fate as Jesus (Jn. 13-17).[97] Besides final exhortations in the farewell discourse, Jesus predicts to his disciples the same scenario of opposition and persecution (16:2). Such anticipated threat from the Jews as predicted by Jesus proves that the threat of persecution will continue for his followers even after his physical departure.

So, the crises of controversies, excommunication and persecution on account of the Johannine community's expression of faith in Jesus reflects the time and setting after the time of Jesus' early ministry. That is after Jesus' death and after the Roman war and "at the time Judaism was engaged in a process of self-definition and retrenchment."[98] It was then a controversy that was triggered by the Johannine community's convictions and beliefs concerning the Messiahship of Jesus and a time when "the Johannine Jewish Christians probably sharpened and refined their understanding of Jesus in response to opposition and controversy."[99] Such controversies, says Larry W. Hurtado:

> ... often has the effect of sharpening and intensifying the efforts of groups to assert and define their core commitments. As a religious group defends its beliefs and practices against the ridicule and refutation of outsiders, the group clarifies for itself what is central and nonnegotiable, thereby making more emphatic the "boundary markers" that identify the group, the sorts of distinguishing marks and clear expressions of group identification that are essential for the

95 Jesus himself clearly is a Jew (4:9). John presents two opposing sects of Judaism in his Gospel – The Johannine Jews who primarily oppose Jesus' claims concerning his role, authority, and mission are 'the Jews' (although sometimes 'the pharisees') and another Jewish group who accept and follow Jesus are called 'disciples' (who are also the Jews). So the epithet "the Jews" in John's Gospel do not present a solid front against Jesus. 'The Jews' or the 'pharisees' could then be virtually equated, as oppose and against Jesus and his followers. It is also observed that in John's Gospel Sadducees, Scribes, Herodians and Zealots are not mentioned which probably clues a time after the disastrous Roman war and the destruction of the Jerusalem temple (i.e., post 70 C.E.).

96 D. Moody Smith, *ANTC: John* (Nashville: Abington Press, 1999), 35.

97 Cornelis Bennema, *Excavating John's Gospel: A Commentary for Today* (Delhi: ISPCK, 2005), 14.

98 Smith, *John*, 36.

99 Hurtado, *Lord Jesus Christ*, 350.

> survival and growth of any group. Also, as a group deals with internal disagreements in beliefs and practices, there are efforts (on all sides of controverted matters) to articulate those beliefs and practices more clearly over against unacceptable versions of them ("heresies," in the sense that the term came to acquire in early Christianity).[100]

In the initial years of the community's life, these believers continued to live and move within the world of Judaism, maintaining its membership in the synagogue and participating in Jewish festivals,[101] all the while keen enough to convince their fellow Jews that Jesus was the long promised and expected Christ/Messiah.[102] But, the majority of the Jews did not adhere to their claims about Jesus and Judaism eventually was fragmented. Certain Jews within Judaism have ascertained and assimilated the significant truth about the person and role of Jesus. This belief has evoked schism within Judaism and in effect the life and faith of Judaism was threatened and those who have paid their allegiance to Jesus and believed that the Messiah had come in the person of Jesus of Nazareth were expelled from the participation in the Synagogue.[103]

It is rational to assert on the basis of the nature of the text that the Gospel was formed/shaped during which there was a tension between Jewish Christians and Judaism. Thus, the Johannine community was occasioned by its changing situation. Or to put in another word, the community was in a sort of transitional period and eventually the community's tradition was borne. The prime single factor that resulted in conflict with the synagogue and the consequent formation of the tradition was Christological. As a result, those who confessed their faith

---

100 Hurtado, *Lord Jesus Christ*, 350-51.

101 Rensberger, *Johannine Faith and Liberating Community*, 25.

102 Richard B. Hays, *The Moral Vision of the New Testament: A Contemporary Introduction to New Testament Ethics* (New York: HarperCollins, 1996), 146.

103 The Greek derivation of the term indicates simply a gathering, void of any religious connotation. However the Babylonian exile (where a large number of the prominent Jewish inhabitants of Jerusalem were deported to Babylon) brought certain modification in Jewish religious life. The then Jewish exiles were deprived of land, temple and cultic priestly ministrations. The Jews living outside of Jerusalem could not participate regularly in the Temple worship. Therefore, for most Jews, the religious life began to be centered on the local synagogue as an alternative. So, it is believed that Synagogue worship began during the Babylonian exile. For some Synagogue arose in late 152-142 B.C.E. (Roger T. Beckwith). The exact date for the origin of the Synagogue cannot be certainly recovered though. Whatsoever, Synagogue served as a meeting place for Jewish social life and as well as a house for prayer and study of the Scripture. So Synagogue today is the place of assembly commonly used by Jewish communities primarily for public worship and instruction. Roger T. Beckwith, "The Pre-history and Relationships of Pharisees, Sadducees and Essence: A Tentative Reconstruction," *Rev Q* 11 (1982): 27; I. Sonne, "Synagogue," *The Interpreters Dictionary of the Bible*, edited by George Arthur Buttrick *et al.*, (Nashville: Abington Press, 1962), 476; Burkett, *An Introduction to the New Testament*, 40.

in Jesus were excommunicated and the Johannine community was truly born.[104] The Johannine community found itself estranged from its parent world being excluded from the Synagogue (Jn. 9:22; 12:42; 16:2).[105] The community of John's Gospel experienced split from its fellow Jews both in the local scale and against the religious authorities. Francis J. Moloney contended that one cannot deny the fact that the Gospel of John was written against the backdrop 'of a painful breakdown between two groups in the larger Jewish community.'[106] The community of John was nonetheless evolving a new 'identity,' working out its continuity and discontinuity at the same time with their Jewish past in regards to the issue of Christology.[107] It is for that reason difficult to suggest that the Johannine community in totality had parted ways and is improbable therefore. But that the community saw themselves as part of Judaism in some aspects but with a significant shift in perception about the person of Jesus is very telling. Nevertheless the threat of expulsion from religious participation in the synagogue have paved way for the formation of a new community and be isolated and naturally the newly formed community needs to consolidate and define its identity from a new light.

The evidence to a complete expulsion of anyone confessing Jesus as the Christ is most clearly described in the experience of the man born blind whose parents refuse to speak for their son 'because they were afraid of the Jews, for the Jews had decided that anyone who acknowledged that Jesus was the Christ would be put out of the synagogue' (Jn. 9:22). This expression 'to be put out of the synagogue' (ἀποσυνάγωγος γένηται) is found only in the Fourth Gospel. So, the final rift between the Johannine community and their original heritage found within Judaism is reflected in the story of the man born blind. As such the conversation between the Jews/Pharisees and the parents of the blind man to figure out his real identity (Jn. 9:18) is considered the single most primary bit of evidence for the circumstances of the origin of the Johannine community.[108] Other places where we are able to read the process of putting believers of Jesus out of the Jewish place of worship is mentioned in John 12:42 and 16:2. So, an originally Jewish-Christian (Johannine) community now had to continue its life within the context of the threat and hostility from parent Judaism.[109] There seems

104 Painter, *John: Witness & Theologian*, 16.

105 See Raymond E. Brown, *The Community of the Beloved Disciples* (New York: Paulist Press, 1979), 36-47; David Rensberger, *Overcoming the World, Politics and Community in the Gospel of John* (London: SPCK, 1989); J. Louis Martyn, *History and Theology in the Fourth Gospel,* 3rd edition (Louisville, London: Westminster John Knox Press, 2003), 145-167.

106 Francis J. Moloney, *The Gospel of John: Text and Context* (Leiden: Brill, 2005), 41.

107 Raimo Haloka, *Identity Matters: John, the Jews and Jewishness*, NovTSup 118 (Leiden: Brill, 2005), 290.

108 Smith, *John*, 194-196.

109 Moloney, *Belief in the Word*, 16.

to be a fear to be separated from the synagogue if any Jewish people confessed their belief that Jesus was the Messiah (Greek here is *Christos*) because the Jews had already decided to expel such people who will confess Jesus as the Messiah (Jn. 9:18-22). The aftereffect of the expulsion and the trauma the small circle of Johannine community has faced is aptly described by David K. Rensberger in the following lines: Expulsion would have meant social ostracism, loss of relationship with family and friends, economic dislocation, religious dislocation. The Synagogue meetings, thc public liturgy, the festivals and observances were all now denied them, and the authoritative interpretation of the sacred scripture itself was in the hands of their opponents.[110] The Johannine community as believers and followers of Jesus had to live out the social consequences of the uncompromised allegiance[111] to Jesus as their Lord (King).

To counter the threat of division, pressure was brought to bear on all who confess that Jesus is the Christ (Messiah). And so about C.E. 85 'The Test Benediction' (*Birkath ha-Minim*) was published to provide basis for excluding 'heretics' from the synagogue.[112] This benediction was added to the Twelfth Benediction under the leadership of Rabbi Gamaliel II at Yavneh that dates somewhere between 80 and 115 C.E. But, the Test Benediction decree itself cannot be dated precisely.[113] So, also we cannot establish with precision that the expulsion was the direct result of the insertion of the new clause to the Eighteen Benediction of the Synagogue prayer to curse the heretics, as Marytn holds that the expulsion is to be identified specifically with the *Birkath ha-Minim* that which was promulgated at Yavneh (Jamnia).

But, the expulsion/excommunication from the Synagogue, which was mainly on christological ground goes unchallenged. The confession of Jesus as the Christ was the basis for the excommunication of the Jewish Christians. It likely appears that the threat of expulsion was designed to discourage converts[114] so that unity of Judaism will remain intake and not breakdown. And so in some ways the threat of expulsion from the Synagogue encouraged Jewish believers to keep close their faith in secret to remain within the fold of Judaism. How far it was possible to keep one's faith secret in Jesus is difficult to ascertain though. Such typical instances can be mentioned of Nicodemus (Jn. 3:1ff cf. 12:24) and Joseph of Arimathea who remained a secret disciple of Jesus because of the fear of the Jews (Jn. 19:38). On the other side of the coin, the man (born blind) overcame intimidation from the Jewish leaders for which he was excommunicated for his confession of belief in Jesus. There is no mention of the man's name except for 'the man born blind' which is a literary characterization device for John to achieve

---

110 Rensberger, *Johannine Faith and Liberating Community*, 26-27.

111 Hays, *The Moral Vision of the New Testament*, 148.

112 Painter, *John: Witness & Theologian*, 13.

113 Ashton, "Introduction: The Problem of John," 13.

114 Painter, *John: Witness & Theologian*, 13.

his purpose of advancing belief in Jesus.[115] The Gospel records that this 'man born blind's confession has inevitably led to his consequent break with Judaism. The tradition of the Johannine community was shaped in such situation of hard decision making time – to choose to believe in Jesus is to break away from Judaism.[116]

Martyn expounds the history of the Johannine community into three periods – the early period comprises the conception of a messianic group within the synagogue community that is the so called Johannine group (community/ Christians/schools) were still part of the local synagogue, the middle period features part of the group becoming a separate community experiencing excommunication from the synagogue and martyrdom (two major traumas), and in the late period the community is characterized by a movement toward firm social and theological configurations.[117] Martyn attempted an elaborate reconstruction of the Johannine social complexity during which the Gospel was written as represented by the "social and theological configuration in which the Johannine community found itself was… at least quadrilateral." First, the Johannine community; second, the community sharply differentiated from the parent synagogue to the point of being polarized with a breakdown in communication; thirdly, the community came to be even more sharply differentiated and alienated from a group of the so-called Christian Jews who remain within the parent synagogue; fourthly, the Johannine community hopes for unification with other communities of Jewish Christians who have also suffered excommunication.[118] In effect, the text reflects not a single history of the community but different phases of the Johannine community with different strata of historical circumstances.

The historical setting of the Fourth Gospel plays a very significant role in shaping the moral values of the then Johannine community. During the formation of the developing Johannine community, that is, during the late first century, the community was experiencing a tension with her parent synagogue. The Jewish Christians who constituted the major chunk of the Johannine community had

---

115 Bennema, *Excavating John's Gospel,* 12. Characterization as a literary tool is a referential description of characters in the Fourth Gospel. The tool is utilized as a technique to achieve his end that is to promote faith in Jesus. Characterization creates a sense of being in the shoe of the character described. So it assists and persuades the reader to identify him/herself with the described character who believes in Jesus rather than the opponent character (most often the unbelief character/s).

116 Here note must be taken that the Jews who believed in Jesus as the Christ did not necessarily intent to break away but rather it is the elite Jewish leaders who execute excommunication. And so naturally believing in Jesus necessitates breaking away from the life and faith of legalistic Judaism. The formation of the Gospel was then determined by the situation faced by Jews who believe in Jesus within the larger umbrella of Judaism at least in origin.

117 J. Louis Martyn, *The Gospel of John in Christian History* (New York: Paulist Press, 1979), 93, 102, 107.

118 Martyn, *History and Theology in the Fourth Gospel,* 3rd edition, 145-167.

faced excommunication from their formal religious hearth. The community was the minority who believed in Jesus as the one fulfilling the Jewish messianic expectation and their relationship with the Synagogue was then severed. The text also gives a potential indication that the ardent believers in Jesus' Messiahship faced even martyrdom (Jn. 16:2). The conflict or say the crisis John addresses is a conflict within Judaism, a crisis concerning belief and unbelief that is a response to Jesus as the Messiah and the claims made for Jesus.[119] The Jewish community was confronted with a choice to come into the light or remain in the darkness. They were left with a decision to opt either for the truth over against falsehood, to choose between life and death. They were made to decide to make the choice in their response to Jesus either 'to believe' or *not* 'to believe' in Jesus as the Messiah. And this was a crucial ethical decisive and defining moment to decide one's own impending judgment. Against this Jewish religious background, we must try to understand the ethics of the Gospel of John.

The situation of the community then was in such hostility with her parent synagogue. It is within this conflict context that the community had to live out its distinctive identity with its full eschatological hope. There was in fact an increase of threats and persecution; this is reflected in the structural arrangement of the narratives and events recorded in the Gospel. Initially the signs performed by Jesus drew no much conspiracy but as the narrative advances, the leaders of the Jews felt being threatened of their religious belief and later decided to put any one who would profess Jesus as the Son of God and the ultimate decision was to put Jesus to death. There was there and then a prominence of the Jews hostility towards Jesus and his disciples. It is supposed that the Gospel purports two-level drama. The first level reflects to tell the story of Jesus and his disciples in the 30s and the subsequent situation of the Johannine Christians in the last quarter of the first century where the community had faced exclusion from its parent Jewish synagogue.[120]

In the light of this, the Johannine community probably comprised of two transitory phases. The former phase was occasioned by the fact that the Johannine Christians were bonafide members of the Jewish Synagogue, a closely knitted Jewish community who had come to accept Jesus as the Messiah. The latter phase is characterized by the intra-communal disagreement on Christological issue have parted ways and since then become a minority whose participation in the synagogue then was restricted resulting in the expulsion. The controversies and the subsequent expulsion of the Johannine Jewish Christians from the synagogue was

---

119 Allen Verhey, *The Great Reversal: Ethics and the New Testament* (Michigan: Wm. B. Eerdmans Publishing Company, 1984), 142; Smith, *The Theology of the Gospel of John*, 51.

120 Tuckett, *Christology and the New Testament*, 153-154; Barnabas Lindars, *The Gospel of John* (Michigan: Wm. B. Eerdmans Publishing Company, 1987), 36-37. It was first published in London by Marshall, Morgan & Scott Publishing Limited in the year 1972.

then the effects of their ardent claims about, and reverence of, Jesus which became unbearable to other fellow Jewish community (esp. Jewish religious leaders).

The Jewish/Johannine Community which had once come under the umbrella of Judaism lacked no political security as long as it was considered as members of Judaism but once the separation was marked, it had lost the protection of the Roman government.[121] John's community then had experienced alienation from its Jewish cultural context. The community had felt social alienation from its established and parent society, Judaism.[122] So, there was an estranged relation between these two communities, that is, Johannine community and Jewish community.[123] The existence and its life experience of the Johannine community must then be studied in the context of its contemporary Jewish community.

The conflict thus mirrored in the Gospel is Christological mainly on the issue of the identity of the Messiah between the ardent followers of Jesus (Johannine community of believers) and the post - C.E. 70 Judaism.[124] The Christology of John's Gospel "developed in the bosom of a community that underwent several changes."[125] It was a question of believing in the person of Jesus and the revelatory works (signs) he did perform. Faith in Jesus as the unique (only) Son of God in Johannine term was blasphemous to Judaism. And to say more, the Jews had charged Jesus with blasphemy for claiming to be one with God which was considered a perilous threat to Jewish monotheism. The Christological dispute was then on the question of the significance and authority of Jesus, and this conflict is extended on in terms of Jesus' relation to Judaism.[126] Christology, henceforth, became the major conflicting issue between the Johannine Jewish Christians and the synagogue authorities.[127]

The Johannine dialogues indicate that the order of Johannine community development is dialectical as observed by Meeks: "the christological claims of the Johannine Christians resulted in their becoming alienated, and finally expelled, from the synagogue; that alienation in turn is "explained" by a further development of the christological motifs (i.e., the fate of the community projected onto the

121 Lohse, *The First Christians*, 99.

122 Kare Sigvald Fuglseth, *Johannine Sectarianism in Perspective: A Sociological, Historical, and Comparative Analysis of Temple and Social Relationships in the Gospel of John, Philo, and Qumran* (NovTSup 119; Leiden: Brill, 2005), 373-374.

123 Adele Reinhartz, *Befriending the Beloved Disciple: A Jewish Reading of the Gospel of John* (New York: Continuum, 2001), 51.

124 Lindars, *The Gospel of John*, 37. In John's Gospel, we hear no mention of the Sadducees, the leading party in Jesus' time, or of the Zealots but only of the Pharisees who became the undisputed leaders after 70 C.E. The Pharisees were left in sole possession of Jewish loyalty.

125 Frank J. Matera, *New Testament Christology* (Louisville: Westminster John Knox Press, 1999), 216.

126 Painter, *John: Witness & Theologian*, 135.

127 Keener, *The Gospel of John*, vol.1, 202; Smith, *The Theology of the Gospel of John*, 51.

story of Jesus); these developed christological motifs in turn drive the group into further isolation. It is a case of continual, harmonic reinforcement between social experience and ideology."[128] Thus, the life of the Johannine community had resulted in persecution and conflict because of her messianic confession in Jesus.

However, the opponents who are called 'the Jews' in the Gospel are not to be taken as a generic term to include all the Jews in every time and place or all the Jews contemporary with Jesus but as a historical entity and symbolic representation of human rejection of God's revelation in Jesus.[129] In fact 'the Jews' must be understood as a reference to the Synagogue leaders with whom the Johannine Christians were in conflict.[130] The conflict that was Christological basically concerning the Messiah and the claims made for Jesus[131] and Jesus' own statement about himself as equal with God (Jn. 5:18; 10:30) also must have precipitated the expulsion of the ardent Christians who have pledged their allegiance to him from the Synagogue.[132] This was the first accusation of blasphemy put on Jesus by the Jews. In effect, the synagogue Jews see and conceive as a threat to their traditional monotheistic belief. It is reasonable to deduce that the Johannine Jewish Christian community might have lived in a closed set up as they have been expelled from the Jewish Synagogue to which they had once belonged. The community has to find its true identity to prove the worth of their belief in the person of Jesus in whom there is life eternal. It must have been a real crisis for the community as a minority. It can be rightly assumed that the Johannine community must have suffered much to have been persecuted by its own Jewish people. It is amidst the socio-cultural surrounding that the Johannine ethical values have to stand out to be a distinctive faith community of Jesus.

The ethical values by which the community has to live by, was on the basis of faith in Jesus as the One sent from God, the Father (Jn. 3:16; 20:30-31). Jesus was accepted as their ethical standard of living because he revealed and he himself is the source of morality. This is to suggest that the ethical aspect and Christological aspect in the Fourth Gospel is closely inter-connected. Either aspect is to be studied in the light of the other aspect. There was an intra-communal crisis within the Jewish sect. So, within Judaism the two poles exist – Believing Jews and Unbelieving Jews – based on the Jewish response to the Messiahship of Jesus. The Johannine community was thereby confronted with a choice to believe or not

---

128 Meeks, "The Man from Heaven in Johannine Sectarianism," 194.

129 Rudolf Bultmann, "πιστεύω, πίστις, πιστός," *TDNT*, πε-ρ, vol. 6, edited by Gerhard Friedrich (Michigan: Wm. B. Eerdmans Publishing Company, 1968), 225; D. Moody Smith, *The Theology of the Gospel of John* (Cambridge: Cambridge University Press, 1995), 56.

130 Keener, *The Gospel of John*, vol. 1, 146.

131 Smith, *The Theology of the Gospel of John*, 51.

132 Brown, *The Community of the Beloved Disciples*, 36-47, 174; John Ashton, *Understanding the Fourth Gospel*, 1st edition (1991), 167.

to believe whereby an individual's outcome is to live in the light or darkness, truth or falsehood, which subsequently is a matter of choosing life or death.

2.4. Jewish Law and Traditions as the Moral Background for the Johannine Community

The Jewish law which basically is contained in the Torah is understood as containing historical events with religious significance. For the Israelites (Jews), the Torah sets forth God's will and purpose for them.[133] It is in the Torah that the "extremely concrete and detailed system of regulations is embedded in a narrative of events, which are presented in the guise of "mighty acts of the Lord."[134] For, these acts of God established, what is described as the "covenant," between the 'People of God' and the God who delivered them from the bondage of slavery from the hands of the Egyptians. Thus, for the 'People of God', the classical moral law finds its expression in the following recorded words - "I am the Lord your God, who brought you out of the land of Egypt, out of the house of slavery; you shall have no other gods before me" (Exod. 20:2-3 cf. Deut. 6:12, 14). The Torah as such provides the basic framework for the ethical living for the covenantal Jewish people of God. Even before the second century B.C.E., academic learning had been established in the land of Israel. The scrolls of the Bible were studied and the law was analyzed in an effort to understand what God wanted from the people. Often in this academy of learning, discussions were both based on biblical texts and oral law (popular interpretations of biblical law and customs). These traditions were memorized and passed from generation to generation (orally). Sometime in 165- 163 B.C.E., during the rule of the Maccabees (Hasmonean Empire), a group of the Jewish philosophers called the Pharisees, made the decision to write down the oral law.[135] It is told that Johanan ben Zakkai, one of the greatest scholars of Jerusalem established a new academy in a small city called Jabneh (which is also Jamnia).[136] From there, he proceeded on to the teachings of the sages, ensuring that the laws of the people (laws contained in the Torah) would be followed even in the absence of the physical presence of the city Jerusalem and its Holy Temple (68-70 C.E.). And Simon Bar Kokhba (132-135 C.E.) led a final rebellion against Rome and ruled briefly and after 3 years was defeated (132-134 C.E.) and immigration to other lands increased. This decision to write down the

133 Bruce Chilton and Jacob Neusner, *Judaism in the New Testament: Practices and Beliefs* (London and New York: Routledge, 1995), 1.

134 Dodd, *Gospel and Law*, 11.

135 Taitz, *Judaism*, vol. I, 8-9. Also see Morton Smith, "Palestinian Judaism in the First Century," reprint in *Essays in Graeco-Roman and Related Talmudic Literature* (New York: n.p., 1977), 195-196.

136 A centre of Jewish learning and after the disastrous event of Jerusalem in 70 C.E., the Great Sanhedrin moved from Jerusalem to Jabneh, but in 80 C.E. it moved to Usha in Galilee, in 116 C.E. it moved back to Jabneh.

oral law proved vital for the survival of the Jewish life.[137] Since then oral law was organized into a series of six books called the Mishnah, and its main object was the "preservation, cultivation, and application to life of 'the Law' (Torah).[138] The Mishnah technically is the first book of commentary on biblical law which was compiled and finalized by one of the great scholars of the law, Judah ha Nasi, the patriarch in the year 200 C.E.[139]

Henceforth, the Torah served as a guiding principle for the well being of the covenantal 'People of God.' It was perceived as the only and ultimate God's revealed word that cannot be altered but to observe diligently. And so any faithful Jew was expected to revere the Torah and so the Israelites as God's chosen people were to keep the Torah in all details. The people appealed to the Torah and validated their faith by carefully studying and keeping it. The religiosity of the people of Israel as such solely centers on this Torah. God is known more through this given Torah and in the light of this given Torah the Jews were expected to conduct their life in accordance to the moral precepts laid down in it. The Jewish faith, therefore, is inseparable from their way of life.[140]

It is quite clear that John features his audience's continuity with their Jewish heritage and more significantly as the people of God.[141] The Johannine community's faith is thus pictured as the valid continuation of the Judaistic faith. This is to admit that the author of the Fourth Gospel does not negate Judaism in its entirety rather it enhances the concept and proves that it points and culminates in the Messianic role and authority of Jesus. So, Jesus is portrayed as the higher and ultimate truth to which Judaism was pointing at. Early on though "the Jews" were condemned and blamed for the crucifixion of Jesus "John valued Israel and definitely adhered to the Torah as he read it."[142] The Scripture and Moses whom the Jews rely on as their central locus for God's revelation and God's agent respectively have in fact pointed beyond themselves to bear witness to Jesus (Jn. 5:39, 46).

In the Johannine community's context, Moses is conceived by the evangelist as one who has borne witness to the truth about Jesus (Jn. 5:46). The Jews are at fault when they appeal to Moses to oppose Christ (Jn. 9:28) because Moses

137 Jacob Neusner, *There We Sat Down: Talmudic Judaism in the Making* (New York: K'tav, 1972), 36-38.

138 *The Mishnah,* translated from the Hebrew with Introduction and Brief Explanatory Notes by Herbert Danby (Oxford: Oxford University Press, 1933), xiii.

139 Taitz, *Judaism*, vol. I, 9-10.

140 Eugene B. Borowitz, "Judaism: An Overview," *The Encyclopedia of Religion*, vol. 7, edited by Mircea Eliade *et al.*, (New York/London: Macmillan Publishing Company/Collier Macmillan Publishers, 1987), 134.

141 D. A. Carson, *The Gospel According to John* (Michigan/U.K: Wm. B. Eerdmans Publishing Company, 1991), 63; Lindars, *The Gospel of John*, 36.

142 Chilton and Jacob Neusner, *Judaism in the New Testament*, 5.

who is a witness to Christ will himself be their accuser (Jn. 5:45).[143] The Gospel emphasizes that the Scriptures are in fact a witness to Jesus now and here rather than to a history of salvation in the past. This is not to ignore the historical past though.[144] And it is in and through Jesus that God's good will and purpose for humanity is truly made known more than the Scripture does because God the Father is perfectly embodied personally in the Son.[145] But, ironically, the Jews failed to see this truth. God is made known through the Scripture but God is not made known as much as He is made known through Jesus. Jesus is the perfect representation of God here on earth.

Jesus is presented in the Fourth Gospel as the "divinely warranted guarantee of the promise of Israel for all people."[146] It is to this unrecognized truth that the author of the Fourth Gospel attempts to bring out the truth on the surface for the people to accept and thereby promote, retain and strengthen their faith in Jesus. More than the Greek ethics the Jewish moral tradition is assimilated in the lives of the Johannine community. It may sound too much to suggest that the Jewish ethics has influenced the ethical outlooks of the Johannine community. But, those certain core precepts of the Jewish ethics are reflected as a sign of continuation of Jewish moral tradition in the latter community which is religiously oriented.

The body of the written material as found in John's Gospel represents the core beliefs of Jewish Christian of its time and so can access the best traditions that identified the particular Johannine Christian community prior to the internal crises and controversies.[147] The text of the Gospel projects familiarity with Jewish thought and religious observances. It acknowledges Judaism[148] as the locus where Christian faith had begun ("salvation is of the Jews," (see Jn. 4:22). There is a vast knowledge of the geographical set up in Palestine and of festival customs much associated with temple worship. And there is much agreement with Hebrew Old Testament (mainly in christological texts).[149] The Johannine community having originally stemmed from its parent Jewish set up had the Jewish law and tradition as its moral background. The main divergent however from the mother Judaistic

143 Nils Alstrup Dahl, "The Johannine Church and History," *The Interpretation of John*, 2nd edition, edited by John Ashton (Edinburgh: T&T Clark, 1997), 155.

144 Dahl, "The Johannine Church and History," 153.

145 Chilton and Jacob Neusner, *Judaism in the New Testament*, 120.

146 Chilton and Jacob Neusner, *Judaism in the New Testament*, 121.

147 Hurtado, *Lord Jesus Christ*, 354.

148 The term Judaism is first found among the Greek-speaking Jews of the first century C.E (II Macc. 2:21: 8:1; Ga. l 1:13-14). Judaism refers to the creative, dynamic elements as portrayed in the different civilizations and cultures of the Jews at the varied stages of their history – such as Hellenistic Judaism, Rabbinic Judaism, Medieval Judaism, and, from the 19th century, Orthodox, Conservative, and Reform Judaism. For more details on Judaism please see Rabbi Louis Jacobs, "Judaism," *Jewish Values* (Jerusalem : Keter Books, 1974), 3-26.

149 George R. Beasley-Murray, *WBC*: John vol. 36 (Texas: Word Books Publisher, 1987), lviii.

belief, is belief in the person of Jesus as the 'Son of God', who himself is the expected Messiah (the theme that will be taken up in the fourth chapter). Belief in Jesus who was first introduced as the *logos* of God is now the Christ/Messiah, the 'Son of God', and who also is the 'Son of Man' has come to save the world is the standard and the starting-point for a new way of life in a newly established community of faith.

The fundamental faith of the Jewish religion is of its unique characteristic of belief in one single God (monotheistic belief). This fundamental monotheistic envision, and concept, of God is a springboard to their entire development of ethical system, which is based on the revelation at Mount Sinai through Moses and is expressed in the Torah (Deut. 4:44 cf. *Perke Aboth* 1:1).[150] The Torah is very central to the religious Jewish life.[151] The religious imperatives content in the Torah is required to be translated into everyday term involving human beings' conduct both toward God and his/her fellow created members. The strict observance of the Torah is so crucial that the negligence of the commands of it was accounted to be a great sin,[152] while the practice of it gave life in this world and the world to come (*Pirke Aboth* vi. 7).[153] The moral values of Judaism were still binding upon the newly formed Messianic community of the Johannine Gospel. Viewing from this end, the Johannine community did not altogether divorce from its Jewish heritage in terms of its moral value systems. Their belief and advocacy to the Messiahship of Jesus did not automatically make them non-Jewish or anti-Jewish. Rather, they continue to live as Jewish, socially and culturally. The Law which is central to the Jewish religiosity still holds true for the Johannine community as well. There was no new set of rules to govern the life style of the Johannine community. The only thing that was new is 'new commandment' that directs from the Lord (detail about the 'new commandment' is left unattended for the next chapter). The tradition that goes along the Jewish practices are observed and respected. The Gospel of John while affirming the Jewish law and tradition, centers her ethical reflection on the moral world of God in and through Jesus, which intrigues a response of faith from human beings (this aspect of Jesus as the archetype moral agent will be discussed in the next chapter). This implies that the Johannine community shares the same moral values as that of Judaism in its law and tradition in its essence. For the Johannine community and its author Jesus is presented as the perfect and true symbolic representation of the Torah. In other words, Torah has its truest and definitive interpretation in the light of the new revelation, wrought in and through the person of Jesus.

150 *The Mishnah*, 460.

151 Carson, *The Gospel According to John*, 334.

152 Canon Sell, *The Talmud, Mishnah and Midrash* (Madras: SPCK, 1928), 78.

153 *The Mishnah*, 460.

2.5. Messianic Community: A Johannine Community's Identity

Identity is a collective aspect of the set of characteristics by which a thing is recognizable or known. It is also the distinct personality of an individual regarded as a persisting entity. Thus, identity is one very essential part of an individual or a community's hallmark. What is that distinctive characteristic of the Johannine community by which it stood out amongst others? The identity of the Johannine community is to be understood against the imperative given by the master, 'love one another' so that people will know that they are what they are as disciples of Jesus (Jn. 13:35). Love is the motivating factor that undergirds the distinctive trait of the identity of the community of John's Gospel. This love is the love that comes from the Father through the Son. The Son is the One sent as the One anointed, the Messiah. In this case, it is the Messiah who has demonstrated love by living out his love for the disciples to emulate. The disciples have learnt what matters most by looking at Jesus who has set a good example for them.

Johannine community is relegated as a 'messianic group within the community of the synagogue' by Martyn so also Ashton.[154] This reference is discussed within the early period of the community's history. The community has been rooted in the belief in Jesus as the expected Messiah and continues to carry its ardent belief (messianic) till it receives its distinctive community name as 'Johannine community.' The community centers around, and is established around the belief in the very person and work of Jesus. That is, the Johannine community is a group of believers who have come to see and believe that in Jesus their expectation of a Messiah is being fulfilled. Jesus is the Christ. This community built its confidence on the fact that they knew God in and through the Son (Jn. 14:7ff; 10:30, 38 b; 12:44, 45, 49, 50) and it is through the only begotten Son that they get accessed to God (Jn. 14:6). The community sees herself as the community of faithful believers. The faithfulness in their belief in Jesus as the expected Messiah have eventually got them detached from Judaism and something more for the community is that their faith in Jesus also suggests a "change in social location."[155] "One of the primary functions of the book" says Meeks "…must have been to provide reinforcement for the community's social identity."[156]

There appears a sectarian consciousness among the Johannine Christian community, a sense of exclusiveness, a sharp delineation of the community from the world.[157] In dealing with the issue of the Johannine community as sectarian D. Moody Smith has rightly commented that any reading of the Gospels and Epistles

154 Ashton, *Understanding the Fourth Gospel*, 2nd edition, 108.

155 Meek, "The Man from Heaven in Johannine Sectarianism," 193.

156 Meek, "The Man from Heaven in Johannine Sectarianism," 193.

157 D. Moody Smith, *Johannine Christianity: Essays on its Setting, Sources, and Theology* (South Carolina: University of South Carolina Press, 1989), 3.

of the New Testament shows evidences of a sectarian consciousness, a sense of exclusiveness, a sharp delineation of the community from the world[158] and this is much true for the Fourth Gospel as it has been also often tagged as 'Sectarian' although not unanimously agreed upon this characterization. This explanation suggests the natural response of any social group in the face of the threat that threatens the integrity of the said social group. Nevertheless on reading certain portions of the Gospel suggest the inclusive communal aspects of the Gospel (e.g., Jn. 10, 15, 17). In this case, one cannot appropriate the Johannine community simply as an esoteric community. Though it may not be wrong to assert the nature of the Johannine community as a closed community it would also be right to say that the community was *not* closed off but was open to receive anyone who may profess the same faith in the community. In this case the Johannine community which constitutes a continuing community of Jesus and later of his disciples as well is a welcoming community. The prime criterion, in the Gospel of John, is to have faith in Jesus which in fact is the hallmark for true discipleship and for the subsequent formation of a Messianic Community.

2.6. Basic Socio-cultural and Religious Practices of the Johannine Community

As has been mentioned earlier, the Johannine community originally was basically Jewish, who initially continued to conduct themselves as part of the larger Jewish community. But, they were later expelled from the local Jewish community because of their emphasis on, and strong assertion about Jesus as the Messiah.[159] Subsequently, it goes without saying that many Jewish practices were still part of the Johannine community's practices too. In this case, the latter continues to sustain the socio-cultural heritage of its Jewish ethnicity. Mention must be made that though the Johannine community might have made herself aloof from the main umbrella of the so called Synagogue Judaism, some continuity of customs and practices with broader Jewish life were still maintained. Here we briefly discuss some of the very core Jewish practices reflected in the text.

2.6.1. Marriage: A Wedding at Cana

Marriage is indeed the most significant rite of passage in the life of the Jewish people probably because it is rooted in the biblical commandment to "be fruitful and multiply" as recorded in the Genesis creation account (Gen. 1:28).[160] So, marriage for the Jewish people is a union sanctified by God.[161] Marriage is considered to be "the prototypical act of creation"[162] and the Jews considered it to be every

158 D. Moody Smith, *Johannine Christianity* (Edinburgh: T&T Clark, 1984), 3f.

159 Wayne A. Meeks, "The Man from Heaven in Johannine Sectarianism," *JBL* 91 (1972): 68-72.

160 Taitz, *Judaism*, 97.

161 www.myjewishlearning.com. Accessed on 30-08-2017.

162 Anita Diamant, *The New Jewish Wedding* (New York: Summit Books, 1985), 97.

man's duty in order to perpetuate the name of his family.[163] Tractate *Ketuboth* (pl. *Ketubbah* in Hebrew) of Mishnah is entirely devoted to the marriage contract. One of the hallmarks of the Jewish marriage is to present the marriage contract (*Ketubbah*) to every bride. Jewish marriage laws are complicated. Talmudic laws regulate whom one can marry, stipulate the safeguards guaranteed to the wife, and lay out the husband's requirements. Ketubbah remains an important symbol of Jewish marriage. The Jewish wedding ceremony lasts for seven days, one day for each of the seven traditional blessings of marriage, among observant families.[164]

John 2:1-11 records one of the Jewish social institutions or events - marriage, a wedding celebration. Marriage is a social event which is socially recognized institution that is celebrated with much jubilation and feasting. Marriage is one such domestic special occasion that marks off one of the high points of human living.[165] In ancient Mediterranean world a wedding was celebrated as the marriage of two families and not just the two individuals. Marriage in the Mediterranean world was arranged, sometimes between kins[166] as practice in some parts of our country today. Marriage celebration was a sort of public demonstration that speaks of the status of the two families' honor. Marriage then can be spoken of as an exchange of honor between two families.

A wedding was arranged in such a way that everything will be in order and sufficient and even surplus of festive food or wine is prepared so as to keep and bring family public honor. During marriage ceremony, the house which remains normally a private space is open to all and thereby open to public scrutiny.[167] In order to save the family from serious loss of honor, the wedding ceremony was therefore conscientiously arranged. Honor is one fundamental social value in Mediterranean society. It implies the opinion someone has of his/her own worth and an appreciation of how one is rated by relevant social group.[168]

In ancient Mediterranean world, marriage was not a public institutionalized form of celebration in feasting where the whole village was included and thereby the arrangements were quite elaborate.[169] Thus, wedding ceremony was a solemn occasion which marked off the special time for both the families given into marriage. The concern here nevertheless lies not to discuss comprehensively how marriages were arranged or held in Mediterranean cultural world but to see how

---

163 Herbert Waddams, "Marriage," *A Dictionary of Christian Ethics*, edited by John Macquarrie (London: SCM Press, 1967), 206.

164 For more details on Jewish concept of marriage and its related rituals please see Taitz, *Judaism*, vol. 1, 97-106.

165 Bruce J. Malina and Richard L. Rohrbaugh, *Social – Science Commentary on the Gospel of John* (Minneapolis: Fortress Press, 1998), 65.

166 Esler, *The First Christians in their Social Worlds*, 33.

167 Malina and Richard L. Rohrbaugh, *Social – Science Commentary on the Gospel of John*, 70-71.

168 Esler, *The First Christians in their Social Worlds*, 25.

169 Esler, *The First Christians in their Social Worlds*, 25.

the Jewish wedding festivities came alive in the community under study. It is one such special time that is recorded in John 2, a wedding at Cana in Galilee,[170] which sufficiently also tells the Jewishness of the ceremonial act (purification) and custom. The first miracle story of turning water into the best wine explains well the miracle within a specific socio-historical event that took place in Cana in Galilee (2:1 'on the third day a wedding took place...') and at the same time its intention within the framework of self-disclosure of Jesus' identity. Especially verse 6 describes the Jewish requirement for the kind of ceremonial washings of hands and vessels - "Nearby stood six stone water jars, the kind used by the Jews for ceremonial washing, each holding from twenty to thirty gallons" (2:6). It shows the Jewish purificatory water that stood in the six stone water jars that was turned into wine.[171] According to the Jewish religious tradition vessels made of stones were deemed not susceptible to uncleanness (*Kelim* 5:1 cf. *Parah* 3: 2).

The record of the wedding at Cana is in fact the beginning of the manifestation of the glory of Jesus before the world unlike chapters 13-17 which records the manifestation of Jesus' glory before believers.[172] John chapter 2 records an initial geographic outline (region of Galilee) of Jesus' public ministry "where the glory of the Son of Man takes shape in the miracles of the abundance of wine (2:1-12)."[173] The miracle is the sign of the 'self- revelation' of Jesus' glory (2:11 cf. 1:14) and this story of this first *semeion* is the beginning point for Jesus' entire self-revelation which is given through *semeia* (cf. Jn. 12:37; 20:30). John remarked that this miracle is the beginning of the *semeia* which points forward to the following *semeia* to come[174] and also speaks of Jesus' *semeia* as proof and witness of his origin that he has come from, and sent by God (2:11, 16 cf. 5:31, 36 ff.) and even if they (the Jews) do not believe in him, they must atleast believe the *erga* (Jn. 10:37 f.). The miraculous signs which Jesus performed as recorded, play a significant decisive role in the Christology of the Fourth Gospel and cannot be ignored (2:11, 23 cf. 20:31). The following important theme that dominates the entire gospel is made visible here in this section of the Gospel – that is, the

---

170 The story of the wedding at Cana has enjoyed divergent ways of interpretations – symbolically, allegorically, as an expression to certain notion of faith (ahistorical interpretation), an extract from *semeia* source where miracles are considered the evidence regarding only the spiritual significance. For further information on this complex of problems see W. Nicol, *The Semeia in the Fourth Gospel* (Leiden: E. J. Brill, 1972), 123.

171 Kanagaraj and Ian S. Kemp, *The Gospel According to John*, 52. See tractate *Kelim* of the sixth division, Tohoroth of Mishnah, which reads, "An oven of stone or of metal is not susceptible to uncleanness; yet this last is susceptible by virtue of being a vessel of metal...(*Kelim* 5:11).

172 Rudolf Bultmann, *The Gospel of John: A Commentary*, translated by G. R. Beasley-Murray, R. W. N. Hoare and J. K. Riches (Philadelphia: Westminster Press, 1971), 77.

173 Herman Ridderbos, *The Gospel of John: A Theological Commentary*, translated by John Vriend (Michigan: Wm. B. Eerdmans Publishing Company, 1997), 97.

174 Rudolf Schnackenburg, *The Gospel According to St. John*, vol. 1, translated by Kevin Smyth (Kent: Burns & Oates, 1968), 323.

focus on the identity of the "person of Jesus and the eschatological hour of the promised time of salvation...revealed in the transcendent glory of the Messiah of Israel as the 'Son of Man' descended from heaven and as the 'Son of God' sent by the Father."[175]

Signs have profound effects on those who follow Jesus. For John, the miracles are all 'signs' pointing beyond themselves (signifying a transforming power that is associated with the performer Jesus) and are thereby recorded because he believed it did happen.[176] In the same manner, Herman Ridderbos argues against those who maintain that much of John's materials are unreliable, stated that faith did not produce the story but rather the story produced the faith. He further asserts that John adds interpretations to the facts, gives theological exegesis of what he records without distorting the facts.[177] The miraculous sign of Jesus as recorded in John chapter 2 thus projects historical, christological and the spiritual significances because faith rests exclusively on such *semeia* performed by Jesus (2:23 cf. 3:2; 4:48). Signs are revelatory – revealing the aspects of Jesus' identity, authority and mission. John appropriately records the first of Jesus' signs at Cana in Galilee unmasking the glorious public ministry of Jesus. Miracles are validating signs and pointers to the unique character of Jesus' mission both in the personal-christological (Jn. 5) and soteriological (Jn. 6) sense of the word.[178] So, for John, Jesus is the one object and content of faith.[179] All that is demanded of man is faith in Jesus the *logos* who is later identified as the Christ, the 'Son of God' and the 'Son of Man.' Consonantly faith according to the Gospel is a decisive ethical moment which is also the basic attitude demanded from the viewers of the 'signs' Jesus performed and the readers of the first century community (and us today).

2.6.2. Food Fellowship and Foot Washing

A meal often time is consumed for nourishment and besides a meal (love feast) was eaten for the purpose of fostering and expressing brotherly love, by early Christians.[180] But, there is something more than this that is indicated in the Fourth Gospel. So, the simply mention of 'the meal' was probably and generally known in

---

175 Ridderbos, *The Gospel of John*, 99.

176 Leon Morris, *The Gospel According to John: The English Text with Introduction, Exposition and Notes* (Michigan: Wm. B. Eerdmans Publishing Company, 1971), 176.

177 Ridderbos, *The Gospel of John*, 1-16.

178 Ridderbos, *The Gospel of John*, 9.

179 Schnackenburg, *The Gospel According to St John*, vol. 1, excursus vii, 563.

180 William F. Arndt & F. Wilbur Gingrich, *A Greek- English Lexicon of the New Testament and Other Early Christian Literature*, 4th revised & augmented edition (Illinois/Cambridge: University of Chicago Press/Cambridge University Press, 1952), 6; Cf. *A Greek- English Lexicon of the New Testament and Other Early Christian Literature,* 3rd edition, revised and edited by F. W. Danker based on Walter Baur's (Chicago & London: University of Chicago Press, 1957, 1979, 2000), 7.

the tradition (Jn. 13:2 cf. 21: 20).[181] It was the last meal of Jesus with his disciples and the setting for the farewell discourse was the night he was to be betrayed.[182] The last meal/supper took place on Thursday evening (Nisan 13) prior to the death of Jesus on Friday (14th).[183] This evening meal is significantly used as an important mode of communicating a message of great significance. The central focus is Jesus' relationship with his disciples, in regard to both what is to take place (stereological significance) and the scene following his physical departure (Jn. 14-17).[184] So, the last supper described in John 13 is not a Passover meal. It is the Last Supper taken before the day of Passover (Jn. 13:1).[185] Whatsoever, it is an important occasion both for Jesus and his disciples. It basically served to share a fellowship undergirded by love and respect for each individual partaking the supper and more importantly, it tells of the oneness and mutual solidarity of Jesus and his disciples. Oneness in the purpose of Christian ministry is strongly implied in this episode of the narrative setting of the last supper and washing of the disciples' feet.

While the final meal of Jesus with his disciples in the Synoptic Gospels symbolizes the meaning of his impending death (Mk. 14:12-25), in the Fourth Gospel the disciples of Jesus are reckoned as friends and Jesus reveals what he knows of the future.[186] John describes the distinctive nature of the last supper that which is clubbed with Jesus washing his disciples' feet and toward the end of the supper Jesus gives the new commandment "love one another" (the detail of this important ethical theme will be discussed in the following chapter). The scene of the meal is dominated with the theme of discipleship where feet washing serve as the basis for the relation of master and disciples (Jn. 13:12-20).[187] Most fervently, the evening meal in the Gospel is dominated by the exemplary act of Jesus washing the feet of his disciples, to which we turn our attention now. And

---

181 Lindars, *The Gospel of John*, 442.

182 Ridderbos, *The Gospel of John*, 458.

183 Ridderbos, *The Gospel of John*, 454. The Synoptic identifies this meal, held at the beginning of Nisan 15, what we know as the evening of Nisan 14, assuming that the day of the death of Jesus took place on the first day of the Passover. However the Gospel of John chapter 13 does not call the meal the Passover meal and therefore Jesus' death did not happen on the Passover. Everything is said to have occurred a day earlier – the evening meal on Nisan 13 and Jesus' death on the 14th so that "only after Jesus' body was in the tomb did sunset mark the beginning of the feast when the Passover meal could be eaten." See Raymond E. Brown, *The Gospel According to John: The Anchor Bible,* vol. 2 (London: Doubleday & Company, 1966), 555f.

184 Ridderbos, *The Gospel of John*, 451.

185 Gail R. O'Day, "The Gospel of John: Introduction, Commentary, and Reflections," *The New Interpreter's Bible,* vol. 9 (Nashville: Abingdon Press, 1995):719; Kanagaraj, *The Gospel of John*, 428; Lindars, *The Gospel of John,* 444, 448.

186 Malina and Richard L. Rohrbaugh, *Social-Science Commentary on the Gospel of John*, 72; Smith, *John*, 251-252; Lindars, *The Gospel of John,* 442.

187 Lindars, *The Gospel of John,* 442.

yet our focus here is just to showcase the Johannine community's practices as a continuity of the parent Jewish cultural practice. So, the ethical significance of the foot washing is also left for the next chapter's concern. Nonetheless we will briefly look into its cultural background.

Foot washing was a customary act in Judaism as in other cultures[188] especially washing the feet of the guests at a meal. Probably it was also an act of hospitality undergirded by loving kindness.[189] We have an Old Testament instance where Abraham saw three men standing and to which he rushed to offer them water to wash their feet and offered them meal too (Gen. 18:1-8). Another instance is of the narrative of Lot, to whom appeared two angels, who offered water to wash their feet and then later prepared a meal for them (Gen. 19:1-3, see also Gen. 24:32-33). Again in Genesis 43:24 we read that, "when the steward had brought the men (Joseph's brothers) into Joseph's house, and given them water, and they had washed their feet...." In antiquity, says Thomas, whether Jewish or Greco-Roman, washing the feet of another was considered an act of servitude, basically performed by a person of inferior rank or status.[190] Foot washing was, then, considered a menial task usually performed by slaves or low-status servants[191] probably a Gentile slave was required for the task.[192] So, the washing of another's feet is an act of humiliation and servitude.[193] Even a Jewish slave could not be required to wash the feet of his master as indicated in the *Midrash Mekhilta* 21.2.82a on Exodus 21:2.[194] It is probable to interpret John 13:4 that the meal was already underway when Jesus got up to wash his disciples' feet. It was a customary practice to recline and not be sitting at table meals fellowship.[195] The practice of fellowship at meals was a necessary activity during Jesus' own period. Jesus laid down an example that his disciples continue to engage in such practice. It can be supposed that even after Jesus' death and resurrection, this practice of fellowship at meals and foot washing was continued in keeping with the legacy of the Lord Jesus. And it is practiced even in many Christian churches today.

---

188 Gail R. O'Day, 'The Gospel of John: Introduction, Commentary, and Reflection:" 722.

189 Lindars, *The Gospel of John*, 446.

190 John Christopher Thomas, *Footwashing in John 13 and the Johannine Community* (JSNT Sup 61; Sheffield: Sheffield Academic Press, 1991), 26-42; Jerome H. Neyrey, *The Gospel of John in Cultural Perspective* (Michigan: Wm. B. Eerdmans Publishing Company, 2009), 364-368.

191 Malina and Richard L. Rohrbaugh, *Social-Science Commentary on the Gospel of John*, 219; M. H. Shepherd, "Foot Washing," *The Interpreter's Dictionary of the Bible, E-J*, edited by George Arthur Buttrick *et al.*, (Nashville: Abington Press, 1962), 308.

192 Beasley-Murray, *John*, 233.

193 Smith, *John*, 253.

194 Barrett, *The Gospel According to St. John*, 440.

195 Kanagaraj, *The Gospel of John*, 433.

2.6.3. Jewish Religious Festivals

The Jewish religious festivals are an important theme in John's Gospel because they provide chronological frameworks for delineating the timing of Jesus' ministry here on earth and secondly they provide a topical framework for the Gospel, a background for Jesus' ministry and depicting Jesus as the fulfillment of what these Jewish festivals stood for.[196] There are three very essential annual festivals of the Jews recorded in the Fourth Gospel – the first is the Passover, the second the Feast of Booths and thirdly the Feast of Dedication. These three festivals are in fact pilgrim Jewish festivals that required every male to travel to the ancient Temple in Jerusalem.[197] So, during these annual Jewish festivals one especially a Jew man was obliged to travel to Jerusalem, the central city of Judea. Jerusalem occupies a central religious locale for the Jewish people and so is center for the Jewish life. All significant religious festivals were taking place at Jerusalem and for which any Jews living outside of Jerusalem would have to travel to Jerusalem to worship God on such auspicious religious festivals (Jn. 11:55).[198] The festivals have their origin in divine commandments. Leviticus commands, besides the Sabbath, the appointed feasts of the Lord (Lev. 23). "Feast of the Lord" (Hos. 9:5) or "a feast to the Lord" refers to Passover, Shavuot (Feast of Weeks or Pentecost)[199] and as well to Sukkot (Feast of Booths/Tabernacles). These are the three biblically based pilgrimage

---

196 Bennema, *Excavating John's Gospel*, 15-16; Thomas Vallianippuram, *New Society in John's Gospel* (Aloor, Kerela: Biblia Publications, 2008), 119-121.

197 Jerusalem is considered the most sacred city. The first Jewish Temple was built in this specific territory on Mount Zion by King Solomon (I Kgs. 5:8; 2 Chron. 2-7). As such Jerusalem Temple held the prominent place as the centre of faith. The Temple is regarded as the place where YHWH lived and ruled. That is the presence of God is most believed to be in the Temple. It is also considered the dwelling place of the glory of God where his presence is manifested, and abiding virtue, and where men meet him in adoration and worship. Congruently, the city of Jerusalem becomes a central point of every aspect of Jewish religious and national life. See Sanders, *Judaism Practice and Belief*, 249; R. E. Clements, *God and Temple* (Oxford: Basil Blackwell, 1965), 2-3; G. A. Barrois, "Temple," *Interpreter's Dictionary of the Bible, R-Z* , edited by George Arthur Buttrick *et al.*, (Nashville: Abington Press, 1962), 560; Rabbi Daniel Kohn, "What are Pilgrimage Festivals? http://links.myjewishlearning.com. Accessed on 05-10-2017.

198 Burkett, *An Introduction to the New Testament and the Origins of Christianity*, 40.

199 Feast of Weeks commemorates the revelation of the Torah on Mount Sinai through Moses to the Jewish people. So it is also known as the festival of the giving of the Torah or the gathering of Passover. It occurs on the 50th day after the 49 days of counting Omer. So, it is observed on the 6th to 7th of the Jewish lunar calendar of the month of Sivan (i.e., 14 May – 15 June). The festival marks the culmination of the redemption since the exodus of the Hebrew people from Egypt was intended to lead to the revelation of Sinai, the goal of Passover is the giving of the Torah. What is Shavuot?, https://toriavey.com> what-is-shavuot; Shavuot – the Feast of Weeks, www.hebrew4christians.com. Accessed on 30-08-2017.

Jewish festivals.[200] They are important festivals of the Jewish expressions both of their theology and national aspiration as 'People of God.'[201] The festivals focused on key aspects of Israel's story, retelling and commemorating their deliverance from the bondage by the God of the covenant.[202] Thus, the covenantal people of God were to keep up the tradition of what God had done for them (that is the experiences of God's grace and love for them in the past) through these feasts.

2.6.3.1. The Passover Feast

The Passover[203] also called the festival of unleavened bread is a Jewish festival observed annually in commemoration of Israel's deliverance from the Egyptian bondage. It is to commemorate the occasion on which the angel of the Lord slew the Egyptians but passed over the Israelites' household without killing them when the blood of the Passover lamb was smeared on their lintels and doorposts. It was a milestone in the Israelite's history as a nation (Exod. 12:14, 24-27; 13:14). The Passover feast also ushered the commencement of the barley harvest. It was designed for rest and worship on the first and last of the seven days wherein people were commanded to eat the unleavened bread (Exod. 12: 14-20).[204] The Passover feast holds such a high religious place of honor that every Jew was required to make a pilgrimage to Jerusalem once in a year.

Jesus is said to have traveled to Jerusalem for the Passover feast for three times that equals to his three year ministry based on the record of the Fourth Gospel. This comes clear to any reader that Jesus participated in religiously held important festivals such as this. John is the only Gospel that records a visit by Jesus to Jerusalem three times for the Passover Feast (2:13; 11:55-12:12; 18: 28, 39).[205] Jesus being a Jew must have visited Jerusalem in keeping with the Mosaic command to go on pilgrimage.[206] Every Jew male was obliged to go to the

---

200 Moshe David Herr, "Festivals," *Jewish Values* (Jerusalem: Keter Publishing House, 1974), 288-290.

201 Gerry Wheaton, *The Role of Jewish Feasts in John's Gospel* (Cambridge: Cambridge University Press, 2015), 83-157.

202 Wright, *The New Testament and the People of God*, 234.

203 There are three particular references mentioned – John 2:23; 6:4, and 11:55-56.

204 Kanagaraj, *The Gospel of John*, 105-106.

205 Jesus is said to have appeared in Jerusalem often times for the feasts of the Jews in the Fourth Gospel (mostly at Passover, unnamed feast recorded in John 5:1, Hanukkah (Jn. 10:22) and Feats of Booths/Tabernacles (Jn. 7:1-52). Jesus' first visit to Jerusalem for the first of the three Passovers takes place at the beginning of his ministry and he cleanses the Temple (Jn. 2: 13-22). The second Passover occurs at the close of his public ministry and the third Passover during his crucifixion time. The episode of the cleansing of the Temple is found in all the Gospels except in its difference in chronology. In the Synoptic Gospels Jesus visits Jerusalem at Passover once just before his death (Matt. 21:12-13; Mk. 11:15-17; Lk. 19:45-46).

206 Pilgrimage is a religious undertaken journey to some hallowed shrine. Normally it entails persons travelling to sacred places to experience the divinely sacred and that the journey is

Jerusalem Temple thrice a year to appear before the Lord with gifts proportionate to the blessings one has received from God during the annual festivals (Passover Feast, Feast of Weeks, Feast of Tabernacles (Deut. 16:16; Exod. 23:17; 34:23).

The Gospel of John portrays Jesus as the Passover lamb, through whose death salvation is wrought for the world and its inhabitants (Jn. 13:1-38; 1:29, 35; 19:36; cf. 1 Cor. 5:8).[207] There is dual significances: theological-historical relating to the past experience of the Israelites, and christological, where Jesus' life and ministry liberate those who believe in him (Jn. 3:16).

2.6.3.2. The Feast of Booths

The Feast of Booths also known as the Feast of Tabernacles or Sukkoth was considered the most holy and most popular feast for the Jews. This so called Festival of Booths or Tabernacles was feast of thanksgiving basically for God's blessings in the grape harvest[208] which was celebrated for seven days (during which dwelling in booths was obligatory throughout these seven days), from the fifteenth to the twenty-first of Tishri in the fall (September- October).[209] The first day of the feast was held on a Sabbath and on the eight day, it concluded with a special holy convocation (Lev. 23:34-36 cf. Num. 29:35).[210] The Feast was originally observed with special allusion to the blessings received during the wilderness wanderings when the Israelites had lived in booths or tents (Lev. 23:39-43; Deut. 16:13-15), the time when God the Yahweh was pleased to reveal Himself in the tabernacle in the Old Testament times. The tabernacle was considered a symbolic representation of God's presence (*shakinah*)[211] and subsequently regarded the centre of the manifestation of God's glory to his chosen people (Exod. 40:34) and especially at the sacrifice hour (Lev. 9:6, 23).[212] The Fourth Gospel records the presence of Jesus at the Festival of Booths or Tabernacles in John chapter 7 (the story shifts the geographical location from Galilee to Judea, specifically Jerusalem, the center place of Jewish religious life (7:1, 2, 10). The fifth discourse on the 'Life- Giving Spirit' (7:1-52) until Jesus' public ministry depicts a steadily

most probably understood as sacred time of period. In Israel there were shrines rooted in Israelite kinship religion. For instance, the tombs of the Patriarchs in Hebron, David's tomb in Jerusalem, tomb of Joseph in Samaria, Rachel's tomb near Bethlehem and the like. And there was the central shrine of political religion in Jerusalem. For further details see Malina and Richard L. Rohrbaugh, *Social – Science Commentary on the Gospel of John*, 75.

207 Kanagaraj, *The Gospel of John*, 428.

208 Kanagaraj, *The Gospel of John*, 232.

209 Ridderbos, *The Gospel of John*, 253; Kanagaraj, *The Gospel of John*, 231, 232; *The Mishnah*, footnote 10 in pp., 172-173.

210 Ridderbos, *The Gospel of John*, 257.

211 G. Henton Davies, "Tabernacle," *Interpreter's Bible*, edited by George Arthur Buttrick *et al.* (Nashville: Abington Press, 1962), 506; Morris, *The Gospel According to John*, 392.

212 Davies, "Tabernacle," 498; Edwyn Clement Hoskyns, *The Fourth Gospel,* edited by Francis Noel Davey (London: Faber and Faber Limited, 1947), 148.

and eventual deepening hostility of the Jews against the Messianic claims of Jesus which is central for John. It is tenable to suppose that as the Old Testament tabernacle was considered the symbolic representation of the presence of God, Jesus is that actual representation of God with us.

John probably had brought altogether in chapters 7-8 most of what Jesus has to say in response to Jewish objections raised to Jesus' messianic claims. Indeed the objections to the Messiahship of Jesus are all met in this section of the Gospel.[213] Only the Fourth Gospel records that Jesus visited Jerusalem at a time other than the final Passover during which he was finally crucified.[214] The probable fact that Jesus stayed in Jerusalem from the time of the Feast of Tabernacles to the Feast of Dedication is a way to prepare readers for his presence at the coming Passover, when the hostility of the Jews reached its climax at crucifixion.[215] The significance of the recording of the Tabernacle feast in the Gospel might probably meant to suggest that the manifestation of God in the tabernacle in the wilderness, in the temple is now transposed to the actual and perfect manifestation in the person of Jesus, "whose ministry would result in God's dwelling neither in a tent nor in a temple, but in men's hearts by His Spirit."[216]

So, while the Old Testament tabernacle was understood as the symbolic representation of God's presence, John's Gospel which equates Jesus as one with God (Jn. 10: 30 cf. 1:1-2) is now the one in whom this image (tabernacle) of Old Testament faith is fully realized in the person of Jesus. Jesus is the true and final meeting place between God and human beings.[217] Consequently, the readers of this Gospel are called to believe in this tangible tabernacling and revelation that culminates in the person of Jesus. Jesus stands in the place of God because he is the actual and perfect representation of God's presence in his very being.

---

213 C. H. Dodd, *The Interpretation of the Fourth Gospel* (Cambridge: Cambridge University Press, 1958), 346. See the constant pressure of the opposition that Jesus met that his life was in danger (Jn. 7: 1, 13, 19, 25, 30, 44; 8:37, 40, 59).

214 Smith, *John*, 167.

215 Kanagaraj, *The Gospel of John*, 342-343.

216 Morris, *The Gospel According to John*, 392.

217 Carson, *The Gospel According to John,* 62-63.

2.6.3.3. Feast of Dedication

The Jewish festival of Dedication also known as the Feast of Hanukkah[218] is a post-biblical festival.[219] It is celebrated in commemoration of the purification and rededication of the Temple in 164/165 B.C.E.[220] by the Jewish revolutionary Judas Maccabeus after Antiochus Epiphanes, the Syrian King defiled it by setting up 'an abomination of desolation' on the altar in 167 B.C. (1 Maccabees 1:54; 4:36-61).[221] This festival is also known as the Feast of Lights (Josephus, *Ant. 12.325*), centered on Jerusalem and celebrated the dedication of the Temple, the restoration of worship, and the return of the presence of God.[222] The feast took place in Jerusalem beginning on 25th kisleu[223] in winter about November - December in our calendar (Jn. 10:22) and lasted for eight days.[224] It is told that the altar was desecrated by Antiochus Ephiphanes (1 Macc. 4:41-61). After its three year of desecration, the temple was cleansed and rededicated by Judas Maccabeus by rekindling the altar fire on the same day when the 'abomination of

---

218 Hanukkah though not biblically ordained took on great significance because of its connection with the Jewish concept of temple, which is considered the most sacred place where God's presence is understood to be present. The origins of Hanukkah can be traced back to the rule of Maccabees in 165 B.C.E. This Maccabees family organized a rebellion against the Syrian-Greeks rule and its harsh insistence on the Greek religion, and they succeeded in driving out the Greek/Syrian kings from their tiny land of Judah. This war was led by Mattathias and his five sons. The middle son, Judah, was chosen as the military leader. So, along with his brothers and a bunch of followers, Judah managed to defeat the Syrian- Greek forces in what was basically a civil war between Jews who wanted to adopt Greek/Hellenistic culture and Jews who wanted to maintain a traditional way of life. So after defeating King Antiochus IV, the then ruler of the land of Israel at that time, the Maccabee brothers and their army reclaimed the Holy Temple in Jerusalem, defiled by Syrian soldiers during the course of the war. After cleaning and its restoration, Judah Maccabee pronounced a weeklong holiday on the 25th of the month of Kislev. So the name Hannukkah or Rededication evolved. The legend of Hanukkah, as it has come from the Talmud narrates that when the Jewish soldiers came into the desecrated Temple they sought immediately to rekindle the eternal light, lit with consecrated oil, that was kept burning always above the alter. A soldier was sent to find more oil, because there was no enough oil to last for a single day. But, the single cruse of oil did not get extinguish as thought. It is related that the single cruse of oil continued burning for eight full days,, until new oil was obtained and brought to the Temple. See Emily Taizt, *Judaism,* vol. I, 123-124.

219 Wheaton, *The Role of Jewish Feasts in John's Gospel*, 165-171.

220 The year of commemoration differs – it is given 164 B.C.E. (Bennema) and for some it is dated in 165 B.C.E (Ridderbos, Kanagaraj).

221 Bennema, *Excavating John's Gospel*, 120; Ridderbos, *The Gospel of John,* 367; Smith, *John*, 202; Malina and Richard L. Rohrbaugh, *Social – Science Commentary on the Gospel of John,* 184.

222 A Guilding, *The Fourth Gospel and Jewish Worship* (Oxford: Claredon Press, 1960), 127-129.

223 There are different spellings, for instance - Kislev (Ridderbos); Chislev (Dennis Bratcher); Chisleu (Morris); kisleu (kanagaraj).

224 Morris, *The Gospel According to John*, 517.

desolation' had been set up.[225] This festival is the last of the great festival scenes in John and it occasions the last of Jesus' debates with Judean opponents. The feast is said to be celebrated every year in the manner of the feast of Tabernacle (2 Macc 10:1-9)[226] but not so much important as that of great pilgrimage feasts like the Passover and the Tabernacles.[227]

The Johannine community in many important aspects still held to their Jewish socio-cultural and religious beliefs and practices. The Johannine community was still living in a Jewish environment and so we find familiar concepts and practices. Therefore, we will not be wrong to state that the community was still familiar with essential facets of the Jewish heritage informing us of its continuity from Jewish traditions and its subsequent moral world. And besides, the central focus is Jesus' confrontation with the Jews concerning his identity. It is significant to note that in all these three recorded Jewish festivals; Jesus is seen as the fulfillment of all that the feasts stood for (Jesus as the visible and tangible presence of God, Jesus as the Passover lamb who sacrifice his life for humankind's redemption, and Jesus as the eternal light that illuminates the life of everyone).

It is also fascinating to note that Jesus' central identity as the Messiah; the Son of God dominates the discourses which occur in the context of these Jewish religious festivals and the discourses that followed wherein the question of belief in Jesus comes into focus to bring humans to believe in him. It is very likely that John wants us to see in Jesus as the fulfillment of all that these Jewish feasts stood for or signified.[228] The christological significances that the Fourth Gospel brings out to persuade and convince the readers and to promote faith in Jesus by the miraculous signs he performed and by his (Jesus) teachings as the fulfillment and superseding these Jewish feasts is intriguing. The Johannine community in essence is in continuity with the Jewish tradition without which the former cannot be fully understood nor appreciated where it had stood then.

Conclusion

The Johannine community initially evolved from Judaism. As such it primarily had Jewish members and later extended and incorporated other members from outside the Jewish community (Samaritan/Gentile Christians). It is quite logical, from the structural composition of the Gospel, to suppose that the Samaritan Christians formed the priori to constitute the Johannine community (Jn. 4). The Johannine community encompasses more of an inclusive nature of community composition. This fact probably is virtually right because of the tenet of what entails true discipleship according to the Fourth Gospel. True disciple is one who

225 Kanagaraj, *The Gospel of John*, 342.

226 Morris, *The Gospel According to John*, 517.

227 Ridderbos, *The Gospel of John*, 367.

228 Morris, *The Gospel According to John*, 517.

truly affirms/ alleges his/her Messianic confession of Jesus as the expected and promised Christ and thereby paying undivided allegiance to Jesus as the only one who came from God the Father.

The Johannine community is a closely knitted community who has come to confess Jesus as the expected Messiah. So, the Johannine community constitutes members of a clearly defined community who sees themselves as being in the light because they have believed in the Son of God, Jesus the Christ. They have transited their past familial, social, and religious ties from Judaism and now live in close familial community determined by their belief, and not by their ethnicity, in Jesus as the Christ/Messiah. The community as such was not closed off but was opened to and for anyone who would believe in Jesus. The Community of John's Gospel is an inclusive community that embraces all people who believed in Jesus as the One coming from God and is One with God.

And so was the composition of the Gospel audience multi-ethnicity not restricted to Jewish Christians but includes those of the Samaritan and Gentile Christians too. This is to maintain that the Gospel readers were both Jews and non-Jews. There was no strict guard against any assimilation with the community outside. The primal criterion probably was 'belief' in Jesus as the long awaited Christ. So, anyone who would believe and profess Jesus as the Son of God having sent by the Father would ideally be part of the Johannine community. The Johannine community in deed is a caricature of a multi-ethnic, socially variegated and all inclusive community as both the object and achievement of God's love and of Jesus in his mission to bring God's divine love into the world.[229]

This eventually produced a characteristically sectarian situation in which the community was turning in on itself. It is noted that the Johannine community has experienced expulsion from the Jewish synagogue where they had formerly belonged. The Christians in John's community thereby were at the point of a transitional period from being Jews to Christian Jews. That means the Johannine community's experience of trauma results in a dramatic change in their situation (a changing one). But, in due course of time the community turned towards the world and sets out its mission work (Jn. 17). Consequently, by the time the Gospel was published, the presence of the Gentile and Samaritan Christian is envisaged.

By way of conclusion we can recall that the Johannine community had undergone conflict with the Synagogue. This conflict was religious in its outlook. It was a christological conflict driving a wedge between the community of believers as against the world of unbelief. Subsequently, the Johannine community was defining itself against its own parent fellow Jews who were primarily characterized

229 Richard A. Burridge, *Imitating Jesus: An Inclusive Approach to New Testament Ethics* (Michigan: Wm. B. Eerdmans Publishing Company, 2007), 341. Also see Fernando F. Segovia, *What is John? Literary and Social Readings of the Fourth Gospel*, vol. 2, edited by Fernando F. Segovia (Atlanta: Scholars Press, 1998), 183-209.

by their unbelief. This concrete historical situation of the community has served as an impetus for the community to turn to itself and maintain its own distinctive identity as one of the faithful Messianic Jewish community. The experience that the community had undergone must have had contributed much in the development of its rich theological articulation and its ethical conduct (i.e., its faith articulation or simply a reflection of its belief in concrete way of behavior).

The Community of the Fourth Gospel in many significant areas continues to be Jewish especially in its basic socio-cultural and religious festivals. This is a strong indication that the Johannine community is in continuity with the Jewish practices and beliefs though the community has undertaken a shift in her major theological articulation and eventually consolidates her identity as community of believers in Jesus' messianic role.

Chapter 3

Major Ethical Pointers In John's Gospel A Thematic Approach

Introduction

The present chapter will delve into few but selected passages in the Gospel according to John that seem to have bearing on ethics or in other words that have ethical appeals extrinsically or intrinsically. Perhaps the researcher's attention is devoted and inclined more towards the literary narrative text *in front*. However, to ensure that the important aspects are not overlooked, the researcher will try her best to read the text *behind, in and in front of the text* as a reader. Meanwhile note must be taken that the literary genre of the Gospels does not contain the primary ethical text in the manner of the Aristotle's philosophical understanding and explanation of ethics.[1] Leander E. Keck has correctly noted that "the vocabulary of ethics used in major philosophical traditions is generally absent from the New Testament."[2] The Gospel of John does not contain explicit codes of conduct. Nevertheless ethical appeals definitely are embedded in the narratives with its character portrayal, specific directives, and images which provide critical reflection on human response and action.

However, no attempt will be made to present the fully rounded sketch of the ethics of the Johannine writings but limit my focus to the ethical indicators/pointers as implied in the Gospel of John. Ethics is a veritable aspect of any social life of a community. So, one cannot isolate the study of the ethical values without considering the social world of the given community and this social aspect are

1 Richard A. Burridge, *Imitating Jesus: An Inclusive Approach to New Testament Ethics* (Michigan/Cambridge: Wm. B. Eerdmans Publishing Company, 2007), 33.

2 Leander E. Keck, "Rethinking "New Testament Ethics,"" *JBL* 115/1 (1996): 9.

gleaned from the text. So, as to uncover the insightful meaning of the text the social and narrative worlds are to be held together because any interpreter cannot entirely grasped in a single-sided studies whether it be of social history or narratology.[3] The sociological approach as one exegetical method to the interpretation of the Bible is appropriated in this research because it attempts to situate the texts in its social milieu in which God-human encounter takes place. The method is valid to the extent that it serves as a window through which to view the human existential context. This approach is more apt because the Gospel clearly reflects this aspect of God becoming human (Jn. 1:14). The Gospel of John reflects an application of ethics in a particular and defined situation (of the Johannine community). The element bearing on ethics in the Gospel has to be defined at the outset and so the analytical framework must be first worked out.

3.1. Defining Hermeneutical Terms for the Ethical Interpretation

It is of paramount importance to set out the analytical framework for further investigation into the ethical elements present in the text of the Gospel of John. Delineating what entails ethics in John's Gospel calls for a closer examination by reading in between the lines as we have the text in front and before us. The categories used to analyze ethical material in the Gospel are of fundamental importance for the ethical materials seem to be embedded in a number of ways. It is conveyed through narrative events, metaphors, images, arguments and the like. Johannine ethical significance can thus be grasped when the story is fully read.[4] As such, the quest for the Johannine ethics strives to consider not only the explicit moral instructions but the whole story that gives out a ray of value system and its moral conceptions which eventually lead the reader towards certain moral conduct. So, at hand consideration is to take into account evidences from the Gospel which act as a catalyst or give way to discovering ethical indicators explicitly or implicitly. As a result, in analyzing the text not only direct ethical statements should receive attention but also to such statements and references that convey ethical messages implicitly.

Careful reading of the Gospel exposes the centrality of the Christology that takes precedence over all other theological themes. Thereby any Christological references with an emphasis to believe in Jesus will serve as a working definition to find the ethical thrust of the Gospel. So, an overview of some of the relevant texts for the ethical pointers/indicators in the Gospel demands attention. A closer examination of selected passages, terms/words, or phrase will help us to advance and sharpen our understanding in regard to the ethical elements present in the Gospel. In effect, the present chapter endeavors to unearth the themes that account for the presence of the ethical elements in the Gospel either explicitly or implicitly

3 Gail R. O'Day, "Toward a Narrative Study of John," *Interpretation* 49 (1995): 345.

4 Richard B. Hays, *The Moral Vision of the New Testament: A Contemporary Introduction to New Testament Ethics* (New York: HarperCollins, 1996), 140.

(subtle indication). It is to explore the motivated principles according to which the community is supposed to live. Or in other expression, we are to look for such ethical pointers which may lead us to understand the ethical principles or even exhortation to which the community in a particular historical setting 'ought to' or 'should' abide by. Consequently, concept related verbal equivalents of ethics (such as work/s or 'signs', 'doing the work of God' or ethically loaded verb "to believe") will be traced to unravel the ethical aspects of the Gospel of John.

Nonetheless, *no* linguistic exegesis is considered as the mode of exposing, but a thematic approach is adopted, to unearth the ethical dimensions as found in the Gospel distinctive narratives. It is believed that selected terminologies and passages under study will certainly throw light to ascertain valuable ethical aspects present in the Fourth Gospel. Ethics as an imperative command or exhortation will be the analytical category to identify what entails 'what one ought to do' and is expected to do. In cases where explicit commands or moral instructions are absent, we will try to locate the subtle ethical pointers which lead the reader toward certain moral actions.

3.2. A Thematic Analysis of Ethical Pointers

The attempt in this section will be to find passages that inform the ethical values. In analyzing the ethical elements our attention will not be only to the ethical words of Jesus but also to his deeds 'ἔργα' (σημεῖα)[5] which serve as a paradigm (ὑπόδειγμα). Burridge rightly alleges that one may compile the ethics of Jesus by considering his deeds as an example.[6] Since ethics is a reflection upon the question of how to properly act, one should look for explicit evaluation of the actions (deeds) of Jesus as portrayed in the text by the Gospel of John.[7] So, the question, 'How does John display or speak about Jesus' deeds or actions?' is of prime importance in seeking to unravel the ethical concepts in John's Gospel.

3.2.1. 'To Believe:' A Decisive Ethical Moment

The term πιστεύειν "believe," "have faith," "come to faith," "put faith" is considerably frequent in the Gospel of John and at times used along the word γινώσκειν "know," "realize" (Jn. 6:69; 17:8 cf. 14:7 & 10).[8] It is used both transitively (means 'to entrust,' it occurs once in 2:24 but devoid of any specific significance) and intransitively ('to give credence to,' 'to believe,' and 'to have

---

5 The terms ἔργα' and σημεῖα are used interchangeably in this research, to refer to the miraculous deeds of Jesus which posses a revelatory function to incur faith in the actor.

6 Burridge, *Imitating Jesus*, 31.

7 Karl Weyer-Menkhoff, "The Response of Jesus: Ethics in John by considering Scripture as Work of God," *Rethinking the Ethics of John: "Implicit Ethics" in the Johannine Writings*, edited by Jan G. van der Watt and Ruben Zimmermann (Tubingen: Mohr Siebeck, 2012), 160.

8 Raymond E. Brown, *The Anchor Bible: The Gospel According to John*, vol. 1 (New York: Doubleday & Company, 1966), 512-514.

confidence in', 'to trust').[9] It is to the latter meaning that the Johannine expression of faith is in place. The lexical meaning of πίστις is given as faith, confidence, fidelity, guarantee, loyalty. Having given the meaning of faith no secular text accounts a parallel to the expression of the Biblical faith that inspired the conduct of the biblical ancestors (the Greek literature in contrast has greater inclination towards intellectual phenomenon though both moral and intellectual elements encompass the sense of the word faith).[10] Faith then implies confidence expressed in human relationship as fidelity, trust, assurance, oath, proof, guarantee (cf. Heb. 11: 1).[11] The Johannine concept of faith is occasioned and concerned about presenting the right intention on the view of salvation, characterized by the term life (ζωή), for the world back then was in quest of life as salvation.[12] The occasion of John's community struggles to define and affirm its own identity as belonging to its own Jewish community but who excommunicated them from the Synagogue (the central place of worship where they get religious teachings imparted to them by the religious leaders). The Johannine community was denied of the religious benefits for having believed in Jesus as the Messiah. There is a strong emphasis on the role of faith in adherence to Jesus.[13] In situation such as this, it calls for a particular actions and determine specific behavior that would stand out as the true followers of Jesus and also an indication of John's community's identity. As such, faith in Jesus as the Messiah constitutes the most fundamental and dominant character to define the community's character. Consequently, the content of belief is the role, authority and divinely ordained mission of Jesus (Jn. 8:24; 13:19; 11:27, 42; 14:11; 15:27; 16:27, 30; 17:8; 20:31).[14]

In the Gospel of John, Jesus explicitly talks about himself and his teachings focused on his own personal identity with its allied authority and mission. Besides, Jesus is presented as the object of faith more succinctly (than it is in the Synoptic Gospels) and the highest personalization of revelation (Jn. 1:14; 11:27;

---

9 C. H. Dodd, *The Interpretation of the Fourth Gospel* (Cambridge: Cambridge University Press, 1953), 179; Ceslas Spicq, "πίστις," *Theological Lexicon of the New Testament,* παι - ψευ, vol. 3, translated and edited by James D. Ernst (Peabody, Massachusetts: Hendrickson Publishers, 1994), 110-111.

10 Dodd, *The Interpretation of the Fourth Gospel,* 179-180.

11 Spicq, "πίστις," 110-116; Dodd, *The Interpretation of the Fourth Gospel,* 183.

12 Rudolf Bultman, "πιστεύω, πίστις, πιστός," *TDNT,* πε – ρ, vol. 6, edited by Gerhard Friedrich (Michigan: Wm. B. Eerdmans Publising Company, 1968), 223; Jey J. Kanagaraj, *The Gospel of John: A Commentary* (Secunderabad: OM Books, 2005), 23-27.

13 Barnabas Lindars, *The Gospel of John* (Michigan: Wm. B. Eerdmans Publishing Company, 1987), 35. It was first published in 1972 in London by Marshall, Morgan & Scott Publishing Ltd.

14 Dodd, *The Interpretation of the Fourth Gospel,* 183.

20:31).[15] Faith[16] in John remains more as a fundamental and comprehensive decision towards the eschatological envoy of God and his saving revelation in the person and work of Jesus.[17] It is quite fitting that John begins (thus the prologue 1:1-18) and closes (purpose statement 20:31) the Gospel with direct and explicit presentation on the person of Jesus. As a result, 'belief in Jesus' is one significant governing theme and is Christologically determined[18] and it has a saving effect.[19] The narration of the miraculous work of Jesus design to incur faith in him is chronicled at the beginning of his public ministry (that has been touched upon in chapter - One). Belief is both stanched with religious and ethical notion in John's Gospel. It strongly demands action. It is therefore an ethical catalyst to translate itself into concrete action. There is a dynamic interconnection between faith and action. The good works done in the light is prompted by the belief in Jesus (Jn. 3:19-21 cf. 12:46). This is to acknowledge that there is coherence between faith and love (Jn. 13:34; 15:12) and the eyes of faith beholds Jesus as the revealer and bringer of God's divine love (Jn. 3:16).[20]

True identity as followers of, and belonging to, Jesus is one very important factor in John's Gospel. And it is determined by the word 'belief' and the content is in the nature, mission and status of Jesus as the Christ.[21] Believing is a term which "describes the kind of relationship of Jesus and another person that enables a person to execute the works of Jesus."[22] It has been mentioned earlier that no set of rules or codes of conduct are systematically presented in the Fourth Gospel yet they are embedded predominantly in the various Christological narratives and discourses that permeated the literary content of the Gospel. In line with this, the catchword 'believe' in John's Gospel is determinative of what one ought to

---

15 E. C. Blackman, "Faith," *The Interpreter's Dictionary of the Bible, E-J*, edited by George Arthur Buttrick *et al.,* (Nashville: Abington Press, 1962), 222; Bultman, "πιστεύω, πίστις, πιστός," 227.

16 The words 'faith' and 'belief' connote the same notion. So, the words *faith* and *belief* are interchangeably used in this research work. Faith is a human response to Jesus, in whom all God's intended revelatory events took place. So, faith is a response of human beings which is to be perfected in love. It is the perfection of commitment of believers in Jesus Christ. John's Gospel recognizes the supreme importance of faith.

17 Rudolf Schnackenburg, *The Gospel According to St John,* vol. 1, translated by Kevin Smyth (Kent: Burns & Oates, 1968), excursus vii, 558.

18 Bultman, "πιστεύω, πίστις, πιστός," 228.

19 Dodd, *The Interpretation of the Fourth Gospel*, 186.

20 Bultman, "πιστεύω, πίστις, πιστός," 228.

21 Dodd, *The Interpretation of the Fourth Gospel*, 183. See John 8:24; 11:27, 42; 13:9; 14:2; 16:27, 30; 17:8; 20:31.

22 Weyer-Menkhoff, "The Response of Jesus," 165; Dodd, *The Interpretation of the Fourth Gospel*, 180.

or should be. The Greek verb πιστεύω[23] 'to believe' used in the Fourth Gospel is remarkable because for John it is highly probable that he thought of faith as an activity which takes humans right out of themselves and makes them one with Christ.[24] So faith 'πίστις' according to the Gospel 'is an ethical action' (6:29)[25] and it requires of believers in Jesus to alter the fundamental way in which they know and understand themselves.[26] That is, faith in Jesus involves a change of realm from darkness (immoral) into the light (moral world). Faith predominantly is a religious concept bound up with an element of moral concept in John's Gospel. πιστεύω 'to believe' is frequently followed by εἰς with the accusative (i.e., accusative preposition πιστεύειν εἰς 'Ιησουν) and so it can be regarded as the distinctive Johannine expression.[27] 'To believe' in someone expresses a 'moral element of personal trust' (Jn. 14:1)[28] and it embraces knowing who Jesus is and where he comes from (i.e. to recognize the claims of Jesus as God's truest revelation).[29] Accordingly, for the Fourth Gospel 'faith' is a human's response to

---

23 The Greek verb πιστεύω "to believe" in the Gospel occurs 98 times (but the noun form πίστις is never used) against 11 times in Matthew, 14 in mark, and 9 in Luke's Gospel, Acts 37 times and 54 times in Paul. The numerical frequency speaks volumes of the significant place the verb "to believe" is given by the Evangelist. The noun form is not used may be partly because of its usage by heretical thinkers. It is assumed that some of the pre-Gnostic systems of the day gave it unhealthy associations and rendered the word suspect with John). It is also important to note that 'to believe' in Jesus takes up a large part of the center section of the Gospel's content. It appears that John's favorite construction is the usage of the verb πιστεύω with accusative (πιστεύειν εἰς with accusative 36 times), πιστεύω with dative (18 times), πιστεύειν ὅτι...(13 times), πιστεύειν used absolutely (30 times) and πιστεύειν with neuter accusative (11:26b). The verb πιστεύω with accusative seems to be the key expression for John in the Gospel which is almost exclusively directed to the person of Jesus except in John 14:1, where Jesus speaks of God as the object "πιστεύετε εἰς τὸν θεόν." See Leon Morris, *The Gospel According to John: The English Text with Introduction, Exposition and Notes* (Michigan: Wm. B. Eerdmans Publishing Company, 1971), 99, 335; Blackman, "Faith," 223-225; Bultman,"πιστεύω, πίστις, πιστός," 222-228.

24 Morris, *The Gospel According to John*, 336.

25 Rudolf Schnackenburg, *The Gospel According to St. John*, vol. 2 , translated by Cecily Hastings, Francis McDonagh, David Smith & Richard Foley (London: Burns and Oates, 1980), 260.

26 Frank J. Matera, *New Testament Ethics: The Legacies of Jesus and Paul* (Louisville, Kentucky: Westminster John Knox Press, 1996), 103.

27 Dodd, *The Interpretation of the Fourth Gospel*, 183; Blackman, "Faith," 224. Outside of the Johannine writings is found only in Matt. 18:6; Acts 10:43; 14:23; Rom 10:14; Gal 2:16; Phil. 1:29.

28 Morris, *The Gospel According to John*, 336; Dodd, *The Interpretation of the Fourth Gospel*, 182.

29 Dodd, *The Interpretation of the Fourth Gospel*, 183; Bultmann, "πιστεύω, πίστις, πιστός," 227; Blackman, "Faith," 233. The nature of faith in Jesus in John's Gospel takes two important concerns. Firstly, faith in Jesus is to believe as the One sent into the world by God. By faith people who believe in Jesus affirm Jesus as the Revealer, the only-begotten son (1:18). Secondly, for those who believe in Jesus as coming from God (origin of Jesus) believe that Jesus is the Savior of the world (4:42); Jesus is the Holy one of God who has the words of life everlasting

Jesus' revelation from many aspects (cf. 1:12; 2:23: 3:18) and with considerable urgency (e.g., the story of the Samaritan woman in John 4).[30] And so "to believe" in Jesus is not to merely accept the claims of Jesus, "by intellectual assent, but to acknowledge that claim by yielding allegiance"[31] and by way of obedience to his commandments (whereby obedience takes the form of visible action). There is therefore an inalienable relationship between faith in Christ and the practice of that faith in everyday affairs of one's life.

As such, 'to believe' in Jesus is very central to the Fourth Gospel and is loaded with profound ethical implications.[32] 'To believe' in Jesus is an active and actual commitment to whatever causes Jesus stood for.[33] The primary significance of belief in Jesus is stated in John 3:15-16 and the σημειᾶ Jesus performed are the decisive miraculous works in establishing faith in Jesus as the Christ, the Son of God (Jn. 20:30-31).[34] At the same time, there is a basic ethical demand by the call of Jesus, the revealer of God's truth which however "does not need to be elaborated in structure and content but which can be identified by the response of faith and love."[35] Johannine ethics corresponds to the practical application of the faith in Jesus in daily living. At the heart of the Gospel's purpose there is a call to people to evaluate the works (σημεῖα) Jesus has performed which specifically signified his real identity.[36] So for John, both men and women are responsible for

---

(6:68-69); the descent-ascent movement of the Son of Man that is believe in Jesus as the Son of Man who comes from God the Father and he will return to where he belongs (1:51; 9:35-38); Jesus is the Christ/Messiah , the Son of God (11:27; 20:31). So Johannine faith or belief is more than a mere trust.

30 Schnackenburg, *The Gospel According to St John*, vol. 1, excursus vii, 558.

31 Dodd, *The Interpretation of the Fourth Gospel*, 184.

32 Matera, *New Testament Ethics*, 103. Several examples of those who put their faith in Jesus are recorded in the Gospel. For instance, the disciples who believe in Jesus, The Samaritans (Jn. 4), Royal officer and his whole household whose son was at the point of death was made to live (Jn. 4:43-53), a man born blind (Jn. 9), Sisters of Lazarus (Jn. 11), the crowds who witness the raising of Lazarus who was buried for four days (Jn. 12:10-11) and Nicodemus though a secret believer came to anoint Jesus' body for burial (19:39). In deed the case of Nicodemus is interesting whose faith in Jesus involves a struggle. He came to Jesus at night to know the truth but was not able to believe in the mysteries that Jesus discloses (3:1-14). But, then in the middle of the narrative of the Gospel he is presented as defending Jesus from a summary condemnation by the religious leaders (7:51) and at the end of the Gospel narrative he is presented as a secret disciple (19:39).

33 Jose Maniparampil, *Reading the Fourth Gospel* (Bangalore: Claretian Publications, 2000), 34.

34 Renstorf, "σημεῖον," *TDNT*, vol. 2, edited by Gerhard Friedrich (Michigan: Wm. B. Eerdmans Publishing Company, 1971), 250.

35 Michael Labaln, "It's Only Love"- Is That All? Limits and Potentials of Johannine "Ethic" - A Critical Evaluation of Research," *Rethinking the Ethics of John: "Implicit Ethics" in the Johannine Writings* (Tubingen: Mohr Siebeck, 2012), 18.

36 Christos Karakolis, "Semeia Conveying Ethics in the Gospel According to John," *Rethinking the Ethics of John: "Implicit Ethics" in the Johannine Writings,* eds. Jan G. Van der Watt and

believing in Jesus and unbelief is considered "morally culpable."[37] Belief or faith is the bond which binds the believer to Jesus, the Revealer.[38] The call to believe in the significance of the σημεῖα and accordingly belief in Jesus[39] is in fact a gate way to life 'ζωή' eternal (Jn. 20:3-31 cf. 1 Jn. 5:13). Life eternal through believing in Jesus is both soteriological and ethical in nature[40] (this theme will be taken up in detail in the subsequent chapter). In this case, faith can be equalized as the life-giving vision, or knowledge, of God[41] in Jesus (Jn. 11:40 cf. 22:25-29).

Belief in Jesus serves as an ethical force. That is, belief in Jesus is a driving force to the ethical expression of the hearers in their attitudes and values. Interestingly, belief in Jesus is working the works of God (Jn. 6:28-29)[42] and it "becomes the major ethical action persons can perform."[43] Faith in Jesus enables the believer to do the same works of Jesus or even better (Jn. 14:12 cf. 5:20) which suggests a strong moral notion. Thus, good works appear to be the consequence of faith (Jn. 14:12).[44] Accordingly, believers are enabled to work the works of God (that is to act rightly)[45] when they believe in Jesus. 'To believe' in Jesus is a moral act because for John the single moral 'work' that God requires from human kind is 'to believe' in Jesus (Jn. 6).

The Johannine community's identity is shaped by their belief in Jesus. Those who believe in Jesus as God's messenger of salvation have already passed through the critical moment and have obtained eternal life: "I tell you the truth, whoever hears my word and believes him who sent me has eternal life and will not be condemned; he has crossed over from death to life" (Jn. 5:24 cf. 11:25-26). Their behavior is defined and is faith oriented, directed in the person and work of

---

Ruben Zimmermann (Tubingen: Mohr Siebeck, 2012), 193.

37 D. A. Carson, *The Gospel According to John* (Michigan: Wm. B. Eerdmans Publishing Company, 1991), 99.

38 Rudolf Bultmann, *The Gospel of John: A Commentary*, translated by G. R. Beasley-Murray (Oxford: Basil Blackwell, 1971), 615; Craig S. Keener, *The Gospel of John: A Commentary*, vol. 2 (Peabody, Massachusetts: Henrickson Publishers, 2003), 941.

39 Karakolis, "Semeia Conveying Ethics," 195.

40 Cornelis Bennema, "Virtue Ethics in the Gospel of John: The Johannine Characters as Moral agents," *Rediscovering John: Essays on the Fourth Gospel in Honour of Frederic Manns*, edited by L. D. Chrupcała (Milan: Terra Santa, 2013), 167–181.

41 Dodd, *The Interpretation of the Fourth Gospel*, 186.

42 The ἔργα of Jesus as σημεῖα and the work of God are affected in the ἔργα. The ἔργα of Jesus as σημεῖα are at the same time the ἔργα of God (4:34; 5:36; 9:3f; 10:32; 14:10; 17:4). See Rengstorf, "σημεῖον," *TDNT*, vol. 2, 248.

43 Jan G. van der Watt, "Ethics and Ethos in the Gospel According to John," *ZNW* 97 (2006): 158.

44 Hermut Lohr, "Εργον as an Element of Moral Language in John," *Rethinking the Ethics of John: "Implicit Ethics" in the Johannine Writings*, edited by Jan G. van der Watt and Ruben Zimmermann (Tubingen: Mohr Siebeck, 2012), 242.

45 Weyer-Menkhoff, "Ethics in John," 165.

Jesus. Belief, therefore, is the ethical response of the believers in relation to Jesus' self-revelation through the working of σημεῖα. Johannine ethical implication thus evolves from believing in Jesus. Subsequently, the decision of the people to believe or not to believe in Jesus bears corresponding ethical consequences.[46] A positive response of faith in Jesus then intuitively leads one towards certain good moral action. Glen Lund avows that, "the ultimate test for Johannine moral acceptability could perhaps be described as intimate connection to Jesus/God through belief and faithfulness to his testimony within the Spirit-guided community."[47]

The Gospel according to John portrays Jesus as the object of faith. The Johannine Jesus summons for faith in him through the σημεῖα he did perform. The 'signs' served as an important pointer and indicator to the self-disclosure of Jesus as the expected Messiah, the 'Son of God' and the 'Son of Man' who has come to offer life. Therefore, the σημεῖα are the backbone of the Johannine narrative.[48] So, the act of believing in Jesus according to John entails a profound outcome of faith that results in the gift of life eternal. The Hebrew concept 'to do truth' is to do the prescriptions of the Law faithfully according to the Old Testament and Qumran but this concept of truth in John is transposed to refer to embrace to the truth of Jesus.[49] Thus, to believe in Jesus is to acknowledge the truth and this acknowledgement of the truth "calls not only for theoretical acknowledgment but the ethical action that necessarily follows from it"[50] and that is to do good works which corresponds to doing the will of God according to the Fourth Gospel.

The Johannine discourse on the bread of life (Jn. 6) resolves the relation between faith and work which was the early Christian struggle (Paul, James). The crowd's ethical question, Τί ποιῶμεν ἱνα ἐργαζώμεθα τὰ ἐργα τοῦ θεοῦ; "what must we do to perform the works of God ? (Jn. 6:28) focuses on behavior and seeks to identify actions that are in conformity with the will of God.[51] Jesus replied that τὸ ἐργον τοῦ θεοῦ consist in believing in the one whom the Father has sent. 'Ιησοῦς καὶ εἶπεν αὐτοῖς, Τοῦτο ἐστιν τὸ ἐργον τοῦ θεôυ, ἱνα πιστεύτηε εἰς ὃν ἀπέστειλεν ἐκεῖνος (6:29). 'To believe' in Jesus as the revelation of God is a moral

46 Karakolis, "Semeia Conveying Ethics," 212

47 Glen Lund, "The Joys and Dangers of Ethics in John's Gospel," *Rethinking the Ethics of John: "Implicit Ethics" in the Johannine Writings*, edited by Jan G. van der Watt and Ruben Zimmermann (Tubingen: Mohr Siebeck, 2012), 278.

48 J. N. Sanders and B. A. Mastin, *The Gospel According to St. John* (Peabody, Massachusetts: Hendrickson Publishers, 1968), 5.

49 Ignace de la Potterie cited by Raymond E. Brown, *The Community of the Beloved Disciple* (New York: Paulist Press, 1979), 129.

50 Georg Strecker, *Theology of the New Testament*, translated by M. Eugene Boring (Berlin: deGruyter; Louisville: Westminster John Knox, 2000), 430.

51 Labahn, "It's Only Love" – Is That All?," 32.

act in that it acknowledges the true identity and ἐργον τοῦ θεοῦ and Jesus.[52] It is interesting to note Jesus' response nails to the heart that the singular ἐργον God requires is πιστεὺειν εἰς' Ιησοῦν. That is, faith is the only and the essential human response to God's Son, the true revealer and bringer of salvation. It is a requirement to believe in Jesus as the Messiah. Faith in God's representative (Jesus) is the human attitude willed by God in response to his action (Jn. 14:1).[53] πιστεὺω then is the proper moral response that people should render to God.[54] The centrality of belief in Jesus is affirmed in every narrative passages and discourses beginning from the prologue to the epilogue.[55] And especially the purpose statement of the Gospel succinctly tells that all the miraculous *signs* Jesus performed were intended as a vehicle to reveal his glory and subsequently lead to believe in him. Doing the works of the Father is one prime ethical conduct required. So, believing in Jesus becomes a fundamental ethical behavior one can carry him/herself.[56] 'To believe' in Jesus indeed is a stairway or an impetus to the right ethical living. As such, belief in Jesus as sent by God the Father is the required work of God (Jn. 6:29). And this theme of faith or belief, in the Gospel according to John, is intricately connected to the theme of Judgment. A person is judged either by believing or refusing to believe in Jesus as the One sent from above, the Father. If one believes he/she becomes the child of God and belongs to the family of the Kingdom of God and enjoys life eternal brought forth by the person and work of Jesus. And if one refuses to believe in Jesus he/she incurs judgment of condemnation on him/herself (Jn. 3:18; 5: 24 ff). Human's response to Jesus in faith or disbelief leads to one's own verdict of life or death.[57] So, the coming of the Son is the ὡρα of κρίσις. In other word, Jesus coming to the world has brought the future into the present (judgment).[58]

One's appropriate response to God's divine revelation is to believe in Jesus according to John. There are three very important consequences of believing in Jesus. In the first place, one who believes in Jesus is given the power to become God's child (Jn. 1:12-13). This person will become part of the family of God.

---

52 Cornelis Bennema, "Virtue Ethics in the Gospel of John," 167–181. The works of God are the works of Jesus because Jesus does whatever the Father commanded him (10:37, 38;12: 49-30; 14: 10, 11, 24, 31).

53 Schnackenburg, *The Gospel According to St John*, vol. 2, 39.

54 Jan G. van der Watt, "The Gospel of John's Perception of Ethical Behavior," *In die Skriflig* 45 (2011): 433-435.

55 Larry W. Hurtado, *Lord Jesus Christ: Devotion to Jesus in Earliest Christianity* (Michigan: Wm. B. Eerdmans Publishing Company, 2003), 351.

56 Jan G. van der Watt, "Radical Social Redefinition and Radical Love: Ethics and Ethos in the Gospel According to John," *Identity, Ethics, and Ethos in the New Testament*, edited by Jan G. van der Watt (Berlin: Walter de Gruyter, 2006), 114.

57 Bultmann, "πιστεύω, πίστις, πιστός," 224.

58 Bultmann, "πιστεύω, πίστις, πιστός," 226.

Secondly, those who believe in Jesus will not remain in darkness (Jn. 12:46). The third central significance is that whoever believes in Jesus as the Son of God will have eternal life (Jn. 3:16; 20:31). Congruently, those who believe and remain in Jesus will spontaneously do what is good (Jn. 3:20-21). Thus, faith in Jesus becomes a springboard to a virtuous living and it promises life (Jn. 3:16, 36; 5:24; 6:40, 47; 20:31) whereas unbelief will not *see* life (3:36).

The community is invited to believe and live according to what Jesus had said and done. Jesus' life and ministry is a reflection that illuminates the will of God the Father. Jesus calls people to behave according to Scriptures that which is interpreted and understood in the light of his life and ministry. The Scripture comes afresh and alive in and through Jesus who is sent by the Father (Jn. 5:39). The will of the Father is exemplified, interpreted in the presence, life and work of Jesus. The miraculous signs illustrate that Jesus is the Son of God and calls for faith in action. Faith in the Gospel, thus, has multifaceted significances - soteriological, Christological, and ethical character, the aspects are equally important and closely associated.[59] Since Jesus illumines the Father in all aspects, people are invited to believe in him and henceforth live accordingly. Believing precedes action so believing in the person and work of Jesus is determinative for a code of conduct for Johannine community of believers. This suggests that the Johannine ethics is Christologically determined. Jesus is the interpretative focal point for a believer's conduct.

Unlike the Synoptic Jesus,[60] the Johannine Jesus calls for a response of faith in him. The object of faith is Jesus the 'Son of God' sent from above into this world below.[61] He is the means (belief) to the end (life eternal). For John, life 'ζωή'[62] is the ultimate and the highest good which everyone must long for. And yet, this life cannot be obtained by him/herself but by believing in Jesus. The raising of Lazarus is a sign that particularly displays Jesus as the source of life.[63] So, for John, believing in Jesus as the Son of God who has been sent to offer life eternal is one very important ethical moment in a person's life. The Johannine Jesus calls for a response of faith that is 'to believe' in him and the signs 'σημεῖα' are indeed the vehicle manifesting his glory and a testimony that he comes from God. All who believe in Jesus must undertake a profound change in the attitude of life and the way they perceive the world in which they live.[64]

59 Schnackenburg, *The Gospel According to St John*, vol. 1, excursus vii, 567.

60 Jesus in the Synoptic gospel proclaimed the Kingdom of God and a corresponding call to repentance.

61 D. Moody Smith, *The Theology of the Gospel of John* (Cambridge: Cambridge University Press, 1995), 2; Bultmann, "πιστεύω, πίστις, πιστός," 223, 227; Blackman, "Faith," 234.

62 Much more details will be discussed in chapter 5 under the heading 'Ethics is life.'

63 Sanders and B. A. Mastin, *The Gospel According to St John*, 5. cf. 1:4; 3:15f.; 5:24, 26, 29, 39, 40; 6:35, 63, 68; 8:12; 10:10, 28; 11:25; 14:6; 17: 2-3; 20:31).

64 Matera, *New Testament Ethics*, 97.

Accordingly, belief is a decisive step and which is demanded of an individual in the Fourth Gospel (6:28). In its truest sense faith is an act and has the character of obedience (which can be described as a τηρεῖν of the ἐντολαί given by Jesus) and this obedience must be expressed in one's conduct (15:10 cf. 1 Jn. 2:3f; Deut. 4:30).[65] As such, 'to believe' in Jesus as sent by God is one prime ethical challenge of the Gospel of John.[66] The Father-Son relationship is an ethical paradigm for every believing community. Cordial relationship is built on the basis of the belief in the person of Jesus. Eventually, belief in Jesus is one of the important guiding criteria for the community's behavior of John's Gospel. Belief in Jesus determines the actions of an individual so it becomes a decisive factor for one's eternal life or condemnation. So, choice and decision lie in an individual's hand. If one believes, he/she has passed from death to life but unbelieving leads to condemnation. So, believing in Jesus is a decisive ethical moment which will forever decide the individual's future judgment. As such one's belief or unbelief becomes a moral ethical decision inculcating judgment to him/her either by believing or refusing to believe in Jesus whom the Father has sent into the world.

The new existence of believers results from a belief in Jesus that brings them into a new reality of being belonging to the fold/family of God. Belief in Jesus is a springboard to the desiring ethical behavior. In other words, Jesus acts as a motivator and a model for the believers' ethical behavior. Whereas, the failure to believe in Jesus is connected with doing evil works and not the good works of God (7:7).[67] Faith or belief in Jesus is an affirmation of standard moral norms because the Gospel presents Jesus as the one who speaks the truth and himself being the truth at the same time.[68] Consequently, belief or faith in Jesus serves as the primary ethical conduct and this is what God, the Father who sent His only begotten Son, wants His people to do. It is also of great significance, theologically, that the Johannine faith is always referred to witnesses and testimony.[69] The Johannine community of disciples is obliged to bear witness and testimony (15:27) to the salvific plan of God that is revealed in and through the person and ministry of Jesus Christ. And this witness and testimony has to be lived out in everyday life in consonant with the new commandment of Jesus. No individual in the community of believers is thus spared of the need for his/her personal decision in believing in Jesus, for Jesus himself is the ultimate revelation of God (i.e., the eschatological presence of the Father-God in the Son-Jesus).

---

65 Bultmann, "πιστεύω, πίστις, πιστός," 225-227.

66 Matera, *New Testament Ethics*, 97.

67 Karakolis, "Semeia Conveying Ethics," 198-199.

68 Lohr, "ἔργον as an Element of Moral Language in John," 240.

69 Schnackenburg, *The Gospel According to St. John,* vol. 1, 562.

Faith is, therefore, a prominent moral element of decision to be made by an individual in the Fourth Gospel. This faith is intrinsically ordained to confessing and which is to be expressed in Christological confessions which must be projected in the face of unbelieving world is given importance in the Gospel.[70] Believers must hold to the teaching of Jesus (Jn. 8:31) which is closely linked up at once with the moral element of faith, the "keeping of the commandments" of Jesus,[71] working out or living out that faith in love. Belief in Jesus is not a matter of a onetime effect but a continuous process that has to be lived out every day (that is one has to live his/her faith on a daily basis - it is, a lifestyle, lifelong).

The Gospel of John is full of "instructions on the faith" which are concerned with the object of faith and also with the life of faith itself, as it is demanded of the minority community of believers in the midst of an unbelieving world.[72] According to the Fourth Gospel, 'πίστις' is that escorts to the attainment of eternal life (20:31). Subsequently, Johannine ζωή is an active receipt of knowledge and a work to be engaged which necessitates an ethical imperative.[73] Without belief in the Son Jesus Christ, there is no proper understanding of what is ethics in essence. It goes well to affirm that ethics, in John's Gospel, is fundamentally a reflection on the content of faith, faith in Jesus the *logos* who is the Christ, the 'Son of God', the 'Son of Man' and its attached role, authority and mission. Precisely, for reasons to induce faith in, to persuade and strengthen the readers, Jesus performed *semeia* in the presence of his disciples (the later to be witnesses of this truth) duly appointed, selected, and specifically documented (Jn. 20:30, 31 cf. 10:37, 38). The fundamental fact here is that 'faith' did not produce the story but rather the story produced the faith.[74] And this fact of belief in Jesus ought to mirror through the believers' action. Belief in the Gospel of John is therefore not a mere thought process but

70 See the various records of the confession of faith by individuals (Nathanael in 1:49; Simon Peter in 6:68 f; the blind man 9:38; Martha, Lazarus' sister in 11:27; and not the least Thomas called Didymus in 20: 24) and even of groups (the Samaritans or the people of Sychar in 4:48 and the Galileans after witnessing the miraculous sign of the multiplication of the loaves in 6:14).

71 Schnackenburg, *The Gospel According to St. John*, vol. 1, excursus vii, 564-565.

72 Schnackenburg, *The Gospel According to St. John*, vol. 1, excursus Vii, 573.

73 J. P. Miranda, *Being and the Messiah: The Message of St John* (Maryknoll, New York: Orbis Books, 1977), 148; Wayne A. Meeks, "Man from Heaven in Johannine Sectarianism," *JBL* 91(1972): 58; Also see Timothy J. M. Ling, *The Judean Poor and the Fourth Gospel* (Cambridge: Cambridge University Press, 2006), 208. The implication of the Johannine vitality of new life begotten in and through Jesus is fully worked out in the apparent perfectionism of I John 3:9, where an individual having born of God can no longer sin. This involves an intense commitment resulting from the belief to the ultimate goal of attaining eternal life.

74 Herman Ridderboss, *The Gospel of John: A Theological Commentary,* translated by John Vriend (Michigan: Wm. B. Eerdmans Publishing Company, 1997), 7 & 14.

is action oriented and has to be actualized in the behavior of every believer in every aspects of life.

3.2.2. "Doing the Works of God": Ethical Determinant

D. C. Jones defines Christian Biblical ethics as "a way of life that conforms to the will of God as revealed in the historical Jesus Christ and the Holy Scriptures."[75] According to the Gospel of John 'doing the works of God' in the first place is to do the will of God. What is then the will of God according to the Fourth Gospel? The will of God is to πιστεύω εἰς Ἰησοῦν as the Son of God and sent by God. And 'believing in the one sent by God' is equated as doing τὸ ἔργον τοῦ θεοῦ (Jn. 6:29). Then in Johannine understanding, belief in Jesus is to do the works of God (Jn. 6:28-29). The ἔργα τοῦ θεοῦ are works required to correspond with God's actions (cf. works 'done in God' (Jn. 3:21) and 'to do the works of him who sent me' (Jn. 9:4).[76] The Greek ἔργον refers to any deed that demonstrates a consistent moral character.[77] So, the phrase "doing the works of God" has a strong ethical implication because it is the works required to correspond to the actions of God.

The exclusive function of Jesus is to accomplish the work of the Father.[78] In short to do the works of God is to believe in Jesus (Jn. 6:27).[79] In other words, belief in the person of Jesus is understood as fulfillment of the works of God.[80] And in the second place, doing what is true is what determines doing the works of God. So, doing the works of God has a Christological overtone and a Christological outlook too. Doing the works of God and doing what is true are intricately linked to the person of Jesus. For doing what is true is doing the work of God and is to be in the light, who is Jesus. It implies that Jesus is set as the ultimate moral standard for the believing community. The theme of light loaded with ethical consequences is foretold in the prologue of John's Gospel (1:4-6, 9) and is embedded in the very person and activity of Jesus. The term 'light' is reckoned as the key to unlock the treasury of the ethical teaching in the Gospel.[81] Jesus is the light that came into the world. This moral value (light) that characterizes the Son Jesus and directs his actions, must also determine the believer's character and

75 D. C. Jones, *Biblical Christian Ethics* (Michigan: Baker, 1994), 16.

76 Schnackenburg, *The Gospel According to St. John*, vol. 2, 39.

77 W. Bauer, W. F. Arndt, and F. W. Gingrich, "ἔργον," *A Greek-English Lexicon of the New Testament and Other Early Christian Literature, 2*nd edition, revise and augmented by F. W. Gingrich and F. W. Danker (Chicago: University of Chicago Press, 1979), 390.

78 Karakolis, "Semeia Conveying Ethics," 197.

79 Jan G. van der Watt, "Ethics of/and the Opponents of Jesus in John's Gospel," *Rethinking the Ethics of John: "Implicit Ethics" in the Johannine writings,* edited by Jan van der Watt and Ruben Zimmermann (Tubingen: Mohr Siebeck, 2012), 188.

80 Labaln, "It's Only Love"- Is That All?," 31.

81 R. Newton Flew, *Jesus and His Way: A study of the Ethics of the New Testament* (London: The Epworth Press, 1963), 150.

conduct. The theme of truth and light dominates the thought in John's Gospel. The sign of the healing of the man born blind fairly is a dramatic illustration that Jesus is the light.[82] John chapter three is often documented as Johannine concept of ethical dualism. The dualism of doing evil and doing what is true is ethically documented here in John 3:20-21. Those who believe in Jesus will do what is good, because Jesus is the source of truth.[83] And those unbelieving will do evil because they love darkness. One's faith or unbelief in Jesus incurs in him/herself an eschatological judgment which nevertheless has already begun to operate in the present. The Gospel supposes that those who do good will be rewarded and those who practice evil will be punished (Jn. 5:29). So, the decision of the believers to or not to believe in Jesus foreshadows the eschatological judgment of God upon oneself.[84]

Jesus comes as the light to the world and this light is life and those who walk in this light will not come under darkness (Jn. 8:12 cf. 12:35). And the theme of light comes vibrantly clear when Jesus refers to himself as the light of the world who comes to give life during the feast of Tabernacles (Jn. 8:12; 9:5). But, if they fail to believe he is the Light, in sin will they die (Jn. 8:21, 24 cf. 12:35). The dualism in the Gospel of John is moral, not metaphysical.[85] The metaphor of light bears ethical implication. Belief here becomes an ethical decisive moment to live in the light and that death will not overtake the believing individual (contrast 8:24). This belief is 'to believe' in Jesus as sent by God as the light of the world and will not come to judgment but pass from death to life (Jn.5:24).

For the Johannine Gospel 'light' is inherently good which entails ethical element. Light always has a moral content in the Fourth Gospel.[86] One is called to come to the light and thereby refrain from evil works and practice truth. The importance of good deeds and bad deeds are highlighted and yet it is 'curiously intertwined with Christology.'[87] Light and truth complement one another and at the same time both belong to one coherent virtue. The light symbolizes goodness as opposed to darkness which is used as a symbol of moral evil.[88] Light then entails

82 Sanders and B. A. Mastin, *The Gospel According to St. John*, 5. Cf. 1:4, 5; 3: 19-21; 8:12; 9:5; 12:35, 36, 46.

83 Sanders and B. A. Mastin, *The Gospel According to St. John*, 5. Cf. 1:14, 17; 4:23, 24; 5:33; 8:32, 40, 44-46; 14:6, 17; 15:26; 16:13; 17:17, 19; 18:37-38.

84 Matera, *New Testament Ethics*, 99.

85 Francis J. Moloney, *The Gospel of John,* edited by Daniel J. Harrington (Minnesota: The Liturgical Press, 1998), 282.

86 Wilbert Francis Howard, *Christianity According to St. John* (London: Duckworth, 1943), 61. Cited by Flew, *Jesus and His Way*, 150.

87 Raymond E. Brown, *The Community of the Beloved Disciple* (New York: Paulist Press, 1979), 129.

88 T. B. Matson, *Biblical Ethics: A Guide to the Ethical Message of the Scriptures from Genesis to Revelation* (Georgia: Mercer university Press, 1967), 228. John shares this concept of dualism with the Qumran text (Rule of the Community (1QS). The use of antitheses – light verses

ethical function which has a basic illuminating function. Jesus sent by the Father as the light is to give eternal life to whoever may believe in him (Jesus) and so 'to believe' in Jesus as having come from God is the 'ethical challenge' of the Gospel of John.[89]

To walk or to do good means living according to the will of God and subsequently doing the will of God is to abide in the word of God and this Word is Jesus according to the Gospel of John. Koester's contention that the verb 'walk' in John 8:12 points to the ethical dimension of discipleship is persuasive.[90] The acceptance or rejection of the Son of God projects a strong moral emphasis. One who accepts Jesus chooses light and lives no longer in darkness. The injunction in John 12: 35, "walk while you have the light, before darkness overtakes you" conveys a pattern of moral behavior in a journey of moral growth. The dualism here is used to imply that human are called to decide for the light or else ultimately one decides for darkness. This is a "decision dualism"[91] that if one does not come into the light he/she is in the dark opting for evil rather than good.

The decision is for allegiance to, or rejection of Jesus corresponding to distinguish good and doing good or reject Jesus and choose to do evil. There is no mid-way and is exclusively a question of an alternative. There is a sequential result in the perspective of one's way of life resulting from the choice one makes: light or darkness.[92] The contrast between light and darkness is pointedly described in John 3: 19-21. The moral impact of the light and darkness symbolism is sharpened here in this passage. In here, unbelief is attested to be due to moral failings. Men's attachment to evil averts their coming to the light.[93] And their passions and actions prove that they are the devil's children (Jn. 8:44). One does evil actions because he/she is in the dark while one who is in the light spontaneously carries out good actions.[94] The people's work is evaluated according to their ethical quality. Their attitude with regard to the light is analogous to their works or even dependent upon them. The works as ethical actions reveal the moral character of the people who perform them.[95] There is therefore a very strong moral emphasis

---

darkness, life versus death, love versus hatred, truth versus falsehood, etc., are found both in John and at Qumran. The conflict is between good and evil and in this conflict one is summoned to the crisis of decision (In the Gospel of John it implies allegiance to or rejection of Jesus in his personhood and his subsequent role (messianic) whereas at Qumran it involves acceptance of the community's interpretation of the Law).

89 Matera, *New Testament Ethics*, 97.

90 C. R. Koester, *Symbolism in the Fourth Gospel: Meaning, Mystery and Community* (Minneapolis: Fortress Press, 1995), 143.

91 John Painter, *John: Witness & Theologian* (Delhi: ISPCK, 1974), 6.

92 Thomas Vallianippuram, *New Society in John's Gospel* (Aloor: Biblia Publications, 2008), 259.

93 Schnackenburg, *The Gospel According to St. John*, vol. 1, excursus vii, 574.

94 Vallianippuram, *New Society in John's Gospel*, 261.

95 Karakolis, "Semeia Conveying Ethics," 198.

in the Johannine dualism of light verses darkness.[96] This dualism is inherent in the distinction between good and evil, right and wrong, and whereby doing the works of God is to believe in Jesus and that which has to be accompanied by doing good works.

3.2.3. Jesus the Moral Archetype of God

The eighth chapter of John's Gospel (esp. vv. 39–47) records an account of Jesus' dispute with the Jews where a strong antagonism is established. The dynamics of identity and behavior are clearly brought forth, and the distinct focus between two mutually exclusive families (God verses devil) is brought forth. The argument is that children bear the characteristics of their respective parent (father).[97] And this thought of the children bearing the characteristic of their father in words and deeds is very significant for the minds of the Hebrew people (especially when it comes to moral likeness of the son to the father).[98] When 'the Jews' claim that Abraham is their father, Jesus says that if this were the case they would demonstrate corresponding behavior (Jn. 8:39, 42). Identity and behavior are co-related (identity demands matching behavior and behavior reveals identity). The conduct of 'the Jews' is characterized by sin (Jn. 8:24), lie (Jn. 8:35, 55) resembling their father (of lies). They claim themselves as descendants of Abraham but their mode of conduct shows that they belong to the devil (Jn. 8:44). They are against the truth and do not understand the words of Jesus nor of the Father God (Jn. 8:43, 45, 47). The dispute or say an argument that proceeds has "more explicit moral values."[99] The works of God and Abraham are taken or judged positively and the opposite is true of the devil (Father of lies). There is an indication of a close connection that exist between the 'works' and the origin of those who enact them (cf. Jn. 8:39, 41, 44). The underlying assumption is that children do the things or works their parents do. Children are prompted to imitate the deeds of their parents.[100] So, are the children of the devil who do evil like their father (Jn. 8: 41, 44) or the children of God who will abide and live by and according to the works of God.

Now, who does the 'works of God' is a significant question to be attended. Johannine Jesus is portrayed as complying with the Father's ἐντολὴν (Jn. 12:49-50; 14:10-11, 31). The portrayal of Jesus as saying and doing exactly as the Father does is an implication that Jesus' life and activity are shaped, guided

96 Jan G. van der Watt, *Family of the King: Dynamics of Metaphor in the Gospel According to John* (Leiden: Brill, 2000), 237.

97 James Montgomery Boice, *An Expositional Commentary: The Gospel of John,* vol. 4 (Michigan: Baker Books, 1999), 1042.

98 T. E. Pollard, *Johannine Christology and the Early Church* (Cambridge: Cambridge University Press, 1970), 17.

99 Lohr, "ἔργον as an Element of Moral Language, 240.

100 Lohr, "ἔργον as an Element of Moral Language, 240.

by God (Jn. 14:44-45). In simple term, Jesus as God's emissary implements the Father's commandments. Behind the saying and doing of Jesus stands the authority of God.[101] In Jesus the Son is manifested the moral likeness of the Father-God, for Jesus reproduces exactly the words and activities of his Father. We can say, hence, Jesus in obedience lived the words and deeds of the Father. In simple words, the ethics of Jesus is the ethics of God, for, Jesus lived by what God commanded him. This is to sanction that Jesus is the moral archetype of the Father. The mutual relationship that exists between the Father God and the Son Jesus is an ethical paradigm for the community of believers to emulate. Jesus as the Son lives the will of the Father till the way to the cross of Calvary. The ethics of Jesus is a response to what God the Father was doing in and through him (or working in Johannine term). As the Father has loved the Son, so the Son loved the disciples and urged them to remain in his love and obey his teachings as he has been to the Father (Jn. 15:10 cf. 14:23). Therefore, our response in faith to what Jesus has commanded is equally a response to God and thus is at the heart of Johannine ethics.

Jesus' injunctions which are summed up in the term "commandment" are inseparable from his personhood (identity). The words Jesus uttered and the acts he performed (behavior) are seen together (Jn. 8:28; 14:10). What he says and does are thereby binding upon the hearers and viewers of his words and deeds respectively. John presents here the ethical dualism, depending upon the choice one makes, he/she either belongs to the devil or to Jesus (Jn. 8:42-44).[102] Jesus confronts people with the will of God through his teaching as representative coming from and sent by God. Jesus is depicted as the moral prototype of God's work. The works carried out by Jesus are the works instructed by the Father and are of the Father's (Jn. 10:32, 37).[103] Whatever 'works' Jesus performed are shown and given by the Father (Jn. 5:20, 36; 17:4). This entails the loving and mutual coherence that exists between the Father and the Son, their common work, their communion in all things, and their complete oneness of being.[104] There are no works that Jesus has done independently but all have been by and through the Father's knowledge. If Jesus exclusively 'said' and 'did' as God the Father has commanded, then it is very coherent and fair to stress that ethics originated from the moral world of God and the Son Jesus becomes the moral archetype of God in this physical world. This is to indicate that Jesus' words and deeds are not autonomous but originates from the Sovereign God.[105] The

101 Schnackenburg, *The Gospel According to St. John*, vol. 2, 424.

102 S. S. Smalley, "Diversity and Development in John," *NTS* 17 (1970): 278.

103 Schnackenburg, *The Gospel According to St. John*, vol. 2, 424.

104 Schnackenburg, *The Gospel According to St. John*, vol. 2, 177.

105 Doing God's will is so pertinent in the Gospel that it is equalized with human's most basic requirement for sustenance i.e., food. Nothing stands out against this human inevitable daily diet (food) so Jesus' highest craving is to please the Father by doing His will. See for references

Fourth Gospel's most distinctive ethical teaching then is that the ethical conduct is related to the person of Jesus and 'the norm of morality is one's relationship to Jesus.'[106] Jesus as the Son fulfills the ethical demands of God in every minute detail even to the point of death and this is expected of the community of believers who pay allegiance to him through faith, for, in the Gospel of John, moral behavior of the community of believers springs from, and is rooted in, the person and work of Jesus.

The presence of God, the Father is with Jesus and truth is thereby determined by his presence and revelation[107] (later the Spirit-*Paraclete* continues the mission of revelation). Jesus claims to have come from and represents God, the Father. Jesus' works are in fact the fulfillment of his Father's will (Jn. 4:34). He is the revealer who reveals his Father's will to the world (Jn. 5:20). He accomplishes and fulfills his Father's works in obedience (Jn. 5:36 cf. 17:4). The Father's commands are fulfilled in obedience to what God works and not by what man works.[108] His obedience in fulfilling his Father's works speaks of their relatedness and mutual indwelling. The ἐργα Jesus worked are a manifestation of his relationship with the Father, and the Father-Son to the world, and also connects back the world to the Father. Besides, Jesus' claim that he will return to where he had come from[109] suggests that he is the genuine mediator between the Father, Son and believers in the world. For the Father has revealed, entrusted and bestowed on him authority in everything (Jn. 3:35; 5:22, 27; 13:3). In this case, whatever Jesus has commanded and whatever his earthly life and ministry have entailed, speaks of the moral world of the Father (Jn. 12:49-50; 14:31). This points out that the ethical demand has a divine origin and is being mediated in and through Jesus because Jesus is the only Son, in the bosom of the Father, who came to dwell amongst us (Jn. 1:14) and has made Him known (Jn. 1:18). This implies that Christology (Jesus Christ), in the Fourth Gospel, directs our attention to theology (God) through his way of life (virtuous behavior).

In the Gospel of John, there is a crystal clear presentation of what God has done for men (Jn. 3:16 known to be the classical statement). It effectively describes three important things. It succinctly tells what God did (gave us His Son), the quality of his act (which is love – the untranslatable Greek word - *agape*)[110] and its direction (or say purpose which is directed towards the perfection of life in

---

where everything Jesus has said and did was in tuned with the divinely ordained, designed and operated in his very own life and ministry. John 4:34; 5: 19b-20b, 36; 6:36; 7:16-17; 8:26b, 28b, 29, 55b; 10:18b; 12:49-50; 14:10b, 24, 31; 15:10,15; 17:7

106 Matera, *New Testament Ethics*, 94.

107 van der Watt, "Ethics of/and the Opponents of Jesus," 191.

108 Bultmann, *The Gospel of John*, 222.

109 John 13:3; 14:28; 16:5,10,17; 17:5; 20:17.

110 The quality act of God's love is made realized and completed in the sacrificial act of Jesus on the cross.

God's creation that is eternal life). The virtuous life of the Johannine community of believers is based on Jesus' teaching. Nonetheless, the teaching of Jesus and his life examples are not in a form of specialized code of regulations but is based upon the revelation of the nature of the eternal God, the Father, from which all moral obligations flow. Therefore, according to the Fourth Gospel, God is the source and foundation of ethics, manifested in and through the life and activity of Jesus Christ. God acts in and through Jesus and Jesus in turn acts through us by the power of the Holy Spirit. This idea of the one and the exact replication of the words and deeds can however be stated as a paradox like any other terms like 'now and then,' 'here and now' etc., in John's Gospel.

The Gospel of John portrays Jesus as a model for ethical living. Jesus having come from God reveals the truth about God. He provides the exact, intensive and extensive interpretation of obedience to God in and throughout his life and ministry on earth. Jesus' ethics is God's ethics. In this sense, Johannine ethics can be tagged as 'ethics of truth' which is revealed (for further elaboration see 5.3.4). Jesus fulfills and enhances the significance of ethical demand of God's will, in and by humble and submissive obedience in words and deeds (Jn. 12:49, 50; 14:31). The relation of the Son to Father in obedience serves as a significant ethical paradigm for us, as believers in Jesus, for Jesus is the moral archetype of God. This leads us to the next important discussion on Jesus as the definitive paradigm for moral behavior.

3.2.4. Jesus, the Classic Paradigm for Ethical Behavior

It is significant to note that as Jesus comes to the close of his public ministry he now exclusively turns to the close circle of his disciples making his farewell address impinge with ethical imperatives, exhortations and encouragement. Jesus' farewell discourse has series of ethical implications for the believers. Matera has correctly summarized the ethical implications of Jesus' departure – the disciples must continue to believe in Jesus despite his physical absence – they must love one another as they have been loved for 'to love one another' serves as a mark and touchstone of discipleship – they must show their love for their master by keeping his commandment and must rejoice that he returns to the Father for their good.[111] It could universally be true, but especially for our context like India, the farewell words and deeds of a dying person is significantly weightier and dear. The last words of a departed soul have significant ramifications (though it is beyond explanation) in the lives of the living family and friends. And thus, an individual feels much obliged to fulfill the wish of the dying person.[112] So, the importance of the farewell discourses of Jesus can be well appreciated and appropriated in the lives of the community of believers now and then. We shall hereafter examine closely the passage where ethical significances can be marked out from the farewell

111 Matera, *New Testament Ethics*, 107.

112 Kanagaraj, *The Gospel of John*, 428.

discourses of Jesus. Firstly, we will examine the act of Jesus (feet washing) and thereafter the word of Jesus (which is imperative).

3.2.4.1. Feet Washing: An Exemplary Behavioral Conduct (13:1-17)

The foot washing presupposes the *Sitz Im Leben* of the socio-cultural practice of the first century Christian. It was measured to be a hospitable act extended to guests upon arrival at the home of their host, while the guests were reclining at table (Lk. 7:44 cf. 1 Tim. 5:10).[113] It was customarily performed by servants to wash their master's foot. That is, a foot washing was considered a menial job for Jewish slaves, Gentile slaves, wives and children.[114] Besides, washing of the guests' feet was also a common practice of loving kindness (1 Tim. 5:10 cf. 2.6.2 of ch. 2). It was a usual customary practice that the host supplies water for the guests to wash their hands or feet when they arrived for a meal. It was a symbolic token of social acceptance, recognition and honor. And the act of feet washing was a usual way of showing an act of courtesy.[115] Such historical context showcase the relationship between servants and masters and John purports this foot washing to the love relationship of Jesus to his disciples. The textual setting of the foot washing took place in the context of a meal which dominates the narrative during which Jesus demonstrated his love for his disciples by assuming the role of a household servant. The passage like washing of the disciples' feet has incurred different interpretations.[116] Jesus Himself gave two interpretations of his act. The first is theological in nature, pointing towards Jesus' saving death on the cross (Jn. 13:6-10) that has to do with the salvific interpretation. The second interpretation is paraenetic in nature (Jn. 13:12-20).

Jesus' act is an act of humility and service that proceeds from his love for his disciples.[117] Jesus after washing his disciples' feet says that he has given them a *hypodeigma* which provides for the disciples to serve one another (that is to become servants to one another).[118] Jesus washing the disciples' feet is a pattern or an example of concrete behavior to be emulated. The explicit indication of Jesus in John 13:15 is set as an exemplary behavioral action to be emulated by the immediate disciples as recounted in the narrative needs special attention.

113 Oscar Cullmann, *Early Christian Worship* (London: SCM Press, 1953), 105-110; Lindars, *The Gospel of John*, 446.

114 George R. Beasley-Murray, *WBC: John,* vol. 36 (Texas: Word Books Publishers, 1987), 233; Rudolf Schnackenburg, *The Gospel According to St. John*, vol. 3, translated by David Smith and G. A. Kon (London & Kent: Burns & Oates, 1982), 399; M. H. Shepherd, "Foot Washing," *The Interpreter's Dictionary of the Bible, E-J,* edited by George Arthur Buttrick *et al.,* (Nashville: Abington Press, 1962), 308.

115 Morris, *The Gospel According to John*, 612; Lindars, *The Gospel of John*, 447.

116 See for details, Kanagaraj, *The Gospel of John,* 429-448.

117 C. K. Barrett, *Gospel According to St. John: An Introduction with Commentary and Notes on the Greek Text* (London: SPCK, 1960), 363.

118 Matera, *New Testament Ethics*, 105.

The most obvious indicative ethics is followed by an imperative ethics. It is here that the ethical directive is translated into concrete form of behavior, an action undergirded by love (that does not hesitate to serve others in spite of the social expectation based on social status) and humility (a humble service even to the point of humiliation). Customarily, a socially lesser person ought to wash the more important person's feet. And yet Jesus had turned this usual social practice the other way round by taking the initiative in washing the feet of his disciples showcasing humility and willing attitude to serve one another.[119] The humble service of Jesus wipes out all possible arrogance that might have probably be part of the disciples' personality. So, we can audaciously exclaim that the notion of love takes concrete expression in the humble service of the master in the Fourth Gospel (13:1-20). This concrete action of the washing of the disciples' feet has clearly become the ethical model for the immediate disciples of Jesus and for those who will come to believe in him in the subsequent generation(s).

Jesus himself has defined the right ethical perspective in dramatic picture of action in concrete and historical situation and it is intended to appeal to the conscious by way of actual action. The act of Jesus which gives ethical lesson must however be viewed in the light of the life, death, and resurrection of Jesus. "The washing of the disciples' feet rests upon and interprets the death of the Lord, and is not a detached action containing in itself a merely ethical action."[120] Jesus washing the feet of the disciples "provides a graphic illustration of love in action."[121] Feet washing is a significant action, an acted parable, says Morris, setting out that great principle of lowly service which finds its supreme embodiment in the atoning death of Jesus as the Son of Man on the cross.[122] And it complements the governing theme of love that undergirds the whole Johannine theology of love. Thus, the love command in John 15:13-14 calls for an imitation of the love of Jesus demonstrated for his disciples, which are concretized in terms of self-giving by laying down his life to the point of death.[123]

The particular form of foot washing is an intense symbolic expression and gesture of love and close solidarity that existed between Jesus and his disciples.[124] In deed the foot washing and the following commands of Jesus to follow his action is fleshed out by detailed instruction how they might practically be applied.[125] The essence of love is demonstrated in servanthood. It teaches us

119 Kanagaraj, *The Gospel of John*, 433.

120 Edwyn Clement Hoskyns, *The Fourth Gospel*, 2nd edition (London: Faber and Faber, 1961), 443- 446.

121 Russell Pregeant, *Knowing Truth, Doing Good: Engaging New Testament Ethics* (Minneapolis: Fortress Press, 2008), 204.

122 Morris, *The Gospel According to John*, 612 - 613; Shepherd, "Foot Washing," 308.

123 Pregeant, *Knowing Truth, Doing Good*, 204.

124 Moloney, *The Gospel of John,* 370-376.

125 Lund, "The Joys and Dangers of Ethics," 278.

an ethical lesson of humility – a spirit and an attitude that must be in our being as was in Jesus' being and had accomplished by his action. It is rightly commented that the true essence of Christian authority lies in humility.[126] Jesus as the Master has patterned this virtue of humility by a concrete illustration. He exercised his authority in humility by washing his disciples' feet. And mutual humility is expected from amongst the company of believers. The behavior of the believers must be conditioned by mutual humility (cf. Matt. 10:24; Lk. 6:40). There is seemingly a danger when the act of feet washing is perpetuated externally as a ritual without its spirit in many churches today. Care must be taken not to sideline the spirit and the attitude required to live through this life as followers of Jesus Christ. So, Jesus patterned the act of humble service by washing the feet of his disciples and instruction to do the same as he has done to them leads naturally to the new commandment to love one another just as they have been loved, which leads us to the immediate concern.

3.2.4.2. 'Love One Another:' A Basis for New Identity

The Greek word for love 'ἀγάπη'[127] is an important element of Jesus' teaching and fundamental to the doctrine of Johannine writings (Jn. 3:16).[128] The love command in John's Gospel which regulates the ethical conduct of the community of believers is distinctive of Johannine usage and subsequently is one dominating theme.[129] Congruently, it functions as one important key to interpret what underlies ethical behavior within the community of believers. John prefers to concentrate the direct ethical statements in one single word love. Love is the bond

---

126 Edwyn Clement Hoskyns, *The Fourth Gospel*, edited by Francis Noel Davey (London: Faber and Faber Limited, 1947), 440.

127 The English term 'love' translates a group of Greek words in the New Testament. The two most dominating word families are the ἀγαπή family and φιλέω family, of which agape is given the highest and final expression of love. Other Greek words for love – *eran* and *stergeo* were used in the first century, of these *eran* is not used in NT. However it is debated whether the appearance of the concept of *eros* does. *Stergeo* appears only in the compound word φιλόστοργος (Rom. 12:10). For further details please see William Klassen, "Love in NT and Early Jewish," *The Anchor Bible Dictionary*, vol. 4, edited by David Noel Freedman *et al.* (New York: Doubleday, 1992), 381-396.

128 Klassen, "Love in NT and Early Jewish," 381, 389.

129 The term ἀγαπή is most often used by John. There are two expressions of love in the Johannine corpus – ἀγάπαω and φιλέω. Both these words are interchangeably used (*agapan* in 3:35; 14:23; 11:5; 13:23; *philein* in 5:20; 16:27; 11:3; 20:2). This implies that there is no much significant difference in meaning. The verb ἀγαπαω 'to love' appears 35 times in the Gospel and 28 times in 1 John. The noun form of love "ἀγαπη" appears 7 times and 18 times in the Gospel and the first epistle of John respectively. And the adjective 'beloved' ἀγαπητος appears 6 times in first John. The verb φιλέω occurs 13 times in the Gospel. See Klassen, "Love in NT and Early Jewish," 389; Raymond E. Brown, *The Anchor Bible: The Gospel According to John,* vol. 1 (New York: Doubleday & Company, 1966), appendix 1: Johannine Vocabulary, 497-498.

that binds and holds the family of God in oneness. The use of ἐντολὴ in John's Gospel, unlike the Synoptics (Matt. 22:36-40; Mk. 10:17f ; Lk. 10:26, 28) and Paul (Rom. 13:9-10) which refers to the ordinances of the Mosaic Law, refers to God's commandment which Jesus bears and implements by himself.[130] The command of God directs the entire mission of the Son Jesus into the world to bring life eternal (cf. Jn. 12:50).[131]

The passage of John 13 has often been equated as the most (and sometimes *only*) explicit moral rule recorded in the Gospel of John. Consonantly, it is considered the central and essential commandment of Jesus and is equated as the Gospel's ethics. The 'new commandment' (ἐντολὴν καινήν) 'love one another' (ἀγαπατε ἀλλήλους) in John's Gospel is a special characteristic of the last discourses (13-17). This ἐντολὴν καινήν remains a legacy of the departing Jesus to his disciples until these days. The command is new in a sense that it corresponds to the command that regulates the Father-Son relationship (Jn. 10:18; 12:49f; 14:31; 15:10)[132] and also new in that it was delivered in and for the new age inaugurated by Jesus' very life and death because to have love for one another especially for one's neighbor had already been propagated in the past history within the Israelite nation (Lev. 19:18; Deut. 6:5).[133] Precisely, the commandment is 'new' because of the reality and situation Jesus had inaugurated. As such, Jesus' command 'to love one another' is unquestionably a focal point of his ethical instruction (Jn. 13:34; 15:12).

This new command 'ἀγαπατε ἀλλήλους' which is imperative (for the disciples) is founded on the indicative (of what Jesus himself has done and proved). Jesus' love for them is the reason that they must love one another (Jn. 13:34; 15:12). The imperative love command rests upon an indicative of God's

---

130 Brown, *The Anchor Bible: The Gospel According to John,* vol. 1, 504; Barrett, *Gospel According to St John,* 362; Schnackenburg, *The Gospel According to St John*, vol. 2, 424. There is a strong affinity of Moses' and Jesus' role in executing the commands of God. For instance, compare John 12:49 with Deuteronomy 18:18-19. Deuteronomy reads, "I will raise up for them a prophet like you from among their own people; I will put my words in the mouth of the prophet, who shall speak to them everything that I command. Anyone who does not heed the words that the prophet shall speak in my name, I myself will hold accountable." It is possible that Jesus is presented as the eschatological prophet like Moses (6:14 contrast 7:40, 52; cf. 1:21-25 cf. Deut. 30:15, 19; 32:47), who speaks the words and commandments of God, presenting a choice between life and death, before the people. However, Johannine formulation is typical in presenting Jesus incomparably greater than Moses. He is sent by the Father while Moses was called. He speaks from a direct knowledge of God and speaks what He heard straight from the Father (8:26 cf. 3:32).

131 Matera, *New Testament Ethics*, 106.

132 Schnackenburg, *The Gospel According to St. John,* vol. 2, 172-174; C. H. Dodd, *The Interpretation of the Fourth Gospel*, 196.

133 Barrett, *Gospel According to St John*, 377; Hoskyns, *The Fourth Gospel*, 451; Boice, *The Gospel of John,* vol. 4, 1038-1039. Hillel also said: Be of the disciples of Aaron, loving peace and pursuing peace, loving mankind and bringing them nigh to the Law (*Pirke Aboth* 1:12).

love for Jesus and the love of Jesus for the Father and Jesus' love for the circle of his disciples.[134] Hence, the love command is based on the prior love of Jesus himself that basically flows from the Father (Jn. 13:34-35; 15:9). Jesus' love was shown practically (as an example) by washing his disciples' feet (Jn. 13:1-15) and later in the discourse the love command looks toward to his sacrificial love (crucifixion on the cross (Jn. 15:12-13). The love of Jesus for the world was demonstrated and translated into action on the cross of Calvary. The love of God and the Son Jesus always finds its way in action (cf. 1 Jn. 3:16-18). Jesus' command "to love one another" is a basic obligation laid on the community of believers. The obligation to reproduce in human action the quality and the direction of God's work (giving us His Son by which we are saved).[135] This is to postulate the motive that entails the deeply rooted ethical precept of obligation to be followed in obedience. Nonetheless, obedience is to be preceded by faith. For instance, we see that there is an attempt to evoke a response of faith from all personal characters in the Gospel narratives.[136] Johannine Jesus is the model who has set the pattern to be emulated. He is the revealer and to certain extent the unique embodiment, or the incarnation of the one and only God. He is the classic paradigm both in word and deed.

This led us to assert that the new commandment comprises the divine relationship (vertical indicative) that is transfused to human relationship (horizontal imperative). The command 'love one another' does not necessarily suggest to hate, nor is there any provision prohibiting loving, others.[137] Love which must be translated into action must fore-mostly begin from within, inside and naturally it will overflow to neighboring fellow humans. This could be best explained against the backdrop of the Johannine community's historical circumstance where they were expelled, hated for their belief in Jesus as the bearer of God's truth.[138] The disciples as a community of believers believed and received Jesus as against the unbelieving Jews.[139] It is in this context that the

---

134 Allen Verhey, *The Great Reversal: Ethics and the New Testament* (Michigan: Wm. B. Eerdmans Publishing Company, 1984), 143.

135 C. H. Dodd, *Gospel and Law* (Cambridge: Cambridge University Press, 1951), 71.

136 Nathanael (1:45-46), Nicodemus in John 3, The Samaritan Woman in John 4, The paralyzed man at the pool (Bethesda) in John 5, adultery woman in John 8, The Man born blind in John 9, Lazarus' sisters in John 11, Peter (13:6-10, 21:15-22). John's Gospel is filled with personal beloved characters whose characters are real and also serve as ideal characters. Such response of their faith and conviction about Jesus is immensely exemplary.

137 Boice, *The Gospel of John,* vol. 4, 1039.

138 Burridge, *Imitating Jesus,* 325-334.

139 The Johannine use of the term 'the Jews' have been often exploited for anti-Judaism or anti-semitic purposes. But it is congruent to acknowledge that the bitter words spoken against 'the Jews' are directed against Judaism as a religious entity (denying or unbelieving or rejecting Jesus as the Messiah sent by God) and not against the Jews as a race. Because the author of the Fourth Gospel probably himself was a Jew who was faithful enough to observe and transmit

Johannine Christian Community came to be viewed as the only sphere within which life and love could be found and valued. The Johannine love command has nowhere in the Gospel promulgated that the community of believers in Jesus Christ are to reciprocate the antagonism (hatred for hatred e.g., the Qumran community of the Dead Sea Scrolls).[140] Because of this we should see and try to read and interpret the love commandment in the light of other references within the Gospel itself. That is we must look at the broader purpose and theological framework of the Gospel literature. Notably John 3:16 one of the world's best loved and quoted verses tells us that the world is the object of God's love and the mission upon which His son Jesus Christ is sent as the Savior of the world (cf. Jn. 4:42; 6:51; 12:46). And what is more in consonance to the Father's will is that the Son sends the disciples as witnesses to proclaim to the truth and prays for the future *disciples* who will come to believe in him through their testimony (Jn. 17:18; 20:21 cf. 15:27). It is thus congenial in all probabilities to infer that the commandment was given to the disciples and yet never with an intention to hate the unbelievers.

The call and an exhortation to love one another must henceforth be read as a response to a communal crisis of identity and an appeal that called for unity within an oppressed minority community and not of exclusivist as some would suggest. Hays rightly expressed that the distinctive appeal for love within the believing community is a poignant cry for solidarity beset by external and internal stress[141] and not otherwise. Brian K. Blount who writes from his African American context speaks loud enough in explaining the reason for the limitation of the command. His interpretation is that the command 'love for one another' enables the believing community "to sustain itself and simultaneously resist the hostile world around…by energizing an alternative reality and a competing force for change, transform that world."[142] And yet other references to God's love for the world have an embracing outlook to accept whoever may believe in Jesus (Jn. 1:12; 3:16; 17: 20f).

Consonantly, this new commandment given by Jesus basically serves as the ethical basis which guides the behavior of his followers. As a result, this new commandment of Jesus determines the followers' future lines of expected action (Jn. 15:10, 12, 17).[143] The basis of this love springs from well defined relationships that are expressed in actions and not merely an emotion[144] that at

---

the Jewish socio-cultural values (number of references to Jewish religious practice and festivals) in his writings as we have them now.

140 Burridge, *Imitating Jesus*, 334.

141 Hays, *The Moral Vision of the New Testament,* 146-147.

142 Brian K. Blount, *Then the Whisper Put on Flesh: New Testament Ethics in an African American Context* (Nashville: Abington Press, 2001), 108.

143 van der Watt, "Ethics and Ethos in the Gospel According to John," 115.

144 T. Larsson, *God in the Fourth Gospel* (Stockholm: n.p., 2001), 276.

times cannot be explained scientifically or mathematically but by experience which is a part of life's mystery. Love finds its way in action. It is action oriented. Love is readable when it becomes visible through actions. So, Jesus commanded his disciples that they love one another so that everyone will know that they are his disciples. Jesus showed his love practically (as an example) by washing his disciples' feet (13:1-15) and that which culminated to his sacrificial love (crucifixion on the cross (15:12-13).

The love of God in and through Jesus for the world was demonstrated and translated into action on the cross of Calvary. So the love command in the Fourth Gospel is based upon the precedent love of Jesus for the believers, illustrated and illuminated by his paradigmatic act of humble service by washing his disciples' feet and his sacrificial love to the point of lying down his own life on the cross.[145] The real explanation and the full picture of what love entails in the Fourth Gospel "can be found only in its portrait of Jesus."[146] The Christological reference constitutes the essential novelty of this new Commandment.[147] van der Watt rightly posits that the basis of love is not emotion but relationships that find its way in action. Love is a matter of action that exists in activity.[148] When God says He loves the world He proves it by sending and sacrificing His one and only begotten Son Jesus (Jn. 3:16).

This love command is patterned after Jesus' own displayed love and is characterized by "an element within a set of relationships defined by reciprocity."[149] God the Father loves the Son (Jn. 3:34; 10:17; 17:23, 24, 26) and the world (3:16) and those whom He has given to the Son (Jn. 17:21 f). The Son reciprocates the love of his Father by loving Him back (Jn. 13:31). The Son extends his love to those whom God has given him as a response to the love of God for him (Jn. 15:9). The love of God is revealed and manifested in Jesus. In fact this love displayed by Jesus is "also paradigmatic of its nature and manner" (13:34 cf. 15: 12).[150] So, to follow the steps of Jesus is "to have before us a truly human example, but it is also to have the divine pattern made comprehensible and imitable. Hence, the imitation of Christ, being the imitation of God himself so far as God can be a model to his creatures, becomes a model of absolute ethics."[151] Jesus' act of humble and loving service in washing the feet of his disciples preconditions

---

145 Johannes Nissen, "Community and Ethics in the Gospel of John," *New Readings in John: Literary and Theological Perspectives*, edited by Johannes Nissen and S. Pedersen (Sheffield: Sheffield academic Press, 1999), 102-103.

146 Burridge, *Imitating Jesus*, 327.

147 Raymond F. Collins, *Christian Morality: Biblical Foundations* (Notre Dame, IN: University of Natre Dame Press, 1986), 116.

148 van der Watt, "Ethics and Ethos in the Gospel According to John," 116-117.

149 Pregeant, *Knowing Truth, Doing Good*, 200.

150 Wolfgang Schrage, *The Ethics of the New Testament* (Philadelphia: Fortress Press, 1988), 307.

151 Dodd, *Gospel and Law*, 42.

for his disciples' acts of love. This act of Jesus' love not only serves as a model but also as an "enabling force of their love."[152] For John, love is never devolved "into a sentiment or an emotion. Its expression is always moral and is revealed in obedience"[153] is highly remarkable.

Love in action is actualized in Jesus washing his disciples' feet signifying humble service and unrestraint self giving.[154] The lack of specific injunction to be imitated in the command 'love one another' except for the paraenetic feet washing does not mean that it does not cover a wide range of ethical implications because as long as one lives in this world we are prone to unexpected challenges in every way in every day. From the spiritual perspective the biggest challenge would be the danger of losing faith in Jesus when we are in despair (challenge of unbelief). There are uncountable and unpredictable ways where the practice of the commandment 'love one another' can take practical range of behavior and the first epistle of John records one of those in the sharing of the materials world's goods (I Jn. 3:17). There are critics who said that the love command in John's Gospel is vagued.[155] To this, let me quote Georg Strecker who made his notable comment on the lack of specificity saying that the gift of love '*agape*' includes the gift of freedom and responsibility to those who believe. Anyone who responds in faith 'are called to do the right thing at the right time' to do good works (1 Jn. 2:29), the time of every new situation' and challenges in which they [we] are called upon to decide what action is appropriate to that love that proceeds from the Father (3:21) mediated through the son and has brought them [us] near to God.[156]

The inclusive community of disciples (which covers future believers of Jesus) is asked to conform to the conduct of Jesus and to his love whereby the one who truly believes in Jesus will pattern his/her entire way of life after Jesus - by keeping his commandment (Jn. 14:21, 23; 15:10). The social nature of love within the community must be a reflection and correspond to the filial Father-Son relationship expressed in their mutual love for one another. The concern here, then, is stressed with the relationship between the Father and the Son and the disciples (believers). So, it is a relationship established with the Father through faith in the Son.[157] It is said that relationships not only affect but also influence

152 Volker Rabens, "Johannine Perspective on Ethical Enabling in the Context of Stoic and Philonic Ethics," *Rethinking the Ethics of John: "Implicit Ethics" in the Johannine Writings,* edited by Jan van der Watt and Reuben Zimmermann (Mohr Sieback: Tubingen, 2012), 120.

153 Barrett, *Gospel According to St. John*, 385; Lindars, *The Gospel of John*, 35.

154 Shepherd, "Foot Washing," 308.

155 For instance, Wayne A. Meeks, "The Ethics of the Fourth Evangelist," *Exploring the Gospel of John: In Honor of D. Moody Smith,* edited by R. Alan Culpepper and C. Clifton Black (Louisville, Kentucky: Westminster John Knox Press, 1996), 318.

156 Strecker, *Theology of the New Testament*, 515.

157 Hoskyns, *The Fourth Gospel*, 464.

one's subsequent behavior and relationships.[158] Johannine love which is relational is a love which is mutual and also demands a response. Its nature is reciprocal; one is loved to love back. 'To love' is made possible by the love of Jesus which indicates that the expected mutual love within the community rely on the love given by God in and through his Son, Jesus. Living what is commanded is made possible by the grace and power of God through Jesus and through the Spirit. There is an active involvement of the power of Christ in the lives of the believing community. The right ethical conduct of a believer is therefore always determined and guided by Jesus through the Spirit-*Paraclete*.

Therefore, it is suitable to promulgate Johannine love as the bedrock of all ethical conduct for it looks back to God from whom it proceeded and got manifested in the person of His Son Jesus' life and activities that culminated on the cross. For John, *agape* is characteristically used theologically, Christologically and ethically and which is to be understood as a reciprocal love and also specifying the mutual relationship (a sort of circular web is formed).[159] The Gospel explains the significance of love 'agape' in the light of the divine mission with its focus on Jesus Messianic role. The whole Gospel is oriented to the fact that the love of the Father is revealed in His Son Jesus. It goes well together to say that the foundation for the ethic of the Gospel of John is in accord with the love of God manifested in Jesus.[160] This love is based on the prior love of God and the love of Jesus for the disciples (13:14) which is confirmed on both side of the command by his humble service (washing his disciples' feet) and his sacrificial love demonstrated on the cross. So, the full picture of what love is found in its portrait of Jesus.[161] To Rabens, John 13:34 which contains the New Commandment of the Gospel conveys both the content and the enabling power behind John's ethics in a nutshell.[162]

Mention has to be made here that often times the Johannine love command is critique as narrow and have interpreted as the consequence of negative attitude to the world and being exclusivism. Yes, the commandment has its immediate location in the interrelationship within the Jewish community to which it had once belonged. And it has to be understood in the social and religious circumstance of the community.[163] Nevertheless, nowhere in the Gospel of John, is written that

158 Robert A. Hinde, *Towards Understanding Relationships* (London: Academic Press, 1979), 4.

159 Willi Marxsen, *New Testament Foundations for Christian Ethics*, translated by Jr. O. C. Dean (Minneapolis: Fortress Press, 1993), 287. God the Father loves the Son and the Son reciprocated the Father's love. The Son Jesus loves the disciples and the disciples love the Son. The Father God loves the disciples and the disciples love the Father God. See for references John 14:15, 21, 31; 15:9, 10, 12, 13; 16:27; 17:23, 24, 26.

160 Strecker, *Theology of the New Testament*, 512.

161 Burridge, *Imitating Jesus*, 327.

162 Rabens, "Johannine Perspective on Ethical Enabling," 120.

163 James H. Charlesworth, "The Gospel of John: Exclusivism Caused by a Social Setting Different from That of Jesus (John 11:54 and 14:6),"*Anti-Judaism and the Fourth Gospel*, edited by R.

the community of believers in Jesus Christ is asked to reciprocate the antagonism (hatred for hatred e.g., the Qumran community of the Dead Sea Scrolls).[164] In fact, love command serves as a prism that spreads light on the spectrum of Johannine ethics says Rabens.[165] He further quotes Jorg Frey who opines that the love command is a call "for unity in the face of internal diversity (cf. 11:51-52; 17:21-23) and demands the reconciliation of social, ethnic and other differences in the new 'family' or 'community' of friends."[166] It finds its expression in its willingness to exercise what may benefit the other besides itself. In deed love is an active determination of the will.

The love of Jesus is an ethical force that drives the behavior and attitude of his disciples and future believers. Jesus' love is exemplified in the unconditional and self-sacrificing moment in his life ministry and death on the cross of Calvary. Love is prominently and is the essence of Jesus' ethical teaching.[167] Love serves as the decisive criterion for right ethical behavior and takes a complex form. It also reflects the right Christological understanding because Jesus explicated and modeled in a concrete action. Rabens aptly opines that "love experienced in intimate relationships transforms and empowers people for ethical life in accordance with the values."[168]

It is therefore logical to construe that the ethics of Jesus is found in the love command 'love one another'[169] as I have loved you' and his love is the guiding ethical principle. The self-sacrificing example of Jesus which incurs ethical implications is the best epitome example to be followed.[170] As such, love determines believers' attitude and must also find its expression in self-sacrificing actions that honors God. All other ethical aspects indeed hang on this crucial love command. Indeed, the concept of love "is a many-splendored thing."[171] Love is the undergirding virtue to keep all other ethical directives that could be spoken of. If not for love, everything seems just too impossible. After Jesus' physical departure, the Spirit-*Paraclete* takes over the responsibility to lead and guide the believers to truth. So, there is also an active participation of the Spirit in the lives of the believing community for its ethical conduct.

Bieringer, D. Pollefeyt, and F. Vandecastelle-Vanneuville (Louisville: Westminster John Knox Press, 2001), 247-278.

164 Burridge, *Imitating Jesus,* 334.

165 Rabens, "Johannine Perspective on Ethical Enabling," 120.

166 Rabens, "Johannine Perspective on Ethical Enabling," 120.

167 George Arthur Buttrick, eds., *The Interpreter's Dictionary of the Bible* (Nashville, New York: Abington Press, 1962), 168.

168 Rabens, "Johannine Perspective on Ethical Enabling," 130.

169 Hans Kvalbein, "The Kingdom of God in the Ethics of Jesus," *StudiaTheologia* 51 (1997): 65.

170 Burridge, *Imitating Jesus*, 330.

171 Raymond E. Brown, "The Paraclete in the Fourth Gospel," *NTS* 13 (1966): 118.

3.2.5. The Spirit-Paraclete: Moral Guide to Ethical Behavior (John 14-16)

The Greek word παράκλητος is peculiar to the Johannine corpus and it has traditionally been identified with the Holy Spirit.[172] It is derived from the verb παρακαλέω meaning 'one who is called to someone's aid.' So, etymologically it renders a forensic meaning of an advocate (*advocatus* (Latin) in legal setting. So, the technical gives the passive rendering 'lawyer,' 'attorney' and which is rare. But, the Greek interpreters of the Fourth Gospel render the active sense of the word, so given the meaning mediator, intercessor, helper who appears in another's behalf.[173] So, the active sense of the Greek noun παράκλητος is more suitable in all occurrences of the Johannine literature, whereby the verb παρακαλέω takes the particular force of 'to console,' 'strengthen by consolation,' 'comfort.'[174] There are five *Paraclete* – passages in the Gospel (14:15-17, 26; 15:26- 27; 16:7b-11, 13-14) and one in the first epistles of John (I Jn. 2:1). In the epistle Jesus is παράκλητος who serves as a heavenly intercessor with the Father.[175] In these sections of the Gospel Jesus not only promise his divine presence to the disciples but are also exhorted to continue to have faith in God and also in him (14:1), and to keep his commandments (14:15, 21, 23; 15:10). The promise of the divine presence of Jesus through the *Paraclete*[176] *is one of the most comforting promises for the community of believers (14:16). Captivatingly, Jesus informed his disciples of their privileges and obligations*[177] while cautioning them of the consequences of being his followers (15:1-16:4a).

Johannine's distinctive theology of the Spirit-*Paraclete* has to be understood in the context of the delay of *parousia* and the death of the first generation

172 Brown, *The Anchor Bible: The Gospel According to John,* vol.1, xxvi-xxviii; Idem, "The Paraclete in the Fourth Gospel," 113.

173 *A Greek- English Lexicon of the New Testament and Other Early Christian Literature,* 3rd edition, revised and edited by Frederick William Danker base on Walter Bauer's (Chicago & London: University of Chicago Press, 2000), 766; Brown, "The Paraclete in the Fourth Gospel:" 113-132; Hoskyns, *The Fourth Gospel*, 465-470.

174 Hoskyns, *The Fourth Gospel*, 467. An active noun form παρακλήτω from the verb παρακλαλέω existed and was used in the LXX of Job 16:2 for Job's comforters but later Jewish translators (e.g. Aquila and Theodotion) of the OT used παράκλητος. This tells that the word meaning was not controlled by its etymological or technical meaning.

175 Brown, "The Paraclete in the Fourth Gospel," 113, 117.

176 The Johannine Paraclete is the Holy Spirit also called the spirit of Truth and is the Spirit whom the Gospel speaks regularly (cf. 3:5f. 34; 4:23; 6:63; 7:39; 20:22).

177 Jesus' disciples have been witnesses of his works during his life ministry. On the basis of this fact the disciples' faith is established and is urged to continue to carry out the progress of his works on earth even after his physical departure (esp. 14:12). The disciples are given the moral precepts to be carried out in the days ahead to keep Jesus' commandments by loving one another so that they will be identified as his disciples (14:15). There is a strong emphasis on the connection between faith and work. The involvement of the disciples in the progress work of Jesus is to be prompted by their continued believe in Jesus.

eyewitnesses[178] precisely the time between Jesus' physical departure and his return. So, beginning with the time when the disciples are left behind on earth till the Lord will make his second coming, *parousia.*[179] *Considering the full account of the contexts, it is then reasonable to say that, in Johannine Paraclete* are converged three concise meanings - (i) the *Paraclete* as a vindicating and punishing witness; (ii) one who aids and supports; (iii) a counselor and teacher.[180] The work of the Spirit-*Paraclete* is, thus, related both to Christ and to the life in flesh of Jesus who is the ultimate and true revelation of God.[181] The dominant idea of the *Paraclete* is that he assists in a situation when the need is utmost in the physical absence of Jesus,[182] in this perspective, the Spirit can be called 'Comforter,' 'Counsellor' and considering John 14:16 where Jesus speaks of ἄλλον παράκλητον, it gives a natural inclination that the *Paraclete* can be called 'Advocate' as well. In short, in Spirit-*Paraclete* as the Spirit of Truth is captured the complexity of the functions of the comforter, counselor, and an advocate (i.e., the natural and obvious meanings of these terms are seen in the *Paraclete*).

Robert Kysar advanced that the Spirit-*paraclete* of the Fourth Gospel "became a christocentric understanding of the Spirit by which John provide an intellectual link between the historical revelation believed to have occurred in Jesus of Nazareth and the contemporary experience of the vitality of that revelation in the Johannine community…the community is the locale in which the work of God begun in Christ is continued."[183] Jesus in the Gospel offers repeated reassurance that his physical departure will not leave the community as orphaned (14:18). Jesus reminds the disciples of what he has taught them and encourages them

178 Raymond E. Brown, *The Anchor Bible: The Gospel According to John,* vol. 2 (London: Geoffrey Chapman, 1971 [Reprinted 1982, 1984]), 1142-1143; Schnackenburg, *The Gospel According to St John,* vol. 2, 436.

179 Ridderbos, *The Gospel of John*, 496.

180 Hoskyns, *The Fourth Gospel,* 467-468. There is also an opinion shared that in the Johannine *Paraclete* is fused the prophet's figure who bears witness, bestows counsel, and teaches and discloses the future.

181 Hoskyns, *The Fourth Gospel,* 468. In all occurrences of the Paraclete contexts in the Gospel, the *Paraclete's* work in relation to Christ can be derived in the following points – Christ who prays to the Father on behalf of the disciples for *Paraclete* (14:16); the Paraclete will be sent by the Father in Christ's name (14:26); He himself will send the *Paraclete* from the Father (14:26), following his physical departure from His disciples (16:7). The *Paraclete's* work in relation to Jesus who is the revelation of God can be summarized as follow – The *Paraclete* as the Spirit of Truth reveals in history the ultimate truth of God, teaching and bringing remembrance to this truth (14:16); Bear witness to Jesus , so also will the disciples for they have been with Jesus from the beginning (15:26, 27 cf. 1:14); Guide the disciples into all the truths (wherein the revelation of the Truth is also focused upon Jesus (16:13-15); Convict the world of sin, righteousness and judgment (14:17).

182 Brown, "The Paraclete in the Fourth Gospel," 118 f.

183 Robert Kysar, *The Fourth Evangelist and His Gospel: An Examination of Contemporary Scholarship* (Minneapolis: Augsburg Publishing House, 1975), 239-240.

to remain faithful to his commandments. Jesus foretold the probable upcoming hostility they will face from the unbelieving world after his departure (Jn. 15:18-25; 16:1-4; 17:14). He assures them that his return to where he had come from will not however leave the community of faith in dismay but that he will send the *Paraclete*, the Spirit of Truth to be with them (Jn. 14:15- 18; 15:26; 16:7-15).

So, the promised *Paraclete* acts as Jesus' 'successor and remind the disciples of everything what he has said'[184] revealed and taught them earlier during his earthly ministry (Jn. 14:15, 23, 25 cf. 8:51f; 15:20; 17:6). All that the *Paraclete* did was the continuation of Jesus' own work and is determined in content by his work.[185] The Spirit- *Paraclete* is modeled on Jesus.[186] The function of the *Paraclete* is to teach the community, to remind Jesus' followers of what he had taught, to testify and witness about him before the world (Jn. 15:26; 16:7-11) and above all to provide continuing guidance even matters that are yet to come (Jn. 16:12-14). This confirms the view that the promise of the *Paraclete* is the promise of the continuation of the revelation that which had begun in Jesus.[187] The *Paraclete* brings home the personal presence of Jesus and his transforming love to the disciples.[188] So, the Spirit-*Paraclete* provides the Father-Son's continuing presence and also acts as a source of continuing revelation.[189] It also appears that the intimate presence of Jesus by the *Paraclete* enables the disciples to keep the commandments even after Jesus' ascension to heaven (14:15-17; 16:6-7).[190]

John gives special emphasis to the fundamental role of the Spirit-*Paraclete* in the lives of the immediate disciples of the Johannine community. Jesus offers his communion by the Spirit-*Paraclete* in their lives, be on their life's journey together with him. The disciples are not left as orphans even in the physical absence of Jesus because he is understood to be present in spirit amongst them. The promise of Jesus which is fulfilled by the power of the *Paraclete* and its presence is assured. The *Paraclete* is with and in them (both disciples and later believers) to guide and protect them. It is this *Paraclete*, the Spirit of Truth which functions to bring to the inner consciousness and understanding of the disciples the words of Jesus as supervision for their life and belief.[191] The Spirit does not act independent apart from Christ as though he were picking up the task which Jesus begun and had now relinquished but continues the work that had begun.

184 Matera, *New Testament* Ethics, 104.

185 Ridderbos, *The Gospel of John*, 502.

186 Max Turner, *The Holy Spirit and Spiritual Gifts - Then and Now* (Carlisle: Paternoster, 1999), 79.

187 Bultmann, *The Gospel of John,* 617.

188 Rabens, "Johannine Perspectives on Ethical Enabling," 120,

189 Hays, *The Moral Vision of the New Testament*, 151.

190 Rabens,"Johannine Perspectives on Ethical Enabling," 127.

191 John W. Pryor, *John: Evangelist of the Covenant People* (Illinois: InterVarsity Press, 1992), 159.

The Spirit-*Paraclete* is to bear witness to Christ (Jn. 15:26), to make operative what Christ had already effected or accomplished.[192] Much of Jesus' early work or ministry was obscured and enigmatic to his immediate disciples, but they came to understand in the light of the Resurrection (Jn. 2:22; 12:16). Now this obscurity and enigma of Jesus' words are now being made to be understood by the conviction of the Holy Spirit, the *Paraclete*. It is this Spirit in John's Gospel who teaches all things and reminds the then disciples (believers) of all that Jesus has said (14:26) and also leads them to the full truth of the revelation of Christ (16:13).[193] The *Paraclete* will convict (ἐλέξει)[194] the world. The *Paraclete* is functionally identified as Jesus by the author of the Gospel that is the Paraclete is understood as Jesus' personal presence.[195] It is inseparably bound to the person Jesus Christ. Because it is only through Jesus that the Spirit came to exist for the community (Jn. 7:39) and it is from him that the community of believers in the Fourth Gospel received the Spirit (Jn. 20:22).[196] In deed the Spirit- *Paraclete* is the eschatological *continuum* in which the work of Jesus Christ, initiated in his ministry and awaiting its termination at his return, is fashioned out.[197] The behavior of the disciples specifically and the Johannine community at large is understood to be driven and guided by the *Paraclete*.

The *Paraclete* provides comfort and moral confidence for the community of believers. It is the *Paraclete* who will guide and teach them all things (basically all truths). This implies that the *Paraclete* of John's Gospel plays a central and crucial role in guiding and shaping the behavior of the Johannine community and the believers' behavior at large. That is, Johannine *Paraclete* functionally has an ethical importance in guiding the behavior of the believers in the right direction. The *Paraclete* plays important role in sustaining the disciples in the empowering relationship to Jesus and his love in which they are to abide.[198] The *Paraclete* helps the followers of Jesus to live in accordance with the will of God the Father.

---

192 Barrett, *the Gospel According to St. John*, 76.

193 Schnackenburg, *The Gospel According to St. John*, vol. 1, excursus, 570. This is clearly meant to be addressed to later believers as well, who are to regard and accept the testimony of Jesus' earthly companions and that of the Paraclete as a single unity (cf. 15:16 f).

194 The word ἐλέγχειν means "to expose", "to bring to the light of day", "to show a thing in its true colors." It is the activity of the judge and prosecuting counsel in one. The questions reserved by the apocalypses for treatment at the last day: sin, righteousness, and judgment are here treated by John adding that the paraclete will announce to you the things to come (τά ἔρχόμενα ἀναγγελειύμιν 16:13). The spirit already proclaims the truth that will one day be manifested, and the judgment that will then be carried out.

195 Rabens, "Johannine Perspectives on Ethical Enabling," 118.

196 Schnackenburg, *The Gospel According to St John*, vol. 3, 149.

197 Barrett, *The Gospel According to St. John*, 76.

198 Barrett, *The Gospel According to St. John*, 139.

There was a strong distinctive theological belief of the active presence of the Spirit-*Paraclete* within the Johannine community of faith.[199] It is appropriate to infer that the community of John is inspired, taught and guided by the risen Jesus by the power of the Spirit-*paraclete*. The community of believers in John perceives the Spirit *Paraclete* as her teacher and interpreter. And most significantly the Spirit-*Paraclete* appears as the enabling agent in the Gospel of John. The Spirit is thus the illuminating and strengthening power of God which enables the community to continue to remain faithful, and thus belong, to God and to possess the truth.[200] The notion of Spirit-*Paraclete* guided ethics forecasts a process of discernment. So, the community of believers must count on the Spirit not only to guide them in all the truth but also inspire and empower them in the process of discerning the truth and the good.[201]

In the words of Jose Maniparampil, "the risen Lord continues to refashion the traditions."[202] So, the community of John's Gospel is a group of believers who are guided/led and empowered by the Spirit-*Paraclete*. The community of believers is constituted by the power of the revelation that is at work in it but need to remember that the community has its power only in its faith in the invisible, not in what can be proved or controlled. The Spirit-*Paraclete* is visible only to faith and faith alone. It is impossible to understand revelation outside of faith because the Spirit that is at work by the power of the revelation cannot be "at work in world-history as a factor in the history of ideas, and such as could be detected by the historians in institutions or persons, in cultural advancement or social achievement, etc."[203] Accordingly the Spirit-*Paraclete*, of the Fourth Gospel, is a moral guide for the community of believers in the physical absence of Jesus.

So in John's Gospel, *Paraclete* plays an important role in guiding the community of believers to do what is right and which eventually is truth. Unlike other New Testament documents that emphasize on the didactic teaching on moral values, John's Gospel shows a more specific involvement of the Spirit of Truth that proceeds from the Father and Son to continually lead the community to what holds to the truth. John's ethics is more relational wherein Jesus' personal interest in guarding the moral life of the community after his departure becomes one of his chief concerns. The community of believers anticipated the *parousia* of Jesus. But, the interim presence of the *Paraclete* as a moral guide is suggestive and promising, to guide the disciples in their ethical conduct.

---

199 Hays, *The Moral Vision of the New Testament*, 149.

200 Schnackenburg, *The Gospel According to St. John*, vol. 3, 149.

201 Pregeant, *Knowing Truth, Doing Good*, 209.

202 Maniparampil, *Reading the Fourth Gospel*, 89.

203 Bultmann, *The Gospel of John*, 617.

3.2.6. Abiding in Jesus: Ethics of Discipleship (John 15)

Discipleship is central to the Fourth Gospel and the Gospel takes up this important correlation of the vine and the branches to relate the underlying importance of its existence (mutual indwelling) and its permanency of relationship between Jesus and believers in him.[204] The disciples are compared to branches on a vine (Jesus) whereby an intimate mutual relationship is established between them. And most importantly, "the symbol of the vine suggests a unity like that of a living plant, in which a common life, flowing from the central stem nourishes all the branches and issues in life."[205] Discipleship is distinctively characterized by me,nein "remain," "abide," "stay," "dwell on" in Jesus (it occurs 40 times in the Gospel, probably the highest frequency of occurrence).[206] The urgency of the allegorical message of this parable is the emphasis laid on the concept of being *in* (Jesus) *Christ*, which makes stern ethical demand (cf. Rom. 8).[207] The Gospel view of discipleship is deeply rooted in Christology. So, the discourse on the Vine and the branches is of central significance which is instructive as an example of the influence of Christology on ethics.[208] One's moral life must be lived within a community and not as an isolated individual and to live this moral life, according to the Gospel of John, is impossible apart from Jesus (15:5). Abiding in Jesus is the important grounding for Johannine discipleship.

The discourse signals the general relation between Jesus and his disciples. The Fourth Gospel does use an analogy to describe the intimate relationship established between Jesus and the disciples as the branches are to the vine. The verb me,nein translated 'to abide' or 'to dwell' is employed as a 'key expression of dwelling reciprocity' – the abiding of the Father in the Son and the Son in the Father, and of the Son in the disciples and the disciples in the Son (triangle

---

204 The Johannine doctrine of the indwelling can be compared to the Pauline concept 'in Christ.' The Pauline understanding of 'in Christ' is exemplified in the 'body of Christ' and in the olive-tree which is the symbolic representation of the true people of God. From the olive-tree is severed off all the unfruitful branches so that through faith new branches might be crafted into the tree (Rom. 11:16- 24; 8). Both for John and Paul, the inherence of an individual in Christ Jesus is inseparable from the unity of individual believers with one another in the company of the believers (Church). So, for both of them the concept of being 'in Christ' is strongly emphasized (Jn. 15 cf. Rom. 8). See Dodd, *The Interpretation of the Fourth Gospel,* 196; Lindars, *The Gospel of John,* 35-36; Raymond E. Brown, *The Anchor Bible: The Gospel According to John,* vol. 1 (New York: Doubleday & Company, 1966), 510.

205 Dodd, *The Interpretation of the Fourth Gospel*, 187-200; Kanagaraj, *The Gospel of John*, 494-506.

206 Brown, *The Gospel According to John,* vol. 1, 510.

207 Lindars, *The Gospel of John,* 36.

208 Schrage, *The Ethics of the New Testament,* 299; James M. Gustafson, *Moral Discernment in the Christian Life,* edited and with an Introduction by Theo A. Boer and Paul E. Capetz (Louisville, London: Westminster John Knox Press, 2007), 41.

relationship).[209] So, as the Father dwells in the Son (14:10) so is the Son (Vine) to the disciples (branches) (15:5, 9-11). The ethical fruit of disciples precisely flows from this reciprocity of their abode in Jesus and Jesus in them.[210] The moral life of the disciples depends so much on abiding in Jesus, for their moral life is not possible without Jesus. Just as the branch cannot bear fruit so the disciples cannot bear fruit without abiding in Jesus (15:5).

So, abiding in Jesus is a basic requirement to bear fruit. That means Jesus is the source of the disciples' moral life.[211] As such, Jesus' injunction "abide/ remain in me" forms the basis of the new ethics that the post-resurrection, exalted Christ demands of his followers.[212] A disciple of Jesus cannot bear fruit devoid of abiding in Jesus and Jesus abiding in those who believe and thus belong to him. This 'abiding' is an active every day abiding (not a mystical union) and utter dependence on Jesus that issues into fruit bearing.[213] So, to remain in Jesus is more than simply believing in him[214] because just as the Son abides in the Father and replicates exactly what the latter asks him to say and do, so also an individual who remains in Jesus must reflect the character of Jesus. The disciples' identification with Jesus is metaphorically presented as the vine and the branches and has a very strong ethical implication.

This symbolical representation of the relationship between Jesus and believers is that if one has to remain as a branch on the vine; one must remain in the love of Jesus (15:9). The relation between Jesus and the disciples rests upon their mutual love. And this concept of ἀγάπη in John does not "devolve into a sentiment or an emotion" but "is always moral and is revealed in obedience."[215] So 'obedience to keep Jesus' commandments' will be the proof and consequence of the disciples' love for their master Jesus (14:15, 21). And this love must be articulated in love for one's fellow believer (15:12).[216] Jesus entrusted the disciples to carry on the task of mission and contending the same experience of rejection he had faced at the hands of the world (15:18-21). The abiding of Jesus thus "makes it possible for those who belong to him to abide in him." There is a reciprocal interdependence on the theme of abiding in Jesus and Jesus abiding in those whoever believes and this is a very noteworthy phenomenon to be taken note of it.

---

209 Dodd, *The Interpretation of the Fourth Gospel*, 196.

210 Pregeant, *Knowing Truth, Doing Good*, 208.

211 Matera, *New Testament Ethics*, 108.

212 Chrys C. Caragounis, "Abide in Me:" The New Mode of Relationship between Jesus and His Followers as a Basis for Christian Ethics (John 15)," *Rethinking the Ethics of John: "Implicit Ethics" in the Johannine Writings*, edited by Jan G. van der Watt and Ruben Zimmermann (Tubingen: Mohr Siebeck, 2012), 263.

213 Caragounis, "Abide in Me," 261.

214 Beasley-Murray, *WBC: John*, 272.

215 Barrett, *Gospel According to St John*, 385.

216 Brown, *The Gospel According to John*, vol. 1, cviii.

This relational concept of abiding in Jesus is one basic characteristic of discipleship in John's Gospel. Henceforth discipleship receives a new emphasis in the Gospel according to John. In the synoptic Gospels, the disciples are asked to deny themselves and take up their cross and follow Jesus but in John's Gospel disciples are expected to abide and dwell in Jesus. The allegory of the vine and branches (15:1-17) in John's Gospel indicates that remaining in Jesus is not a mystical experience but will have its outworking in obedience to the commands of Jesus.[217] When Jesus instructs his disciples the primary paradigm is his own relationship of love and obedience and harmony with the Father - a relationship of such kind that they are alleged to remain in each other (Jn. 14:10).[218]

There is indeed the dialectic between the indicative (Jesus loves) and the imperative (love one another). The imperative finds its basis in the indicative and so the indicative takes precedence over the imperative. Nevertheless, abiding in Jesus is itself based on Jesus' abiding in those who have come to believe in him and thus belong to him. In John's allegory of the vine and the branches, there is no merging of the two (Vine and branches/Jesus and disciples) but both remain distinct. It puts forward that the identity and the life of the community is vitally dependent on its relationship with Jesus, a relationship expresses in obedience.[219] They are expected to be like and do the things the master does (except for the cross). Jesus' death was redemptive, the only means to life eternal, and no human being can embrace such atoning death.[220] The cross for John's Gospel is a crowning glory from which flows life. It is not a place of humiliation but a place of exaltation (3:14; 8:28; 12:34). Jesus' death on the cross is a return to the Father where both have initially shared the glory even before the foundation of the world (17: 5).

The mark of discipleship is stamped with the Master's command to love one another. This love command is grounded on being loved. Now the ethics of love in the Gospel stands and falls exclusively on God's redeeming love manifested by sending his begotten Son (3:16). Love for one another, as a remarkable display of being Jesus' disciples is a live witness to the world, and is the "touchstone of discipleship"[221] in the life of the Community of John. So, love for one another serves as a pertinent mark of discipleship in the Johannine community. The disciples' norm of morality depends on their relationship to Jesus. They are expected to showcase their mutual relationship and prove their abode in Jesus by keeping his love commandment. The love command in Johannine perspective is therefore "a call to distinct action(s) led by the principle of love."[222] Above all,

---

217 Brown, *the Gospel according to John,* vol. 1, 510-512.

218 Pryor, *John: Evangelist of the Covenant People*, 161.

219 Pryor, *John: Evangelist of the Covenant People*, 126.

220 Kanagaraj, *The Gospel of John*, 440.

221 Matera, *New Testament Ethics*, 107.

222 Michael Labahn, "It's Only Love"- Is That All? Limits and Potentials of Johannine "Ethics'- A Critical Evaluation of Research," *Rethinking the Ethics of John: "Implicit Ethics" in the Johannine*

the life of a disciple is to orient his/her life toward Jesus as the One having come from the Father.

Abiding in Jesus is another form of an expression of one's faith. If one lacks faith in Jesus, there is no question to abide in Him. Faith is one such sublime aspect in determining one's choice–to accept or reject the person of Jesus and his word. Faith is action oriented and therefore ought to be active, bringing forth fruit. Here the belief must become visible in their life in the fruit they are expected to bear. Nevertheless, the bearing of the fruit is the result of abiding in Jesus and not vice versa. This suggests that Christology has direct consequences for ethics in the Gospel of John. Whoever confesses faith in the person of Jesus is called to keep his command and this command is to love one another which serve as a hallmark for Johannine discipleship. Jesus' command is based on what he himself has demonstrated and his injunction thereby is not beyond what he himself has done (exercised).

The immediate disciples are urged to do as much as Jesus has done for them and he does not command the disciples to do more than he has accomplished for them. And the disciples are to keep Jesus' command and to show the world their distinctive characteristic by abiding in their master's word. It is reasonable to suppose that the disciples' faith in Jesus must be equated and qualified by their action for "faith must find an outlet in action."[223] Faith and action go hand in hand, they belong together. We have seen the strong emphasis on the connection between faith and the anticipated involvement of the disciples in the progress works of Jesus (Jn. 14:12). Faith is manifested through action and action is the manifestation of faith. Those who have believed in Jesus must remain in him and hence forth exhibit their faith to the world by their fruitful life (produce concrete action). Faith is not a mere philosophical abstract but action oriented. Believers are urged to demonstrate their faith by good works. Faith (in Jesus) becomes the means to an end (good work).

The fourth Gospel conveys that the ethical responsibility is the natural outcome of a new relationship built with Jesus. This relationship, said Flew, is both ethical and religious. It is ethical, because the love which is unique and incomparable is given by Jesus for the everyday life of believers in him. It is religious too, because life is meant to be lived out in loyalty to Jesus who offers the true knowledge of God the Father, and life eternal.[224] There is a strong Christological motivation that the disciples (believers) should abide in Jesus and remain in him so as to bear fruit (fruit of good service). Ethics of abiding in Jesus

---

Writings, edited by Jan G. van der Watt and Ruben Zimmermann (Tubingen: Mohr Siebeck, 2012), 25.

223 Eduard Lohse, *The First Christians: Their Beginnings, Writings, and Beliefs*, translated by Eugene Boring (Philadelphia: Fortress Press, 1983), 85.

224 Flew, *Jesus and His Way*, 151.

elevates above a list of rules and principles to reciprocal interpersonal relationship that is constantly ready to bear fruit a productive activity.

John affirms that the Johannine community as believers is to continue the task of carrying his mission, patterning their lives after his and sharing his destiny (12:26). As such, the bond between Jesus and the disciples (or believers at large) is determinative for the Johannine community's ethical norms.[225] For John, authentic discipleship entails abiding in Jesus (which is relational) as branches is to the vine. The imagery of the vine and the branches (John 15:4-10) clearly unfolds the truth that it is only in their union with Jesus Christ that the disciples can bear fruit. And the spiritual indwelling made available to the community of the disciples will result in obedience to Jesus (15:7).

3.2.7. Ethics of Perfection (John 17)

Jesus said, ἐμὸν βρῶμά ἐστιν ἵνα ποιήσω τὸ Θέλημα τοῦ πέμψαντός με καὶ Τελειώσω αὐτοῦ τὸ ἔργον "My food is to do the will of him who sent me to complete his work" (4:34). The ἔργον is a singular whole that comprises the miraculous works of Jesus (i.e., σημεῖα). The ἔργα of Jesus as σημεῖα and the ἔργα of God are effected in the ἔργα[226] βεχαυσε τηε ἔργα of Jesus is regarded as the ἔργα of God (4:34; 5:36; 9:3f; 10:32; 14:10; 17:4). Jesus in the priestly prayer utters, ἐγώ σε ἐδόξασα ἐπὶ τῆς γῆς τὸ ἔργον τελειώσας ὃ δέδωκάς μοι ἵνα ποιήσω "I glorified you on earth by finishing the work that you gave me to do" (17:4). Jesus' acclamation that he has finished the ἔργον given by God who has sent him has an immense ethical implication that cannot be overlooked. Jesus had a moral obligation to bring into perfection the ἔργα of God, which were indeed the commandment of God (Jn. 12: 49, 50; 14: 31). The verb 'τελέω' meaning "to finish" is the same verb Jesus used when he explains concerning his *ergon* to be done (Jn. 4:34) and when he accomplished that *ergon* on the cross, Jesus exclaimed, τετέλεσται (Jn. 19:30). On the other important side of the coin, there is at the heart of the Gospel the motif of replication/imitation of Jesus (cf. giving up lives for the sake of other (Jn. 12:23-26); disciples are sent just as Jesus is sent by the father (Jn. 17:18: 20:21-22). Perfection here does not mean self-righteousness, rather more of fulfilling God's mission that is God's will. It is goal-oriented, accomplishing the divine purpose of God. Jesus is both the model and criterion as he brings it to completion the divine mission God the Father has assigned. Jesus is the best example of his own teachings.

The ethics of obedience mediated by Jesus has indeed determined and colored the community's ethics. The hearers and the disciples therefore must abide by the command Jesus has pronounced. On the part of the disciples is required responsive obedience. Obedience to the commandments is demonstrated as keeping the new commandment to love one another as warranted and exemplified

225 Hays, *The Moral Vision of the New Testament,* 1996, 143.

226 Renstorf, "σημεῖον," *TDNT,* vol. 2, 247.

by Jesus' love for them (Jn. 13:33-34; 15:9-17).[227] Disciples are to be in the Son as the Son is in the Father. Here imitation of Jesus is directive. Imitating Jesus in obedience just as he himself has been in obedience to God the Father and has exactly explicated what the Father has commanded him (Jn. 12:49; 14: 31). Jesus' life vocation and mission was directed by the self-consciousness that he has been sent by the Father and that he was utterly committed to carry out the will of his Father's divine mission in obedience till the ultimate accomplishment on the cross and utters the victory exclamation 'it is finished' (Jn. 19: 30).

By following the footsteps of Jesus, who has obediently tread the road of obedience and submission to the Father's will, believers will know and translate the distinction between what is 'from above' and what is 'from below' and can in fact move on to the path of perfection. This suggests that 'from above' would, in simple interpretation may mean what is good and right and the other the opposite side of it. Disciples of Jesus must follow the example of Jesus in obedience and believe that the Father and the Son are mutually inter-dependent. Jesus does the work of the Father (Jn. 5:36; 10:37) where 'the works of God' (*erga tou theou*) becomes the task for Jesus to bring it to completion (human redemption on the cross, the zenith accomplishment). The commitment of Jesus to his Father is undergirded by the fact that no activity or work is done on his own. All of what Jesus did (i.e., the works) therefore have their origin in God, the Father.

The works Jesus did are in actuality the works of God produced through him. This means that the Father's works are "embodied in the deeds of Jesus."[228] Jesus truly reflects God's way of doing and sayings things. John 17:18 underlines the obligation to continue the mission of Jesus by his followers (cf. 13:12-20). To carry on the legacy of mission is yet another important habitual action mainly for the Johannine community (group of believers). Followers (believers in Jesus) are to continue his mission as belonging to the same family of God because Jesus has commanded them to do so (which is ethics). Jesus' disciples are therefore believers with a mission like their Lord and master who is sent by the Father (Jn. 17:18; 20:21).

Conclusion

It has become clear from the analyzed passages that there are more of ethical implications than it has been supposed. The Gospel of John is not designed as ethical treatises nonetheless it is loaded with ethical implications in the narratologies. There is a greater emphasis in summoning the community of believers to live their moral life which distinctively is and must be characterized

227 William R. G. Loader, "The Law and Ethics in John's Gospel," *Rethinking the Ethics of John: "Implicit Ethics" in the Johannine Writings,* edited by Jan G. van der Watt and Ruben Zimmermann (Tubingen: Mohr Siebeck, 2012), 153-154.

228 Marianne M. Thompson, *The God of the Gospel of John* (Michigan: Wm. B. Eerdmanns Publishing Company, 2001), 237.

by *faith* and *love*. Sapping and accumulating the ethical significances as found in the narratives, the most dominating and profound ethical categories seem to be faith and love. Both of these ethical elements work together to create a profound ethical perspective and are treated theocentrically and christocentrically. Thus, faith and love appeared and served as the most regulating ethical principles in the Gospel of John.

This moral life is explicitly related to the words and deeds of Jesus, who has been sent by the Father for the salvific revelation. The closely examined words or phrases are ethically loaded and have thereby served as valuable ethical indicators in understanding the Johannine community's ethics in significant relationship to Jesus. As such, Johannine ethics is an ethics which is oriented and founded on a Christologically based indicative. Every implied ethical and moral demand from God is explicated in and through the Son Jesus Christ. The ethical principles discussed are based upon and directly related to the identity and work (behavior) of Jesus whose very life has served as an ethical model and a guide to his disciples. This is to postulate that ethics in John's Gospel does not stand aloof from the person and work of Jesus.

The analyzed thematic study of the ethically related terms, phrases and passages have significantly pointed to the fact that John's Gospel has so much to tell us in regard to ethical messages. The theme of ethics is not betrayed. In reality, the theme of ethics is wrapped up in the theme of Christology. Gospel's ethical exhortations or directives or teachings are intricately merged with Christological materials. This is to surmise that Johannine ethics has to be studied in close relation to Johannine Christology because it is in the Christology that ethics is so embedded and articulated. Ethics in John's Gospel is embodied in Jesus' personal life and that has become truism for the community to emulate.

It is the character, life and work of Jesus that revolutionized the Johannine conception of morality. Jesus' life creates the community's conception and value of moral behavior. Believing in Jesus as the unique Son of God who has come to fulfill the Messianic expectation of the then Jewish eschatological hope is significant. It is the belief in Jesus that lies the ethical decisive moment of the believing community to consolidate themselves into a messianic community in the face of the unbelieving Jewish community. So, only those who believe in Jesus would be qualified to be his true disciples practicing faith, love and obedience to God through Jesus. Thus, faith in the person of Jesus as the Christ and loving one another are the fundamental ethical expression of the Johannine community. So, John saw the importance of reporting the facts of Jesus' ministry which in fact calls forth for a decisive choice of acceptance or rejection with its underlying ethical significances. Those who responded to Jesus in faith placed themselves as members of God's family. For John's Gospel, ethics is rooted in a right response to the faith in Jesus as Christ the Son of God who brings along life eternal. In effect, faith in Jesus is the fundamental ethical conviction for the community of John's

Gospel. The right ethical conduct of the community is thereby grounded upon faith in Jesus which must be reflected in their conducts by loving one another.

The ethical pointers present in the Gospel of John are sufficient enough to concur that ethics is essentially important which lead us to even more fundamental motives for action. As Zimmermann articulates, "John does not want to solve individual problems of daily life itself. Instead he wants to carry out ethical work at a more fundamental level that enables the reader in the end to find a happy life, or in Johannine terminology, an "eternal life' which nevertheless starts from daily life"[229] right here in the present. The concrete acts of believers in the Gospel are connected with the deeds of Jesus and eventually and finally to the works of God.[230] This is to endorse that Johannine Christology and Johannine ethics belong together. In John's Gospel "ethical life is empowered through the experience and example of love in an intimate relationship to Jesus and the Father."[231] It becomes clear that Johannine Christology is the basis for developing Johannine ethics.

It is also apt to reiterate that Johannine ethics is and must be interpreted in the light of Johannine Christology. In other words, Johannine ethics has to be interpreted and evaluated in the light of the words, (teaching) and works (*erga*) of Jesus. Jesus' performances of σημεῖα act as demonstration of his identity and his core mission (Jn. 10:38; 12:37). That is, Johannine ethic basically is rooted and revolves around the Johannine Christology. The ethical precepts in the Gospel of John take on a fresh aspect. They became the standard by which the believer's behavior is judged and it as well served as guideposts in the course of living out the moral standards in the "new society"[232] pattern after the life and teaching of Jesus. The aspect of Johannine ethic in the Gospel is a relational concept because the addressees are called to believe in Jesus. Johannine ethic is and must be operated within the belief in Jesus, who has functioned as a model for the ideal ethical behavior. Johannine Jesus being the ultimate moral agent of God models the perfect paradigm of ethical behavior in every aspect. All in all Johannine Christology serves as a hermeneutical key to unlock the Johannine ethics in the Gospel of John.

We may reasonably bring to a close that ethical indicators or pointers are distributed in the Gospel narratives which nevertheless requires a deeper sensibility

229 Ruben Zimmermann, "Is There Ethics in the Gospel of John? Challenging an Outdated Consensus," *Rethinking the Ethics of John: "Implicit Ethics" in the Johannine Writings*, edited by Jan van der Watt and Ruben Zimmermann (Tubingen: Mohr Siebeck, 2012), 79.

230 Zimmermann, "Is There Ethics in the Gospel of John?," 80.

231 Rabens, "Johannine Perspective on Ethical Enabling," 134.

232 Vallianippuram, *New Society in John's Gospel*, 129 - 154. He considers chapters 5 and 9 of John's Gospel as the proposal of Johannine theology of forming a New Society. Here in it is probable to consider the thought process of forming a new society not as an exclusive society but a transform society within the circle of the same existing society where its ethical precepts are drawn from the life and teaching of Jesus, who is the Christ, the Son of God.

to discover that ethical precepts are embedded in the Christological narratives. Johannine ethics is neither self-contained nor self-sufficient in itself but finds its fulfillment in Jesus Christ. And not the least it is often a Johannine style to convey his message implicitly and therefore John's ethical perceptions are clothed in his style which is implicit rather than explicit.

The Johannine Jesus is the primal ethical actor/model of the ethical life in whom lies the true essence of the norms of theological morality because it is in and through him that the fundamental and foundations of the moral life is mediated (Jn. 6:28ff). The ethical indicators employed in the Fourth Gospel to drive home the ethical principles are, 'to believe' (in Jesus as sent by God), 'to do the works of God' which is the will of God (and that is to believe in Jesus), 'to love one another' as an index for true meaning of discipleship, 'to abide' (in Jesus so as to bear fruit which suggest moral responsibility), to continue the mission work of God undergirded by his profound love for the plight of humanity to grant life eternal (which is salvation). Having stated this, the fundamental ethical demand of the Fourth Gospel can be summarized as a call to faith, to love which is the will of God. This is to emphasize that the ethics of Johannine Gospel hangs under the two most distinctive ethical domains of 'faith' and 'love.' There is a dynamic connection between these two virtues. In them we see the connection between religious message ('to believe in Jesus') and moral obligation (love in action), the rooting of ethics in faith and God-given existence and the need for faith to be implemented in moral action (1 Jn. 3:23).[233] Faith and love go together in fulfilling the ethical concept and thereby must prompt a believer to do good works and continue the work of witnessing and mission by the enabling power of the Spirit-*Paraclete*, a moral guide for the believers following the physical departure of Jesus Christ (14:12; 15:26,27cf 17:18; 20:21 cf. 1 Jn. 3:23).

The validity of Johannine Christology that pertinently impacts the ethical behavior of the Johannine community is well supported by several pieces of the material, language and thought contained in the Gospel. Christology becomes the interpretive and defining key to right ethical living in the Johannine community and which is still binding for our contemporary society today. Congruently, it is an attempt to draw how ethics and Christology are inter-connected and to find out how either have influenced or shaped the other (or one another) and the subsequent impact thus resulted in the lives of the believing community. Though some scholars would still say Johannine community is esoteric and eventually the ethical implication was restricted to the core Johannine community. The researcher would however go in line with the thought development that Johannine ethics has a wider implication for all humanity that includes our 21st century society today. The following chapter will concentrate on the contours of John's Christology that intrigue and inform us to further explore the ethically loaded Christological categories.

233 Schnackenburg, *The Gospel According to St. John,* 260.

Chapter 4

Christology of John

Introduction

The identity of the person of or who is Jesus is central to our Christian faith, for reason that Jesus plays a central and an ultimate role in God's dealings with all humanity. There would have been no much study, as much as it is now, without the person and the work of Jesus Christ that has impacted the life of every believing individual and of the believing community at large as much as it has been for the early first century Christians. Congruently, the study of the person of Jesus (Christology) has been and is one of the prime interests in the study of the biblical theology as was the central focus of early Christian proclamation concerning the theological interpretation of the person and work of Jesus of Nazareth.[1] The person or identity of Jesus Christ is evidently the focus of thought both in the Gospels and the Pauline corpus.[2] As such, Christology lies at the heart of the New Testament theology which is especially true for the Gospel of John.

The Fourth Gospel's presentation of who Jesus is, lies at the heart of all that is distinctive in the Gospel.[3] It is rightly recognized that the Gospel of "John is the

---

1 Richard N. Longenecker, ed., "Christological Materials in the Early Christian Communities," *Contours of Christology in the New Testament* (Michigan: Wm B. Eerdmans Publishing Company, 2005), 47; John Drane, *Introducing the New Testament*, revised (Oxford: A Lion Book, 1999), 175.

2 Ben Witherington III, "Jesus as the Alpha and Omega of New Testament Thought," *Contours of Christology in the New Testament,* edited by Richard N. Longenecker (Michigan: Wm B. Eerdmans Publishing Company, 2005), 28.

3 D. A. Carson, *The Gospel According to John* (Michigan: Wm B. Eerdmans Publishing Company, 1991), 95.

most overtly theological of the Gospels, and Christology is its central focus."[4] The Gospel of John has its soul concern with the identity of Jesus as the *logos* incarnated who is the Christ, the 'Son of God', and the 'Son of Man.' The Gospel records the controversies of Jesus with the Jews and their religious leaders through his proclamation with such titles. Herman Ridderbos went to the extent of saying that,

> the question on which the whole of the Fourth Gospel is focused, is: who is Jesus?...the question that every confrontation with Jesus ends with...For everything that Jesus gives, everything that one may expect of him, and everything that he asks in the way of faith, obedience, and love is finally determined by who he is.[5]

The identity of Jesus – both in Christological and soteriological senses are equally the central focus in explicating the ethical implications of the Gospel. Following here we will discuss the christological perspective that informs ethical concerns in the Gospel of John.

4.1. An Overview of Johannine Christological Perspective

In the words of Martin Hengel, "Christology is the doctrine concerning God's revelation in [Jesus] Christ and the salvation wrought through Christ."[6] In simple words, Christology is an expression of people's conviction about the person of who Jesus is to them. So, it is a consciousness about the reflection of the person of Jesus. And in a more extended way it is also the question of what Jesus thought of himself as he is in relation to his very being. Therefore, there are two ascertainments in regard to Christology: What Jesus thought about and claimed himself to be, and others thought about and attributed to him. These two assertions are equally important for the proper understanding of who Jesus is. The self-consciousness of Jesus, and the consciousness of people about Jesus, act as a guiding principle for the determination of one's destiny in the salvation plan of God. However, we will not deal in details concerning the profiles and prospects about these ascertainments.

The Gospel of John documents about the person of Jesus in a narrated form with high Christological tones which in deed is the striking characteristic of the Gospel. Rudolf Bultmann in his deliberation about the characteristics of the Gospel of John states:

> The Gospel of John fundamentally contains but a single theme: the Person of Jesus. The entire Gospel is concerned with the fact of his

4 R. Alan Culpepper, "The Christology of the Johannine Writings," *Who Do You Say That I Am? Essays on Christology in Honor of Jack Dean Kingsbury*, 1st edition, edited by Mark Allan Powell and David R. Baur (Louisville, Kentucky: Westminster John Knox Press, 1999), 66.

5 Herman Ridderbos, *The Gospel of John: A Theological Commentary,* translated by John Vriend (Michigan: Wm. B. Eerdmans Publishing Company, 1997), 6-14. Quotation is from page 11.

6 Martin Hengel, *Studies in Early Christianity* (Edinburgh and New York: T&T Clark, 1995), vii.

> presence, the nature of his claim, whence he comes and whither he goes, and how men relate themselves to him. The miracles supply information about Jesus himself; the speeches are concerned with the speaker; the discussions devolve about the person of Jesus.[7]

The person of Jesus occupies a central focus in the Gospel of John. Everything that John writes or narrates in the Gospel centers around the person and work of Jesus Christ to the extent that Christology dominates the Johannine proclamation. Johannine distinctive Christology perhaps is the most characteristic aspect of Johannine theology.[8] For the Gospel of John, according to G. R. Beasley-Murray, "salvation, eschatology, God's dealings with his people and the world, and the mission of the Holy Spirit are all set in relation to Christ, and so aspects of the function of the Christ. But the unremitting concentration of the Evangelist on the person through whom God acts makes it plain that for him "function and person are inseparable."[9] That is, the behavioral pattern/conduct and identity of Jesus are integral part to each other. Jesus' identity of his *being* is reflected and is recognized in his way of conduct, which is why the co-relation of his identity (Christology) and functional aspects of his ministry (soteriology) cannot be studied in isolation.

The central affirmation for the Gospel of John lies in the fact that Jesus is sent by God. He is the perfect and ultimate revelation of God and one with God.[10] The distinction between the historical Jesus of Nazareth and Jesus the Christ of the early Church is synthesized in the Gospel of John.[11] Consequently, the consciousness and conviction of who Jesus really is - has been the center of the proclamation of the early Churches and of our present twenty first century as well. And most importantly, the ethical implication is imbedded and grounded in the very *being* and works of Jesus. Often, the statement made on Johannine theology as nothing but Christology, and his Christology his soteriology, is notable.[12] According to Rudolf Schnackenburg:

> The Johannine Christology is essentially ordained to soteriology. Everything that the Johannine Jesus says and does, all that he reveals and all that he accomplishes as "signs," takes place in view of man's attaining salvation, in view of gaining eternal life. And this salvation is

---

7 Rudolf Bultmann, *The Gospel of John*, translated by G. R. Beasley-Murray, R. W. N. Hoare and J. K. Riches (Philadelphia: Westminster Press, 1971), 5.

8 D. Moody Smith, *ANTC: John* (Nashville: Abington Press, 1999), 43.

9 George R. Beasley-Murray, *WBC: John* 36 (Texas: Word Books, 1999), 18.

10 C. H. Dodd, *The Interpretation of the Fourth Gospel* (Cambridge: Cambridge University Press, 1954), 185.

11 Jose Maniparampil, *Reading the Fourth Gospel* (Bangalore: Claretion Publications, 2004), 89.

12 D. Moody Smith, *The Theology of the Gospel of John* (Cambridge: Cambridge University Press, 1995), 174.

> inextricably linked with Jesus, for he reveals himself in word and deed, all his work is interpreted "Christologically" by the evangelist.[13]

The function of Jesus which is endowed with revelatory overtone to reveal God the Father and his ontological being as the Son are inseparable, i.e., the function and the person of the Son is inseparable. Ethics is to be found in this aspect of John's theology which is Christology and that which is his soteriology too.[14] The purpose of the writing of the Gospel revolves around the person of Jesus.

A belief in the person of Jesus is of vital significance in the Johannine community. On the other end, understanding the person of who Jesus is also plays very crucial and significant role in determining one's belief. In turn, this belief determines one's whole perception about his/her ethical conduct. This chapter tries to bring out how ethics is reflected in the Christological articulations in John's gospel. One must be able to see the bits and pieces of John's artistry articulation where ethics cannot be adequately discussed without taking the broader context of Johannine Christology. Nevertheless, a note has to be taken not to vie to which of the Christological title is to be considered the central or the ultimate against other christological contours. The Christological titles of Jesus complement to one another and neither of them is exclusively complete in itself. The prerogative of God to give life eternal is transposed to the Son's authority. For instance, to bestow life eternal on the believers by the Son of Man in John 3:14, 15; 6:27 is also linked to the activity of the Messiah and the Son of God in John 20:31. John depicts a very high Christology and that Jesus' identity is central to the Gospel of John (20:30-31; 3:15-36).[15] The Johannine Christological perspective serves as the springboard to other theological aspects such as soteriology, ecclesiology and eschatology.[16] From the very beginning of the Gospel, Jesus is portrayed as the divine revelation of the Father who has come into the world to bring light and life. Jesus as the incarnation of the divine word (*logos*) is directly related to God. God comes alive to His creation through His Son, Jesus. Therefore, Jesus' identity remains no secret to the world though many failed to believe in him. Jesus is depicted to talk so much more than the other three Gospels about his identity and to say more Jesus is projected as God's equal in the Gospel according to John.

The Gospel is stamped by the Christological thrust and so is the ethical dimension of the Gospel so connected to it. Christology is so central to Johannine Gospel but the realization about the ethical significance embedded in Johannine

---

13 Rudolf Schnackenburg, *The Gospel According to St. John,* vol. 1, translated by Kevin Smyth (Kent: Burns & Oates, 1968), 155.

14 Birger Gerhardsson, *The Ethos of the Bible,* translated by Stephen Westerholm (Eugene, Oregon: Wipf & Stock Publishers, 1979), 95.

15 Carson, *The Gospel According to John,* 95.

16 Maniparampil, *Reading the Fourth Gospel,* 88.

Christological articulation has been silently buried. Johannine Christology is crucial for interpreting Johannine ethics because it is in Christology, that the ethical messages are implanted. The fundamental structure of ethics in the Gospel of John must, therefore, be approached from the right understanding of Christology. As a result, the present chapter is to unravel the range of Christological elements or perceptions that inform us about ethics in John's Gospel. Accordingly, we will focus our attention on four significant titles that have considerable importance and have stood out and impacted on the understanding of Johannine ethics. In John's Gospel, often the Christological terms seem to overlap or merge into each other. As for instance, "some of what is said of Jesus as 'Son' or as 'Son of God' applies to Jesus as 'Son of Man.'"[17] There are at times no explicit Christological terms used to ascribe to Jesus but are potentially and significantly implied without any such specific Christological title/s. As such, attention will be limited to Christological contours that have direct, or implied prominent, bearing on ethics in the Gospel of John.[18] The four christological titles (*Logos,* Christ, Son of God and Son of Man) may suffice for our present purpose of the research because they enjoy a certain primacy of importance when it comes to ethical significance in the Fourth Gospel.

4.2. Johannine Jesus in Relation to the Father

The Johannine Christological identity primarily needs to be understood in relation to the Father who does the sending of His only begotten Son. Jesus is therefore the key to understand God's saving purpose wrought through him to offer eternal life (Jn. 3:16). Jesus is the ultimate personal representative of God, the Father. Indeed Jesus is God himself (God's very own deity is revealed in the Son) for he was exactly saying and doing as God. He is the perfect image of what God is like.[19] Johannine Christology is the indispensable aspect of the Johannine Father- Son relationship (filial relationship). Jesus' statement of God as his Father implies his divine sonship and his consistent self-consciousness of God's fatherly concern for him and his mission. His consciousness of a relationship with God as his Father is virtually a unique one (*monogenes* Jn. 1:18).[20] The Gospel of John tells it all, by Jesus' insistence, that he neither said nor did anything on his own authority but everything according to the will of the Father from whom he proceeds (Jn. 12:49,

17 Christopher M. Tuckett, *Christology and the New Testament: Jesus and His Earlier Followers* (Edinburgh: University Press, 2001), 159.

18 A sketch presentation of Christological titles in the Gospel of John is as follow – The *Logos* (in the prologue), Messiah (with translation in 1:41;4:25), Christ (note Jesus Christ in 1:17; 17:3), The King, the Holy One of God, The Chosen One of God, The Son, The Son of God, Son of Man, Lamb of God, The Savior of the World, Lord, The Only begotten(1:14,18), The Only begotten Son of God (3:16,18), God (1:1,18; 20:28).

19 Drane, *Introducing the New Testament,* 72.

20 Jey J. Kanagaraj, *The Gospel of John: A Commentary* (Secunderabad: OM Books, 2005), 53-63.

50 cf. 4:34; 3:34). This means Jesus' sonship in John's Gospel projects a moral sense wherein the son Jesus replicates the thought and action of his Father (Jn. 5:19 f).[21] Jesus is the true bearer of God and henceforth whoever rejects him is rejecting the Father who sent him (Jn. 7:28-29). The Johannine Jesus is portrayed as one with a special relationship with God - he is the Son and God his Father and only through the Son do human get access to God (Jn. 14: 6; 6:37) and it is only in the Son Jesus that God the Father is truly made known because he personally embodies Him (God). Jesus is the only begotten Son [22] (Jn. 1:14-18). Jesus often refers to God as 'my Father' and God is the Father of Jesus (Jn. 2:16; 5:17, 43; 6:32). He enjoys special relationship with the Father. The Father is at work in His only begotten Son. The Father and the Son share such a closeness that the latter says and does everything in consonance with the Father's will. There is a mutual relationship between them. It also expresses an element of unity between them (Jn. 10:30 cf. 12:44-45; 14:9). Jesus said that whoever has seen him has seen the Father (Jn. 14:7, 9) implying the nuance of Jesus being the revealer. He is the ultimate revelation of God (Jn. 1:18) and on the other side of the truth, Jesus is the self-manifestation of God himself.

The unity between the Father and the Son is anchored on total obedience and dependence on the part of the Son to the Father (Jn. 5:19-20; 14:28). John 5:19-30 explicate well, the relation that exists between the Father God and the Son Jesus. Painter commented that the Son is neither subordinate in his being nor inferior to the being of the Father. Jesus in his obedience to the Father is his relation one of subordination to the Father and it is his very obedience that makes him the ultimate revealer.[23] This is to infer that the Son is subordinate to the Father in obedience. For John, says Tuckett, "Jesus' unity with God is shown precisely *in* dependence and subordination to God."[24] The dependence of the Son on the Father does not however imply the inferiority of the Son to the Father rather the identity of purpose between them. The absolute unity of the Father and the Son is as essential as the dependence of the Son on the Father.[25] The being of God the Father and the being of the Son Jesus are not identical but the Father cannot be fully known except in and through the Son Jesus. Though the Father and the Son are not identical, they are not entirely distinct either. The will and

---

21 C. K. Barrett, *The Gospel According to St. John: An Introduction with Commentary and Notes on the Greek Text*, 2nd edition (SPCK: London, 1978), 72. Cf. T. E. Pollard, *Johannine Christology and the Early Church* (Cambridge: Cambridge University Press, 1970), 17-18.

22 There are two variant readings - μονογενὴς θεός or μονογενὴς υἱός. The second reading (υἱός) is more in consonant with the Johannine usage (cf. 3:16; 1 Jn. 4:9). Barrett, *Gospel According to St. John*, 141.

23 John Painter, *John: Witness & Theologian* (Delhi: ISPCK, 1974), 139.

24 Tuckett, *Christology and the New Testament*, 162.

25 Donald Guthrie, *New Testament Theology* (Illinois: InterVarsity Press, 1981), 314.

purpose are identical though, because the Son does nothing beyond that which has not proceeded from the authority of the Father who sent him.

4.3. John's Christological Contours that Inform Ethics

We will limit our focus on selected Christological categories. This, however, is not to deny the importance of other Christological categories ascribed to Jesus, but for the purpose that informed essentially about the ethical significances. The four Christological categories that are considered prime important for understanding the ethical aspects of John's Gospel are – The *logos*, the Christ/Messiah, 'Son of God' and the 'Son of Man'. Significant comment needs to be mentioned before further deliberation of these four titles. Jesus in John's Gospel is featured with confidence about his origin (where he comes from) and destination (where he is going). He precisely knows well, who he is (being) and where and why he is for (purpose). Let us now see the four Christological categories one after the other and bring out their ethical significances implied in each of them.

4.3.1. Jesus the Logos

We begin with John's characteristic description of the *logos*- Christology which is placed at the beginning of his Gospel. The *logos* in John's prologue gives expression to the idea of revelation which permeates the rest of the Gospel.[26] The Gospel of John uses the absolute term *logos*[27] as a title to refer to Jesus who eternally pre-existed in the divine sphere (dwell with, and self-expression of God himself) and who equally incarnated to the sphere of the human (came to men and tabernacle with men) (Jn. 1:1 -14).[28] The *logos* is made known and portrayed by the historical figure in its full reality in the person of Jesus (Jn. 1:14)[29] who existed before creation implying that the *logos*-Jesus was not created.[30] John holds together the full divinity and the humanity of the *logos*–Son and chose *logos* to introduce the content of the Gospel of Jesus Christ, the Son of God.[31] The *logos*

26 Bultmann, *The Gospel of John*, 13, 32.

27 The term logos has been believed to be rooted in the Old Testament doctrine of the Word of God, '*debhar Yahweh*' which is thought to be powerful, creative, revealing, and accomplishing. And often the term *logos* bears the meaning of 'message' elsewhere in the New Testament (i.e., the message of the Gospel (Acts 8:25; 1 Thess. 1:6). Whereas in John's Gospel Jesus is the *logos* and therefore he himself is the message (cf. 1 Jn. 1:1). For elaborate understanding of the use of the term *logos* in John see Kanagaraj, *The Gospel of John*, 35-40.

28 Leon Morris, *The Gospel According to John* (Michigan: Wm. B. Eerdmans Publishing Company, 1971), 78; Kanagaraj, *The Gospel of John*, 34-35.

29 Barrett, *The Gospel According to St. John,* 2nd edition, 155; Dodd, *The Interpretation of the Fourth Gospel*, 295.

30 Morris, *The Gospel According to John*, 74, 77; Schnackenburg, *The Gospel According to St John*, vol. 1, 232.

31 Pollard, *Johannine Christology and the Early Church*, 6, 19; Also see similar idea in Dodd, *The Interpretation of the Fourth Gospel*, 285; Schnackenburg, *The Gospel According to St. John*,

is the Word of God and the self- manifestation of God himself (Jn. 1:1) which is dynamic in its function and nature.[32] God manifest himself in his very being and was personally embodied in the *logos* in the person of Jesus (Jn. 1:14). His message and dealings with humanity "was not just written in a book, it was displayed in the very person of God"[33] (Jn. 1:1, 14). This is to suggest that the *logos*-Son is the *logos*-God. The *logos* is creative, accomplishing, revealing, and the means of life through faith in whom humans may have life eternal. That is the immanence of John's *logos* has internal force following the believing and receiving of the *logos* by human beings by faith.[34] The prologue of the Gospel of John explicates threefold mediatorial activity of the *logos*- Son: In *creation* (Jn. 1: 3, 10 cf. Gen 1:3,6,9; Ps. 33:6); in *revelation* as the true light and the only Son who is in the bosom of the Father is the only ultimatum to make known the Father (Jn. 1:18); in *adoption* (salvation) to all who received him and believed in his name are given the power to become children of God (Jn. 1:12-13) and have life eternal.[35]

The personal character of the *logos* who is identified as the light and source of life is the typical Johannine idea (cf. Jn. 8:12; 9:5; 12:46).[36] The *logos* is manifested in the tangible earthly existence in the person of Jesus of Nazareth, who is the final and self expression of the divine being so physical eyes of human beings could perceived.[37] Jesus being the *logos*-Son is an expression of both the moral likeness and an essential identity with the Father.[38] He was with God the Father from the beginning and through him all things were made through him (Jn. 1:3). The *logos*- Son was the light who illuminates all lives lived in the darkness and was consequently the life of everyone who believed and received him for who he was (Jn. 1:5, 9, 12). There are good numbers of ideas in the prologue that are central in the body of the Gospel. Such as life, light (verse 4), witness (v. 7), true (v.9), world (v. 10), glory, truth (v. 14).[39] This implies that much of John's Christology is concentrated in the term *logos* which is used much in a Christological sense. Of

---

vol. 1, 221-224; Kanagaraj, *The Gospel of John,* 54; Dodd, *The Interpretation of the Fourth* Gospel, 296.

32 Cf. Barrett, *The Gospel According to St. John*, 73. Kanagaraj, *The Gospel of John*, 37, 39.

33 Drane, *Introducing the New Testament*, 72.

34 Kanagaraj, *The Gospel of John,* 41.

35 Pollard, *Johannine Christology and the Early Church*, 14-15; Jan A. Du Rand, "The Creation Motif in the Fourth Gospel: Perspectives on its Narratological Function Within a Judaistic Background," *Theology and Christology in the Fourth Gospel,* edited by G. Van Belle, J. G. Van Der Watt and P. Maritz (Leuven: Leuven University Press, 2005), 25

36 Morris, *The Gospel According to John*, 82; Schnackenburg, *The Gospel According to St. John*, vol. 1, 233.

37 Bultmann, *The Gospel of John,* 20; Morris, *The Gospel According to John*, 123; Kanagaraj,*The Gospel of John*, 41, 57-58.

38 Barrett, *The Gospel According to St. John*, 72; cf. Kanagaraj, *The Gospel of John*, 39.

39 Barrett, *The Gospel According to St. John*, 151; Kanagaraj, *The Gospel of John*, 33.

these central ideas – life, light, true, truth have essential ethical significances. Most significantly, Jesus being the *logos*-Son is the visual expression and manifestation of the moral likeness of the God with whom the logos eternally pre-existed. And the *logos*- Son being the light has come to illumine the world living in the darkness (to dispel darkness).[40] Light denotes good ethical behavior as against darkness which represents evil behavior (cf. Jn. 3:19; 8:12; 12:35, 46).[41] The *logos* who is timeless[42] has come in the world (of humankind and her affairs) as the light to show us the truth and give life (salvation).[43] The coming of the *logos*-Son brought along the moral responsibility of proving oneself to be part of God's family by accepting the *logos*-light and life in faith.[44] The *logos* as the light, life and truth contain in brief the substance of ethics of which John presents at the start of his Gospel which is the central purport of the Gospel. *Human* beings must therefore walk in the light and do good to substantiate their belief and acceptance of the *logos* as the light and source of life for the *logos* is God himself in truth (cf. Ps. 36:9). So, the ultimate goal of human beings search for ethical living lies in believing and receiving the *logos*-Son for he is the light and life of everyone who is the truth. The *logos* is the self-incarnation, revelation and manifestation of God and the exact moral representation of the Father who sent him.

4.3.2. Jesus the Christ

The title "Christ" the equivalent of the Hebrew 'Messiah' comes from a Greek term *Christos* meaning the anointed one. It was not a title Jesus used to refer to himself nor did he explicitly claim he was but on significant occasions people called Jesus 'the Christ' and he obviously accepted.[45] Jesus indeed was the Christ in whom is fulfilled the prophecies contained in the Old Testament. In the Old Testament, the idea of anointing a person for a specific post or mission had various applications though it was mainly of kings (1 Sam. 10:1; 12:5; 16:6; 2 Sam. 1:14; even to a heathen king, Cyrus (Isa. 45:1) and priests (Lev. 4:3), and also of prophets (1 Kg. 19:16), patriarchs (Ps. 105:15 cf. 1 Sam 24:6f; 26:9f).[46] Later, the concept of anointing came to indicate to a more technical sense of the

---

40 Morris, *The Gospel According to John*, 84.

41 Kanagaraj, *The Gospel of John*, 43.

42 Barrett, *The Gospel According to St. John*, 153. Cf. Morris, *The Gospel According to John*, 73; Schnackenburg, *The Gospel According to St John*, vol. 1, 232- 233.

43 Beasley-Murray, *WBC*: John vol. 36, 11; Kanagaraj, *The Gospel of John*, 45.

44 Schnackenburg, *The Gospel According to St. John*, vol. 1, 262; Kanagaraj, *The Gospel of John*, 41.

45 Perhaps the term 'Christ' is used so many times in the Gospel of John as compare to the synoptic gospel. Probably because by the time John's Gospel was written the Messiahship was so self-evident that Jesus could be well identified with the title 'Messiah/Christ' devoid of the need for further definition or qualification. See Drane, *Introducing the New Testament*, 66, 69.

46 Kanagaraj, *The Gospel of John*, 87.

one who, *par excellence,* is the chosen instrument of God who would have come to deliver his chosen people.[47]

Later, the meaning of the term underwent certain modifications in the intertestamental period, where the technical sense of the Lord's anointed one became even more central (Ps Sol.17-18).[48] The expectation of the coming messianic age was great. The hope of the coming deliverer that predominated was that of the Davidic king, who would set up an earthly kingdom for the people of Israel and lead them to victory. Richard N. Longenecker has pointed that the Semitic mind prefers to think of functions rather than person.[49] The dominant expectation of the people then was of a political agent with a religious bias. So, the concept of the term Christ (or basically the Messiah) carried a mixed connotation of both a nationalistic and spiritual hopes of the people of God.[50] There are dual Messianic hope in the Qumran literature, one of Aaron and another of Israel (1 QS 9:11). However, Messiah of Aaron took precedent over the latter for the possible reasons that the Qumran community was a priestly community.[51]

The Apocalypses of Ezra and Baruch (4 Ezra 12:32-34), both of which were contemporary with the emerging church seems to be linked with the Davidic son idea as in the intertestamental period. While there was a widespread understanding of the Messianic expectation, there however was no clear understanding with regard to the origin and character of the coming Messiah.[52] As a result, there was a tendency to visualize by different groups a Messiah who will fit their own tenets. For instance, the priestly groups like Qumran in priestly terms and nationalist groups in political terms. Considering the political scenario of the New Testament time, there is high probability that the popular expectation would heavily lean towards the hope of a political Messiah who would deliver the people (Jewish) from the oppressive Roman rule.[53]

---

47 Guthrie, *New Testament Theology*, 237.

48 Kanagaraj, *The Gospel of John*, 87.

49 Longenecker, *The Christology of Early Jewish Christianity*, 63 f; Drane, *Introducing the New Testament,* 69.

50 Guthrie, *New Testament Theology*, 237.

51 Guthrie, *New Testament Theology*, 237

52 Guthrie, *New Testament Theology*, 238.

53 Kanagaraj, *The Gospel of John*, 87; Drane, *Introducing the New Testament*, 69. The Gospels supply explicit information with regards to the present messianic expectations. For instance the first Gospel, Matthew reports that the Jewish counselors of King Herod were able to tell the whereabouts of the birthplace (Bethlehem) of the Messiah (Mt 2:3-5). Luke 3:15 recounts the populace confusion over whether John the Baptist was the expected Messiah. John's Gospel gives even more definite evidence concerning the Messianic expectation. It is recorded that John the Baptist emphatically denied that he was the expected Messiah (Jn. 1:20). The Samaritans also showed up a messianic expectation (Jn. 4:29ff) though were vague about the form that any restoration would take. John's account of the feeding of the multitude

In the Fourth Gospel, we read that the Jews send priests and Levites from Jerusalem to Bethany, beyond the Jordan, to John the Baptist to inquire who he is (Jn. 1:18-19). John's testimony that he is not the Christ and further reference to "the one who is coming after me" is the direct implication of the Messiahship of Jesus (Jn. 1:27 cf. 3:28). And he ends his testimony that this Jesus, who is the Christ, is ὁ υἱὸς τοῦ θεοῦ (Jn. 1:34). Following the scene in which John the Baptist declared Jesus as the ἀμνὸς τοῦ θεοῦ 'Lamb of God,' (Jn. 1:36) lead two disciples to follow Jesus. One of these is Andrew who said to his brother Simon Peter, "εὑρήκαμεν τὸν Μεσσίαν" (Jn. 1:41). These categories are juxtaposed as attributing to the one figure (i.e., Jesus).

The Gospel of John reports that in Jerusalem, there was a confusion regarding current Messianic expectation because of the tradition that the origin of the Messiah would be hidden, whereas, from where Jesus has come was no secret (Jn. 7:26ff). There was also a predominant belief that Messiah will perform σημεῖα as a proof to a Messianic office (Jn. 7:31 cf. Isa. 35:5; Matt. 11:5; Lk. 7:22). Therefore, 'signs' were expected with the coming of the expected Messiah.[54] Accordingly, there is a connection between 'signs' and the Messiah with its anticipated results in the belief in Jesus (Jn. 20:31). The significance of the σημεῖα in the Fourth Gospel is primarily to reveal the δόξα of Jesus and which eventually must lead to faith (Jn. 2:11 cf. 20:30-31). The full significance of the *signs* nonetheless is beneficial only to those who believe (cf. Jn. 6:26, 36; 11:40; 12:37). The central significance of Christology for ethics is that faith is established or grounded on the revelatory events ('σημεῖα') and sayings of Jesus. For the self-disclosure of Jesus reveals something of his divine dignity and power and always has an invitation or a call to decision making (to believe). Besides, a promise is assured to those who respond which is highly ethical (moral response). The purpose of the writing of the Gospel of John suggests that John employs the title 'Christ/Messiah' and qualified it by a further explanatory title 'Son of God.' Thus, the title designated to Jesus as Messiah is to lead others to πιστεῦω in him. And the *signs* he performed act as a means to incur the intended faith and reveal his glory.

The Gospel of John brings up two précised occasions, both in the early ministry to apply the title Christ/Messiah to Jesus.[55] It was in the case of the first disciples, on the lips of Andrew who tells his brother Peter, "We have found the Messiah." And immediately later Philip tells Nathanael, "We have found

---

links with the popular messianic expectation to make Jesus King and his escape from such a design results in the withdrawal of his many previous followers (Jn. 6:66).

54 Rengstorf, "σημεῖον," *TDNT*, vol.vii, edited by Gerhard Friedrich (Michigan: Wm. B. Eerdmans Publishing Company, 1971), 246.

55 The application of the title Messiah to Jesus first appeared in the lips of the first disciples and of the Samaritans. John also notes the confession of Martha, the sister of Lazarus (Jn. 11:27) where messiahship is linked with the 'Son of God' title (cf. 1:49; 20:31).

him about whom Moses in the law and also the prophets wrote..." (Jn. 1:45). It signifies that in Jesus is fulfilled the prophecies of the Old Testament. This further indicates that among the early disciples there was a Messianic understanding against the backdrop of the Old Testament. John at the same time preserves both the Aramaic and gives the Greek translation (Jn. 1:41; 4:25).[56] In contrast to the current speculations about the messianic expectation John's Gospel impress upon the readers that Jesus is the expected Messiah "in a new spiritual sense which is unintelligible apart from the filial consciousness of Jesus."[57] Jesus as a Messiah is bound to humility and obscurity as he is necessitated in the end to suffer on the Cross (as the Lamb of God) for the forgiveness of the sins of the world (Jn. 1:34-35).[58]

The Messiahship of Jesus in John is both hidden and revealed (cf. Jn. 1:41, 45, 49; 10:24; 12:24, 27, 39). It is hidden from the unbelieving and is revealed to the eyes of faith.[59] The Messiah remains forever, making his abiding place with those who believe and receive him. With them he does abide forever. This is the beauty of John's presentation of the Messiah. While God revealed himself in the person of his Son, there is much ethical obligation on the part of an individual to perceive and believe in Jesus as the anointed one. Nevertheless, the affirmation that Jesus was identified as the Messiah is appropriated only after his resurrection and "exalted to heaven, and that he would come again as the Son of Man on the clouds of heaven."[60] Jesus in his person (being) and functions fulfill the long awaited and expected messianic hopes of the people, though not of the political aspirations of the people.

John's Gospel attested that Jesus is the anointed One who is expected to come and has come to make his dwelling amongst us (Jn. 1:14). Jesus serves as God's anointed through whom God intervenes and breaks through into the present for the divine salvific purpose. It is rightly posited that the "messiah is a preexistent, transcendent figure, whom the Most high has been keeping for many years."[61] The Messianic office of Jesus was then a combination of his Messianic acts (ministry) and Messianic death (exaltation on the cross).[62] Messiah is a prophetic category bounded with the line of David and the expectation of the prophets which also connotes the profoundly revelatory work of God's promised

---

56 Kanagaraj, *The Gospel of John*, 87.

57 Guthrie, *New Testament Theology*, 245.

58 Barrett, *The Gospel According to St. John*, 146 – 47.

59 Barrett, *The Gospel According to St. John*, 61.

60 Adela Yarbro Collins and John J. Collins, *King and Messiah as Son of God: Divine, Human, and Angelic Messianic Figures in Biblical and Related Literature* (Michigan: Wm. B. Eerdmans Publishing Company, 2008), 207.

61 Collins and John J. Collins, *King and Messiah as Son of God*, 97.

62 Guthrie, *New Testament Theology*, 251.

servant.[63] Thus, the messianic presentation of Jesus in the Gospel of John plays an important role in determining the gateway to one's destiny (Jn. 20:31).

4.3.3. Jesus the Son of God (or simply the Son)

Reflection or consciousness about Jesus as the 'Son of God' has taken ground since the early times of Christianity. And this understanding has in fact affected the approach of every believer now and then. In the Old Testament, the consciousness of divine Sonship is applied in a number of ways. To briefly sketch the occurrences we begin with the angelic and heavenly beings described as sons of God (Gen. 6:1-4; Job 1:6; 2:1; Ps. 29:1). Israelites collectively are called sons of God (Deut. 14:1-2; Jer. 3:19-20; Hos. 1:10; Eccls. 4:10). Hosea 11:1 records, 'out of Egypt I called my son' implying a corporate (the whole nation of Israel) father-son relationship that which was true of the people individually. The idea of sonship then was also applied to the theocratic king. For example, a promise to David's son (Solomon) that God will be his father and David's son will be God's son (2 Sam. 7:14; Ps.2:7).[64]

In the intertestamental period, the references to divine sonship are admittedly slight. The only use in the early apocalyptic Judaism comes in Enoch 105:2 which reads "and my son will be united with them forever."[65] And in the later Apocalypse of Ezra there is an identification of a Messiah as the Son of God (7:28f; 13:32, 37, 52; 14:9).[66] It is also worth giving a consideration to the evidence from the Qumran literature though even here the references are slight. In 4Q *Florilegium,* The text of 2 Samuel 7:14 is applied to David's branch.[67] It can be assumed that 'Son of God' as a title was taking ground to be thought of as having a Messianic sense.

The passage that has more references about Jesus as the 'Son of God' or simply Son is John 5: 17 ff. This categorical title 'Son of God' is often attached to Jesus as having been sent by the Father. The title reveals the Father-Son (parent-child) unique and intimate relationship (Jn. 15:23; 10:30).[68] He is God's Son and ultimately he is the Father's unique, ultimate, historical and eschatological

---

63 Carson, *The Gospel According to John*, 96; Drane, *Introducing the New Testament,* 68-69.

64 Kanagaraj, *The Gospel of John*, 83-84; Drane, *Introducing the New Testament,* 70.

65 There is however a doubt about the pre-Christian date of this passage because it does not occur in the Greek version in the Sixth-century Chester Beatty papyrus.

66 This Apocalypse of Ezra of apocalyptic Judaism is dated late in the first century and so it is often spoken as having less contribution to the understanding of the use of the title in Judaism in the time of Jesus and the then emergent Christian church. See Guthrie, *New Testament Theology*, 302.

67 Guthrie, *New Testament Theology*, 303.

68 Kanagaraj, *The Gospel of John*, 83.

revelation to the world.[69] The concept of Jesus as 'Son of God' dominates the other Christological titles in John's Gospel. Specifically and probably because the purpose of the Gospel of John is to lead readers to believe that Jesus is the 'Son of God' (Jn. 20:31). The title signifies that Jesus is the one sent and authorized by the Father God indicating the sovereign authority.

The origin of the term 'Son of God' can be looked within the Jewish circle and so the phrase is not foreign to Palestinian Judaism.[70] The title 'Son of God' connotes a Messianic tone in the early Christian usage[71] and thereby has its royal origin and a Messianic term.[72] Nathanael's confession of Jesus as the 'Son of God', the king of Israel (Jn. 1:49) tells it plain that the term 'Son of God' (or simply Son) primarily expresses a royal designation. Both these terms (Son of God and Messiah) are virtually related by virtue of the fact that both refer to Jesus' identity and function (Jn. 11:27; 20:31). The title 'Son of God' has its roots in Jewish messianic traditions and the language of 'sending' is rooted in prophetic traditions of the Old Testament. So, Jesus is portrayed as a true prophet figure.[73] But, in John, the 'sending' aspect has a higher significance because of its filial relation to the Father who does the sending of the Son (Jn. 2:16; 5:17, 43; 6:32, etc.). Jesus' filial consciousness is more clearly expressed in the Fourth Gospel. The Son comes from the Father and says and does exactly as the saying and doing of the Father (Jn. 5:27, 30 cf. 6: 38, 40).

There are striking characteristics of Jesus as the 'Son of God.' Let us here make a brief run through the striking characteristics of Jesus in relation to the Father. They are outlined as follows - the Son is sent by the Father (Jn. 3:34; 5:36, 38; 7:29; 11:42), Father's love for the Son which leads him to show everything he does (Jn. 5:20; 3:35 cf. 10:17), Son's dependence on the Father (Jn. 5:19, 30 cf. 14:31; 15:10), the absolute unity of the Son and the Father in purpose (Jn. 10:30; 17:11 cf. 14:11,20; 5:19ff) and Jesus as the unique Son is the ultimate revelation of the Father (Jn. 6:46; 8:19; 14:8,9); the Son returns to the Father (Jn. 14:12, 28; 16:28 cf. 16:16 f.).[74]

---

69 Daniel Rathnakara Sadananda, *The Johannine Exegesis of God: An Exploration into the Johannine Understanding of God* (Berlin, New York: Walter de Gruyter, 2004), 45.

70 Martin Hengel, *The Son of God* (London: np, 1976), 45; Drane, *Introducing the New Testament*, 70.

71 John Ashton, *Understanding the Fourth Gospel*, 2nd edition (Oxford: University Press, 2007), 166.

72 Tuckett, *Christology and the New Testament*, 160.

73 Tuckett, *Christology and the New Testament*, 161.

74 Rudolf Schnackenburg, *The Gospel According to St John,* vol. 2, translated by Cecily, Hastings, Francis McDonagh, David Smith & Richard Foley (London: Burns & Oates, 1980), 173-177.

4.3.3.1. Son of God in Relation to Sonship

The uniqueness of Jesus as 'Son of God' is distinctive of John' Gospel. The divine sonship of Jesus (i.e., the divine Father-Son relationship) is stressed more strongly in the Gospel of John.[75] There are four instances where Jesus is described as the *monogenes* son[76] (Jn. 1:14, 18; 3:16, 18). Jesus as the Son is unique in a sense that he is the sole reflection of the love and life- giving power of God. This precisely may mean that Jesus shared the actual characteristics, nature and prerogatives of God.[77] It is reasonable to allude that the adjective *monogenes* especially in John 1:14 qualifies Jesus as a unique and special kind of sonship.[78] This concept of the unique kind of sonship is supported by the clear statement of the risen Christ in John 20:17, "my father and your father.'[79] Jesus as the 'Son of God' is the ultimate revelation of the divine God. No one but Jesus the Son alone (Jn. 1:14, 18) gives the concrete expression of the divine taking the form of a human. The Son expounds to the full the extent of the Father's grace and truth.[80] Jesus offers the true knowledge of God the Father. He is the special and ultimate revelation of the God of all ages.

The close connection between the Son and the Father is unmistakable. This is in accord with the statement of his words saying that he comes to do the will of his Father (Jn. 6:38). The Father-Son relationship permeates the content of the Gospel of John than any other three Gospels (Synoptics). There are widespread occurrences of the Father-Son relationship in the speech of Jesus throughout his public ministry. Father's love for the Son which leads him to show everything he does (Jn. 5:20; 3:35 cf. 10:17), so that whatever is done by Jesus as Son is in effect, the ἐργον τοῦ θεου/.[81] In short, the works of Jesus are the works of God. There is complete harmony between the Son and the Father in purpose (Jn. 10:30; 17:11 cf. 14:11, 20; 5:19f.).

The 'Son of God' who incarnates as Jesus of Nazareth inhabited eternity with the Father. And this notion is qualified by the thought of a fundamentally moral relationship between the Father and the Son. The Father-Son relationship works out in their sharing the role of life-giving and judgment, and also in their

---

75 Pollard, *Johannine Christology and the Early Church*, 16.

76 Of course there are varying opinions to the translation of the adjective *monogenes*. See Raymond E. Brown, *The Gospel According to John*, vol. 1 (New York: Doubleday, 1966), 66.

77 Drane, *Introducing the New Testament*, 72.

78 Kanagaraj, *The Gospel of John*, 57.

79 Guthrie makes a point clear that the distinction Jesus made is significant because it rules out the view that Jesus' Sonship was of the same kind as man's, but developed to a greater intensity. He further asserts that others may be given power to become sons of God (Jn. 1:12) but Jesus has no need for this since he is Son of a different kind i.e., he is essentially a son. Guthrie, *New Testament Theology*, 313.

80 Kanagaraj, *The Gospel of John*, 57.

81 Rengstorf, "σημεῖον," 246.

sharing the honor (Jn. 5:21-23), which however is put in the context of the Son's dependence and obedience to the will of the Father.[82] Both moral likeness and essential identity are clubbed in John. For instance, the Son does nothing by himself but reproduces the Father's actions and words (Jn. 5:19f.). The Son in its ultimate completeness reveals the Father's character so that to see Jesus is to see the Father (Jn. 14:9).[83] This consciousness of sonship is expressed in his words and in his acts. The moral likeness of the son to the father is of primary importance to the Jewish mind because a true son is one who reproduces the thought and actions of the father (Jn. 5:19f cf. 8:39b f).[84] This is one dominant feature in Johannine Christology when compared to the other three Gospels. Jesus as the Son replicates the thought and action of the Father (Jn. 10:18; 12:49 f.; 15:15 cf. 14:24) and even more (the nature of his Father-God (Jn. 8:19; 14:9). This entails that the moral world of God is made manifested in the life and ministry of Jesus, who has been sent, to let the world know the truth. And the truth will set the world free (Jn. 8:32) for the truth will transform the immoral human world of darkness to the moral world of the good and the light.

4.3.3.2. Son of God in Relation to Mission

The Fourth Gospel is very unique in its presentation about Jesus as the One who is sent (Jn. 7:27-29). The notion underlying the sending motif is the aspect of mission in the Gospel of John. Jesus as the 'Son of God' is conscious of himself been sent by, and from, God the Father. He has come on a mission to accomplish the salvific task assigned by his Father. In John 8:28, Jesus makes a statement that he can do nothing on his own authority but to say and act on the authority of the Father. This is a strong implication that the mission of the Son and the Father is one. On the other side of the coin, a theme of revelation plays an essential role as part and partial of the mission of God.

What is this revelation we are talking about? It is a revelation concerning the unique filial relationship between Father (God) and Son (Jesus).[85] There is no doubt that Jesus was conscious of this fact of the relation between him and the Father. Jesus was conscious that he has been sent to carry out the will of the Father and thereby fulfilled the obligation (Jn. 4:34; 6:38; 17:4; 19:30). His suffering and dying on the cross serves as the crowing climax and conclusion of the entrusted mission[86] fulfilling in obedience to the will of the Father (Jn. 17:4). That is why Jesus' outcry in the passion narrative of the Fourth Gospel was not an emotional cry but a cognizant affirmation of fulfillment and triumph (Jn. 19:30

82 Sadananda, *The Johannine Exegesis of God*, 48.

83 Barrett, *The Gospel According to St. John*, 60.

84 Pollard, *The Johannine Christology and the Early* Church, 17; Edwyn Clement Hoskyns, *The Fourth Gospel* (SPCK: London, 1956), 92.

85 Kanagaraj, *The Gospel of John*, 83.

86 Sadananda, *The Johannine Exegesis of God*, 38.

"it is finished"). The mission victory heralding in perfecting the Father's will in obedience[87] which finds its expression that he had come to accomplish and has thereby accomplished it (Jn. 17:4 cf. 19:30). In John 8:54, the Father glorifies the Son and it can be seen connected with the climax of the mission which is the exaltation of the Son on the cross. Thus, the consummation of the mission is the exaltation of the Son.

The sending of the Son to the world to save the world by the Father is the central affirmation of the Gospel of John.[88] The 'sending' is equivalent to the 'mission' and this sending or mission of Jesus into the world not only determines the Johannine Christology but also an aspect of "an ethical category."[89] It is attention-grabbing that the Gospel presents the 'sending' in the more general 'world.' The Father sent the Son and the Son in turn sends his disciples into the world (Jn. 3:16-17; 17:18; 20:21).[90] This sending motif in the Gospel is paradigmatic. There is a mutual coordination between the Father-Son and the disciples in working out the mission aspect of the Father. The Gospel advocates that the disciples are *not* to renounce nor leave the world but engage themselves embracing the inhabitants of the literal world (Jn. 3:16, 17; 4:42; 6:33, 51; 17: 15, 21). The central motif behind this sending is to grant eternal life to those who may believe in Jesus who is the Son of the Father God (esp. Jn. 3:16; 17:21; 20:31b).

4.3.3.3. Son of God in Relation to an Agent

The basic Jewish understanding of agency is that an agent is akin to the one who did send him.[91] So also "agency" plays a significant role in the portrayal of Jesus in the Gospel of John. Jesus is sent who is one with the sender (Jn. 10:36-38; 17:20-23). Jesus acts as an agent or emissary, mouthpiece of God and even more to this is that Jesus as the 'Son of God' is God's very own deity (Jn. 12: 44, 45; 14:7, 9-10). The miracles are the evidence that Jesus is in the Father and the Father is in Jesus. The Father and Son are one (Jn. 10:30). Jesus as the 'Son of God' is God's unique agent with a mission.[92] Richard Bauckham rightly commented that.

---

87 M. M Thompson, *The Humanity of Jesus in the Fourth Gospel* (Philadelphia: Fortress Press, 1988), 109.

88 Frank J. Matera, *New Testament Ethics: The Legacies of Jesus and Paul* (Louisville, Kentucky: Westminster John Knox Press, 1996), 97.

89 Willi Marxsen, *New Testament Foundations for Christian* Ethics, translated by Jr. O. C. Dean (Minneapolis: Fortress Press, 1993), 291.

90 A. J. Kostenberger, *The Missions of Jesus and the Disciples According to the Fourth Gospel* (Michigan: Wm. B. Eerdmans Publishing Company, 1998), 190-198.

91 Peder Borgen, "God's Agent in the Fourth Gospel," *The Interpretation of John*, 2nd edition, edited by John Ashton (Edinburgh: T&T Clark, 1997), 84; James F. McGrath, *John's Apologetic Christology: Legitimation and Development in Johannine Christology* (Cambridge: Cambridge University Press, 2001), 89.

92 Sadananda, *The Johannine Exegesis of God,* 43.

> It is not sufficient to suppose that God sends *some one else* to act as his agent in salvation. What this agent does is not something that God can delegate to someone other than God, since it belongs to the uniquely divine prerogatives of the one God. Only one who truly shares the unique divine identity can give eternal life and reveal God's glory in the world.[93]

So, the Gospel of John portrays Jesus as the 'Son of God' and who himself is truly God in the fullest sense, passes or reveals the truth about Him (God). He is the sole agent for revealing and a pathway to the Father (Jn. 14:6). The Son in his very existence discloses the perfect image of what God the Father is like. By being the person of God the Son[94] and by being in the world (Jn. 1:14), the Son Jesus who is the Christ reveals the Father to the world. Jesus as the Son is the fully authorized agent of God, the Father (Jn. 3:27-30; 31-36 cf. 5:19-23). He has the full powers to act for God and at the same time stands in for God because he is equal to God as is evident in the Gospel (Jn. 5:17-30). He stands in the place of God before us. Jesus is truly the agent of God to reveal the truth and who saves the inhabitants of this planet earth to grant us eternal life. God did his part and humans have to do their part – πιστεύειν εἰς' Ιησοῦν – the most ethical decisive moment to either remain in the dark or transit from darkness characterized by devil (Jn. 3:19-20) into light. For John, light is a moral good or quality that illumines people and bestows life eternal (Jn. 1:4–5, 9).[95]

4.3.4. Jesus the Son of Man

The title 'Son of Man' is a literal expression of the Greek ὁ υἱος τοῦ ἀνθπώποῦ which occurs 70 times in the Gospels referring to Jesus[96] and the expression is absolutely a Semitism. The expression is a generic term which corresponds to Hebrew כנ ארמ (e.g. Ps. 8:5) or Aramaic כר אנש (Dan. 7:13) both of which simply means "human being" or "someone."[97] However in the Gospels, the expression

93 Richard Bauckham,"Monotheism and Christology in the Gospel of John," *Contours of Christology in the New Testament*, edited by Richard N. Longenecker (Michigan: Wm. B. Eerdmans Publishing Company, 2005), 159.

94 Maniparampil¸ *Reading the Fourth Gospel*, 90.

95 Cornelis Bennema, "Moral Transformation in the Johannine Writings." *In die Skriflig* 51/3 (2017): 2.

96 Adela Yarbro Collins, "The Origin of the Designation of Jesus as 'Son of Man,'" *HTR* 80 (1987): 396. Reprinted in idem, *Cosmology and Eschatology in Jewish and Christian Apocalypticism* (Leiden: Brill, 2000), 145.

97 Collins and John J. Collins, *King and Messiah as Son of God*, 75; Dodd, *The Interpretation of the Fourth Gospel*, 241-249; Drane, *Introducing the New Testament*, 64 - 65. The epithet 'Son of Man,' in the Hebrew Bible (Jewish religious tradition), is typically employed in two ways. Firstly, it simply means human beings as distinct from God emphasizing the weakness and poverty of ordinary mortals in contrast to the greateness of God (Nums.23:19; Job 25:6; Psalm 8:4; 146:3; Isaiah 51:12). At times prophets were summoned as 'son of man' by God; this

takes a different stance referring to a specific individual (not a collective symbol[98] or simply say a generic terminology) several of which envisions the 'Son of Man' coming on the clouds of heaven (as in the Synoptic (Mk. 13:26 cf. Lk. 22:69)[99] and in the Fourth Gospel presents the ascent - descent motif.

The figure of the 'Son of Man' is originally at home in apocalyptic thought (cf. Dan. 7:13 which describes "one like a son of man" coming with the clouds of heaven. It came to be used as a Messianic title in the first century C.E. (Enoch 37-71; 4 Ezra 12:32, 34).[100] So the prime evidence for the apocalyptic title 'Son of Man' tradition in ancient Judaism is found in the *Similitudes of Enoch and Ezra*.[101] In the Gospels, the title 'Son of Man' is identified and exclusively used by Jesus himself and in addition the term is used more often than any other to describe to Jesus to his person and work.[102] There are three common aspects of the 'Son of Man' title that the Gospel of John and the Synoptic Gospels shared. Firstly, it is an exclusive term used by Jesus to designate himself. Secondly, the 'Son of Man' is the apocalyptic term who undergoes suffering according to the Scripture (Jn. 3:13; 12:24, 32-34 cf. Mk. 8:31 par) and thirdly, the 'Son of Man' is the eschatological judge (Jn. 5:26-27 cf. Matt. 25:31-46).[103] The Gospel of John however has a unique portrayal of the characteristics of the 'Son of Man'[104]

---

however was to highlight the difference between them and the ultimate source of their message (Eze. 2:1; Dan. 8:17). The term in another sense is used to describe the supernatural figure sent from God having dominion and glory over all the people (Dan. 7 cf. 1 Enoch 37-71).

98 T. W. Manson, "The Son of Man in Daniel, Enoch and the Gospels,' *Bulletin of the John Rylands Library* 32 (1950): 171-193.

99 Collins and John J. Collins, *King and Messiah as Son of God*, 75; Drane, *Introducing the New Testament*, 66.

100 Jey J. Kanagaraj and Ian S. Kem, *Gospel of John* (Bangalore: Asia Theological Association, 2000), 70.

101 Collins and John J. Collins, *King and Messiah as Son of God*, 79, 86-94. In the ancient Judaism the title 'Son of Man' which is found in an apocalypse of 4 Ezra (written sometime at the end of the first century) contains three dialogues and four visions. Of course 4 *Ezra* does not employ the title 'Son of Man' nonetheless it is clearly adapting and reworking the Danielic 'Son of Man' vision. And the other most important and extensive depiction of a figure called 'Son of Man' in a Jewish text apart from Daniel 7 is the *Similitudes* (the *Similitudes* contains three parables) *of* 1 *Enoch* 37-71 (its date and Jewish origin is doubted because this section of 1 *Enoch* is not attested in the Dead Sea Scrolls. Early or middle first century C.E. is plausible though not conclusive about when it was written).

102 Drane, *Introducing the New Testament*, 65. There is only one incident where others used the term 'Son of Man' concerning Jesus. It was his listeners are requesting clarification of his own use of it (Jn. 12:34); and only once outside the gospels in Acts 7:56.

103 Kanagaraj and Ian S. Kem, *Gospel of John*, 70.

104 The 'Son of Man' is the pre-existent being with God. He originally belongs to the heavenly realm and incarnated in human form. That means the 'Son of Man' existed with God in heaven before his incarnation. The 'Son of Man' is the link between heaven and earth, i.e., he is the contact point between God, the ultimate Truth and the seekers of truth.

and the title is an enigmatic way of referring to himself (Jesus) that his hearers often time do not understand.[105]

The Passages where the Christological title 'Son of Man' is recorded in John's Gospel are as follows: (1) the angels ascending and descending upon the 'Son of Man' (1:51). (2) Jesus teaches Nicodemus in which the ascent and descent and the lifting up of the 'Son of Man' are retold (3:13-14). (3) 'Son of Man' has the authority to execute Judgment (5:27). (4) Discourse on the bread of life (6:27, 32, 38). (5) Eating the flesh and drinking the blood of the 'Son of Man' (6:53, 54, 62). (6) Jesus' dialogue with the Jews concerning the lifting up of the 'Son of Man' (8:28). (7) Question to the healed blind man "Do you believe in the 'Son of Man'?" (9:35). (8) Encounter of Jesus with the Greeks (12: 23, 34). (9) Jesus with his disciples at the upper room: the time has come for the 'Son of Man' to be glorified (13:31). Having mentioned the occurrences of the 'Son of Man' title it is worth mentioning the characteristics of the 'Son of Man' in John's Gospel which can be grouped under three different headings. (i) *The origin and destiny of the Son of Man* (1:51; 3:13 and corresponding idea (of a connection between his suffering and the celebration of the Eucharist (6:53) in 6:62 cf. 1:14; 2:11; 5:41; 7:18; 8:50; 11:4; 12:41; 17:1f, 22,24). In here the pre-existence of the 'Son of Man' and also the glorification of the 'Son of Man' are echoed (12:23; 13: 31). (ii) Essential facet of the *authority of the Son of Man* (6:27) to bestow life eternal and also judgment (5:26). (iii) Statements forecasting the *lifting up* (ὑψόω) *of the Son of Man* referring to the suffering (in the crucifixion 3:14; 8:28; 12:32-34) as well as to the glory and exaltation (12:23; 13:31).[106]

John 1:51 is the first passage that records the first logion on the 'Son of Man' which speaks of the angels of God ascending and descending upon the 'Son of Man.' It is the most distinctive 'Son of Man' saying alluded to Old Testament Jacob's ladder (Gen. 28:12).[107] Jesus as the 'Son of Man' is *the* only link between heaven and earth (1:51; 3:11-13 cf. 14:6), the only one true mediator.[108] Through his sojourn on earth, the 'Son of Man' bestows upon human kind the revealed knowledge and life eternal. This function of the 'Son of Man' is in consistent with his death, since his death according to John's Gospel represents at once his plunge into the depths of humanity and his ascent to the glory of the Father and is congruent with his eschatological functions.[109] The Johannine 'Son of Man' is elaborated as the link between heaven and earth in the crucifixion which is indeed exaltation, "that crucifixion is ascent to heaven, and that when Jesus is

105 Bauckham, "Monotheism and Christology in the Gospel of John," 156.

106 Drane, *Introducing the New Testament*, 67.

107 Kanagaraj, *The Gospel of John*, 93; Smith, *The Theology of the Gospel of John*, 175. The ascent-descent motif of the Son of Man is the hallmark of John's Gospel (also cf. Phipp. 2:5-11).

108 Craig S. Keener, *The Gospel of John: A Commentary*, vol. 1 (Peabody, Massachusetts: Hendrickson Publishers, 2003), 489.

109 Barrett, *The Gospel According to St. John*, 61.

lifted up he will draw all people to himself. The crucifixion of the 'Son of Man' is also a revelatory event (Jn. 8:28).[110] Jesus is the connecting link between the material world of human and spiritual world of God.[111] These first words of revelation on the 'Son of Man' are then followed by others which develop the Son of Man's theology.[112] It is significant to note that, apart from its allusion to Jacob's ladder there is also an expectation of the Son's pre-existence (Jn. 6:62), though enigmatic.[113]

The designation 'Son of Man' is the one who dispenses judgment at the eschatological age and also at present. He is the Judge, endowed with the power to exercise judgment (Jn. 5:27 cf. 9:39). Martyn has contended that "in some respects, John 5:27 appears to be the most "traditional Son of Man saying in the whole of the New Testament."[114] At the heart of the 'Son of Man' Christology is the most striking feature of the term – ascent-descent motif. This motif eventually is the key to his identity and also the primary content of his exclusively self-knowledge which distinguishes him from the men of this world (Jn.7: 27 contrast 28-29, 37-52; cf. 8:14; 9:29; 19:9).[115] The Gospel pictures Jesus as the 'Son of Man' having the heavenly abode and has come to earth (descent motif) and is destined to return where he belonged (ascent motif). The 'Son of Man' incarnated as a human not only to deliver the heavenly knowledge to human beings but also to reveal God's truth and glory that is the reality of God. In the descent of the 'Son of Man,' humans are able to see and experience God. He is the truest revealer of the heavenly truth concerning the Father and thereby the locus of revelation.[116] The Son is the only intelligible presence of God on earth. He is "the place of God's presence and action; God's eschatological action is realized in him."[117] The 'Son of Man' is an intermediary who connects the way for human to God[118] and believing in the 'Son of Man' subsequently results in eternal life (Jn. 6:35-58).

Jesus as the 'Son of Man' serves as the warrant for the impenetrable revelation. He is the revelation of God's glory on earth in and through whom the real communion and communication of God and human beings is made

---

110 Collins and John J. Collins, *King and Messiah as Son of God*, 211.

111 Kanagaraj, *The Gospel of John*, 93.

112 Schnackenburg, *The Gospel According to St, John*, vol. 1, 322.

113 Guthrie, *New Testament Theology*, 282.

114 J. Louis Martyn, *History and Theology in the Fourth Gospel*, 3rd edition (Louisville, London: Westminster John Knox Press, 2003), 133.

115 Wayne A. Meeks, "The Man from Heaven in Johannine Sectarianism," *The Interpretation of John,* 2nd edition, edited by John Ashton (Edinburgh: T&T Clark, 1997), 184.

116 Craig S. Keener, *The Gospel of John: A Commentary,* vol. 2 (Peabody, Massachusetts: Hendrickson Publishers, 2003), 1014.

117 Schnakencburg, *The Gospel According to St. John*, vol. 1, 522.

118 Kanagaraj and Ian S. Kemp, *The Gospel According to John*, 136-137.

possible.[119] Only he can reveal the heavenly truth because he descended from heaven – and no one but he alone has ascended.[120] This motif of descent-ascent works together. One motif (ascent-return to the Father) "cannot be completely detached," says Ashton, from the other motif (descent – coming into the world) (13:13).[121] Jesus the 'Son of Man' comes from heaven above (Jn. 3:13) signifies the heavenly moral world of God. Heaven above is where he belongs (Jn. 6:62) implying its place of origin. Heaven serves a proper locale for the figure 'Son of Man.'[122] The identity of Jesus as the 'Son of Man' then is bound up with the pattern of his coming into the world from heaven and going back there through his exaltation (crucifixion). All in all, the title 'Son of Man' embodies the aspect of Jesus' heavenly status of origin and destiny[123] which eventually demonstrates his unique relationship with the Father.[124]

'Son of Man' language in the Gospel is much closely linked with soteriological aspect, the functionary aspect. Important occurrences of the term 'Son of Man' seem to be dominated by the exaltation and glorification concepts (as for instance Jn. 3:14; 8:28; 12:23, 34; 13:31). The Johannine 'Son of Man' Christology portrays some of the very profound aspects on the role and person of Jesus. The Greek verb ὑψόω signifies double meaning. One is 'to be lifted up on the Cross' and the other 'to exalt in glory.'[125] This suggests that the death of Jesus is one of John's central features in projecting the 'Son of Man' doctrine and at the same time the death of Jesus is his glory. Thus, the Gospel of John typically presents the 'Son of Man' in combination of the themes of suffering and of glory (12:23; 13:31).[126] So, the true meaning of glory, according to John, precisely lies in the sufferings of the 'son of Man.'

The Christological title 'Son of Man' points us to Christ's conception of himself as of heavenly origin and as the true revealer of heavenly glory. And at the one and same time the title indicates his lowliness and sufferings for humankind.[127] Congruently, John typically presents the 'Son of Man' being 'lifted up' in death, glorified through death through whom life eternal is made available to whoever believes in him. So the 'Son of Man' in John is both a mediator in that he is a redeemer of human beings and also a mediator in an ontological sense, since

119 Kanagaraj and Ian S. Kemp, *The Gospel According to John*, 72.

120 Meeks, "The Man from Heaven in Johannine Sectarianism," 176.

121 Ashton, *Understanding the Fourth Gospel*, 244.

122 Martin, *History and Theology in the Fourth Gospel*, 132.

123 Ashton, *Understanding the Fourth Gospel*, 243.

124 Meeks, "The Man from Heaven in Johannine Sectarianism," 183.

125 Barrett, *The Gospel According to St. John*, 61.

126 Keener, *The Gospel of John*, vol. 1, 304.

127 Morris, *The Gospel According to John*, 173.

he is related both to God and to human beings.[128] We can wrap up saying that the Johannine 'Son of Man' Christology "is essentially an exalted, glorified and authoritative figure."[129] "Nowhere is Jesus' glory more splendid than in the Fourth Gospel. …And nowhere else does the Son of Man, clothed with all power, descend more deeply, realistically, and scandalously into human flesh (cf. 6:27, 53)."[130] The 'Son of Man' in John's Gospel is identified as the heavenly figure loaded with the prerogatives of God who descended from above to the world below. The 'Son of Man' is equally identified with the *logos*, the Christ and the 'Son of God' too.

4.4. Jesus the Determinative Reason for Ethics

Johannine ethics is Christologically motivated. John stresses the importance of ethical notions in the present more than in the future. John does not supplant the future with the present requisition but that it emphasizes the present reality because the present decision determines one's future. In the words of Hays:

> Both the warrants and norms for ethics are to be located almost exclusively in conformity to the person of Jesus. Future rewards and punishments play a minimal; role in motivating ethical conduct; the thing that matters is living in the present in a way that authentically manifests the love of God in Christ. The specific behavior that issues from union with Jesus need not be spelled out in detail, for those who abide in Jesus will intuitively know what is right and do it[131] and be fruitful (cf. 1 Jn. 3:9).

Johannine Christology has a relational aspect/dimension which subsequently affects the ethics of John in functional dimension. So, the functional dimension is built upon the relational dimension, which means that Johannine ethics is built upon Johannine Christology. This is to endorse that Christology functions as a determinative reason for the understanding of ethics in John's Gospel. Christology paves way for the dynamics of ethical living. Christology gives direction to the shape of Johannine community's ethics. To quote Willi Merxsen who said, "the quest for John's ethic proves to be a quest for his Christology'[132] is intriguing and impinging for it flavors the understanding that Christology becomes the determinant factor for the right ethical living. Faith in Jesus becomes the determinant factor. Thus, faith comes with a moral and ethical obligation to love one another, to be a continuing testimony of God's love to the world so that every

128 Barrett, *The Gospel According to St. John*, 61.

129 John W. Pryor, *John: Evangelist of the Covenant People* (Illinois: InterVarsity Press, 1992), 138.

130 Ridderbos, *The Gospel of John*, 14.

131 Richard B. Hays, *The Moral Vision of the New Testament: A Contemporary Introduction to New Testament Ethics* (New York: HarperCollins, 1996), 153.

132 Marxsen, *New Testament Foundations for Christian Ethics*, 290.

believer will share the mutual oneness with the Father and the Son (Jn. 17:21) just as the son Jesus explicates the exact character and nature of God the Father.

The Johannine community of believers has put their allegiance to the person of Jesus as the true revealer of God, coming from heaven, and is the Messiah. They become followers of Jesus by surrendering a position of privilege they had seemingly enjoyed in their previous Synagogue membership. As such the alienation of the Johannine community from its parent Jewish cultural context poses fundamental ethical challenges to redefine their own religious integrity in the face of the threat that came from within. Their articulation of their beliefs in Jesus as the expected Messiah becomes the defining moment, and one very important determinative factor to live in the light. It was in their belief in Jesus as the Messiah, and their conviction about Jesus that they were expelled from their former Jewish membership. In fact what lies beneath the ethical and decisive moment for the Johannine community of believers is therefore Johannine Jesus. Congruently, Christology becomes the determinative reason for making their religiously oriented ethical decision. Jesus' own experience of rejection, hatred and death by crucifixion is indeed a precedent experience and also a sign for the social experience of those who will be called his disciples (distinctive Johannine terminology for 'believers').[133] This fact leads us to the immediate concern that ethics is inseparably linked to Christology in John's Gospel.

4.5. Ethics - An Inescapable Part of Christology

Every ethical dimension that has been so far considered comports well into the theme of Christology. Ethics and Christology are indivisible because we cannot think of ethics without Christology for every ethical conduct is to be conformed to the conduct of Jesus as portrayed in the Gospel of John. Ethics is succinctly defined or redefined in the light and context of Christology in John's Gospel. There is no better place to understand Johannine ethics apart from its main theological aspect of Christology. For it is in Christology that ethics is embedded in John's Gospel. Thus, ethics in the Gospel both invites and attests to the responsiveness into believing or having faith in Jesus, who was introduced first as the *logos* in the prologue of the Gospel and was later identified as the Christ who is the 'Son of God' and at the same time the 'Son of Man;' because in Jesus, all the role and functions of these titles are fulfilled.

The centrality of Christology that dominates the theology of the Gospel of John leads us to no surprise that this "concentration upon Jesus also dominates its ethics,"[134] and that "in a word, the Gospel of John exemplifies a Christological implosion so that ethics becomes Christology."[135] Since the dominant theme of

133 Hays, *The Moral Vision of the New Testament*, 148.

134 Richard A. Burridge, *Imitating Jesus: An Inclusive Approach to New Testament Ethics.* (Michigan: Wm. B. Eerdmans Publishing Company, 2007), 293.

135 Matera, *New Testament Ethics*, 93.

John's Gospel is Christology, 'the ethics of the Johannine writings is exclusively christological in a way not encountered elsewhere'[136] is well said. As such, it is not difficult to accept the accepted truth about the content of the Fourth Gospel that the Gospel is truly Christological and it is thereby consonant to recommend that the Gospel of John is truly ethical too. Johannine Christology becomes the basis for unraveling the ethics of John's Gospel because it is in the Christological narratives that ethical values are entrenched.

The relationship between ethics and Christology in the Gospel of John can be said as being blended seamlessly. It is hard to draw a distinct line, a demarcation between theology (Christology) and ethics because they are dynamically intertwined. The Gospel helps us to understand that ethics is theology in practice and this action is undergirded by faith in Jesus. The key to understanding ethics is to understand the person of Jesus in his totality because he is the perfect person and place from which to begin. The narrative words and deeds of Jesus as exhibited in the Fourth Gospel speaks volume that Johannine Jesus is the resource for defining and framing the ethics of the Gospel of John.

The Fourth evangelist focuses much on Christology and has befittingly got the label that the controlling theological concern of the Fourth Gospel is Christology where all other theological concerns are aspects of the one great theme and all are viewed in the light of the dualism that characterizes the Christology.[137] Ethics cannot be explained without considering the aspect of Christology because for the Johannine community, ethics becomes part and partial and always an aspect of Christology that are closely inter-related. The moral and ethical obligation in the Fourth Gospel arises from the belief in Jesus for what and who he is and for what he says and does. The Johannine ethics is distinctive in a sense that it has taken its shape directly related to Jesus as the Christ particularly to the mission that he has come down from heaven to the earth below to fulfill the *erga* of God. The works of God was accomplished in and through him in full obedience which culminated in his death and resurrection.

Ethics in John's Gospel cannot be studied in isolation. Therefore, one's ethical conduct, as mirrored in the Fourth Gospel, is to be guided and interpreted in the light of his/her relation to Christ. The thematic study has featured that all in all the Johannine ethics is fundamentally a reflection on the content of faith in Jesus as the incarnate *logos* who is eventually identified as the 'Son of God', the Christ, and the 'Son of Man' who came to serve and give life eternal in John's Gospel. This Jesus is God incarnated (Jn. 1:14) and he alone formed the heart and defined the object of belief and hence becomes the measure of one's ethical conduct.

---

136 Wolfgang Schrage, *The Ethics of the New Testament*, translated by David E. Green (Philadelphia: Fortress Press, 1988), 298. First paperback edition 1990.

137 Beasley-Murray, *WBC: John*, vol. 36, lxxxi.

The ethical materials in John's Gospel are embedded in the narrative Christological teachings, discourses, conversations (in dialogue or arguments), priestly prayer, events and exhortations. It is this matter of fact that ethics and Christology in John's Gospel are inseparably interconnected. Nevertheless having endorsed this supposition, it is essential to acknowledge that Johannine Christology is primary and ethics is subordinate to Christology in the Gospel of John. Ethics is given a new content and significance by the introduction of distinctive principle points such as 'believe in Jesus', 'doing the works of God', 'love one another', 'abiding in Jesus', 'bear much fruit', 'you are to witness' etc. Johannine ethics is directly related to Jesus Christ. Thus, Johannine ethics illuminates from a consistent understanding and accepting and believing in Jesus who is introduced as the *logos* in the prologue, is the Christ, the 'Son of God' and who is also the 'Son of Man.'

4.6. Ethical Significance of the Christological Titles

Following what has been discussed about the Christology of John's Gospel it is also essential to bring out to the limelight the ethical significance of each of them. The title of Jesus appears under different titles though it refers essentially to one and only the same figure. The different titles of Jesus have a significant coherence within them for they are loaded with ethical implications. We shall here briefly run through the ethical significance of each of the Christological titles under study.

4.6.1. Ethical Significance of the Logos *Christology*

The Gospel introduced Jesus as the *logos* in the beginning of his presentation of the Gospel. This absolute use of the term *logos* to refer to Jesus is unique. This *logos* is identified with the light and source of life. Light 'φως' and life 'ζωή' in John's Gospel are important themes that recur throughout the Gospel. These terminologies have significant ethical significances (this is further elaborated in the following chapter). The *Logos*-Son Jesus which has both the cosmological (eternally existing with the Father from the beginning) and soteriological (took the form of/ became man for the salvation of human beings) significance[138] also has an ethical significance for the *logos* is the light that illumines and emancipate the lives of those who live in the darkness. He is the life zwh, which is regarded the highest moral good for humankind, according to Aristotle (*Nicomachean Ethics* I.2–4). It is sensible to admit John's zwh, as a moral category representing the continual existence of a moral God and thereby a moral objective. So zwh, is the ultimate moral good that people can attain by believing in the *logos*-Son for in the Johannine prologue the *logos* is identified and describes as the source of life.

The *logos* demands that the individuals who are in the world come to believe and receive him as coming from God the Father and in return an individual who in

138 Bultmann, *The Gospel of John*, 25, 28.

faith receive him is incorporated into the family of God (Jn. 1:12). The individual must therefore be separated from the elements of darkness, for darkness represents evil behavior and light and darkness cannot co-exist. The *logos* came to the world in tangible human figure in the person of Jesus of Nazareth as an ultimate and perfect representation of the moral likeness of an eternally existent God for the *logos* is God himself manifested in the *logos.*

4.6.2. Ethical Significance of the Christological Title 'The Christ/Messiah'

It is logically fitting to assume that Jesus being the anointed has come to this earth (Jn. 1:14) to show us the way to the Father (Jn. 14:6). Believing in that 'Anointed One' as portrayed in the Fourth Gospel invites us beyond this belief (the belief in Jesus as foretold and expected Messiah who is to come into the world) wherein the σημεῖα serve as a vehicle to, and also, a proof to believe that Jesus is the Christ/ Messiah (Jn. 20:30-31). The belief in the Anointed One must result in obedience. There is an implied ethical obligation to tread the path of witnessing and bearing testimony to the fact that we really believe in Jesus as the Christ. The end result of believing in Jesus as the Christ/Messiah gives ζωή eternal (Jn. 20:31) that which is the Fourth Gospel's intended purpose. This implies that ζωή is a moral objective, the means for obtaining it (ζωή) is to πιστεύειν εἰς 'Ιησοῦν which for John πιστεύω is a virtue.[139] In other words, πιστεύειν εἰς 'Ιησουν is a moral act, the exclusive and ultimate means by which people must attain ζωή. "Life" eternal is the highest moral good, which in fact is the lone ἔργον God requires (Jn. 6:27-29).[140] So "to believe" in Jesus as the Christ is the proper moral response that people should render to God.

And if it is in Jesus that the aspirations and longings of the people of Israel are fulfilled it is more impinging that the people in turn are obliged to *live out the faith* which is highly ethical. This belief as already discussed in the previous chapter is the most decisive ethical moment in the lives of the believers in the context of the unbelieving world who are already brought to judgment (Jn. 3:18 cf. 5:24) being far from enjoying life eternal as against the believing individual who is promised eternal life. Therefore, the title of Jesus as the Christ/Messiah signifies beyond its signifying title to the extent of believing in him which must again go a further step to prove that faith by being obedient to the commandment of Jesus as he has been committed to the perfecting of the Father's will in obedience. Jesus has laid a pattern of living a life that is in tune with the will of God, the Father. It is in this that the ethical implication is laid so much on the believers whose faith in Jesus as the Christ/Messiah is significantly fundamental.

---

139 Bennema,"Moral Transformation in the Johannine Writings:" 2.

140 Jan G. van der Watt, "The Gospel of John's Perception of Ethical Behavior," *In die Skriflig* 45 (2011), 433-435.

4.6.3. Ethical Significance of the Christological Title 'Son of God'

What ethical significance can be drawn from the Christological contour of the 'Son of God'? The title so designated to the person of Jesus as the Son is very profoundly and significantly depicted in the Fourth Gospel. The Son is to be understood theologically in the light of his filial relationship/bonding with God, as his Father. Jesus being the Son represents God in his being and in his functions as an agent and who is on a mission trip to the world. No one in the world presents God, the Father as best as the Son does. When we try to understand God, we are obliged to understand him not in isolation but in and through the person of Jesus. So, when we try to perceive from the ethical point of view, everything that the Son did and said was all in obedience to the will of God, who sent him. It suggests that the Johannine ethics is neither self-contained nor self-sufficient but it is to be understood in relational terms. The Johannine relation is defined in the light of the Father-Son (parent-child) relationship and it is to be worked out in obedience. As mentioned in chapter two that obedience is a virtue required on the part of human as a response to the divine revelation, instructions and demands from God. As a result, obedience is ethically rooted in the Father-Son relationship. And this Father-Son relationship is an ethical paradigm to be emulated. If the Son Jesus has accomplished whatever the Father desired of him, believers in him must also eventually fulfill what Jesus, as the 'Son of God' has desired of us in obedience. Jesus' new commandment to love one another must be lived-out, that which will stand out as a distinct touchstone of discipleship (Jn. 13:34-35; 14:15, 21, 23, 24; 15:10, 12, 17). A strong moral obligation is vested on believers in Jesus to live in the light and to do good and eventually bear the fruit of salvation.

4.6.4. Ethical Significance of the Christological Title 'Son of Man'

The ethical significance of the 'Son of Man' title in the fourth Gospel brings home the believers in Jesus as he is, must direct our thoughts and ways of living in obedience to him as he is to God the Father. By his life he brought glory to the Father and simultaneously was glorified. Like the master, the subordinates must also emulate the living pattern as modeled. So, it is an ethical obligation for the community of believers to live out the belief in Jesus by being obedient to his commandments and thereby bringing the good works into its fruition. What greater love can fallen human race crave for when the 'Son of Man' has proved that incredible love by his supreme sacrifice? As usual is the Johannine artistry style that there is an implicit obligation on the part of those who believe in Jesus to live out that obligation of faith and obedience to the commandments of Jesus and showcase the ideal community established according to the patterns of Jesus Christ. The end purpose of the coming of the 'Son of Man' is to give life eternal, which is the highest good, in the understanding of the Fourth Gospel. The means to this end is to believe in Jesus that he is the 'Son of Man', who has the power and authority to give life. It is therefore not wrong to interpret that the Johannine 'Son of Man' Christology has an implied ethical significance.

4.7. Summing the Ethical Significances of John's Christology

The Gospel of John depicts Jesus as the *logos* in his pre-existent state and was incarnated in the person of Jesus who is later identified as the Christ and who is the 'Son of God' and as well the 'Son of Man.' The discussed four Christological titles referred to the one person. The fact that ties these four Christological titles in the Fourth Gospel is - they refer to a single figure Jesus, who preexisted, whose origin is in heaven and has come to fulfill the long awaited hope of the people of Israel. This Jesus is the *logos*, Christ/Messiah, the 'Son of God', and also the 'Son of Man' who gives eternal hope to every believer in him. This identification of Jesus as the *logos*, Christ/Messiah, 'Son of God', and 'Son of Man' was gaining ground before and soon after his death and resurrection. Jesus' identity as Messiah and the 'Son of God' is placed, and are regarded, on equal footing (see Jn. 1:27, 29-34; 9:1-37; 10:24f; 11:27; 20:31).

As is the case with the two epithets of Jesus as the Messiah and Son of God, the identity of Jesus as Messiah appears to be equivalent to his identity as 'Son of Man' (of course with its distinctive particular connotations and the 'Son of Man' epithet was enigmatic until the passion narrative comes into scene). When Jesus reveals his pre-knowledge about Nathanael, the latter's response, "Rabbi, you are the Son of God! You are king of Israel!" indicates the epithets on par. Jesus replied that Nathanael will see greater things of heaven being opened and the angels of God ascending and descending upon the 'Son of Man' (Jn. 1:43-51). It is also interesting to note that Jesus being God's son has the authority to execute judgment because he is the Son of Man (Jn. 5:27). So Jesus as the 'Son of Man' has the power to give life and to pass judgment too.

The sequence of narratives in John 1:35-42)[141] suggests that the titles 'Messiah' and 'Son of God' are equivalent in John's Gospel. This equivalence is reinstated in Martha's confession (Jn. 11:27) and in the purpose statement (Jn. 20:31). In the Gospel of John, the titles 'Messiah' and 'Son of Man' are also presented as corresponding to one another. In the healing of the man born blind and the episodes that follow it, Jesus is recognized both as Messiah (Jn. 9:22) and as 'Son of Man' (Jn. 9:35-38). In this scene of episode, Jesus is both the Messiah and the 'Son of Man' at the same time. Messiah is equivalent to the 'Son of Man' which proposes that in Jesus all expected functions are being fulfilled. In short, the four titles '*logos*,' 'Christ/Messiah,' 'Son of God,' and 'Son of Man' are employed as complementary descriptions of Jesus' status and role.[142]

141 Jesus is identified as the Lamb of God and the Son of God. In the next scene Jesus, who is the Lamb of God is identified with the Messiah (1:35-42).

142 Cf. J. N. Sanders and B. A. Mastin, *The Gospel According to St. John* (Peabody, Massachusetts: Hendrickson Publishers, 1968), 13.

Christology occupies the centrality of the overall purpose of the Gospel of John. And so if ethics is linked to theology, definitely the Fourth Gospel contains the closest understanding of ethics because Christology is in the heart of John's theology. Ethics in the Gospel of John thereby has a high degree of contributing to the overall scholarship of the New Testament ethics. The Gospel of John thus has much more to convince us of our deliberation on ethics more efficiently than never before. What is most pertinent is the love of the Father for the Son which acts as a pattern for the Father's love for those who will believe in Jesus (Jn. 17:23). Similarly, the Son's love for his people is set out as the pattern to emulate (Jn. 13:34) in the newly established community. The moral standard of God articulated in and through Jesus has to find its expression in human's belief and its sequential act of faith, that is, behavioral conduct. This is a fine example of the way in which a high Christology is seen to have practical implications of a far-reaching nature.[143] So, to believe in Jesus has to have its existentialism here on earth because we live in the social and cultural context as everyone else lives.

The Fourth Gospel presents the crux of the ethical precepts solely in the life and ministry of the person of Jesus. The readers are invited to partake to understand the ethical significance that is embedded in the Christological narratives through skillful eyes of faith. As a reader engages him/herself in the narrative reading of the text, a potential decision is inculcated in the process of the reading. While a reader comes in contact with the true identity of Jesus, he/she is led through the wider context to exercise his/her decisive faith, to live that faith in human existence. As far as Johannine ethics is concerned, the person and works of Jesus are important and so the self-disclosure of Jesus as the *logos,* the Christ, the 'Son of God' and the 'Son of Man' and the belief and conviction of an individual are integrally important.

The Johannine ethics is formulated, therefore, on the basis of faith in Jesus as the pre-existent *logos,* the Christ, who is the 'Son of God' and the 'Son of Man' as well. And so it is against the world of unbelief that the Johannine community has to stand out justifying their belief by their everyday living. The foursome Christological titles (*logos*, Christ/Messiah, 'Son of God', and 'Son of Man') are significantly important reflecting the deeper truths far beyond who Jesus is in the redemptive plan and will of God to the extent of living a fruitful life by *believing, abiding* and in *obedience* to the teachings and commands of Jesus. There is a specific logical connection between these two themes (Christology and Ethics in the Fourth Gospel). Whoever believes in Jesus as the *logos*, the Christ, the 'Son of God,' and the 'Son of Man' must reflect his/her belief in his/her way of conduct. We have pointed out in the previous chapter the emphasis laid on the connection between 'belief' and 'action' when Jesus told his disciples that if they believe in him, they will continue the works of Jesus and even greater works (Jn. 14:11-12). One's ethical behavior is indeed the index of one's belief in Jesus

143 Guthrie, *New Testament Theology*, 314.

Christ that which must result in bearing much fruits and thus bear a remarkable hallmark as disciples of Jesus Christ by keeping his commandments (Jn. 13:35; 14:15, 21, 23; 15:10).

It is appropriate to remark that the Gospel of John presents various fitting titles to the One person, i.e., Jesus. He is portrayed as fulfilling all and every Christological mandates/office in his life and ministry and even deeper in his personhood. John's definition of Jesus (or Christology) can be thus summed up in the words of C. K. Barrett who says, "Jesus is the beginning and the end, the first creator and the final judge; also he is the ultimate truth both of God and humanity. Being truly God and truly man, and being also the image of God and the archetype of humanity, he is no less a mediator of true knowledge, and of salvation."[144] The Johannine Christology exercised a decisive influence of faith on the response of the people encountered in the Fourth Gospel. It is probably right to understand that the Fourth Gospel has made Christology and ethics as an integral and organic part of one another. The crux of Johannine ethics is the call to believe in the person of Jesus in which his personhood and mission's credentials are heard and seen in his words and deeds and in response live a life of faith. What is significantly paramount is that where Christology is the major focus, the evangelist creatively assimilates the ethical possibilities and values in it. Jesus as the Son, the anointed One and fulfilling the redemptive will of the sovereign is also the 'Son of Man' offering himself. He reveals the truth, relies in this truth and lives the truth. He who reveals the Father himself depends on the Father and has proved himself by living the revealed truth.

The *being* of Jesus in deed is an obvious pointer to the understanding of what ethics is in John's Gospel. It will not be an over exaggeration to postulate that there will be no Johannine ethics without Johannine Christology because it is in the Christology that ethics are intricately embedded. The ethical pointers in John's Gospel come alive in the words and deeds of Jesus. Johannine ethics is thus Christologically oriented and determined. The whole of Jesus' event, i.e., life and ministry attested by Jesus' combined words and deeds evoke and direct the belief of any willing respondent. Jesus is presented as the ultimate ethical character in whom we find the consistency between his words and actions. Jesus' morality is demonstrated by his integrity. Subsequently, Christology is of paramount importance in determining the ethical aspects of the Fourth Gospel. It is the sole standard foundation for the development of Johannine ethics. As such, Christology is of fundamental importance for understanding the ethical motivation of the Fourth Gospel. So, as believers in Jesus Christ, our transformed lives have to be affirmed by living out the ethical aspect and demand of our faith – to love one another – the external hallmark of being true disciple of Jesus.

One has and ought to agree as believers in Jesus Christ that our ethics must be the reflection of Jesus' ethics. So, the importance of deducing ethical

144 Barrett, *The Gospel According to St. John*, 62.

significance from the life and ministry of Jesus is therefore very relevant. To look out for ethics in the Gospel of John vehemently must henceforth begin from the life and ministry of Jesus as *sent* by God (Jn. 4:34; 5:23-24; 6:34-40;8:16-18; 9:4: 11:42; 12:44-45; 13:20; 17:21-25). The identity of Jesus as the *logos,* the 'Son of God' who is the Christ and the 'Son of Man' in his suffering and exaltation stands out as the major thrust to understand the ethical message of the Gospel. Ethical elements are being promoted and articulated in the narrative Christology of the Gospel. Jesus Christ who is the incarnation of the divine God is the pattern after which one ought to interpret and define his/her life after the life and work of the Son of God.

It is also fitting to assume that the ethical aspects of John's Gospel are based on his understanding of the overall vocation (life and ministry) of Jesus. Johannine Christology defines the believers' way of life and is crucial in interpreting and defining ethics in the Gospel of John. It is the key and ultimate basis for understanding what ethics is in essence, according to the Gospel of John. In brief, all Johannine implicit ethical elements hang on the Johannine Christology, i.e., Jesus is the moral standard in and through whom one experiences a transforming change of life – from darkness to light, from falsehood to the truth, from death to life because Jesus is the light, the bread of life, the truth, the way and the life.

The discussion on the four selected Johannine Christological contours have enabled us to draw out the importance of ethical values in the Gospel of John. Our deliberation has depicted that besides the salvific significance of Johannine Christology there is a very strong implicit implication of ethics which contributes to the overall purpose of the writing of the Gospel. Jesus' passion, death and resurrection, and ascension, is the culminating hour in the long history of God's salvific dealing with human kind.[145] The salvation wrought by Jesus for humankind must be reciprocated by loving obedience to his teachings which is morally right.

Conclusion

The Christological exploration has invited beyond its significant revelation of Jesus as the *logos,* as the Christ/Messiah who is also the 'Son of God' and the 'Son of Man' too. Ethics in the Fourth Gospel is taking on a new significance, a significance that is embedded so much so in the person and work of Jesus Christ. The ethics of the Johannine Gospel is exclusively and richly Christological in a way not encountered elsewhere that calls for believing heart and eye.[146] Johannine ethics has to be excavated from the Christological point of view and is worth the Johannine scholarship exploration.

145 Brown, *The Gospel According to John*, vol. 1, cxvi.

146 Burridge, *Imitating Jesus*, 293. See for instance, John 1:19-28; 3:25-26; 7:45-52; 9:13-33; 10:19-21; 11:45-53,55-57; 12:9-11; 20:24-25.

The ethical challenge of the Gospel lies in the fact to evoke a response of faith by believing in Jesus the *logos* who was in the beginning and was sent by God into this world to grant life eternal (Jn. 3:16; 20:31 cf. 1 Jn. 5:11, 12) and believe that he is the Christ, the 'Son of God' and the 'Son of Man' as well. This is to substantiate that in Jesus the Father has put all things under him (Jn. 3:35; 5:20). Belief in Jesus will automatically result in doing good work and all other ethical decisions will follow because Jesus is also the light and whoever follows him will not tread the path of darkness (Jn. 8:12 ; 1:5 cf. 1 Jn. 3:6,9; 5:18). It is impossible to understand ethics in isolation or apart from the life and ministry of Jesus. Johannine ethics is totally engrossed and embedded in the theology of Christology without which there is no proper and better understanding of what entails ethics in the Fourth Gospel. Christology is therefore the hermeneutical key to unlock the ethical principles in the Gospel of John.

There are significant ethical teachings embedded within Christological articulation. The inter-connection of Christology (which is explicit) and ethics (tacitly articulated) are indispensably linked which is so profound to the thought of the author of the Gospel in presenting the ethical obligation for the believing Johannine community. The Christology which is the pertinent inbuilt of the Gospel content serves as veritable model on how to behave in and outside the community. Johannine ethics and Christology are inseparably intertwined in as much as the content of the Fourth Gospel is concerned in explicating the ethical obligation of the community. The drive is to investigate ethics in relation to Christology and thereby bring out the major ethical themes of the Gospel of John. Given recognition that Jesus' identity illuminated by his very deeds generates the motivation for the believers to realize the ethical obligation about the correct ethical response to the circumstances in which they live.

An open option is left to the decisive and defining moment of the implied reader to excavate the implicit implications and obligations and live by then than to force him/her to make a readymade response to the revealed truth/s. Christology in John's Gospel serves as the springboard in fashioning Johannine ethics. It is a challenge to the believers to be open to God's revealing truth in and through Jesus and then worked out one's ethical character in dependence and obedience to the will of the One God. So, our quest for ethics in the Gospel of John begins with the person of Jesus, who indeed is the source of morality. And now what follows this chapter is to assemble the major ethics of John and draw its divine and communitarian parameters.

Chapter 5

Johannine Ethics
Its Divine and Communitarian Parameters

Introduction

The present chapter is devoted to establish the inter-connection between ethics and Christology by deducing its divine and communitarian parameters. It is basically the relationship of ethics to Christology. In the Gospel of John, ethics and Christology are inextricably linked (inter-connected) and belong inseparably together. Jesus being sent by God the Father revealed the Father by the way he himself lived by words (proclamation) and deeds (activity). This is to bring forth an ethical dimension which is implicit and very significant in its nature in John's Gospel that has not gotten its fair share of attention and consideration thus far. As much as Christology is central to the theology of the Fourth Gospel, that much is ethics central to the theology of the Fourth Gospel too.

Christology being one of the most pertinent themes in the Gospel has no lack of the touch of Johannine scholarship. A great and an exhaustive study has already been done on Johannine Christology. It is an unquestioned fact that John's Gospel records the most exalted form of Christology. Yet the heart of its inter-connectedness with ethics in the Gospel of John has not received the attention that it deserves. The inter-connection is so much more than we might have realized than we do now, as we diligently scan through and read between the lines of the Gospel narratives, discourses, etc. It comes to the fore that the fundamental structure of Johannine ethics is to be approached and deduced from the Johannine Christological perspective. We shall now turn our attention to the inter-connectedness between ethics and Christology that possibly can be delineated from the Gospel of John.

We begin with few questions - What important bearing does Johannine Christology have on our understanding of Johannine ethics? What is the relation between Johannine ethics and the Johannine Christology? How they both are connected? In what way and how are they inter-connected? If so, is it an event or a process? Consequently, the inter-connection between Ethics and Christology in John's Gospel is to unpack the relationship that exists between these two important and pertinent themes (the research would suggest, of course Christology without question is the thrust of the overall ruling theology of the Gospel). The idea of the inter-connectedness between these two aspects is the key importance to be taken note. It is because Johannine ethics is constituted by obedience to God as portrayed in the very words and deeds of Jesus.[1] This gives a suggestive glimpse that Christology entails ethics in the Gospel according to John.[2]

Now how this inter-connection between Johannine ethics and Christology is to be understood. This relationship is undoubtedly expressed in and within the socio-historical context of the Johannine community.[3] We will, here, attempt to establish and bring out the ethical dimension of the Fourth Gospel in relation to Christology. Johannine ethics is directly and inseparably linked to Johannine Christology for the former is 'Christology in action.'[4] The Johannine community of believers is invited to affirm and live out their ethical dimension and demands of their faith in Jesus. So ethics, in the Fourth Gospel, cannot be separated from the belief in Jesus Christ. Efforts will be made to sketch out possible characteristic features of the interconnectedness between ethics and Christology in the following headings. But, we shall first bring out the wider context in which Johannine community's moral tradition is banked and then proceed to feature out the characteristics of the inter-connection between ethics and Christology.

5.1. The Johannine Community as the Moral Narrative Context

Aspects of moral thinking and normative values of the first century Christian faith are distinctively chronicled in the books of the New Testament Bible. The Fourth Gospel also in its distinctive and independent way accounts the ethical

1 D. Moody Smith, *ANTC: John* (Nashville: Abington Press, 1999), 44.

2 Willi Marxsen, *New Testament Foundations for Christian Ethics,* translated by O. C. Dean. (Minneapolis: Fortress Press, 2007), 290.

3 Gary M. Burge, "Situating John's Gospel in History," *Jesus in Johannine Tradition*, edited by Robert Tomson Fortna and Tom Thatcher (Louisville and London: Westminster John Knox Press, 2001), 35ff.

4 Compare Ruth B. Edwards, "The Johannine Epistles," *The Johannine Literature*, edited by Barnabas Lindars, Ruth B. Edwards & John M. Count (Sheffield: Sheffield Academic Press Ltd., 2000), 153-162.

norms and precepts. As such, some distinctive ethical patterns are said to find its expression in the new light within the community where the community served as the newly inaugurated avenue for describing the dynamics of ethics in the Gospel of John.[5] Johannine community is the moral locale in which the work of God in and through Jesus the *logos*, the Christ, the Son of God, and the Son of Man is displayed.[6] The Johannine community is taken as a narrative moral horizon of faith and action in the light of the call to believe in Jesus and keep his commandments. So, with respect to the research limitation to John's Gospel we shall propel to study the Johannine community as a moral locale context to deduce the inter-connection between ethics and Christology. The socio-religious milieu of the community has been dealt in chapter two so we will not repeat but keeping at the back of our mind passing comments will be integrated when need arises.

5.1.1. Moral Traditions of the Johannine Community

It is clear from the foregone treatment of the ethical evidences in the Gospel that the Johannine community's moral world is not limited to the explicit moral teaching such as love but its moral elements are embedded in the narratives, theological arguments, symbols, and habitual social practices that shaped their behavioral pattern. Jesus who has come from heaven to reveal the truth of the Father, God to the world below is filled with ethical implications for the community that accepts and receives the message.[7] The ethics of the Fourth Gospel has its setting in Jewish religious monotheistic belief and the future and realized eschatological expectation of the *parousia*.[8] It is fitting that these monotheistic and eschatological concept respectively find way within specific and historical length of time within a particular community of John's Gospel which is characterized by its internal crisis within Judaism.

The identity of the Johannine community rests upon the belief in Jesus, as the Son of God sent by God. The members of the Johannine community are to find in Jesus the objective standard of ethical conduct. John 13:15 tells it succinctly what Jesus had told the disciples, "I have set you an example that you should do as I have done to you." Jesus' love for them is an ethical paradigm. This is not simply a floating imperative but that which has a direct practical basis grounded in Jesus'

---

5 David K. Rensberger, *Johannine Faith and Liberating Community* (Philadelphia: The Westminster Press, 1988); See also David A. Lamb, *Text, Context and the Johannine Community: A Sociolinguistic Analysis of the Johannine Writings* (Bloomsbury: T&T Clark, 2014), 30.

6 Robert Kysar, *The Fourth Evangelist and His Gospel* (Minneapolis: Augsburg Publishing House, 1975), 240.

7 Richard B. Hays, *The Moral Vision of the New Testament: A Contemporary Introduction to New Testament Ethics* (New York: Harper Collins, 1996), 4.

8 Raymond E. Brown, "The Paraclete of the Fourth Gospel," *NTS* 13 (1967): 113-132.

own action (indicative).[9] Jesus in this narrative episode is not only the master teacher but the best paradigmatic model. Jesus' command to love one another constitutes the core of the community's conduct because Jesus himself has set an example by loving them. The community's behavior is thereby motivated by the love of Jesus and to abide in Jesus to share the divine mutual fellowship. Jesus' words and deeds impacted and motivated the behavior of an individual within the Johannine community. The community must live a virtuous life by loving one another as Jesus has loved them and are encouraged to continue to keep his commandment.

John's Gospel Christology poses series of ethical implications for the community of believers. The Johannine community is set on the contrasted backdrop of the slavery of the unbelieving world (Jews). The Johannine community believes in Jesus who is fore mostly introduced as the *logos* the Christ, the 'Son of God' and the 'Son of Man', and the unique and ultimate revelation of God.[10] Thus, they remain in the fold of God's family as against the Jews, who in spite of their claim to be the descendants of Abraham, refused to believe in Jesus. The unbelieving Jews remain the slaves to sin while the Johannine community is free from the slavery of sin by their belief in Jesus (Jn. 8:31-36 cf. Rom. 6; 8:1-4, 21; Gal. 4:21-5:1).[11] As a result, Christology determines and sets the ethical standard for the community of believers. The Community directly derives its moral principles from the teachings and activities of Jesus (Jn. 8:31-32). Subsequently, the Johannine Christology, which is at the centre and the heartbeat of John's theological thought, is not an end in itself but directs and shapes the community's ethical decisions and behavior. There is a dynamic relation between one's faith and behavior for one's ethical decision is informed and enriched by the belief in the words and deeds of Jesus. The ethical behavior of the believing community is thus shaped and fashioned by the belief in the person of Jesus.

John presupposes a community though the word, ἐκκλησια is not used.[12] There is a major emphasis on a community ethic. The audience or disciples to whom Jesus' teachings were addressed stresses on a community ethic that which can never be overlooked because the disciples did not live in isolation but in the company of the world (Jn. 17:16 cf. 15:118). In true sense the disciples were informed to be testifying agents to the world outside of the closed community of believers. Johannine ethical engagement finds its expression in this world because the created world and its inhabitants is the frontier mission field of God (Jn. 3:16

9 Compare John Christopher Thomas, *Footwashing in John 13 and Johannine Community* (London & New York: Bloomsbury & T&T Clark, 2004).

10 Francis J. Moloney, *The Gospel of John* (Minnesota: The Liturgical Press, 1998), 94–97.

11 Edwyn Clement Hoskyns, *The Fourth Gospel*, edited by Francis Noel Davey (London: Faber and Faber Limited, 1947), 337.

12 C. K. Barrett, *Gospel According to St. John: An Introduction with Commentary and Notes on the Greek Text* (London: SPCK, 1960), 78-82.

cf. 17:18; 20:21).[13] Johannine community is the community of believers who have believed in Jesus as sent by God and are sanctified through the laying down of the life of Jesus. The disciples' moral life is to live in relation to Jesus because there is no moral and ethical life apart from Jesus (Jn. 15:5). It is expected of this community that they ought to live a life of good conduct so outsiders see that they are Jesus' disciples (cf. Gal 6:9,10). And that the life of the community must bear fruit which results from the close communion with Jesus Christ.[14] Bearing fruit is the good works of a Christian life following the abode in Jesus.[15] The realm of morality is not limited only to practical behaviour but also includes human's inner consciousness and conviction about the being of Jesus. If a person does not abide in Jesus he/she is bracketed out from bearing good fruit. This is to infer that the attitudes and motives of every faith community are to a degree subject to one's control and be eligible for moral judgment (see Exod. 20:14; Deut. 5:18; 15:9; Lev. 19:17). As far as the community known from the text are believers in Jesus Christ, then those are the elect ones and are thereby obliged to live a life worthy of the calling upon their lives (1 Pet. 2:9). It is within this community of believers that the individual's life ought to be nurtured and cared (1 Jn. 3:17, 18 cf. 1 Cor. 16:16, 17; Heb. 3:13a).[16] The Johannine community is to model a community of believers characterized by their love for one another in keeping with the command from their Lord, the inaugurator of this new community, so that the world will look upon and begin to believe in Jesus as the *logos* who is the light and life is the Christ, the 'Son of God' and the 'Son of Man' who gave his life for the whole world.

John recounts the salvation story in his distinctive literary style mediating the ethic of Jesus in a distinctive way in the Gospel. Consonantly, he has his own particular and distinctive community with particular and concrete situational needs to address. There has never been an individual in isolation but always a community (community of believers (Church) to which and for which it is written. Therefore, the ethical dimension in John's Gospel has a communitarian dimension (community ethic) wherein the moral life is lived within that community of believers.[17] In this line, it will be fascinating to consider and reflect

13 Richard A. Burridge, *Imitating Jesus: An Inclusive Approach to New Testament Ethics* (Michigan: Wm. B. Eerdmans Publishing Company, 2007), 332.

14 George R. Beasley-Murray, *WBC: John*, vol. 36 (Texas: Word Books Publisher, 1987), 273; Rudolf Schnackenburg, *The Gospel According to St John,* vol. 3, translated by David Smith and G. A. Kon (London & Kent: Burns & Oates, 1982), 100; Raymond E. Brown, *The Gospel According to* John, vol. 2 (New York: Doubleday & Company, 1970), 662-663.

15 Jey J. Kanagaraj, *The Gospel of John: A Commentary* (Secunderabad: OM Books, 2005), 494, 498, 500; Barrett, *Gospel According to St. John*, 395.

16 Frank J. Matera, *New Testament Ethics: The Legacies of Jesus and Paul* (Louisville: Westminster John Knox Press, 1996), 134.

17 Thomas Vallaniappuram, *New Society in John's Gospel* (Aloor, Kerala: Biblia Publications, 2008), 125-126.

on the context of the Johannine community as a minor oppressed community of the first century.[18] We therefore need to seriously take the context of the Johannine community who was under hard situation (in today's context we would probably tag them as the marginalized community as against the dominant religious group in India). The ethical or moral teaching of the Gospel according to John is communal. The ethical behavior of the community however must and begin from the disciples Jesus himself has chosen. They are chosen out of the world for a very unique and distinctive purpose and a responsibility towards one another and to the world at large (15:16).[19] The Gospel emphasizes the importance of living in a community of believers who abide in the Son Jesus as the Son abides in the Father.

Johannine ethics springs out of the liberating experience of a community (from darkness to light; from death to life).[20] A liberty and a hope offered in and through Jesus. Jesus said to his disciples not to be dismayed, 'In this world you will have trouble, but take heart I have overcome the world' (16:33b). In another place, Jesus promises a better home, a mansion (14:2, 3). In fact, the hardship faced by the Johannine community is the commencement of envisioning a new community that is built, after, upon the love of, the person of Jesus. The moral behavior of the Johannine community is wholly shaped by the belief in Jesus as sent by God into the world as the Light so that people will no longer walk in darkness and do no more evil (3:19, 21). The moral foundation of the Johannine community is the person of Jesus because it is in Jesus that one has life and to have life is to believe in him and accordingly keep up with his commandment. There is an urge from its community a total commitment concerning one's way of life – a choice to believe or disbelieve in the Son Jesus. The ethical demand is vibrant. Discipleship is reckoned as keeping the commandment of the Master. Love for one another is the hallmark for true discipleship also a serious note needs to be considered that the pre-requisite for being disciple of Jesus is 'to believe' and then the rest of the commands find its worth. The Fourth Gospel uses and expresses the underlying reality of the concept of being a part of the Community and that is discipleship, to which we now turn our attention.

5.1.2. Discipleship as the Immediate Moral Context of Johannine Ethics

The Fourth Gospel employs μαθητής 'disciple' to represent or describe the community of believers. So the term 'disciple' is an image symbolizing the Johannine community of believers. "Jesus said to the Jews who believed in him, ἐὰν ὑμεῖς μείνητε ἐν τῶ λόγω τῶ ἐμῶ, ἀληθῶς μαθηται μού ἐστε and you will know the truth, and the truth will make you free" (8:31-32). It appears that

18 Rensberger, *Johannine Faith and Liberating Community*, 25-26.

19 Craig S. Keener, *The Gospel of John: A Commentary*, vol. 2 (Peabody, Massachusetts: Hendrickson Publishers, 2003), 1015-1016.

20 Rensberger, *Johannine Faith and Liberating Community*, 25-26, 110-118.

μένω 'to abide' in Jesus is the foremost characteristic of true discipleship.[21] So, discipleship is central and is stamped with the concept of 'abiding' in Jesus as he abides in the Father. The verb (μένω) describes the mutual indwelling of Jesus and his disciples.[22] And besides 'to follow' (Jesus) is a key word for the Johannine understanding of discipleship and which is more objective. See for instances in John 1:35-51 (the call of the first disciples of Jesus); 6:1-14, a large crowd following him cf. 21:19, 22 Jesus' last words to Peter). And another very important essence of discipleship is 'to believe' in Jesus which is more or less a subjective response.[23] So, the chief criteria for being disciples of Jesus is 'to believe' and to continue to hold on Jesus' teachings and remain in him (8:31-32). The absolute content of Jesus' teaching is that he is the *One sent.* He is the *logos* of God, Christ, the Son of God, and the Son of Man who has come to do the will of God the Father (4:34; 6:38; 8:29). In Jesus all the roles of these titles are converged in his personhood.

In the Fourth Gospel we find individuals who make their varying response of faith in Jesus and are eventually considered as 'disciples' and others who oppose to his (Jesus) claims and are thereby 'opponents' to the truth.[24] Jesus is the vine and the disciples are the branches. The moral lives of the disciples are determined by their relationship with Jesus. No individual lives an isolated moral life but within a community of believers and this is fundamentally true for the Johannine disciples.[25] Christology is the fundamental ground because it determines the community's behavior. The call to discipleship which is to follow Jesus and to conform to life and works of Jesus is in fact a decisive trait of the ethics in the written document of the Gospel. Congruently, Johannine discipleship is grounded in its distinctive Christology.[26] Disciples are called to follow the trail Jesus had walked through and had left accomplished. In John 12:26 Jesus says, "Whoever serves me must follow me; and where I am, my servant also will be...." The distinctive call of Johannine Jesus is *not* a call to carry the cross but share the joy of the victory he has accomplished[27] and share the portion of the privilege to be honored by the Father[28] to live in the mansion he has prepared for all believers. And yet, till the journey of faith continues here on this earth the moral responsibility as disciples of Jesus is to be continued.

Disciples in the Synoptic Gospels are asked to take up the cross and follow Jesus (Matt. 10:38; Lk. 9:23; 14:27). In the Fourth Gospel, it takes a different

21 Matera, *New Testament Ethics*, 116.

22 Kanagaraj, *The Gospel of John*, 494-497.

23 Burridge, *Imitating Jesus*, 339-341.

24 Burridge, *Imitating Jesus*, 299.

25 Matera, *New Testament Ethics*, 116.

26 Matera, *New Testament Ethics*, 116.

27 Matera, *New Testament Ethics*, 116.

28 Keener, *The Gospel of John*, vol. 2, 874-875.

level, the Johannine Jesus does not speak of taking up one's cross and follow him rather disciples are asked 'to remain/abide' in him as the branches is to the vine (15) and are to share his victory of the cross (for Jesus' death on the cross is the moment of glorification or exaltation in John's Gospel).[29] Johannine Jesus has "made discipleship accessible to a new generation of disciples for whom following the earthly Jesus is no longer possible."[30] The importance to love one another as Jesus loved is emphasized and also the importance of living in a community of disciples who abide in Jesus is stressed. Johannine discipleship defines who we are in relation to Jesus - as his followers. This *being* (the individual person) has to be verified by *doing* (his/her action) that is by abiding in Jesus and keeping his commandment to bear fruit (Jn. 15:4-5, 10). The moral life of the disciples is not possible devoid of Jesus.[31] Just as the branch cannot bear fruit without being crafted on to the vine so are the disciples to Jesus. Apart from Jesus, disciples cannot bear fruit and to bear fruit means to do something, that is, to 'love one another' in action that has been spelled out already in John 13:34-35.[32] Proverbial saying "Words are the blossoms, action the fruit"[33] is rightly said (cf. 1 Jn. 3:18). The Father also plays a role in the moral life of the disciples. That is *kathairein* 'cleansing' them by the word he has spoken, which is the Father's word, so that they can produce much fruit (Jn. 14:24). The emphasis is on the fruit-bearing of the branches (15:1-11).[34] Therefore, the disciples are to remain in Jesus and keep his commandment by loving one another (15:8-10) and thus be productive in good works.

Belief in Jesus is the main initial criterion to be a disciple of Jesus according to the Gospel of John. It is intriguing to learn that 'discipleship' in the Gospel of John is an open invitation. Faith becomes an ethical decisive moment in one's life, to accept or to reject Jesus. Discipleship in John's understanding is crammed with moral obligations to continue to believe in Jesus as sent by God.[35] They must love one another as loved (patterned after Jesus' love for them cf. 13:34 with15:9-11). They are sent to the world as Jesus has been sent into the world by the Father. We see the parallelism between Jesus being sent by the Father into the world, and the disciples being sent into the world to continue Jesus' mission to the world (Jn. 17:18; 20:21). This implies that there is no suggestion of physical separation from the world so much as it is separation from the values of the

---

29 Matera, *New Testament Ethics*, 116.

30 Matera, *New Testament Ethics*, 117.

31 Keener, *The Gospel of John*, vol. 2, 998.

32 Moloney, *The Gospel of John*, 420-422; Kanagaraj, *The Gospel of John*, 499-500.

33 Taken from the devotional book, *Our Daily Bread,* 2017 Annual Edition.

34 Kanagaraj, *The Gospel of John*, 496, 499.

35 Matera, *New Testament Ethics*, 111.

world.[36] The moral decision lies in the fact to whether accept or reject the claims of Jesus i.e. faith in the Gospel of John is the moral decision.[37] Moral dualism is in pictured created by the world's alienation from God by rejecting Jesus and yet the world remains the object of God's saving love (3:16).[38] The disciples will be hated because their Lord and Master was hated. They will be persecuted to the point of being killed but they are encouraged to endure and not to lose heart because Jesus has overcome death, ensuring their peace (Jn. 16:33 cf. 14:27).[39] Jesus is the ultimate foundation for the disciples' assurance that enables them to persevere in the face of the world's hostility.[40] As a result, the disciples' ethical teachings and practices ought to stand in continuity with Jesus and pass it to the next generation of believers through and by their living - testimonies.

5.2. Jesus the Basis and Momentum for the Moral Traditions of the Johannine Community

From where does the Johannine community of believers draw her moral traditions? The answer is no doubt 'Jesus.' There is a general assumption that Jesus was also significantly considered a teacher of morality (often times addressed as 'Rabbi' in the Gospels).[41] In John 6: 29, the plural 'ἐργα τοῦ θεοῦ' is translated in the singular 'ἐργον τοῦ θεοῦ' emphasizing that there is one single demand of God, that is, to believe in the person He has sent.[42] Πιστεύω is the determinant ethical virtue, a moral decision (as already discussed in chapter three) which is directed to Jesus. For belief in Jesus is "the only, and the essential, human answer to God's sending of the revealer and bringer of salvation."[43] Jesus is the true herald, the anointed and expected one (Christ/Messiah) coming from and sent by the Father (is the Son of God) and who is to suffer as the Son of Man on the cross so as to offer ζωὴ αἰώνιος (Jn. 3:16; 6:27, 40 cf. Dan. 12:2; Jn. 20:31). Having said this, it must be remembered that Jesus is not merely portrayed as a moral religious teacher. His ethical teachings must thereby be understood in the light of his obedience in doing

36 Keener, *The Gospel of John*, vol. 2, 1061.

37 Kysar, *The Fourth Evangelist and His Gospel*, 217.

38 Herman Ridderboss, *The Gospel of John: A Theological Commentary*, translated by John Vriend (Michigan: Wm. B. Eerdmans Publishing Company, 1997), 557.

39 Barrett, *Gospel According to St. John*, 415.

40 Rensberger, *Johannine Faith and the Liberating Community*, 121.

41 Dale Goldsmith, *New Testament Ethics: An Introduction* (Elgin, IL: Brethen, 1988), 177; also see C. W. Carter and R.D. Thompson, *The Biblical Ethic of Love*, American University Studies Series 7: Theology and Religion 79 (New York: Lang, 1990), 128. In the Gospels Jesus is regularly addressed as 'Rabbi' or 'Rabboni' (Aramaic) or teacher. See the references in Jn. 1:38,49; 3:2,26; 4:31; 6:25; 9:2; 11:8; 20:16; Matt. 26:25, 49; Mk. 9:5; 10:51; 11:21; 14:45.

42 Rudolf Schnackenburg, *The Gospel According to St. John*, vol. 2, translated by Cecily Hastings, Francis McDonagh, David Smith & Richard Foley (London: Burns & Oates, 1980), 39.

43 Schnackenburg, *The Gospel according to St. John*, vol. 2, 39.

the will of the Father who sent him to this world. Jesus' words and deeds which include his life, death and resurrection and the promise of his continuing presence in the *Paraclete* are all set in one accord.[44] So, the ethical concerns in the Gospel according to John is indispensably integrated within the christological materials which focuses upon Jesus as the ultimate revelation of God[45] and whose (Jesus) life and ministry in its totality has been in perfect obedience to bring into perfect accomplishment of the Father's will (Jn. 4:34; 5:30; 6:38; 17:4; 19:30 cf. Matt. 26:39). So, it is fitting to conceive that the community of John's Gospel draws her moral understanding from the life, teaching and person of Jesus. Johannine Son of man is the Son of God (3:13; 6:62), who is the archetypal man, the inclusive representative of ideal humanity (12:32 cf. 14:3).[46] We can boldly assume that the Johannine community is founded in Christo-centric cultural origin and this origin shaped its appropriation in the everyday living of the community of believers (13:16-17).[47]

In John's Gospel, 'doing the works of God' is 'to believe' in Jesus, whom the Father has sent (6:29) and that believing in Jesus is a moral act required by God of us.[48] There is a dynamic inter-connection between faith and one's behavior and it can be compared with "knowing and doing."[49] It is the combination of these two elements that lead to a complete whole (i.e. true happiness as Boice describes). The content of happiness is to acknowledge Jesus as Lord and man to assume the role of a servant (Jn. 13:16-17).[50] Faith comes alive in action and so ethics is a reflection of belief (theology). And it is the will of God that one's belief must be directed to his Son Jesus whom He has sent (6:29 cf. 3:17; 1 Jn. 3:23).[51] Eventually, to be in tune with the will of God is to be in tune with Jesus first, for Jesus is the visual unique embodiment of God (for nothing less than God can represent the God for our understanding of who God is)[52] and the

---

44 Kysar, *The Fourth Evangelist and His Gospel*, 236; Hoskyns, *The Fourth Gospel*, 450.

45 C. H. Dodd, *The Interpretation of the Fourth Gospel* (Cambridge: Cambridge University Press, 1953), 169, 185.

46 Dodd, *The Interpretation of the Fourth Gospel*, 244. The Son of Man descends and dwells amongst us and gave his life (dies) so that He may draw all men to him (12:32). He ascends to God where he belonged in order that where He is everyone (who believes in him) may be also (14:3). This idea of solidarity being with Christ (also the example of the Vine and the branches in John 15) can be compared with the Pauline doctrine of the body of Christ (1 Cor. 12:12f cf. Matt. 10:49; 25:40; Lk. 10:16 cf. Jn 13:20).

47 James Montgomery Boice, *An Expositional Commentary: The Gospel of John*, vol. 4 (Michigan: BakerBooks, 1999), 1016.

48 Schnackenburg, *The Gospel According to St. John*, vol. 2, 39.

49 Boice, *The Gospel of John*, vol. 4, 1014.

50 Boice, *The Gospel of John*, vol. 4, 1014-1016.

51 Schnackenburg, *The Gospel According to St. John*, vol. 2, 39.

52 Moloney, *The Gospel of John*, 381; Leon Morris, *The Gospel According to John* (Michigan: Wm. B. Eerdmans Publishing Company, 1971), 78.

only way that leads to the Father (14:6). For the will of God the Father is seen, present and is revealed in and through Jesus (14:9f.), who is the only begotten Son (1:18). The 'will of God' is actualized/realized in the life, words and deeds, death and resurrection of the Son Jesus. Subsequently, the Johannine Jesus is concerned much more to affect the behavior than to simply affect the thinking (consider the dominating service motif in the feet washing).[53]

Our focus is to see the characteristic ways in which the community's behavior is to be affected. Jesus is the moral actor, a supreme model, great example,[54] who carries out the *erga* of the Father (Jn. 5: 19, 36 cf. 4:34; 8:28-29; 10:37). His words and works are both relational and responsible to the Father and the same is expected from the believers in the Gospel of John. For the Johannine community the moral tradition is πιστεύειν εἰς' Ιησοῦν, to do the ἔργα τοῦ θεοῦ, to keep the command of Jesus (ἀγαπατε ἀλλήλους). Faith and love serve as the controlling principles for all other ethical behavior. And these virtues are to constitute the nature of the Johannine community. The community is comprised of all who responded in faith to Jesus as the *logos* of God, the expected and promised Christ, the Son of God and the Son of Man.[55] This signifies that the Johannine community is inclusive in its nature by its open invitation to whoever may believe in Jesus and became the member of the family of God not by blood but by choice (Jn. 1:12 cf. 6:70; 13:18; 15:16, 19).[56]

For the Fourth Gospel, Christology remains the only standard for the action of the community of believers.[57] It is inevitable, therefore, to envisage that the Johannine community is established and constituted by the belief in the life, ministry and person of Jesus which correspondingly is the impetus of the moral traditions for the Johannine community. Jesus is the exclusive figure from which the ethics of John's Gospel sprang. This is to construe that Johannine ethics is Christologically convicted theology. This further leads us to the following points of constructing Johannine ethics in the light of the deeply convicted Christological beliefs.

5.2.1. Jesus the Central Focus of Johannine Ethics

There is no denial that all the writings of the New Testament succinctly speak of Jesus. Each of the New Testament writings is unique in its own way with different theological emphases and with varying community circumstances that called for such particular distinctiveness. However, the different style and ways of each of the New Testament writings share the common point of contact. That is, Jesus becomes the motivating factor for the subsequent writings of the Gospels or letters

53 Boice, *The Gospel of John*, vol. 4, 1014-1018.

54 Boice, *The Gospel of John*, vol. 4, 1040.

55 Dodd, *The Interpretation of the Fourth Gospel*, 186.

56 Keener, *The Gospel of John*, vol. 2, 1015-1016; Kanagaraj, *The Gospel of John*, 508.

57 Marxsen, *New Testament Foundations for Christian Ethics*, 296.

of the books of the New Testament. It is obvious that there would have been no single New Testament writings without the person of Jesus. Jesus' submission to the Father's will by way of obedience in words and deeds, especially in the area of accomplishing God' will,[58] is the ultimate paradigm to be emulated (Jn. 14:31 cf. 4:34; 5:36; 8:29; 10:37-38; 17:4). The fact that the Gospel of John presents its ethical element not without Jesus is of crucial importance. Jesus occupies the central stage being the subject in all of the narratives in the Gospel of John. Even when he is not present, the talk is about him.[59] Jesus is portrayed as the ultimate ethical paradigm. The Gospel of John drives us home to see that the ethics of his Gospel is rooted in the realm of Christology. The Gospel that Jesus brings is not merely a theoretical presentation of 'natural morality' nor a 'revealed morality'[60] but a reality that lives amongst us and which confronts and moulds our attitude and behavior.[61]

Jesus is the epitome for the behavior to be emulated by the community of believers. He is the ultimate basis for ethical behaviors within the community of believers which is exemplified through his very own life and deeds (13-17).[62] So, the moral behavior of the community is intricately linked and defined in relation to the life and ministry of Jesus. Jesus models it first – he loves them and they are to reciprocate the love and exercise this love to one another (13:34). The love of the disciples for their Master must be expressed horizontally in their love for one another. This horizontal love, which must be visible to all, is proof of the vertical dimension. Jesus is the full measure of the love for one another (Jn. 13:34 cf. 1 Cor. 13).[63] It is explicated by his very own act of washing the feet of his disciples. This humble act of service performed by the Lord Jesus is unprecedented in a sense that no master does this act because it was considered a work of lower status people's service in the west Mediterranean world then. Jesus of John's Gospel is depicted as taking up the most humble and self-denying service.[64] After Jesus had

58 Hoskyns, *The Fourth Gospel*, 246.

59 Larry W. Hurtado, *Lord Jesus Christ: Devotion to Jesus in Earliest Christianity* (Michigan: Wm.B. Eerdmans Publishing Company, 2003), 351.

60 K. C. Abraham, *Transforming Vision: Theological - Methodological Paradigm Shifts* (Tiruvalla: Christain Sahitya Samithi, 2006), 73.

61 Jey J. Kanagaraj & Ian S. Kemp, *Gospel of John* (Bangalore: Asia Theological Association, 2000), 307.

62 Ruben Zimmermann, "Is There Ethics in the Gospel of John?," *Rethinking the Ethics of John: "Implicit Ethics" in the Johannine Writings,* edited by Jan G. van der Watt and Ruben Zimmermann (WUNT 1/291; Tubingen: Mohr Siebeck, 2012), 53-54.

63 Boice, *The Gospel of* John, vol. 4, 1038.

64 Kanagaraj, *The Gospel of John*, 438-439; Kanagaraj & Ian S. Kemp, *Gospel of John*, 307; Boice, *The Gospel of John*, vol. 4, 1010, likens the Feet washing in John with Christ's humility recorded in Paul's letter to the Philippians (2: 5-11). First, Jesus rising from supper (in John) is compared when Jesus rose from his throne of glory before his coming to the world (Philippians). Second, Jesus letting his garments aside (in John) is analogous to when Jesus came into the world he

enacted the humble service of foot washing, he asked them to do the same as he has done to them (imperative is based on the indicative paradigmatic mode of service '*diakonia*'). They are to wash one another's feet as an act of humble service as Jesus has washed for them (13:1-20). The significance of the feet washing is multiple - historical event in the life of Jesus and his disciples and the sequel exhortation to humility; part of the commemoration of the Passion which is dominated by the thought of the incarnation, the death and the resurrection of the 'Son of God.'[65] Johannine ethics is an ethics that is determined by the teachings and actions of Christ Jesus. So believers' attitude of humility is "dependent upon the humiliation and the glorification of Christ."[66] This is to once again endorse the fact that Johannine ethics is Christologically oriented and determined.

Jesus' teachings and actions shaped the attitude, behavior and life of the community of believers. The moral life is to be lived within a community of disciples and not as an excluded and isolated individual.[67] The commandment of Jesus to love one another therefore does not necessarily mean that the commandment is to exclude others.[68] The life and activities of Jesus is a model and an ideal because the community in the Gospel of John are to learn from him – how they should behave or what must be done. The life example of Jesus calls for an invitation to imitate. There is a sort of obligation that is laid on an individual who has responded in faith in Jesus (probably he/she is a 'changed person'). This obligation is however not an ordered obligation in a sense of duty but enabling obligation which the Spirit-*Paraclete* will enable an individual to fulfill what is given (loved to love) who has by his/her free will responded to the divine call to believe in Jesus who comes from God.

In this way, one's ethical actions would be seen as an accomplishment enabled Christologically through the Spirit-*Paraclete* so that we will not boast but rather be humbled. For only those individuals who have believed in Jesus are the changed and new persons shaped and guided by the life of Jesus. These changed persons who are shaped and guided can *only* pass on this legacy through their own acts of shaping and guiding (that which is ethics). The Lord Jesus shapes the believer and this believer can become a shaper through his/her own actions. Thus, Jesus becomes the source and the route to which a believer must look up for/her ethical behavior in this world of social existence.

---

laid aside his glory (Philippians). Third, Jesus took a towel and girded himself is a garb of a servant, a role Jesus took upon himself (in Philippians). Lastly, Jesus pouring water into a basin and washing his disciples' feet is analogous to the pouring of his blood on the cross for the washing of the human's sin by the atonement.

65 Hoskyns, *The Fourth Gospel*, 446.

66 Hoskyns, *The Fourth Gospel*, 446.

67 Matera, *The New Testament Ethics*, 116.

68 Boice, *The Gospel of John*, vol. 4, 1039.

5.2.2. Jesus the Ethical Point of Orientation for the Believers

The Johannine theme of light is introduced in the prologue and it is the opposite of moral and ethical pole of darkness (Jn. 1:5). This theme of light is picked up again in the Jesus and Nicodemus discourse (Jn. 3:19-21) but not personified until the Jewish feast of Tabernacles/ Booths recorded in John chapter 8. The theme of light was made obvious by Jesus' own self- declaration that he is the light during the Jewish Feast of Tabernacles also called the Jewish festival of Booths. He said, "I am the light of the world. Whoever follows me will never walk in darkness, but will have the light of life" (Jn. 8:12). Immediately following this discourse, Jesus heals the man born blind, which signifies that he is the real and the source of light (Jn. 9).[69] This personified light is related to the identity of Jesus as the Messiah or Christ (Jn. 8:26f).There however was a confusion among the crowds present at the festival to whether Jesus is the Christ/Messiah or do they need to look forward to another figure other than Jesus who will be the Messiah.

Jesus, the Son is the perfect revealer of God, the Father (Jn. 1:18). No one has ascended into heaven except who descended from heaven, the Son of Man (Jn. 3:13). God has spoken to us through his Son, Jesus; it is decisive, final word which has come through him (Jn. 1:45; 5:39, 46 indicate that Jesus was revealed through prophets and Moses earlier). By his unity with the Father, Jesus has the light and *is* the true light.[70] So the appearance or coming of the light poses a profound ethical challenge to the people. The ethical challenge is to make a choice, a decision whether to continue to live in darkness or to come into the light (decision dualism). There is a choice to orient one's life to walk in the light that is to believe in Jesus or disorient one's life and remain in darkness.

Light and darkness are two opposing poles of moral and ethical dualism in John's Gospel. Light is a metaphor for the illumination brought to human existence by the person of Jesus. Majority of the people prefer darkness over the light because their works are evil (Jn. 3:19) but there are also those who come to the light because their works are good (Jn. 3:21). It is significant to note that the light is here on earth for a specific span of time. The light who is personified as Jesus is to return to where he has come from (Jn. 8:14). Jesus straightforwardly is identified as the light and is already making its presence here and now (Jn. 8:12). In the narrative story of the man born blind, Jesus tells his disciples saying, "While I am in the world, I am the light of the world" (Jn. 9:5). And later in the last chapter of the 'Book of Signs' we are told that there were some Greeks who had come to attend the feast and have inquired to meet Jesus (Jn. 12:20-21). We are not informed if Jesus met those Greeks as requested but we read that Jesus started to predict concerning his death. It is here that the christological titles

---

69 J. N. Sanders and B. A. Mastin, *The Gospel According to St. John* (Peabody, Massachusetts: Hendrickson Publishers, 1968), 5.

70 Birger Gerhardsson, *The Ethos of the Bible*, translated by Stephen Westerholm (Eugene: Wipf & Stock Publishers, 1979), 97.

'Christ' and 'Son of Man' are equated as referring to Jesus and Jesus is related to the light (Jn. 12:34-36).

And so there is an urge to walk in the light while the light is still with them, lest the darkness overhaul them. Then Jesus told them, "You are going to have the light just a little while longer. Walk while you have the light before darkness overtakes you. The man who walks in the dark does not know where he is going. Put your trust in the light while you have it, so that you become sons of light" (Jn. 12: 35-36). A little later we read Jesus declaring this, "I have come into the world as a light, so that no one who believes in me should stay in darkness" (Jn. 12:46). So, we see that the light which is recognised as Jesus is the Christ, also the Son of Man who has come from God to make people realize they are living in the darkness and need to come out from the darkness to the light and believe in this light (Jn. 12:36).

Johannine Jesus is then the ethical point of orientation from dwelling in darkness into living in the light. There is a profound ethical challenge and call to live in the light. Jesus of the Gospel of John who sets an example not merely by words or speech but in truth and action is the ultimate pattern of the believers' conduct. Jesus as the only begotten Son of God serves and fulfills the will of God. It is in the person and work of Jesus that the will of the Father is displayed. The Scripture, the *semeia* speak the fact that the teachings and deeds of Jesus are in accordance with God's will. Consequently, the words and deeds of Jesus serve as the ethical point of orientation for the disciples and believers.

Jesus is the light and those who believe in him will not come under darkness but have passed from darkness to light. The act of believing in Jesus as sent by God, the Father necessitates a change in one's life's direction. According to the Johannine terminology it is from darkness to light, a transition from darkness into light, a transformation from unbelieving to believing. The world of humanity has to reorient their lives according to the revelation brought by Jesus in order to enjoy eternal life. Faith in Jesus entails a profound change in one's life, that is, a reorientation of one's life in relation to the personhood, authority and mission of Jesus. Believers are expected to be how Jesus was and do what he had done. Like a branch attached to the vine, so are believers to abide in Jesus so that they will bear fruit to God's glory.

5.3. Major Important Features of John's Ethics

There are few but very significant features of ethics found in the Gospel of John. We shall feature them out in the following headings.

5.3.1. Ethics of Belief in Jesus

In the Gospel of John, the christological rhetoric is striking with emphatic focus on issues on the belief in, and about, Jesus. The focus precisely is so much on the necessity of πιστεύειν in Jesus as Messiah, Son of God and the Son of Man who at the beginning had his preexistent with God as the *logos* of God. In Jesus, is fulfilled, the role and authority of all that these titles entail. 'To believe' in Jesus as the revelation of God is a moral act in that it acknowledges the true identity and ἐργον τοῦ θεοῦ and Jesus[71] and their indwelling mutual relationship. Jesus explains that the singular ἐργον God requires is πιστεὺειν εἰς Ἰησοῦν (Jn. 6:27–29). As such 'to believe' in Jesus is the proper moral response that people should render to God.[72] The centrality of belief in Jesus is affirmed by the usage of the word πιστεύω in every narrative passages and discourses beginning from the prologue to the epilogue.[73] And especially the purpose statement of the Gospel clearly states that all the miraculous *signs* Jesus performed were intended as a vehicle to reveal his glory and subsequently lead to believe in him (Jn. 20:31). 'Believing' in the one God sent into the world is loaded with an ethical allegation to decide to align oneself with the 'above world,' 'light,' 'truth,' and 'life' over against the world below, in darkness, falsehood and death. This entails that 'belief' in Jesus transits oneself from one realm to another spiritual realm (darkness to light). Rudolf Bultmann contended that "it would not violate Johannine meaning to add: faith is 'conversion' or 'repentance.'"[74] Then faith in Jesus is to undergo a profound change and shift. In this case the Johannine meaning of faith can be equated with the Synoptic concept of repentance or say conversion.

John's Gospel exhibits an artistic exhibition of a loyal single allegiance to the commandment given by God in and through the person of His son Jesus. Jesus is the Son who came from God and he is *the* only way to the Father (Jn. 1:14, 18; 3:18, 34; 14:6). John's Gospel thus displays monotheistic faith as an ethical expression. Jesus is depicted as the object of faith in the Gospel (except Jn. 14: 1b). Johannine Jesus is not presented as another deity but one with God: "I and the Father are one" (Jn. 10:30 cf. 1:1, 18; 10:38). It befits to surmise that at the heart of the ethics of the Fourth Gospel lies the call or an invitation 'to believe' in Jesus. This is a call which directs to eternal life (Jn. 3:16; 20:31). And for John, eternal life is the knowledge of God.[75] No one has seen God but he who has seen Jesus has seen the Father (Jn. 14:10-11, 20; 17:21). Σημεῖα act as a vehicle to prove both the identity of the actor (Jesus) and at the same time the salvific significance attached to the performed signs is also loaded with ethical implications. So, whoever responded in faith to Jesus, eternal life is assured (20:31) for God is

---

71 Cornelis Bennema, "Virtue Ethics in the Gospel of John: The Johannine Characters as Moral Agents." *Rediscovering John: Essays on the fourth Gospel in Honour of Frederic Manns,* edited by L.D.

72 Jan G. van der Watt, "The Gospel of John's Perception of Ethical Behaviour," *In die Skriflig* 45 (2011): 433–435.

73 Hurtado, *Lord Jesus Christ*, 351.

74 Rudolf Bultmann, *Theology of the New Testament*, vol. 2, translated by Kendrick Grobel (New York: Scribner's, 1955), 76.

75 Dodd, *The Interpretation of the Fourth Gospel*, 186, 187.

found "in an historic Person of the past, a Person who nevertheless, through it [faith], remains the object of saving knowledge, the truth and the life"[76] who is Jesus the promised Christ.

Another significant question remains - is the belief in Jesus a onetime response to the call or is it a process? To this we may have to respond that it is a continuous process which must be expressed daily in every day behavior. The allegory of the vine and the branches also informs it clear that they (disciples – where disciples in John have an inclusive connotation embracing everyone who believes in Jesus) must abide in the vine to bear much fruit. So, belief in John's Gospel is an ongoing process with a view to bear fruit and to enjoy eternal life here and now and in the fullness of the time to come. Belief in Jesus is an everyday confession of faith and this faith prompts us to live as children of the light to do good and thus bear much fruit. So again it can be sanctioned that 'belief' in Jesus is an ethical decisive moment, a joyful acceptance which leads to eternal life. Johannine ethics is an ethic of faith which requires an ethic of response, response of faith to the revelation of God which is revealed in the person of Jesus. Subsequently for the Johannine community, the personal injunctions of Christ and his very own demonstrated exemplary life served as a guideline. Conformity to the love and life of Christ fully determines the entire course of a believing community's life. This is to ascertain that the Johannine ethics is an ethics of faith in Jesus.

5.3.2. Ethics of Obedience and Loyalty

Jesus said to his disciples, "If you keep my commandments, you will abide in my love, καθὼς ἐγὼ τάς ἐντολάς τοῦ πατρός μου τετήρηκα καὶ μένω αὐτοῦ ἐν τῆ ἀγάπη" (Jn. 15:10). Jesus' saying that he kept the commandments of the Father is a clear expression of obedience. The highest form of, and the most effective expression of love is, obedience which culminates on the cross of Calvary.[77] And "this obedience is the glorification of the Father's name."[78] We read in different passages of the Gospel that Jesus is conscious about his divine mission and to bring into perfection the will of the Father (Jn. 4:34; 6:38; 17:4; 19:30). Jesus himself has patterned a way of obedience and now he instructs the believers to follow his footstep i.e., to keep his commandments (Jn. 14:15, 21, 23; 15:10, 14).[79] The commands of Jesus are not burdensome to those who love Jesus (1 Jn. 5:3). Jesus being mindful of his coming into the world has set every detail of his life and ministry in submission and obedience to the Father's will. The *erga* of Jesus are the *erga* of God[80] for the Father is glorified in the Son's activity since in

76 Dodd, *The Interpretation of the Fourth Gospel*, 186.

77 Kanagaraj, *The Gospel of John*, 505.

78 Hoskyns, *The Fourth Gospel*, 32.

79 Boice, *The Gospel of John*, vol. 4, 1175.

80 Rengstorf, "σημεῖον," *TDNT*, vol. 7, edited by Gerhard Friedrich (Michigan: Wm. B. Eerdmans Publishing Company, 1971), 248.

everything the Son seeks and achieves the Father's glory (Jn. 14:13, 14 cf. 5:31; 7:18; 8:50. 54).[81] Jesus fulfilling the ethical demands of God is presented as doing precisely just as the Father asks him to say and do (Jn. 5:17, 19; 8:29b). There is a complete unity of the Father and the Son in speech and action which is another form of an expression of obedience of the Son to the Father. Jesus is presented as having the frequent claim to have done the will of God. Jesus would have never done it otherwise but the will of God (Jn. 4:34; 6:38 cf. 7:17; 8:28, 29; 10:37; 14:10-11; 14:31; 15:10; 17:4). It will not be an exaggeration to endorse that the Gospel of John presents Jesus at the highest moral level and there is nowhere any clue of fault or failure except for the false accusation which also lacks specific charge (Jn. 18:30 cf. Mk. 15:14).[82] Jesus' "moral purity is inviolable."[83] His obedience is concretized in the miraculous shmei/a he performed (Jn. 14:9-11) and to which he was committed to bring into completion is flavored with specific ethical implications especially in connection with the Gospel's orientation towards achieving a goal.[84] And this goal has to be achieved through obedience to the will of the Father because obedience is the mark of love (See Jn. 14:21). Obedience to God as demonstrated and lived out in the words and deeds of Jesus constituted the core of Johannine ethics, to which the believing community in Jesus must keep up.

Just as Jesus has been obedient to the will of God, so one ought to do what Jesus commands, a command to love one another as he himself has manifested and lived (Jn. 13:34). Jesus gives a new commandment neither to replace nor to nullify the old Mosaic Law (Deut. 6:5; Lev. 19:18) but gives new meaning from the perspective of the newly wrought salvation history in his life and ministry (entirely given new significance by Jesus).[85] This is the reason Jesus commands that the community of his disciples must love one another as a testimony. The love of the Father is made active in the life and ministry of the Son. This love command virtually must be the hallmark to distinguish them from the rest of the unbelieving world (1 Jn. 1:3).[86] Jesus has loved and laid down his life for them and they must be willing to do as much for each other (Jn. 15:12-14). But, this does

---

81 Moloney, *The Gospel of John*, 397.

82 Kanagaraj, *The Gospel of John*, 588.

83 Donald Guthrie, *New Testament Theology* (Illinois: InterVarsity Press, 1981), 231.

84 Moloney, *The Gospel of John*, 396.

85 Boice, *The Gospel of John*, vol. 4, 1038-1040. According to Boice, the new commandment of Jesus was given a *new object* (in Christ's command the relationship is spiritual, where neighbor signifies any believer in Jesus) and most importantly his love is universal i.e., love is not to be held back from unbelievers. In Leviticus the 'neighbor' was nothing more than the physical Jewish neighbor (family relationship). Secondly, the love command is to be exercised according to a *new measure*. God took the human form to demonstrate his love by sending his son (3:16 cf.1 Jn. 4:10; 1 Cor. 13). Thirdly, the new commandment is made possible by a *new power*. It is the power of the Holy Spirit.

86 Hoskyns, *The Fourth* Gospel, 451.

not require the disciples to do more than what the Master has done. Neither are the disciples obliged to lay down one's life for the other but the bottom-line here is the attitude and the willingness to love at any cost.

Jesus' commandment to remain in him and keep his commandment is constituted by his obedience to the command of the Father (Jn. 12:49; 14:31; 15:10). Fittingly, the submission and obedience of Jesus to God that which is lived out in his life and activities made up the Johannine ethics.[87] Jesus who patterned ethics of obedience in his life expects the same from the community of believers. This ethics of obedience (to abide in him and love for one another) and loyalty (to continue to believe in him) thus must be the characteristic of the believing community. To keep the commandment of Jesus is to obey the commandment of Jesus and this has to be proved by their love for one another as an directory for others to know they are truly the disciples of Jesus (Jn. 14:21, 23 cf. 13:34, 35).

To remain or abide in Jesus is not a metaphysical communion of substance nor a mystical experience to be sought but that must result in living a life of obedience to Jesus as Jesus fulfills in his obedience to the Father (Jn. 5:38 cf. 8:31; 15:10).[88] To obey the words of Jesus and to emulate his actions would be the ultimate sign of obedience and loyalty. Jesus is the light who demonstrates what entails proper ethical conduct. It is this Jesus who nourishes individuals in the moral life, and sustains those who abide in him to bear much fruit.[89] Ethical behavior is also established through example, imitation and as well as obedience which nonetheless is grounded in the experience of loving relationships. Love forms the basis on which obedience functions[90] for the fidelity of love is manifested in obedience. The Father loved and gave the Son definite Commandments (Jn. 3:35 cf. 5:20) and the Son showed and proved by absolute obedience even to the point of death (Jn. 4:34; 10: 17, 18; 19:30 cf. Phil. 2:8).[91] Ethics of obedience is founded on the utter submission and obedience of the son Jesus to the divine will of the Father. So, we can remark that Johannine ethics of obedience and loyalty is grounded on the obedience and loyalty of Jesus, who is the Messiah/Christ who has been sent by the Father on the divine salvific mission to the world. Jesus having lived a life of love and obedience to the Father's commandments has likewise loved and gave the commandments to his disciples to love one another, and they must show their love for their master in obedience to the given commandments

87 Smith, *John*, 44.

88 Smith, *John*, 541.

89 Andrew T. Glicksman, "Beyond Sophia," *Rethinking the Ethics of John: "Implicit Ethics" in the Johannine Writings* (Tubingen: Mohr Siebeck, 2012), 101.

90 Volker Rabens, "Johannine Perspectives on Ethical Enabling," *Rethinking the Ethics of John: "Implicit Ethics" in the Johannine Writings,* edited by Jan van der Watt and Ruben Zimmermann (Tubingen: Mohr Siebeck, 2012), 139.

91 Hoskyns, *The Fourth Gospel*, 477.

(Jn. 14:15), then only can they abide in his love (Jn. 14:15,21 cf. 1 Jn. 4:16).[92] There can be no denial that there is a moral obligation for us, Christians today, who profess to believe in Jesus, to carry through the legacy of obedience and loyalty to God, as Jesus has been to his Father and his God. The Father of Jesus is the Father of ours and the God of Jesus is the God of ours (Jn. 20:17). Johannine ethics is an ethics of obedience and loyalty.

Jesus' command is a command that demands obedience. The demand for obedience is still relevant and applicable even for twenty - first millennium readers like us, not by direct vision or sight of Christ whose coming was a matter of history, but by reading and hearing the apostolic testimony (Jn. 17:20) as recorded in the instant Gospel. The command to love one another and to be obedient to Jesus' command is not exclusive. Jesus' command is timeless and neither space bound nor culture bound but composites universal requisite by which one must guard his/her way of life. Jesus' command hence has bearing even upon the twenty - first millennium believers today. As believers in Jesus Christ, one must regard and hold true to the testimony of the earthly disciples of Jesus and the enabling power of the Spirit-*Paraclete* as a single unity working towards the same goal (Jn. 15:26f). The exalted Lord Jesus through the Spirit-*Paraclete* continues to address and command us to follow him in faith and remain faithful and be obedient to his command (Jn. 8:12). Rationally we can suppose that personal encounter and fellowship with the risen and exalted Lord Jesus Christ has much expectation from us, to obey his command as it was expected of his inner circle of the disciples, then.

5.3.3. Ethics of Love

Love is considered the most supreme and vivid commandment of Jesus in the Fourth Gospel.[93] "I give you a new commandment, that you love one another. Just as I have loved you, you also should love one another." (ἐντολὴν καινὴν δίδωμι ὑμῖν, ἵνα ἀγαπᾶτε ἀλλήλους καθὼς ἠγάπησα ὑμᾶς ἵνα καὶ ὑμεῖς ἀγαπᾶ τε ἀλλήλους) (13:34). The basis for this love command 'love one another' is on the love of Jesus for his disciples. The imperative horizontal love command is based on the indicative vertical love of Jesus himself. Jesus' command is given from above that can be realized in the community of believers,[94] who accepts the claim of Jesus as the true and perfect revelation of God. While the object of this love is the company of believers, the commandment to love one another, however, is not to hold back from unbelievers.[95] Therefore, the new commandment is

92 Hoskyns, *The Fourth Gospel*, 477. To abide in, and to keep, Jesus Commandments are two modes of expressing the same thing. That is, there is coherence between these two imperatives given by Jesus.

93 Craig S. Keener, *The Gospel of John: A* Commentary, vol. 1 (Peabody, Massachusetts: Hendrickson Publishers, 2003), 325.

94 Matera, *New Testament Ethics*, 115.

95 Boice, *Gospel of John,* vol. 4, 1039; Matera, *New Testament Ethics*, 115.

"no retrograde and narrow exclusivism"[96] rather to stay united with God in and through Jesus by the mutual love for one another. This new commandment, Jesus "will presently re-affirm as summing up all his commandments and interpret as to be modeled upon his keeping of the Father's commandments (Jn. 15: 10-12)."[97] The love of Jesus grounded on the love of the Father (Jn. 15:9) is the ground on which the community of believers is grounded. Jesus is the ultimate revelation of God's love for the world (Jn. 3:16 cf. 17:23) and the Father loves the Son (Jn. 3:35; 5:20).[98] Jesus reciprocates the Father's love by his utter submission and obedience to the commandments of the Father (Jn. 15:10). And this can also be expressed through the reciprocal Johannine indwelling relationship of the Father-Son, which also tells of the oneness of the Son with the Father (Jn. 14:10-11; 17:12).[99] This is to articulate that the command of Jesus is rooted in the revelatory events of his own life and ministry.

Jesus loves his own and exhorts them to remain in his love and to keep his commandments (Jn. 15:10 cf. 14:15, 21). And this love which is at the centre of Johannine ethics must be in conformity with the commands of Jesus Christ.[100] To remain in Jesus' love and to keep his commandments are coherently the same thing expressed in two modes.[101] His commandment is that they "love one another" (ἀγαπᾶτε ἀλλήλους) just as they have been loved "καθὼς ἠγάπησα ὑμᾶς" (the imperative rests on the indicative). The Johannine ethics of love is central to the Gospel for it is the expression of the love which God has manifested through Jesus.[102] Subsequently, Johannine ethics is an ethics of love patterned on the love of God manifested in and through Jesus the Son. Love therefore must be the underlying motivation of the ethics of the believing community.[103] In connection to this love command, "to remain" in Jesus is of paramount importance that underlies mutual relationship that which is to be established in love and commitment. The climax is in the imperative mei,nate in my love (Jn. 15:9) which is demanded of the disciples meaning continuing in the love they have received.[104] Their existence must be determined by their love for one another for "love is the foundation of obedience, and obedience is the sure outcome and result of love."[105] And to continue in the love received becomes real only in that moment

96 Hoskyns, *The Fourth Gospel,* 451.

97 Hoskyns, *The Fourth Gospel,* 451.

98 Compare John 10:17; 15:9; 17:23, 24, 26.

99 Schnackenburg, *The Gospel According to St. John,* vol. 2, 313.

100 Boice, *The Gospel of John*, vol. 4, 1106.

101 Hoakyns, *The Fourth Gospel*, 477.

102 J. L. Houlden, *Ethics and the New Testament* (London: T&T Clark International, 1992), 125.

103 Boice, *The Gospel of John*, vol. 4, 1106.

104 Kanagaraj, *The Gospel of John*, 505.

105 Boice, *The Gospel of John*, vol. 4, 1107.

in keeping the commandments that results in bearing fruit (Jn. 15:10).[106] Birger Gerhardson observes that the Johannine love commandment is in agreement with the synoptic Gospels' heart of Jesus' teaching (double commandment to love God and neighbor) which links 'in the process love for God with love for one's fellow human beings.'[107]

It is noteworthy that the injunction to love, which is a *new* commandment, is because of the 'Christological reference which constitutes the essential novelty.'[108] The commandment took a new dimension in the newness of the situation, in the context of his sacrificial love on the cross (Jn. 13:34b; 15:13), newness of the time of salvation here and now but not a new love commandment because love for one's neighbor (Lev. 19:18) and for one's fellow (1QS 1:9-11) are already enjoined both in the Old Testament and in Qumran community respectively.[109] This is unique of John's presentation of the new love commandment which has a continuous and lifelong effect in the lives of the believing community.[110] It is new because Jesus sets in a new situation not new as against to something that has existed nor is a replacement of the old. It is also new because it is Jesus who directs a new motive and power which obliges not to simply fulfill this ethical demand but as a consequence of what we have received ('as I have loved you').[111] The Johannine ethics in deed is borne out of the christological and eschatological reality that the community of believers envisions.

There is an obligation laid on the community of believers by Jesus as a hallmark of their identity which projects a greater frequency than the rest of the New Testament. Thus, it is rightly concluded on this new commandment that "the ethical life of the Christian always remain a response to what Jesus has done on their behalf."[112] Jesus rather than simply giving ethical directives to be followed, fairly

> Sought a response to how God was bringing in his reign through his deeds and words. …The fourth gospel coheres with them (Jesus' ethical teachings as preserve in the Synoptic) in looking for his response of faith in action. Empowered by Jesus' example and his prior love, such

106 Rudolf Bultmann, *The Gospel of John: A Commentary,* translated by G. R. Beasley-Murray (Oxford: Basil Blackwell, 1971), 540.

107 Gerhardsson, *The Ethos of the Bible,* 104.

108 Raymond F. Collins, *Christian Morality: Biblical Foundations* (Notre Dame, IN: University of Notre Dame Press, 1986), 116.

109 Burridge, *Imitating Jesus,* 334; Hoskyns, *The Fourth Gospel,* 451.

110 Moloney, *The Gospel of John,* 424.

111 Burridge, *Imitating Jesus,* 327.

112 Patrick J. Harin, "Remain in Me (John 15:15): The Foundation of the Ethical and Its Consequence in the Farewell Discourses," *Neotestamentica* 25/2 (1991): 355.

> extreme love is the mark of the Christian life: 'By this everyone will know that you are my disciples, if you love one another' (13:35).[113]

Jesus said to his disciples, "If you love me, you will keep my commandments" (ἐὰν ἀγαπᾶτε με τὰς ἐντολὰς τὰς ἐμὰς τηρήσετε) (Jn. 14:15 cf. 14:21, 23f; 15:31). Here love for, and obedience, to Jesus' commandments are brought together and yet it is the condition of obedience that flows from love.[114] This implies that 'to love' precedes 'to keep the commandments of Jesus.' A model is provided by himself in his own loving and mutual obedience to the Father (Jn.14:31). Since Jesus models obedience to the Father, there is an obligation on the community of believers to respond to his commandment so that we not only "know the will of God and the clear revelation of what we ought to be, but also to *become* it (Jn. 14:21 cf. 1 Jn. 2:3, 5; 3; 13-14)."[115] This indicates that Jesus' commandments are significantly "Christologically focused: he demands an ongoing commitment to the truth of his person as the Christ, the Son of God."[116] Such a commitment cannot, logically, be lived in individualistic isolation but that its commitment must find its expression and fulfillment within the community who owes her ardent allegiance to the call of faith in Jesus. Explaining the seeming limitation of love within the group or say a sectarian nature of the Johannine community, Hays comment on this perspective is impressive. He says, "with the world inexplicably refusing to accept Jesus as the bearer of God's truth…the community of faith came to be seen as the only sphere within which life and love could be found."[117]

It is therefore not a thing of surprise that Jesus calls his disciples to love one another (Jn. 13:34), and in the context of love for, and obedience to, him (15:9-19). The scope of love should not narrow down just within the community as though love of God in and through Jesus is limited. And besides, the focus to love for one another does not necessarily put a restriction or "does not mark any frontier."[118] So also John W. Pryor commends that "there is no indication that it implies a rejection of obligations to outsiders" and the Johannine Christians remain in the world (Jn. 17:15), probably with a sense of obligation to it.[119] Teresa Okure says that Jesus' witness to the Samaritan woman functions as a model for

---

113 Burridge, *Imitating Jesus,* 328.

114 Boice, *The Gospel of John,* vol. 4, 1105.

115 Boice, *The Gospel of John,* vol. 4, 1107. Boice further explains that loving Jesus and keeping up his commandments can practically be expressed in at least three things – *service, sacrifice, and sharing.* For further details see page 1109.

116 John W. Pryor, *John: Evangelist of the Covenant People* (Illinois: InterVarsity Press, 1992), 162.

117 Hays, *The Moral Vision of the New Testament,* 147. For similar ideas see Burridge, *Imitating Jesus,* 334.

118 Rudolf Schnackenburg, *The Moral Teaching of the New Testament,* translated by J. Holland-Smith and W. J. O'Hare from German second edition of 1962 (New York: Harder and Harder, 1965), 328.

119 Pryor, *John: Evangelist of the Covenant People,* 162.

the disciples in their mission, and that as he was the one who was sent, so are they.[120] Pryor compares the love command that encloses John 15:12-17, in which Jesus invites the disciples to go and bear fruit.

The ethics of love which is in fact the heart of Johannine ethics is distinctively 'oriented to its Christology'[121] which is based on a practical response to the loving example of Jesus himself, who washed the disciples' feet and laid himself down even to the point of death on the cross.[122] Love for the community and openness to the world do not appear to stand exclusive from one another in John's thinking.[123] Therefore the love command in John's Gospel is not necessarily a restriction. The argument that John *restricts* love to members of the community is finally an argument from silence. And so, John's treatment of love does not license hatred outside the community "but focuses on the fulfillment of God's love within the community. Love – even God's love, even *agape* – seeks a response, an answering answer. It seeks mutual love…."[124] The love command of Jesus in the Gospel of John thus projects a very high ethical implication. The world may come to believe by the mutual love of the community (Jn. 17:20-26).

5.3.4 Ethics of Truth

Jesus brings the true revelation from God because it is the Father who has given the Son the words and works.[125] Jesus more than communicating a visual image fully interprets God[126] because he is sent by God (Jn. 6:42) and God is in him, and he is in God (Jn. 12:44-50); and his words and ἔργα are the words and ἔργα τοῦ θεοῦ (Jn. 12: 44-50) for the Father and the Son are one (Jn. 10:30).[127] Jesus said, "…because I have made known to you everything that I have heard from my Father." (…ὅτι πάντα ἃ ἤκουσα παρὰ τοῦ πατρός μου ἐγνώρισα ὑμῖν.) (Jn. 15:15 cf. 17:6-8, 14a, 26). Whatever Jesus said and did were the exact reproduction and replication of the words and deeds of the Father (Jn. 5:17, 19; 8:28; 10: 37; 14:10f). In everything he complied with the Father as he has been commanded (Jn. 12:49; 14:31). Jesus is said to have taught during the feast of the Tabernacles at the temple courts. We do not have the details of Jesus' teaching recorded but he claims the origin of his teaching from "the Father who sent me"

120 Teresa Okure, *The Johannine Approach to Mission* (WUNT 2/31; Tubingen: Mohr Siebeck, 1988), 17.

121 Eduard Lohse, *Theological Ethics of the New Testament* (Minneapolis: Fortress Press, 1991), 170.

122 Burridge, *Imitating Jesus,* 330.

123 Schnackenburg, *The Moral Teaching of the New Testament,* 163.

124 Allen Verhey, *The Great Reversal: Ethics and the New Testament* (Michigan: Wm. B. Eerdmans Publishing Company, 1984), 144.

125 Schnackenburg, *The Gospel According to St. John,* vol. 2, 176.

126 Keener, *The Gospel of John,* vol. 1, 424.

127 Hoskyns, *The Fourth Gospel,* 455.

(ὁ πέμψας με) (Jn. 7:14-16). In one of the Jewish festivals in Jerusalem, Jesus healed an invalid man who had been suffering for long thirty eight years. This took place on the Sabbath and so the Jews brought aggression to him (Jesus). To this Jesus answered, "The works that the Father has given me to complete, the very works that I am doing, testify on my behalf that the Father has sent me" (τὰ γὰρ ἔργα ἃ δέδωκέν μοι ὁ πατὴρ ἵνα τελειώσω αὐτά, αὐτὰ τὰ ἔργα ἃ ποιῶ μαρτυρεῖ περὶ ἐμοῦ ὅτι ὁ πατήρ με ἀπέσταλκεν) (Jn. 5:36 cf. 4:34). Jesus finds the authority and authenticity of his ministry from the Father. Jesus does or works as the Father does. This suggests that the Father and the Son shared the nature and the same role.[128]

Johannine Jesus reveals 'the truth'(ἡ ἀλήθεια) and is the revealer of 'the truth' (ἀλήθεια) and he himself is 'the truth.'[129] What is truth according to the Fourth Gospel? Jesus is the truth '*aletheia*' so he is able to say, "I am the way, and the truth and the life ..." (ἐγώ εἰμι ἡ ὁδὸς καὶ ἡ ἀλήθεια καὶ ἡ ζωή ...) (Jn. 14:6). Truth here is not an intellectual or philosophical concept but it is God's own self - revelation in and through Jesus (i.e., the very nature of God to reveal himself).[130] This is the divine and eternal reality, that which is the ultimate reality as revealed to humankind in and through the person of Jesus.[131] Jesus of course did not leave a rule-book or a written constitution to which we must refer in times when we face ethical issues, but he did leave the truth resounding in his words and deeds. He is the sole revelation of God, for he alone is in the bosom of God and he alone knows God fully (Jn. 3:13; 6:46).[132] He reveals the reality of God and his divine mission to which people must respond in faith is the ultimate ethical decisive moment. The truth that he has said concerning his identity (who he is) and origin (the One sent by God from above into the world below) is speaking the truth as against falsehood (Jn. 8:45). Jesus as 'the truth' has revealed the authentic nature and character of God in and through himself by his life and activities. Congruently, the overall life and ministry of Jesus is the actual revelation of his obedience to the moral commands of the Father (Jn. 12:49; 14:31).

Jesus' very own life is a rule-book for us to imitate. The existence reality of our living is that we do not have the accurate understanding of what is required of us as God's people. And it is the Gospel according to John that lucidly tells that to do the work of God is to believe in Jesus which is correspondingly equal to doing the will of the Father God. There is no clearer message than that is found in John's Gospel narrative where Jesus spent quality time with the disciples implanting in them life affirming values, life requisitions which is and must be guided by the

128 Keener, *The Gospel of John*, vol. 1, 425.

129 Dodd, *The Interpretation of the Fourth Gospel*, 178; Hoskyns, *The Fourth Gospel*, 455.

130 Matera, *New Testament Ethics*, 99; Morris, *The Gospel According to John*, 74.

131 Dodd, *The Interpretation of the Fourth Gospel*, 170- 178.

132 Keener, *The Gospel of John*, vol. 2, 941.

belief in him. Jesus does not simply give a theoretical content of neither ethics nor mere ideals but he revealed it in his very own life example and then only commands the disciples (indicative ethics precedes the imperative ethics in the Gospel). Many have considered love command as the only ethical commandment of Jesus. But, how true and appealing is that contention that the ethics of John is exclusively inward-looking? Sapping the cumulative underlying implication of Jesus' command and other internal textual references to his 'signs' performances designed to draw faith in his identity only prove that the command "to love one another" serves as the underlying regulating ethical principle on which all other ethical precepts are hanged.

The Johannine Ethics of Truth is the ethics revealed. Now the question arises to why tagged Johannine ethics as Revealed Ethics? Jesus being the torch bearer of God came to this world as the light, the truth and the life and those coming to the light are those who do the truth so that their works may be seen as done in God (Jn. 3:21). The priestly prayer of Jesus records praying to the Father to consecrate the disciples (Jn. 17:7) and send them into the world to speak the truth (basically to reveal the truth about God's divine purpose) to the world. Just as the Father sent Jesus, Jesus now sends the disciples to continue the chain of the one divine purpose (Jn. 17:18; 20:21). In short, the commendation to make known the Father's love in and through the Son for the world is a great revelation. This divine revelation has been revealed in the life, works, teachings, death and resurrection of Jesus. The holistic divine mission of God is fully revealed in the person and work of Jesus – and that is why we can daringly speak of Johannine ethics as 'revealed ethics.' It is because the Gospel has significantly presented both the theological and ethical demand being fulfilled in the very person of Jesus by his deeds and his words which includes his activities and teachings. Jesus said, "I declare to the world what I have heard from Him [Father]" (Jn. 8:26b). He continues to say, "...I do nothing on my own, but I speak these things as the Father instructed me" (Jn. 8:28b). Besides Jesus always does what is pleasing to the Father (Jn. 8:29b) and as he was saying these things, πολλοὶ ἐπίστευσαν εἰς αὐτόν (Jn. 8:30). Then Jesus continues to say to the Jews who have believed in him, "If you continue in my word, you are truly my disciples; and you will know the truth, and the truth will make you free" (Jn. 8:31-32). What is right and what is truth? What is the ultimate goal? The Gospel of John offers this ultimatum answer by his terminology 'eternal life.' These ethical related questions are being lived out in and through the person of Jesus in whom is displayed the supreme will of God.

The ethical values are assimilated in the very life and ministry of Jesus. Though, Jesus did not give long ethical directives to be followed he nevertheless "sought a response to how God was bringing in his reign through his deeds and words."[133] Jesus told his closest disciples to do as he has done to them (feet washing),

133 Burridge, *Imitating Jesus,* 328.

which is paradigmatic. This is a call and an insistence upon the imitation of Jesus through a narrative of his words and ways as a way to live a good moral life. The Father loves the Son, the Son loves back the Father by fulfilling the commands of the Father. In the like manner, Jesus loves the disciples and are commanded to love one another. If the disciples love their master, they will definitely meet the terms with their master's command and it is required of them as disciples. This is to assert that the essence of ethical livelihood is released and revealed both in the words and deeds of Jesus which in sequel places an obligation to obey and live out in the everyday life of every believer in Jesus as the Christ, the Son of God, the Son of Man and who pre-existed as one with the eternal God as the *logos* in the beginning of the world.

Jesus loves the disciples as he was loved by the Father, send them on a mission as he was sent. He gave himself in utter submission and obedience to the will of the Father and which is also expected of everyone who claims to be a believer in Jesus. It has been discussed in chapter 3 that the crowd's ethical question "What must we do to do the works God requires? (Jn. 6:28) got an answer from Jesus, "to believe in the one He has sent." (Jn. 6:29). Here the word 'to believe' encompasses not just a single act or one time moment of belief but a process that requires constant or active engagement in the Lord's command that eventually leads one to experience a perfect bliss of attaining life eternal.[134] Of course this is neither an idea of suggesting that eternal life is gained by the active participation of an individual nor suggesting escapism of ethical responsibility.

The act of belief in Jesus has to be endorsed in abiding in him to bear much fruit (Jn. 15) which implies active engagement in living everyday in accordance to God's will . There is nothing that is not revealed, every minute detail of the divine mission of God is revealed whereby the content of the revelation is *truth* (Jn. 15:15; 17:26 cf. verses 8, 14). The most fascinating and striking thing is that Jesus has promised his presence by the *Paraclete* who will guide them into all the truth (Jn. 16:13). The role and function of the *Paraclete* as described in the Gospel is indicative of the fact that the work has to linger on to perfectionism (concerning the work of witnessing to the truth about God's love and God's continuing mission of love through his Son (Jn. 1:29; 3:16; 17: 18, 20-25; 20:21). Johannine ethics is an ethics that is first revealed through Jesus Christ and it is documented by his obedience in fulfilling the will of the supreme God who commanded him to say and do exactly as he has been authorized (Jn. 12:49; 14:31). So, it is justifiable to propose that Johannine ethics is the 'Ethics of Truth' that which is revealed in and through the words and deeds of Jesus.

134 Matera, *The New Testament Ethics*, 94.

5.3.5. *Ethics of Life*

Life is one of the most significant characteristic concepts in John's Gospel[135] and is expressed in two different terms - ψυχή and ζωή.[136] The former is the transient, finite human life (physical, earthly) that can be laid down (Jn. 10:11, 15, 17; 12:25; 13:37-38; 15:13), and the latter denotes the divine, everlasting life of the Father-Son (i.e., life eternal, the gift of God through His Son, Jn. 1:4; 3:15; 5:21, 26; 6:57; 14:6).[137] The life of God is eternity wherein there is no past or future but only present (in the sense of timeless, i.e., eternity, divine reality).[138] Ζωή[139] is the Johannine equivalent of euvdaimoni, a (happiness, well being), which is regarded the highest moral good for humankind, according to Aristotle (*Nicomachean Ethics* I.2–4). Theologically speaking, ζωή is a moral category representing the continual existence of a moral God and thereby a moral objective. In the language of John, ζωή is the ultimate moral good that people can attain by believing in Jesus (Jn. 20:31; 1 Jn. 5:13). Cornelis Bennema rightly sees the ethical aspect of the 'ζωή' besides the soteriological character, of the purpose of the writing of the Gospel (Jn. 20:31). Whereby, 'the good life' is a moral goal and secondly πιστεύειν εἰς' Ιησοῦν is considered moral 'work' for obtaining this moral goal (Jn. 6:29). In the Johannine sense, the ultimate good is to know God (i.e., knowledge or vision of God) in and through Jesus the Son and partake in the divine life that the Father and the Son shares (Jn. 17:3).[140]

The frequent occurrences of the term ζωή (αἰώνιος) in the Fourth Gospel is one major theme.[141] The compound form 'ζωή αἰώνιος' is employed with reference to Jewish idea of the life of the age to come as contrasted with the life

135 Morris, *The Gospel According to John*, 82; Cf. Paul Lamarche, "The Prologue of John," *The Interpretation of John*, 2nd edition, edited by John Ashton (Edinburgh: T&T Clark, 1997), 51.

136 Dodd, *The Interpretation of the Fourth Gospel*, 144. There probably was no idea of immortality in OT and so life means 'earthly life and well-being.' The compound term 'ζωή αἰώνιος' occurs only in the Greek versions of Dan. 12:2, which teaches quite unequivocally the doctrine of a life in the future (i.e., life of the age to come).

137 Schnackenburg, *The Gospel According to St. John,* vol. 2, 353-354; Brown, The Gospel According to John, 506-508.

138 Dodd, *The Interpretation of the Fourth Gospel*, 150; Schnackenburg, *The Gospel According to St. John,* vol. 2, 355.

139 The word ζωή, 'Life' occurs 135 times in whole of the NT. Out of which 36 occurs in John's Gospel; 7 times in Matthew, 5 times in Luke, and 4 times in Mark; Raymond E. Brown, *The Anchor Bible: The Gospel According to John*, vol. 1 (New York: Doubleday & Company, 1966), 505-508; Morris, *The Gospel According to John*, 82; catholic-resources.org/John/Vocab-Life.html, accessed on 24-07-2017.

140 Bennema, "Virtue Ethics in the Gospel of John," 168–172; Dodd, *The Interpretation of the Fourth Gospel,* 186.

141 Dodd, *The Interpretationof the Fourth Gospel*, 144.

of this age.[142] John finds it significantly important to present the life affirming values which is found in Jesus (to quote few Jn. 1:4; 3; 6 esp. v. 47). Jesus said, "the work of God is this: to believe in the one he has sent" (Jn. 6:29). Who is the one sent? It is Jesus. He is symbolically represented as the light (Jn. 1: 3-9; 3: 17, 19-21). The moral crux of John's Gospel seems that believing in Jesus Christ is life which equally means there is life in his name (Jn. 2:31; 5:24; 6:40; 10:10; 12:50). Life in Jesus "is inalienably a life formed and informed by love" of the Father in and through the Son (Jn. 5:20, 24, 26).[143] So life is to be found in Jesus and it is actualized in relation to, and through, Jesus by believing in him. By believing in Jesus, the believer can posses and enjoy zwh, aivw,nioj here and now (Jn. 3:36; 5:24; 6:47; 6:54).[144] The reality of life and relations in Jesus Christ is emphasized more in this present 'eschatological existence' of humankind here and now in this world.

Belief in Jesus takes a believer to a zone of experiencing and attaining life eternal. That is, one has ζωή now in choosing to believe in Jesus who has brought the revelation of the gift offered by God or is condemned in the refusal to believe in Jesus (Jn. 5:19-30). The traditional eschatological age is inaugurated making eternal life a present reality but without being entirely abandoning the final period of time in the last day. The present and future reality overlaps in the Fourth Gospel. The narrative world of the Fourth Gospel presents to us that those narrative characters who are transformed are being brought and accepted into the new community by their affirmation of their belief and thereby living out the ethical dimension and demands of faith in Jesus. Richard B. Hays has correctly commented that a fuller reading of the Johannine narratives is essential to grasp its implications for shaping and fashioning the life of the believing community because the Gospel of John which at the beginning presents Jesus as the *logos* and eventually identified as the Christ/Messiah, the Son of God and also the Son of Man who comes from above is loaded with ethical implications for the community that accepts the message and finds itself being rejected by the world of unbelief.[145] The Fourth Gospel stresses the worth of the belief which results in life eternal.[146] The stress is so oft-repeated to emphasize the importance of the belief and practice of the individual to respond in faith to the ultimate revealer who

142 Dodd, *The Interpretation of the Fourth Gospel*, 146. According to Dodd, there are three distinquished forms of the expression of life in Jewish usage – (1) 'life' as contrasted with death; (2) 'life of the age' as contrasted with life of time; and (3) 'life of the Age to come' as contrasted with the life of This Age. All of these references however refer to life beyond the grave.

143 Verhey, *The Great Reversal*, 143.

144 Dodd, *The Interpretation of the Fourth Gospel*, 149.

145 Hays, *The Moral Vision of the New Testament*, 140 also 4.

146 See for instance, John 3:15f, 36; 4:14, 36;5:24, 39; 6:27, 40, 54,68; 10:28; 12:25, 50; 17:2f; 20:31.

is Jesus the mediator and envoy of God the Father.[147] This depicts the Gospel's unfailing emphasis in Christology. So, ethics being so much rooted in Christology is life affirming because, it is only in and through Jesus that there is an offer of life eternal (Jn. 20:31).

The Johannine community thus in fulfilling the ethical demands of faith eventually attains eternal life (Jn. 3:16; 20:31). The point here is that, life without Jesus is an empty life and this point of reference to life is found in relationships to and through Jesus ("...he who believes has eternal life." Jn. 6:47 cf. 20:31). Accordingly, as people come to believe in Jesus, their faith is understood as fulfillment of the works of God and subsequently must be affirmed by their behavior. And this behavior is what the Johannine narrative suggests saying 'to do the works of God' is 'to believe in the one he has sent' (Jn. 6:28-29). Later in the passage, the consequence of believing in Jesus is to have eternal life (Jn. 6:40). "To do the works of God" is basically behavioral and focuses to identify actions that are in accordance with the will of the Father.[148] The will of the Father is that whoever believes in his Son whom he has sent will receive eternal life (Jn. 3:16 ff; 5:24, 26; 6:40, 47; 20:31) but whoever does not believe in him brings upon oneself judgment that will lead to death (Jn. 8:24).[149] This implies that every individual is responsible for the choice he/she makes to incur in him/herself the blessing of life eternal or eternal judgment.

5.3.6. Ethics of Responsibility and Vocation

Johannine ethics is an ethics of responsibility and vocation. It is an assignment. It can be understood in relation to the mission work given to the disciples, to be a witnessing community of believers. This mission aspect is patterned upon the Father sending the Son into the world and Jesus sending the disciples to the unbelieving world (Jn. 15:27 cf. 17:18; 20: 21; 14:15, 21; 15:10, 14, 17). This responsibility given to the disciples has a strong ethical implication to continue to teach the world concerning the divine love brought by Jesus which in fact is the ultimate truth about God's nature and concern for the world.[150] The truth that Jesus is sent by God displaying *agape* by coming into this world to reveal to us the ultimate truth of God's love is vitally important.

---

147 J. F. O'Grady, "Johannine Ecclesiology: A Critical Evaluation," *BTB* 7 (1977): 43. Also see C. F. D. Moule, "The Individualism of the Fourth Gospel," *NovTest* 5 (1962): 184.

148 Michael Labahn, "It's Only Love" – Is That All? Limits and Potentials of Johannine "Ethic" – A Critical Evaluation of Research," *Rethinking the Ethics of John: "Implicit Ethics" in the Johannine Writings*, edited by Jan G. van der watt and Ruben Zimmermann (WUNT 1/291; Tubingen, Germany: Mohr Siebeck, 2012), 32.

149 Moloney, *The Gospel of John*, 432-433.

150 Matera, *The New Testament Ethics,* 97-113.

The disciples are given the most explicit paraenetic lesson in John 15 (the true vine and the branches). They are to *menein* in Jesus in order to bear fruit.[151] Their responsibility as the disciples of Jesus must pattern themselves after Jesus as Jesus remains in the Father's love and keep his commandments (Jn. 15:9-11 cf. 5:19). The disciples are chosen so that they may go forth and produce fruit in keeping the commandment Jesus has commanded them (Jn. 15:16-17). Those who believe in Jesus through their apostolic preaching and teaching are the fruit of the vine and the branches (cf. Jn. 17:20). In this case, the imagery of the bearing of the fruit is to be understood in the light of the mission to the world.[152] The commandments of Jesus are the commandments of God that directs Jesus' entire divine mission.[153] Jesus himself will enable them to fulfill his command because he abides in them (Jn. 15:4 'Abide in me, and *I in you*...).[154] As such, Jesus' commandment is grounded in his salvific work as the Good shepherd who lays down his life for the sheep (Jn. 10:11, 15, 17-18). Some have pointed out the sectarian approach of the command as esoteric but one must note the other reference found in the same shepherd passage in the Gospel (Jn. 10:16 speaks of bringing other sheep that does not belong to the fold so there will be one flock under one sphere cf. Jn. 17: 20-23 esp. verse 22 'so that they may be one, as we are one'). The sending of the chosen disciples to tell the truth to the world is the outcome of the death of Jesus i.e., the redemptive significance of his death (Jn. 6:70; 3:17 cf. 12:20-24; Lk.6:13).[155] There is a clear ethical obligation for the disciples to carry out the responsibility and legacy of Jesus' mission to make known the divine ultimate truth that he has been sent by God and that whoever believes in him will find life eternal.

The responsibility given is imperative and thereby becomes a vocation for believers and followers of Jesus Christ. The disciples are sent as witness of Jesus and their vocation to bear testimony to and for Jesus is grounded upon their intimate companionship with him 'from the beginning' (Jn. 6:41, 70; 1 Jn. 1:1-4).[156] The responsibility along exhortation comes to them during the farewell discourse which is very significant from the socio-psychological point of view. The disciples are filled with grief knowing that the master they have been following in their whole life was to leave them very soon. It is at this point of emotional instability and situation that the Lord Jesus gave them a sequence of ethical implications and challenges they will be facing (Jn. 16:2, 33; 15:18-25) after his physical departure.

151 Hoskyns, *The Fourth Gospel,* 471, 475. The insistence to remain in Jesus can be understood in the light of the apostasy of the Jews, of Judas, and of the unbelieving disciples (6:41, 51, 60, 66, 70-71).

152 Hoskyns, *The Fourth Gospel,* 476.

153 Matera, *New Testament Ethics,* 106.

154 Hoskyns, *The Fourth Gospel,* 476.

155 Hoskyns, *The Fourth Gospel,* 478.

156 Hoskyns, *The Fourth Gospel,* 481.

The most paraenetic obligation was to remain in their belief that he is sent, he is the Son of God, the Christ, the Son of Man who came from above to grant eternal life (Jn. 14:1ff.) and live according to his commandments and when they remain and believe in him, they will be able to do greater works (Jn. 14:12) and the most comforting speech was that Jesus is going for their good and that he will be back to get them to be with him and with the Father for eternity. Jesus promised his divine presence by and through the Spirit-*Paraclete* in between the time that marks his physical departure and his second coming, *parousia*.

The responsibility is vested upon them to testify to the truth because they have been with him (Jesus) 'from the beginning' is ethically significant (Jn. 15:27). 'From the beginning' means that the disciples have been with Jesus from the start of his earthly ministry.[157] The disciples are consecrated (Jn. 15:3 cf. 17:17, 19), and the resurrected and glorified Jesus Christ appears to his disciples and pronounced benediction twice saying, "Peace be with you" and said "as the Father has sent me, so I send you." When he had said this, he breathed on them and said to them, "Receive the Holy Spirit" (Jn. 20:19-22; 17:18). This suggests that the disciples are empowered with the authority of Jesus. Hence, we can say that the authority of the disciples, thereby, is rooted upon the authority of the Father and of the Son and of the Holy Spirit.[158] The Johannine farewell discourse, priestly prayer and Jesus Christ's appearance following his resurrection from the death are loaded with ethical implications for the disciples. So, we can infer that the Johannine ethics is an ethics of responsibility and vocation given by Jesus to continue his mission of divine revelation. In short, Johannine ethics is an ethics of responsibility and vocation vested on every individual of believers in Jesus.

Conclusion

The major characteristic features of John's ethics speak well for the interconnectedness that exists between ethics and Christology. In the Gospel of John, every ethical aspect centers on the Christological aspects. The Johannine Christian community serves as the moral narrative world wherein the moral life of the community is intricately related to the very *being* and *work* of Jesus. Discipleship is the closest locale of the moral narrative world of the Johannine Christian community. Their moral and ethical life is defined and oriented in their strong belief and conviction about the claims of Jesus as the incarnated *logos* of God, the promised Christ who is the 'Son of God' and the 'Son of Man.' We have seen that the Gospel of John is far concerned to evoke and seek a response of faith than to present blocks of ethical directives because the heart of ethics is Jesus himself. Consequently, it deems that all ethical requirements hang on Christology. Hays

157 Brown, *The Gospel According to John*, vol. 2, 690.

158 Hoskyns, *The fourth Gospel*, 484.

puts it well, affirming that "both the warrants and the norms for ethics are to be located almost exclusively in conformity to the person of Jesus."[159]

Every detail of Jesus' words and deeds are designed to bring glory to the Father who sent him, so much so that his life and ministry is tuned up with the will of the Father in perfect submission and obedience. Subsequently, one is summoned to believe in Jesus who proceeds from the Father. Hence, anyone who believes and accepts Jesus as the *logos* and confesses Jesus as the Christ, the Son of God and the Son of Man, is expected 'to remain' in him to bear fruit and to enjoy life eternal. It is therefore Christology that defines and frames ethics in the Fourth Gospel. Lohr has rightly asserted that moral norms in the Gospel of John "are defined in a new way by their relation to Jesus, at the same time...the main character in the narrative is dependent upon its relation to moral norms... Moral metaphors ...create both new Christological and moral notions at the same time."[160] We can thereby conclude that the content of the ethical elements, in the Fourth Gospel, has its distinctive stamp from a reference to Jesus Christ.

Johannine ethics and Christology are seamlessly blended and are integral part of one another and yet it is crucial to point out that Christology enjoys a place of dominance than ethics. Why? This is because ethics cannot be explicated devoid of Christology and it is in Christology that the ethics of John's Gospel is embedded and articulated and not otherwise. This is to construe that Johannine ethics cannot be distinctively understood apart from the Christological point of view. Ethics can never be entirely divorced from Christology in the Fourth Gospel and at the same time ethics cannot be solely reduced to Christology though.

The ethical demands in John's Gospel are an essential part of the new commandment given by the Lord Jesus. Accordingly, the new commandment has a decisive influence upon the molding of ethics in the Johannine community. In effect love which is the fundamental content of the new commandment governs the rest of the ethical conducts. Love as an ethical entity is the basis and the foundation to all ethical conducts but again it is paramount to acknowledge that while love is divine, faith is what is demanded from human's response. This means 'love' and 'faith' are two dominant ethical ingredients which constitute Johannine ethics. The ethical teachings and practices of the Johannine community stand in continuity with their belief in Jesus Christ. The teaching of Jesus, the revealed ἔργα that is σημεῖα, and the exemplary act of Jesus in the Gospel of John is indeed set on a consistent high moral tone. For Jesus himself lived up the teaching and he executes the words and works of the Father God in utter obedience to the will of his Father. It will not be an exaggeration to postulate that there would have been no ethics without Christology according to John's Gospel. The Johannine

159 Hays, *The Moral Vision of the New Testament*, 153.

160 Hermut Lohr, "'Εργον as an Element of Moral Language in John," *Rethinking the Ethics of John: "Implicit Ethics" in the Johannine Writings,* edited by Jan G. van der Watt and Ruben Zimmermann (Tubingen: Mohr Siebeck, 2012), 241.

ethics is centered on the universal and timeless Truth, i.e., in the person of Jesus. Faith in the Son of God sensitizes and drives the believer for loving action. The moral principles are revealed in his very person and work which correspondingly becomes a guide to the community's ethical action. Jesus is the standard for ethical living.

Effort has been made to establish the inter-connection between Johannine ethics and Johannine Christology. Wittingly we can say that in the Gospel of John, Christology is the birth-place of all ethical concerns especially for all those who believe in Jesus (πιστεύειν εἰς' Ιησοῦν). The aspects of Christology and ethics are essentially important to one another in John's Gospel. Indeed what is required is a sound balance between ethics and Christology in the Gospel of John. Ethics and Christology must be held together in their organic relation within a whole. Of course it calls for a deeper recognition to understand the ethical precepts and admonition in the light of Christology, for ethical implications are reflected and linked organically with the Christology of the Gospel of John. The concept of the Johannine community as the framework for ethical action arises directly out of the belief in Jesus' messianic role. The Gospel recognizes that doing the will of God (service to God) is to reflect in one's ethical conduct in the community i.e., in the social sphere. Ethics in the Gospel of John is therefore directly related to the theological conviction that Jesus is the expected Messiah/Christ, the Son of God and the Son of Man in whom is life eternal and who in the beginning was the *logos*, was with God and was God and then became flesh and lived amongst us and has patterned how one ought to live in relation to God and to fellow believers.

It is worth to infer that the ethics of Jesus is the ethics of God, the *revealed ethics* which is made realized and visualized in the life, ministry and death of Jesus of Nazareth which no one can substitute. It is in and through Jesus' life in totality, that is, in words and deeds that Jesus as the only begotten Son replicates the very divine nature, character and heart of the Father God's love for the world. The ethical demand of God is fulfilled in Jesus and likewise Jesus demands ethical response of faith from us. So 'belief' in Jesus becomes a prior requisite to follow and thereby be a disciple of Jesus constituting a new community – a community of believers – established according to the ethics of Jesus.

John has a unique way of indicating the community's depth of ethical understanding which has to be achieved in the light and in relation to the unique identity of Jesus as the *logos* of God, the one anointed by God (Christ), who is the Son of Man and at the same time the Son of God, who has walked the path of obedience and perfection in the salvific and redemptive plan of God for the whole world. As such, ethics is defined in close connection to the Christology which is essential and intrinsic to the overall understanding of what entails ethics in the Fourth Gospel. Ethics and Christology are juxtaposed like two faces of the same coin and neither Johannine Christology nor Johannine ethics is a substitute for the other. They are closely an integral part to one another but are two different distinct theologies driving towards a common set of goal within the messianic community established by the belief in Jesus the *logos*-Son who eternally pre-existed with God and then was sent by God as the Christ, the Son of God and the Son of Man clad with profound ethical implications for us today.

Another significant dimension to John's understanding of ethics is that, it is of divine origin because it originated or it stems from God in and through Jesus. This is clear when Jesus speaks of fulfilling what the Father has commanded him (discussed in chapter 3). It is Christologically oriented (because it is through the words and deeds of Jesus that the true essence of ethics is exemplified) nonetheless caution has to be taken that, it was Jesus who first accomplished the ethics of God which became his own ethics because they are one and this divinely originated ethics is so patterned on which the ethics of the Johannine community is built religiously and ethically. Jesus in the Fourth Gospel is seen as fulfilling the eschatological thirst of the Jews except that he is in a way which absolutely transcends the human political hopes of Israel.[161] This is to speculate that Johannine ethics is much dependent in drawing its ethical values from the person, words and works of Jesus the *logos*, who is the 'Christ,' the 'Son of God', and the 'Son of Man' who draws all men to himself on the Cross and a new community of believers is established through him.

Faith becomes the ethical criterion in John's Gospel to live a life in the newly established new humanity brought forth by Jesus. Christology therefore is the pillar and the corner stone to advance the ethics of the Gospel of John. Rightly, Christology is tagged 'the heartbeat of the theology of the Fourth Gospel (Robert Kysar)' and since much of the Gospel's content is concentrated upon Jesus, it must not take us by surprise "that this concentration upon Jesus also dominates its ethics."[162] It is logical, then, to construe that ethics gains its true important significance only from the better understanding of Christology. Johannine ethics is also a revealed ethics and hence can be tagged as 'received ethics' because Jesus did exactly as God the Father had commanded him and has set a pattern of obedience. As Jesus, the Christ, the Son of God and the Son of Man aligned himself to the will of God, the Father and obeyed so are disciples to obey and leave a trail of legacy for later believers to tread this road of obedience. Jesus Christ is the starting point because the ethics of God is embodied and revealed in Jesus. In other words, the ethics of God is met in the ethics of Jesus because the ethics of Jesus is the ethics of God.

It befits to recap that Johannine ethics is ethics that primarily stems from God, *revealed* in and through the life and ministry of Jesus, *received* by faith by community of believers and in the physical absence of Jesus the Spirit-*Paraclete* takes over to guide and enables the community of believers in all the truth to

---

161 Rudolf Schnackenburg, *The Gospel According to St. John,* vol. 1, translated by Kevin Smyth (Kent: Burns & Oates, 1968), excursus vi, 549.

162 Burridge, *Imitating Jesus*, 293.

live their faith in this world by loving one another which must result in bearing fruit. The community of believers, as such, is expected to begin to exercise love for one another as they have been loved that must 'take place first in the circle that is closed but not closed-off'[163] but visible enough for outsiders to see and evoke in them the same ethical virtue and then once they practiced this love concretely in their daily life, they are capable and committed to go into the world in continuation of the mission of God, by sending them (inhere 'sent' determines an ethical significance).

This is to conclude that Christology is the key to the ethical interpretation of John's Gospel. Christology serves as the ultimate starting point to envision, approach and understand ethics. The ethical and Christological materials in the Gospel of John validate one another. It is Christology that constitutes the essential novelty of ethics because this Christology of John is Jesus who fulfills the commands of God and who in turn commands us to obey and keep his commandments. Jesus is the bedrock to the accurate interpretation of ethics in its spirit. The obedience in doing the will of God takes priority over everything else for Jesus (Jn.3:34 ...doing God's will is his food) and so it must be for us too, if we claim to believe in him. The ethical demand of Jesus for us today is grounded in what he has done for us (the imperative rests on the indicative). The Johannine ethics is religious in its outlook and is simultaneously conducive to align believing community to her moral behavior.

163 Marxsen, *New Testament Foundation for Christian Ethics,* 289. References for sending which is undergirded primarily by the love of God (1:1,11; 3:16) and the Son as loved and sent by the Father does work together with the Father (15:16) and disciples are sent as the Son is being sent (20:21; 17:18).

Conclusion

The central propagation of this work rests on the fact that Johannine ethics is implicitly embedded in Christological narratives and therefore is better understood in the light of Johannine Christology. Four Christological titles have been selected for this purpose. In the light of what has been studied in the previous chapters, it is worth to bring out some important observations and point out certain implications and relevance of the study undertaken.

Johannine Christology is the genesis and growth of Johannine ethics. Ethics and Christology are seamlessly blended. The theme of ethics is assimilated, transformed and transposed into Christology and yet ethics is not totally reduced to Christology. The belief in Jesus leads to the experience of having eternal life here and now. There is a tremendous confidence outcome of faith, if one believes in Jesus and all moral decisions will follow which will be made possible by the enabling power of the Spirit-*Paraclete* as promised. Believing in Jesus as having come from God the Father is the underlying prerequisite to moral life because it is from this belief that "comes the power to love, and all else besides."[1] 'Faith' and 'love' are two most dominating virtues that play a central and momentous role in understanding the ethics of the Gospel of John. John's Gospel in fact reconciles the Jewish concept of religious life which was practically orientated with the ideas of reflecting one's religiosity in the physical sphere in their moral behavior.

The narrative style of John's Gospel presents the most beautiful and excellent ethical dimension. John tries to lead the readers to explore for themselves the truth and the message that lies beyond the narrative words. We have noted earlier how John would open double meanings in the choice of his words. Even here, it is fitting to see John's intention to understand the double significance of Johannine Christology. The underlying assumption is that when we try to understand the theological presentation of the person and work of Jesus it does not end there (surface meaning of the word) but also the *effect of believing* in his life and ministry has to be inculcated in the lives of the believers which eventually

1 Frank J. Matera, *New Testament Ethics: The Legacies of Jesus and Paul* (Louisville; Westminster John Knox Press, 1996), 113.

must result in living a virtuous life. Believing in Jesus endows a special privilege and by virtue of this privilege also comes a moral responsibility to live by faith and exercise our faith by our daily conducts in love, balancing our proclaimed faith in our sayings and doings as to the will of God. This is to construe once again that Johannine ethics in essence is inseparably linked and intrinsically embedded in the Johannine Christology.

The ethical principles in the Gospel of John are not laid bare when it first met our eyes except for the "love command" which is explicit. Other ethical references or pointers are not presented in a systematic way but are rather distributed in almost every passage of the Gospel. It has become apparent that we cannot limit our search to the particular and systematic form of ethics, when it comes to the Gospel of John. The simple reason is because the Gospel was not intended to be written as an ethical treaty containing a systematic exposition of biblical morality. The present work has advanced the possibility to explore the ethical pointers to be given more serious attention and consideration they deserve. The moral teaching of the Gospel is largely concentrated in the course of narratives by ways of arguments and confrontation between Jesus and different characters (except for the farewell discourse (Jn. 13-17) which is stamped by a long discourse on moral exhortations, command and prayer).

In John's Gospel "to believe" in Jesus rationally is the foremost fundamental ethical pointer and all other ethical pointers follow. And on the same plane is the 'love' virtue that supports and backs up all other ethical dimensions. The implication of these two important ethical virtues is so profound that the two cannot part ways. Love and faith are two essential ethical principles on which every other ethical elements rests upon. Love is divine and faith is human. God loving human beings precedes human beings believing in God. Love virtually takes precedence over faith. And yet both blend together to make a complete whole of the essence of ethics in John's Gospel. God is love and he loved us first (Jn. 3:16 cf. 1 Jn. 3:16). The prime difference between faith and love is this – love originates from God and is directed to us (we are object of God's love). Faith is from the heart of humankind directed to God through Jesus (Jesus is the object of our faith). God loved us first and demonstrated his love by giving his Son Jesus as our Savior. It appears that it was necessary for God to tell the world that Jesus is His own Son sent by Him. So the miraculous evrga 'works' which is σημεῖα 'signs' are used as vehicles to prove God's Son's origin, identity, role, authority and underlying mission to invoke faith in Jesus. No wonder Johannine faith is directed to Jesus because Jesus is God in tangible human form (Jn. 10:30 cf. 1:14). All the 'signs' recorded in the Gospel are for a purpose (Jn. 20:30 records that there are some more signs Jesus had performed) and every recorded sign culminated on the cross. The purpose statement of the Gospel speaks crystal clear that "these (i.e., the miraculous signs) are written that you may believe that Jesus is the Christ, the Son of God, and that by believing you may have life in his name" (20:31). This implies that the '*semeia*' which serve as the means to the self-disclosure of Jesus as the Christ, the 'Son of God', and the 'Son of Man' are the bedrock on which faith rests. Love was manifested first in Jesus who lived amongst men and invited men 'to believe' in him through his deeds/works 'erga.' So, love comes first, and then invokes human response in faith to Jesus. And human's first reaction to God's call is "to believe." That means from human's perspective faith comes first and then love. That is, love automatically will be prompted by faith and this belief must find its expression by loving one another in action as commanded (Jn. 13:34 cf. 1 Jn. 3:24).

Love takes wide ranges of expressions and forms. So, it is viable to suppose why John did not give specific directive/s when it comes to teaching on love. The highest and most expensive form of love is laying down one's life for a friend and Jesus did that on the cross. This love of God in and through Jesus Christ cannot be compensated by anything else in the world but to simply believe in him and keep his commandment to love one another. Faith and love in John's Gospel are profoundly encumbered with ethical implications. This is to validate that faith and love are central component of ethics in John's Gospel. The combination of these virtues results the best in human when they are attended and are saturated in our lives - that is the kind of ethics demanded from us in John's Gospel. In short, Johannine ethics is ethics of faith and love combined resulting in life eternal, the highest good.

We need eyes of faith to unveil the ethical directives in John's Gospel where ethical references are implicit rather than being explicitly and systematically presented. We have discussed some of the major and important ethical pointers and passages that give clue to the essence of ethical dimensions in the Fourth Gospel (in chapter 3). In fact, every ethical horizon in John's Gospel is directed or focused 'to believe' in the person of Jesus. Faith in Jesus is the starting point of all ethical requirements in John's Gospel. So, the foremost essential ethical deed that is required from human is 'to believe' in Jesus. Johannine faith is an attitude towards Jesus and is not a mere faith in general. Faith in Jesus is, therefore, the first and most crucial action required to do the works of God. Without this deed of fully associating with Jesus, persons will remain in moral darkness and die in their sin (Jn. 3:17ff; 8:2). So, Johannine ethics is relational which involves both a choice to believe and a process to walk in the light.

Implications and Relevance

The Narrative of the Gospel of John echoes distant past events, situations and historical circumstances. The temporal and the socio-cultural distance that separate us from the first century Johannine Christian community poses a question of relative validity for our twenty - first century Christian community. How can one relate the Johannine ethical concern with our present ethical issues? Once we realize how Christology and ethical principles of the Fourth Gospel undergird, inform and supply the givens for our specific actions, then we will be prepared to operate our Christian living in faith and love. The first century Johannine Christian community of believers relied and stood firm in their belief in Jesus and lived out their ethics. Believing in Jesus brings people into the family relationship of God. 'To believe' in Jesus is a requisite for the membership of being in the community of believers and this faith must find its way in concrete action. The probable reason why John uses the verb πιστεύω to indicate its action oriented entity rather than using the grammatical noun form πίστις speaks well for his choice of the verb form. Faith is an active and not a passive virtue. Subsequently, 'to believe' in Jesus is not an event but a process that needs to be renewed again and again in the act of living out one's belief in every day and in every way. So the use of the phrase πίστευειν εἰς'Ιησοῦν which speaks of Jesus as the object of faith has unwavering abiding and dynamic influence for us today to live a good moral and ethical lifestyle prompted by our faith in, and love for, Jesus, and love for one another.

The distinctive artistry of the Gospel of John's narrative brings home the ethical pointers directing us to the affirmation of life eternal (ζωὴ αἰώνιος), which is the highest moral good, according to the Fourth Gospel, in and through the life and ministry of Jesus Christ. Just as the Father sends the Son, the Son Jesus sends the believers to the world (Jn. 20:21). This sequel (of sending motif) rationally impinges a very significant ethical implication for us to continue the divine mission of God. Jesus promised the enabling power of the *Paraclete* (Jn. 14:12) as we may engage ourselves in the divine mission of the Father-Son. Believers are exhorted to continue as witnesses and bear living testimony to the unbelieving world. Jesus has set before us ethical tasks which are obligatory as believers and followers of him. Christological motivation becomes the most fundamental paradigm in uncovering the ethical dimensions in John's Gospel. The Johannine ethics is a religiously oriented ethics undergirded by the love of God in and through the person of Jesus the *logos,* the Christ, the 'Son of God', and who also is the 'Son of Man.'

The Johannine community is driven by their belief in Jesus who is the centre of their community ethos. So, ethics in the Fourth Gospel operates in the realm of believing community whose allegiance and devotions are directed to the life and ministry of Jesus. The ways in which the authority of Jesus in Johannine community is anchored should be brought to bear in our contemporary Christian living. Our faith in Jesus must be reflected in our obedience to keep his command to love one another so that we become the fragrance of the *ideal* believing and loving community as inaugurated and intended by Jesus himself. Everything we do must be dictated and motivated by the love we have received from God in and through Jesus. And as we willingly respond to God's love in faith, our actions will automatically be prompted by faith because *faith* and *action* are co-relational aspect, and in areas where we need help, the Spirit-*Paraclete* will lead us into all truths to do what is pleasing in God's eyes.

When we touched the issue of relevancy, the concept of sectarianism automatically pops in. In dealing with the issue of the Johannine community as sectarian, D. Moody Smith has rightly commented that any reading of the Gospels and Epistles of the New Testament shows evidences of a sectarian consciousness, a sense of exclusiveness, a sharp delineation of the community from the world[2] and this is much true for the Fourth Gospel as it has been also often tagged as 'Sectarian' although not unanimously agreed upon this characterization. This explanation suggests the natural response of any social group in the face of the threat that threatens the integrity of the said social group.

How is this peculiarity of 'Johannine Sectarianism" as Meeks[3] had first postulated applicable to a different social world like ours today? Can this so called sectarian nature of the Gospel of John *really* be looked at as indifferent? Can we still consider the Johannine ethics as esoteric/interim/conventicle ethic as some have explicated? Or is there any significant impinging timeless truth that can be delineated from the Gospel of John's ethics? The understanding or interpretation of Johannine ethics as interim or conventicle will definitely determine our concept of ethics today as a Christian. And if we are to hold on to or share the shared view (of course it is not a unanimously agreed consensus), will we disregard the canonical Gospel of John as we have before us today? What if our exegetical knowledge drives us to conclude every book of the canonical Bible as conventicle because it was written to and for a certain group of people in distant past? Definitely we are not, nor will we consider as conventicle rather we have already received every Scripture portion in the Bible as the inspired message preserved for us for our edification and building up our Christian community(2 Tim. 3:16). So the view that the ethics of the Gospel is conventicle or even interim is nullified, because the Gospel has continued to profoundly speak to us today. And so we can confidently advocate that the ethics of John's Gospel is even more relevant and applicable for our twenty-first Christian community especially in pluralistic context such as India.

The theological centrality of the Gospel is Christology and subsequently ethics as aspect of Christology cannot be denied of its implicit significant presence even in the absence of its explicit ethical terminologies/categories. Then should we consider the Gospel of John as a reliable guide to the moral life of believers? We may wittingly answer – Yes! The greatest New Testament principles of ethical behavior were taught by Jesus Christ – to love God wholeheartedly and neighbor as oneself (Matt. 22:37-40). But, the question remains unanswered - How are we to draw out any moral absolutes designed to be applicable to specific situations in totally different times, cultures and complexities in the face of the specificity and particularity of the first century social world? The ethical instruction that were set out at a particular moment in a particular situation is still debatable issue

2 D. Moody Smith, *Johannine Christianity* (Edinburgh: T&T Clark, 1984), 3f.

3 Wayne A. Meeks, "The Man from Heaven in Johannine Sectarianism," *JBL* 91 (1972): 42-72.

that confronts our changing situations with new rampant emerging crisis in the society. Walter C. Kaiser[4] advocates that the specific commands or instructions in a specific context do not exclude the possibility that they are the expression of universal principles. He further asserts that a universal rule is simply one that applies to every case of a certain class, no matter how particular and specific that class maybe. Kaiser's argument though from the Old Testament point of view is true for the Gospel of John's allegation for the expression of the universal principles that guide one's moral conduct in fast changing world like ours today. He rightly points out the issues that the heart takes precedence over issues of external acts of obedience. The particularity of the Bible was not meant to prejudice our use of it but to help us in identifying with it by sensing that the same principles were capable of being worked out in all the concreteness and uniqueness of daily life is well said.[5] Considering the fast changing culture that we are living in, "it is possible to overreact as a result of awareness that cultural change is real, and to forget that cultural continuity is also real. God remains consistent and the conditions of life today are not totally discontinuous with those of the biblical cultures"[6] is convincing.

We have realized that the Gospel of John demonstrates its rich ethical values which are life-affirming because it is directly connected to Jesus who has come to offer life eternal (Jn. 3:16; 20:31). So, Johannine ethics is so much more than it was realized in the past. Johannine ethics is a process that works in reciprocal relationship and therefore active where it requires a daily expression of obedience in our everyday living by faith in Jesus Christ. Johannine ethics hence has a wealth of significance for every believing individual to align oneself to Jesus Christ. The overriding theology of the Fourth Gospel is his Christology and it befits to advocate that as much as Johannine Christology is central to his theology that much is ethics important because it is in Christology that ethics is embedded.

The question still remains. How do we appropriate the Johannine ethics as an ethics applicable to us? Is Johannine ethics still binding for our twenty-first Christian society plagued with alarming frequency of evil practices? How do we enact the application of the Johannine ethics in our situation? How far is the Johannine ethics valid? What timeless truths of the moral and ethical challenges of the Fourth Gospel are relevant for readers like us? ...The then intended readers of the Gospel must have found that this story of Jesus' life and person have impacted their thought processes and their walk of lives. We, as the now and present readers, share that response of the readers of the first century Christian community because the Gospel of John continues to be relevant for us today. As

4 Walter C. Kaiser, Jr., "New Approaches to Old Testament Ethics," *JETS*, 35/3 (Sept., 1992): 289.

5 John Goldingay, *Approaches to Old Testament Interpretation* (Toronto: Clements Publishing, [1981] 2002), 53.

6 Goldingay, *Approaches to Old Testament Interpretation*, 53.

modern readers of the Gospel of John are influenced by the Johannine community of faith and we carry this tradition of having being believers in Jesus as coming from God and is God himself to offer us life eternal which is the indissoluble reality of the kingdom of God. And if this is the case, what has been expected of us, as believing community must live the life of love and faith, which must produce good moral life in this pluralistic world.

In the midst of an imperfect corrupted society, Jesus is the role model to which we must look at and live. As such Jesus' qualities must give character to our present day Christian conduct. Borrowing Paul's terminology 'co-workers' or 'laborers together' (1 Cor. 3:9 ; 1 Thess. 3:2) we as today's Christians likewise must possess this attitude and be guided by this attitude to pass on the good work legacy in our daily actions (ethics) which we have received and learned from the life of Jesus. Jesus did everything that the Father had commanded him to do (Jn. 12: 49, 50; 14:31) and he did accomplish (Jn. 19:30 also see 5:36). His ethical living was based and founded on God and he has lived a life of obedience in fulfilling the will of the Father. Therefore, our ethical behavior and living must be shaped and guided by the very model Jesus has patterned for us to obey and live by it. Our existence here on earth must henceforth be a reflection of Jesus Christ working in us. Our actions must be an action of our Lord Jesus Christ (ethics integrated in Christology).

Let us also remember that the Johannine writings do not come to us as an autonomous ethics based on reasons and impartial to commitments and loyalties but came as a part of tradition that bears the moral identity of the Johannine Christian community and in which that identity is brought to bear both creatively and faithfully on the concrete moral context of that particular community in the face of the threats to be excommunicated or even killed because of their faith in Jesus as the Messiah. As believers in the very being and work of Jesus, we cannot disconnect ourselves from the past history of the faithful community from whom there is much to learn. We are witnessing the threat from other faiths especially the Hindu fanatics and in this similar scenario we can hold on to Jesus' moral exhortation not to lose heart because he has conquered death and continue his mission to spread the divine love of God for the whole world so that they will come to know that Jesus is the Savior, the Messiah who has come from God to offer us life eternal. And the responsible stamped with the imperative to make known to the world that God loves the world and offer his Son to give us life of eternity.

It is appropriate that the imperative exhortation 'love one another' is given as it demands during the time of a communal crisis of identity, the Johannine community had faced. As it is implied and expected that believers in Jesus Christ are exhorted and challenged to live more truthful lives like Jesus who in obedience to the will of the Father carried out the Father's given mission. For the Johannine community, to live in the present matters much because it predicts the future whereby the present living has to be a manifestation of the love of God in and through Christ. The life lived now shadows the life after in John's understanding. It is like living the future at present. We find no specific injunctions on how to live and what is the right thing to do except Jesus' response to the crowds in John chapter six, that is, to believe in the Son who has come from the Father and the works he has done. According to the Gospel of John, believing in the person of the very nature of Jesus is crucial because if one believes in him all other moral decisions and acts will follow. Similarly Hays commented that "the specific behavior that issues from union with Jesus need not be spelled out in detail, for those who abide in Jesus will intuitively know what is right and do it" because the *Paraclete* will guide them to the truth (Jn. 14:16-17; 16:8-11, 13).

The responsibility of any and every believer is not simply to live in the sacred dimension of life (spirit realm) but through all its social structures and process for the accomplishment of those things to which he/she is committed in line with the will of God. Jesus' prayer that he chose his disciples from out of the world and yet they do not belong to the world and that they be protected from the evil one is ethically significant (Jn. 17: 6, 14, 15, 16). The ethics must find its manifestation in the world (physical) and not outside. The command of Jesus to love one another as a distinguishing mark for the disciples is not a short term command but its effect ought to ripple throughout the century as an example to be emulated as a believing Christian community. In this line, the Johannine ethical perspective which is often labeled as sectarian or esoteric can be best explained from the life situation of the community which inevitably has undergirded their thought process and their subsequent world view. The Johannine ethics is a reflection on the content of faith which in a subsequent follow up demands decision – to believe and enjoy eternal life in Jesus or not to believe and face condemnation.

Therefore, the Gospel of John's articulation of ethics is inherently embedded in the person of Jesus vitally taking the form of an address which does not allow one to be a mere listener (to the sayings) or spectator (of the miraculous sign performed by Jesus) but demands faith, which is an ethical decision. The Fourth Gospel in an extraordinary way continues to speak and pose challenges to us today as it did in the earliest times to the readers of the first-century Johannine Christian community of the west Mediterranean world. It appears that the Gospel was written for and with a specific and ardent thrust to bolster the faith of the many believing Jewish Christians not to fear but to make an open confession of their faith in Jesus as the Christ. Their confession and witness to the truth leads to a confrontation and a break with Judaism and even the possible of being hated and killed was obvious because the Lord Jesus himself has undergone these facts.

The ethics as defined in relation to the person of work of Christ in the Fourth Gospel continues to inspire and provide us a guiding principle to live a life of true discipleship. This is to assert that the Fourth Gospel placed before us a substance of both inspiration and a standard of reference which is why the

Gospel has not lost its relevance for our Christian living today. The precepts of Jesus Christ thus become the standards by which our conduct is judged. And it also serves as our guideposts to and in the way we must travel in seeking the true ends of our being in the Kingdom of God. As such the ethics of the Fourth Gospel which is Christologically founded and grounded spells a profound impact to whom it was first addressed and this has not faded away nor lost its relevance for our present circumstances today. The Johannine Christological portrayals and statements have helped us to understand better the ethics of the Fourth Gospel.

Faith in Jesus became the foremost guiding criterion for the living standard of the Johannine Christian community. Faith in Jesus, thus, determines the actions of an individual in the community of John's Gospel. Johannine ethics is an ethics of belief in Jesus which congruently offers eternal life. The ethical demands of Jesus had a far reaching implication for all humankind. Jesus'

> Precepts stir the imagination, arouse the conscience, challenge thought, and give impetus to the will, issuing an action. In so far as we respond, holding the commandments steadily in view, reflecting upon them, and yet treating them not merely as objects for contemplation, but as spurs to action, there gradually comes to be built up in us a certain outlook on life, a bias of mind, a standard of moral judgment. The precepts cannot be directly transferred from the written page to action. They must become, through reflection and through effort, increasingly a part of our total outlook upon life, of the total bias of our minds. Then they will find expression in action appropriate to the changing situations in which we find ourselves.[7]

Jesus established a new community where faith becomes the criterion to become a member in the kingdom he inaugurated (Jn. 1:12). This community hallmark was then to be in unity finding its expression in love for one another just as Jesus himself has propagated, lived and modeled.

The central divine mission of God is to demonstrate 'love' for the desperate need of the world in and through the very life-event of Jesus. And this love is not limited by time, place, or any other thing in the world except the unwillingness and the unbelief of the human's heart. The God in the person of Jesus, the Christ, the 'Son of God', and the 'Son of Man' who has done many *semeia* though *only selected* ones are documented for *reason* that we may πιστεύω in him and have life eternal (Jn. 20:23). And this life eternal is present here and now but the fullness of this beautiful experience still awaits a period of time for the *eschaton*. In this world of pluralism there is only one thing that can knit and bolt us together into one community, a community of faith established in the light of the love of God inaugurated through Jesus Christ. The true membership in the kingdom of God in John is the true believer. A person who believes in Jesus is a true Israelite (Jn.

7 C. H. Dodd, *Gospel and Law* (Cambridge: Cambridge University Press, 1951), 77.

1:47). The family ties is not of blood or carnal lineage (Jn. 1:13), but begotten of water and spirit (Jn. 3:5) because he or she becomes child of God because of his/her faith in the One and Only Son (1:12) who had been sent to pitch his dwelling amongst us (Jn. 1:14). Now these believers are knit into one family by and through faith in Jesus and their love for one another, and they are gathered from the whole world into one (Jn. 11:52 cf. 17:6).

Present reality of eschatological existence is presented very clearly in John's Gospel. For instances, eternal life is a present reality if one hears Jesus' words and has faith in him (Jn. 5:24) and being in the family of God is a gift granted here on earth (Jn. 1:12). There is no suspense in John. Everything is realized though its ultimate realization is yet to be fulfilled in future. John has a very poetic and intriguing appeal to the troubled hearts that tries and strives to find happiness in this world (Jn.14:27 cf. 16:33). Especially in the present scenario of India, the persecution of Christians across the country has a strong appeal to the persecuted Christians. Therefore, in period such as this Johannine emphasis on realized eschatology has an immense message for our troubled society today. John skillfully knits bits of moral and ethical pointers into the Christological narratives without distorting and altering the significant and intended message which he wanted to bring across his readers' mind. He takes heart to bring home the central message of his theology of Christ and the implied ethical decision, to respond in and by faith to the command of Jesus.

The literary narrative style of John is such that ethics is tied to Christology and both are integrally linked to one another for a perfect living here on earth where unbelief poses a big challenge to our faith in Jesus Christ. John's Gospel in its distinctiveness has generated a distinctive and core understanding of what entails ethics in essence by drawing its ethical precepts from the life and examples of Jesus. This probably is what makes distinctive the Fourth Gospel from the rest of the New Testament documents in presenting the highly Christologically oriented ethics for the believers in Jesus of his time. Timothy J. M. Ling remarked that the Johannine social world, which draws on social-scientific resources on 'virtuoso religion,' and enables us to envisage the Gospel's striking ethical and eschatological dualism within a credible indigenous social context without forcing it to the sectarian margins of the social world is impressive.[8]

We must note that the teachings of Jesus are addressed to a series of individuals who compose the community of believers which is the body of Christ (e.g. Jn. 6:53-58; 7:37f). The love of Jesus Christ, his life and ministry which is constituted by his humble submission expressed in obedience to the supreme will of God must be a motivational force that drives us to emulate our Lord's example. M. Carapiet has rightly commented that Christian ethics is "primarily modeled on Jesus Christ whose life and activities are archetypal and paradigmatic for the

8 Timothy J. M. Ling, *The Judaean Poor and the Fourth Gospel* (Cambridge: Cambridge University Press, 2006), 147.

life and actions of his future disciples."[9] Jesus provides the 'perception' to see 'which features of experience are significant,' the 'motivation' for 'how to act' and the 'identity' of 'who we are as Christian.'[10] Subsequently, Johannine Christology is depicted as a catalyst for deducing ethical frameworks in the Fourth Gospel.

The Johannine community is understood as living in the realized eschatological *aeon* but at the same time anticipating the future. "The incarnation [of Jesus] inaugurates the eschatological age and makes eternal life present in the here and now, but there is still a period of time to await the final 'last day.'"[11] That means the 'eschatological existence was experienced and lived'[12] which was brought by Jesus the *logos* who is the Christ, the 'Son of God' and the 'Son of Man' and who was guiding them. Our lives must be based on the life and teachings of Jesus and Jesus is still guiding us today by the *Paraclete* to testify to the truth only if we prove by the way we live each day. There is a danger of ethical laxity in our present generation which calls for an urgent probing. The revelation Jesus brought is the *only* true revelation and no other revelation that we see or hear are nothing but competing spiritual powers in different forms in our own country today.

The purpose statement of the Gospel with an open ended call to believe in Jesus alone is even sufficient enough to explain the inclusiveness of the Johannine community (Jn. 20:30). Love needs to be displayed and be strengthened first within and then only find its way out to the surrounding social human world. Otherwise, it may simply be a verbal expression without being proved first within the lived community (1 Jn. 4:9, 11, 19, 20). So, we can infer that Johannine community is inclusive in its essence and do away with the prejudices that have long blocked the validity of the Scripture. The community of believers is sent by Jesus as he has been sent by the Father and the Spirit-*Paraclete* is promised to enable them to continue the work of witnessing and uniting the world to himself (Jn. 15:16; 17:26; 22). As such, John in his unique artistry rhetoric narrative style "designed to introduce its readers to its special *rhetoric* language and symbolism"[13] is far from being exclusive and impregnable and is "uniquely readable for outsiders."[14] If at all, the nature of the Fourth Gospel is understood as a sectarian group/community then it is best explained by number of Scholars that the reason for its nature is not in its theology but in its social background which is highly notable. The Gospel of John has offered significant and important insights

9 M. Carapiet, "Jesus and Christian Ethics Today," *Jeevadhara* 23 (Kottayam, Kerala: 1993), 442, 449.

10 William C. Spohn, 'Jesus and Christian Ethics,' *Theological Studies*, 56 (1995): 101-107.

11 Burridge, *Imitating Jesus,* 335.

12 This phrase is borrowed from Willi Marxsen, *New Testament Foundations for Christian Ethics* (Minneapolis: Fortress Press, 1993/2007), 86.

13 Ling, *The Judaean Poor,* 164.

14 T. S. Dokki, 'Irony and Sectarianism in the Gospel of John,' *New Readings in John*, edited by J. Nissen and S. Pedersen (JSNTS 182; London: Sheffield Academic Press, 1999), 104.

into the nature of ethics and this being essentially and strikingly a *revealed ethics* in and through the life, ministry and person of Jesus the *logos*, the Christ/Messiah, the 'Son of God' and who is simultaneously the 'Son of Man', the ultimate divine ambassador of the heavenly Father, God.

Johannine ethics is programmatic in Jesus' life and ministry and we are expected to respond in faith and obedience as he has been to the Father who sent him. The ethics of Jesus is the ethics of the Father and the ethics of the Johannine community is to reflect the same. Thus, the inner life of intentions, attitudes, motives and ethical behavior must result from the belief in Jesus which eventually must result in loving obedience to the will of God. But, how are we to grapple with the new emerging ethical issues that did not exist probably when the Gospel was written? The Gospel provides answer for us – the *Paraclete* will guide us to the good and right interpretation (Jn. 16:12). Our part is to believe on the promises Jesus has promised and wait upon the enabling power to meet the hermeneutical challenges as we struggle to understand what the will of God is. Therefore, ethics does not end in just a belief in Jesus but to experience daily in our lives and live out our faith in love and obedience continuing to testify to the truth till Jesus comes back to take us home (Jn. 14:2-3). The enabling power of God/Christ who is the *Paraclete* is promised as the moral guide for the believing community. So till the *parousia* of the resurrected Christ, we as disciples/ believers of Jesus Christ must live within the wider circle of secular world of existence (Jn. 17:15).

The Gospel of John has been a significant interest and importance to challenge and inspire a wider community of believers who have responded in faith and become followers or disciples of Jesus the Christ/Messiah, the 'Son of God' and also the 'Son of Man'. Jesus came to reveal the truth about God who bestows eternal life in and through his envoy, i.e., His Only Begotten Son (Jn. 3:16; 20:31). The literary genre of the Gospel as a narrative Gospel impinges that in the absence of the coherent ethical treatise the ethical implications are embedded primarily in the narrative structure of the Gospel. The central stress is on the call 'to believe' in the *erga* of Jesus, which bear as a testimony that it is the *erga* of God. A 'belief' in John's Gospel is the moral choice and act, an important ethical decisive moment. And so 'doing the works of God' is reciprocating that 'belief' which will eventually lead to the desiring attainment of eternal life, as suggested in the Gospel of John. So, the central presentation of this work is to propagate that ethics is inseparable from the Christology because ethics has to be abstracted and deduced from the theology of the Christo-centric narrative of the Gospel of John. This belief is an ongoing process requiring everyday lives to bear fruit by one's consistent abode in Jesus as branch is to the vine. To determine one's faith is to do the will of God, a determinant ethical factor which Jesus himself has already modeled in his very own life and activities with utmost obedience to the Father God. The Fourth Gospel succinctly puts in writing that selected σημεῖα documented in the Gospel are designed to instill belief in the lives of the readers.

The final or zenith of this response of faith in Jesus the *logos* as the Christ, the 'Son of God' and 'Son of Man' results in eternal life that is found exclusively in Jesus. So Johannine ethics has the other significant aspect of life affirming values. Christology is a catalyst that helps to define, abstract and deduce ethical directives in the Gospel of John. So in discussing the Johannine ethics, what requires of us is to seriously consider the Christological aspects in order to understand the fundamental nature of ethics in the Gospel according to John.

Johannine ethics is fundamentally a reflection on the content of faith in Jesus who was in the beginning the *logos* is now the Christ, the 'Son of God' and the 'Son of Man'. It can be described as an ethics undergirded by a tone of filial relationship – God's ethics which is imperative – is fulfilled indicatively in and through the life and activities of Jesus-and believers are to continue both of this indicative imperative ethics by the enabling power of the Spirit-*Paraclete*. Every individual believer must hold and own responsibility for his/her own actions. Even though Jesus has accomplished everything for our salvation, we must express our beliefs into concrete ethical behavior (what we generally called as Christian ethics). This is to indicate that our claim of faith in Jesus must be incorporated in our everyday conduct. Ethics in John's Gospel which is intrinsically linked to Johannine Christology has a timeless true and *not* for an interim ethical implication/relevance. The writing of the Gospel of John has been influential in the past centuries and even to our times and has authority because it is profoundly christological and that is why it exerts ethical implications for us today right here and now. Our Christian belief must be legitimized by our actions which is ethical because ethics is a reflection and aspect of theology (Christology) according to the Gospel of John.

It is significant to make remarkable impression that Johannine ethics contributes the very core of the New Testament ethics. When Christology is the heart of the New Testament theology, the evangelist of the Fourth Gospel has said it all that the ethical dimension of the Johannine community is fashioned in the light of the belief in the life and teaching of Jesus Christ. When ethicists say that Christian ethics is "theology in action," we can say that the Johannine ethics is "belief in action." Johannine ethics in this sense touches the core, the root of what entails ethics in practical ground. Before an individual implied reader is urged to emulate specially the humble service and attitude of Jesus he/she is prompted first to put his/her faith in Jesus. Then only an individual can be determined to pursue the expected follow-up ethical actions. All in all, the Johannine Christology is then the hermeneutical key to unlock the Johannine understanding of ethics. Christian ethics must be fuelled and motivated by the divine love of God demonstrated in the sacrificial act of his Son, Jesus Christ. Our belief in Jesus must be a continuous process and this belief must be qualified in our everyday living by loving one another in fulfilling the commandment of Jesus (which expresses a close connection between Christology and ethics) and in obedience doing the will of God which in itself is believing in Jesus (circular move). Every individual has to make his/her own decision to whether believe in Jesus and if so we are called to work out that faith in our everyday lives, day after day. Belief is an ethical decisive moment which risks our lives of being hated by those who do not believe in Jesus Christ (especially in our Indian present scenario where the adherents of the Hindu propagators are propagating India as Hindu-stan).

Our Christian ethics has to be legitimated by our belief in Jesus and has to be legitimated further in our daily way of life (visibly). Our lives must be a proclamation of our faith in Jesus whose life and activity was a proclamation of the Father God working in and through him. So, we expect that the God of Jesus is our God who will enable us by the power of the *Paraclete* he has promised and thereby must bear much fruit because the tree is known by its fruit. Johannine ethics which is inseparably linked to Christology is therefore relational and functional as well. Having ascertained the interconnection between ethics and Christology in John's Gospel, there is one question that creeps or recurs before us, i.e., was John's emphasis on ethics or Christology? With no hesitation, one would say it is Christology and the place of ethics is reduced. However, one must remember that for the Fourth Gospel, ethics is always an integral aspect of Christology. John, through Christology attempts to bring home the ethical values. This is to sanction that the ethical aspects in John's Gospel is not an independent entity. Having considered the study undertaken, it is suggestive to propose that ethics can be studied and advance as one important theme in the Gospel of John. In other words, to advance the Johannine scholarship, ethics can be treated as one important theme that is "ethics as a theme."

Summary

The journey began with the thought development that there could be something more than that meets the eyes concerning the ethical aspects in the Gospel of John. The hypothesis is that ethics in the Gospel of John is so widely implied in Christology and that there is an inseparable link between them. So with that presupposition and conviction, the research ventured, reading in between the lines of the Gospel to establish the inter-connection that might have existed between ethics and Christology. For the same, the Johannine Christian community is considered as the moral narrative world of John's Gospel in which the ethos, beliefs and value systems came to be expressed in their socio-cultural and religious circumstances. Primarily, the community's ethics came alive much towards her religious inclination. The motif of belief in Jesus takes precedence over all other ethical behavior that follows. It is in the face of the belief in Jesus that the love commandment is given. Faith and love go hand in hand. They are the two most chief ethical determinants in John's Gospel. 'Ethics as a theme' can be advanced in the Gospel of John, for it propels to a new avenue to advance

Johannine scholarship. As a concluding summary, let me highlight the findings of the research in the following statements.

- Ethics and Christology are blended seamlessly that either of them can never entirely dissociate from the other. Of course, the primacy of Christology over ethics must be acknowledged. They are like different faces of the same coin. So, for the right and better understanding of ethics in the Gospel of John, one needs to have a deep and thorough conviction about the person of Jesus in connection to his divine origin, role, authority, and missional aspect of his coming into the world and that he is risen and is coming back.
- In John's Gospel, ethical exhortation or teaching is merged with Christological materials and so there is a validation between these two themes (ethics and Christology). Faith and ethics are integrally correlated whereby faith is directly connected to Jesus. This has led us to endorse that the ethical dimension in John's Gospel are to be interpreted in relation to Jesus Christ.
- The mutual relationship between the Father and the Son serves as the ultimate ethical paradigm for the community of believers.
- Faith and love are two dominating ethical principles which must journey together, and every other ethical category hanged on them. These virtues work together (or co-exist) to define the ground of ethics in John's Gospel. Ethics of love is met in the ethics of humankind's respond to faith in Jesus Christ. The Father's love is transmitted to human beings through the Son and we are called to believe in this truth i.e. a respond from humankind is demanded. Faith in Jesus as the true revealer of the divine purpose of God is so crucial. As such 'to believe' in Jesus is one prime ethical act demanded by God. This is to say that faith has to be implemented in moral action. Thus, there is a strong connection between the religious message (of God's love for the world) and the moral obligation (on peoples) to live out one's faith in action.
- Faith and love being the ground of Christian ethics, the timeless challenge for us today is to continue to exercise the love of God we have received and respond by faith in and through Jesus Christ, so that the world will know that we are true disciples of Jesus Christ. Love is the need of every human race, and this love is freely given to the world, and we are obliged to bear witness to this unmerited love of God for the whole world. "And this is his command: to believe in the name of his Son, Jesus Christ, and to love one another as he commanded us" (1 Jn. 3:23 cf. Jn. 3:34).
- There is significant importance for us Christians to draw important ethical insights and guidelines for our conducts as we respond to Jesus by faith. The ultimate and supreme revelation of God is revealed in and

through the person and work of Jesus Christ. The ethical implication of the Gospel of John is still bidding to guide and challenge us in viewing our attitudes and actions in the light of our relationship defined by our new identity as believers in Jesus Christ.

- The ethics of John's Gospel is not an in-group ethics intended for few individuals (small group of disciples or Johannine Christian community) but also for the readers who come to believe in Jesus through the testimony of Jesus' inner circle of disciples. This concept of future believers definitely is inclusive of anyone and everyone who believes in Jesus. So, Johannine ethics has an inclusive significance.
- Johannine Christology infallibly informs us about the effective way of Christian living. Ethics in the Gospel, therefore, recommends 'faith' and 'love' to be the chief ethical virtues that coherently work together in fulfilling the command of Jesus. The 'end desire' correspondingly is to attain life eternal which in fact is the highest hope, honor and happiness one could ever imagine.
- In a nutshell, Johannine ethics is fundamentally a reflection on the content of faith in the origin, role, authority, and mission of Jesus as the *logos*-Son who existed eternally with God and became man who is the Christ, the 'Son of God' and the 'Son of Man.' Therefore, Johannine ethics is a way of being in constant relation with God in and through his Son Jesus. John's Gospel contains some of the most crucial aspects of ethics- Ethics of Faith, Obedience and loyalty, Love, Truth, Life, and ethics of Responsibility and Vocation. As a result, the inter-connection between ethics and Christology, in the Fourth Gospel, can be expressed in a maxim "belief in action" where belief is a moral choice to be made by an individual. This is to propagate that there must be a constant balance between our claim of faith in Jesus and everyday life conduct to be worked out through love. John's Gospel in effect seems to contain the essence of Christian ethics that is to be fashioned in dependence to Jesus, who himself is the moral archetype of a moral God. Thus, ethics in the Gospel of John can be advanced as one important theme in advancing the Johannine scholarship i.e. 'ethics as a theme.'
- May God's values and standards as already mirrored in and through Jesus' identity (person) and function (work) be nourished most effectively as we make our choice to continue to have faith in Jesus, who is the *logos* incarnated, the promised Christ, the 'Son of God' and the 'Son of Man.' And thereby be empowered by the Spirit-*Paraclete* to have the right relationship with God and with one another and be able to compose a new kind of social structures that would best replicate God's way of doing and sayings things here on this earth.

Bibliography

Books (Both Single & Joint Author(s)

Abraham, K. C. *Transforming Vision: Theological - Methodological Paradigm Shifts.* Tiruvalla: Christain Sahitya Samithi, 2006.

Ashton, John. *Understanding the Fourth Gospel.* 2nd edition. Oxford: Oxford University Press, 2007.

Bennema, Cornelis. *Excavating John's Gospel: A Commentary for Today.* Delhi: ISPCK, 2005.

Blount, Brian K. *Then the Whisper Put on Flesh: New Testament Ethics in an African American Context.* Nashville: Abington Press, 2001.

Brown, Raymond E. *The Community of the Beloved Disciple.* New York: Paulist Press, 1979.

Burkett, Delbert. *An Introduction to the New Testament and the Origins of Christianity.* Cambridge: Cambridge University Press, 2002.

Burridge, Richard A. *Imitating Jesus: An Inclusive Approach to New Testament Ethics.* Michigan: Wm. B. Eerdmans Publishing Company, 2007.

Carter, C. W. and R. D. Thompson. *The Biblical Ethic of Love*, American University Studies Series 7: Theology and Religion 79. New York: Lang, 1990.

Chilton, Bruce and Jacob Neusner. *Judaism in the New Testament: Practices and Beliefs.* London and New York: Routledge, 1995.

Clements, R. E. *God and Temple.* Oxford: Basil Blackwell, 1965.

Collins, Adela Yarbro. *Cosmology and Eschatology in Jewish and Christian Apocalypticism.* Leiden: Brill, 2000.

Collins, Adela Yarbro and John J. Collins. *King and Messiah as Son of God: Divine, Human, and angelic Messianic Figures in Biblical and Related Literature.* Michigan/UK: Wm. B. Eerdmans Publishing Company, 2008.

Collins, John J. *Introduction to the Hebrew Bible.* Minneapolis: Fortress Press, 2004.

Collins, Raymond F. *Christian Morality: Biblical Foundations*. Notre Dame, IN: University of Natre Dame Press, 1986.

Cullmann, Oscar. *Early Christian Worship*. London: SCM Press, 1953.

Culpepper, R. Alan. *John, the Son of Zebedee: The Life of a Legend.* Minneapolis: Fortress Press, 2000.

DeSilva, David A. *An Introduction to the New Testament: Contexts, Methods & Ministry Formation.* Illinois: InterVarsity Press, 2004.

Diamant, Anita. *The New Jewish Wedding*. New York: Summit Books, 1985.

Dodd, C. H. *Gospel and Law.* Cambridge: Cambridge University Press, 1951.

_______. *The Interpretation of the Fourth Gospel.* Cambridge: Cambridge University Press, 1953.

Drane, John. *Introducing the New Testament*. Revised edition. Oxford: A Lion Book, 1999.

Ehrman, Bart D. *The New Testament: A Historical Introduction to the Early Christian Writings*. Second edition. Oxford: Oxford University Press, 2000.

Esler, Philip F. *The First Christians in their Social Worlds: Social-Scientific Approaches to New Testament Interpretation*. London and New York: Routledge, 1994.

Flew R, Newton. *Jesus and His Way: A Study of the Ethics of the New Testament.* London: The Epworth Press, 1963.

Fortna, Robert Tomson. *The Fourth Gospel and Its Predecessor*. Philadelphia: Fortress Press, 1988.

Fuglseth, Kare Sigvald. *Johannine Sectarianism in Perspective: A Sociological, Historical, and Comparative Analysis of Temple and Social Relationships in the Gospel of John, Philo, and Qumran.* NovTSup 119. Leiden: Brill, 2005.

Gardner, E. Clinton. *Biblical Faith and Social Ethics*. New York: Harper & Row Publishers, 1960.

Gerhardsson, Birger. *The Ethos of the Bible.* Translated by Stephen Westerholm. Eugene: Wipf & Stock Publishers, 1979.

Gill, Robin. *A Textbook of Christian Ethics*. 2nd edition. London: T&T Clark, 1995.

Glatzer, Nahum N, ed. *The Rest is Commentary: A Source Book of Judaic Antiquity*. Boston: Boston Press, 1961.

Goldingay, John. *Approaches to Old Testament Interpretation*. Toronto: Clements Publishing, 2002.

Goldsmith, Dale. *New Testament Ethics: An Introduction*. Elgin, IL: Brethen, 1988.

Gottwald, Norman. *The Hebrew Bible: A Socio-Literary Introduction*. Minneapolis: Fortress Press, 1979.

Guilding, A. *The Fourth Gospel and Jewish Worship*. Oxford: Claredon Press, 1960.

Gustafson, James M. *Moral Discernment in the Christian Life.* Edited and with an Introduction by Theo A. Boer and Paul E. Capetz. Louisville, London: Westminster John Knox Press, 2007.

Guthrie, Donald. *New Testament Theology*. Illinois: InterVarsity Press, 1981.

Haloka, Raimo. *Identity Matters: John, the Jews and Jewishness.* NovTSup 118; Leiden: Brill, 2005.

Hanson, K. C. and Douglas E. Oakman. *Palestine in the Time of Jesus: Social Structures and Social Conflicts.* Minneapolis: Fortress Press, 1998.

Harrington, Daniel J. and James F. Keenan, *Jesus and Virtue Ethics.* New York: Rowman & Littlefield Publishers, 2002.

Hays, Richard B. *The Moral Vision of the New Testament: A Contemporary Introduction to New Testament Ethics.* New York: HarperCollins, 1996.

Hengel, Martin. *Studies in Early Christianity*. Edinburgh and New York: T&T Clark, 1995.

_______. *The Son of God.* London: SPCK, 1976.

Hinde, Robert A. *Towards Understanding Relationships.* London: Academic Press, 1979.

Houlden, J. L. *Ethics and the New Testament.* London: T&T Clark, 1992.

Howard, Wilbert Francis. *Christianity According to St John*. London: Duckworth, 1947.

Hurtado, Larry W. *Lord Jesus Christ: Devotion to Jesus in Earliest Christianity.* Michigan/UK: Wm. B. Eerdmans Publishing Company, 2003.

James, E. E. *Ethics: A Biblical Perspective.* Bangalore: Theological Book Trust, 1992.

Jones, D. C. *Biblical Christian Ethics*. Michigan: Baker, 1994.

Koester, C. R. *Symbolism in the Fourth Gospel: Meaning, Mystery and Community.* Minneapolis: Fortress Press, 1995.

Kostenberg, A. J. *The Missions of Jesus and the Disciples According to the Fourth Gospel.* Michigan: Wm. B. Eerdmans Publishing Company, 1998.

Kysar, Robert. *The Fourth Evangelist and His Gospel: An Examination of Contemporary Scholarship*. Minneapolis: Augsburg Publishing House, 1975.

Lamb, David A. *Text, Context and the Johannine Community: A Sociolinguistic Analysis of the Johannine Writings.* Bloomsbury: T&T Clark, 2014.

Larsson, Tord. *God in the Fourth Gospel.* Stockholm: Almqvist & Wiksell International, 2001.

Ling, Timothy J. M. *The Judean Poor and the Fourth Gospel.* Cambridge: Cambridge University Press, 2006.

Lohse, Eduard. *The First Christians: Their Beginnings, Writings, and Beliefs.* Translated by Eugene Boring. Philadelphia: Fortress Press, 1983.

_______. *Theological Ethics of the New Testament.* Minneapolis: Fortress Press, 1991.

Long, Edward LeRoy. *A Survey of Christian Ethics*. New York: Oxford University Press, 1967.

Longenecker, Richard N. *The Christology of Early Jewish Christianity*. London: SCM Press, 1970.

Maclntyre, Alasdair. *A Short History of Ethics*. Special Indian edition. London and New York: Routledge, 1998.

Maniparampil, Jose. *Reading the Fourth Gospel.* Bangalore: Claretion Publications, 2004.

Martyn, J. Louis. *History and Theology in the Fourth Gospel*, 3rd edition. Louisville, London: Westminster John Knox Press, 2003.

_______. *The Gospel of John in Christian History*. New York: Paulist Press, 1979.

Marxsen, Willi. *New Testament Foundations for Christian Ethics.* Translated by O. C. Dean. Minneapolis: Fortress Press, 2007.

Masih, Y. *A Critical History of Western Philosophy*. 5th revised & enlarged edition. Delhi: Motilal Banarsidass, 1994.

Matera, Frank J. *New Testament Ethics: The Legacies of Jesus and Paul.* Louisville: Westminster John Knox Press, 1996.

_______. *New Testament Christology.* Louisville: Westminster John Knox Press, 1999.

Matson, T. B. *Biblical Ethics: A Guide to the Ethical Message of the Scriptures from Genesis to Revelation*. Georgia: Mercer University Press, 1967.

McGrath, James F. *John's Apologetic Christology: Legitimation and Development in Johannine Christology*. Cambridge: Cambridge University Press, 2001.

McQuilkin, Robertson. *An Introduction to Biblical Ethics.* 2nd edition. Secunderabad: OM Books, 2002.

Meeks, Wayne A. *The Moral World of the First Christians*. London: SPCK, 1986.

Miranda, J. P. *Being and the Messiah: The Message of St. John*. Maryknoll, New York: Orbis Books, 1977.

Moloney, Francis J. *Belief in the Word.* Minneapolis: Fortress Press, 1993.

Morey, Robert A. *The Bible, Natural Theology and Natural Law: Conflict or Compromise?* Millerstone: Christian Scholars Press, 2010.

Neyrey, Jerome H. *The Gospel of John in Cultural Perspective*. Michigan: Wm. B. Eerdmans Publishing Company, 2009.

Neyrey, Jerome H. *An Ideology of Revolt: John's Christology in Social-Science Perspective*. Philadelphia: Fortress Press, 1988.

Nicol, W. *The Semeia in the Fourth Gospel.* Leiden: E. J. Brill, 1972.

Okure,Teresa. *The Johannine Approach to Mission: A Contextual Study of John 4:1-42.* WUNT 2/32. Tubingen: Mohr Siebeck, 1988.

Painter, John. *John: Witness & Theologian*. Delhi: ISPCK, 1974.

Pollard, T. E. *Johannine Christology and the Early Church*. Cambridge: Cambridge University Press, 1970.

Powell, Mark Allan. *What is Narrative Criticism?* Minneapolis: Fortress Press, 1990.

Pregeant, Russel. *Knowing Truth, Doing Good: Engaging New Testament Ethics*. Minneapolis: Fortress Press, 2008.

Pryor, John W. *John: Evangelist of the Covenant People*. Illinois: InterVarsity Press, 1992.

Reale, Giovanni. *History of Ancient Philosophy IV, A: The Schools of the Imperial Age*. Edited and translated by John R. Catan. New York: State University of New York Press, 1990.

Reinhartz, Adele. *Befriending the Beloved Disciple: A Jewish Reading of the Gospel of John*. New York: Continuum, 2001.

Reis, Burkhard, ed. *The Virtuous Life in Greek Ethics*. Cambridge: University Press, 2006.

Rensberger, David K. *Johannine Faith and Liberating Community*. Philadelphia: The Westminster Press,1988.

________. *Overcoming the World: Politics and Community in the Gospel of John*. London: SPCK, 1988.

Resseguie, James L. *Narrative Criticism of the New Testament: An Introduction*. Michigan: Baker Academic, 2005.

Russell, D. S. *Between the Testaments*. Philadelphia: Fortress Press, 1965.

Sadananda, Daniel Rathnakara. *The Johannine Exegesis of God: An Exploration into the Johannine Understanding of God*. Berlin, New York: Walter de Gruyter, 2004.

Sanders, E. P. *Judaism Practice & Belief 63 BCE – 66CE*. London/Philadelphia: SCM Press/ Trinity Press International, 1992.

Sanders, J. N. and B. A. Mastin, *The Gospel According to St John*. Peabody, Massachusetts: Hendrickson Publishers, 1968.

Sanders, Jack T. *Ethics in the New Testament: Change and Development*. London: SCM Press Ltd, 1975.

Schrage,Wolfgang. *The Ethics of the New Testament*. Translated by David E. Green. Philadelphia: Fortress Press, 1988.

Scott, C. A. Anderson. *New Testament Ethics: An Introduction*. Cambridge: Cambridge University Press, 1948.

Segovia, Fernando F. *What is John? Literary and Social Readings of the Fourth Gospel*. Vol. 2. Edited by Fernando F. Segovia. Atlanta: Scholars Press, 1998.

Sell, Canon. *The Talmud, Mishnah and Midrash*. Madras: SPCK, 1928.

Smith, D. Moody. *Johannine Christianity*. Edinburgh: T&T Clark, 1984.

Smith, D. Moody. *The Theology of the Gospel of John*. Cambridge: Cambridge University Press, 1995.

Smith, D. Moody. *Johannine Christianity: Essays on its Setting, Sources, and Theology*. South Carolina: University of South Carolina Press, 1989.

Stephen, M. *Christian Ethics: Issues and Insights*. New Delhi: Concept Publishing Company, 2007.

Strecker, Georg. *Theology of the New Testament.* Translated by M. Eugen Boring. Berlin: de Gruyter; Louisville: Westminster John Knox, 2000.

Taizt, Emily. *Introduction to the World's Major Religions: Judaism.* Vol. I. Edited by Lee W. Bailey. London: Greenwood Press, 2006.

Theissen, Gerd. *Sociology of Early Palestinian Christianity*. Philadelphia: Fortress Press, 1978.

Thomas, John Christopher. *Footwashing in John 13 and the Johannine Community. JSNTSup* 61, Sheffield: Sheffield Academic Press, 1991.

Thomas, John Christopher. *Footwashing in John 13 and Johannine Community.* London & New York: Bloomsbury & T&T Clark, 2004.

Thompson, Marianne M. *The Humanity of Jesus in the Fourth Gospel.* Philadelphia: Fortress Press, 1988.

Thompson, Marianne M. *The God of the Gospel of John*. Michigan: Wm. B. Eerdmanns Publishing Company, 2001.

Tidball, Derek. *An Introduction to the Sociology of the New Testament*. Exeter: The Paternoster Press, 1983.

Titus, Harold H. *Ethics for Today.* 3rd edition. New York: American Book, 1957.

Tuckett, Christopher M. *Christology and the New Testament: Jesus and His Earliest Followers*. Edinburgh: University Press, 2001.

Turner, Max. *The Holy Spirit and Spiritual Gifts – Then and Now.* Carlisle: Paternoster, 1999.

Vallianippuram,Thomas. *New Society in John's Gospel.* Aloor: Biblia Publications, 2008.

van der Watt, Jan G. *Family of the King: Dynamics of Metaphor in the Gospel according to John*. Leiden: Brill, 2000.

Verhey, Allen. *The Great Reversal: Ethics and the New Testament*. Michigan: Wm. B. Eerdmans Publishing Company, 1984.

Wheaton, Gerry. *The Role of Jewish Feasts in John's Gospel.* Cambridge: Cambridge University Press, 2015.

White, R. E. O. *Biblical Ethics: The Changing Continuity of Christian Ethics.* Vol. 1. Exeter: the Paternoster Press, 1979.

Wright, N. T. *The New Testament and the People of God*. Minneapolis: Fortress Press, 1992.

Books (Edited)

Alstrup Dahl, Nils. "The Johannine Church and History." *The Interpretation of John.* 2nd edition. Edited by John Ashton. Edinburgh: T&T Clark, 1997.

Ashton, John. "Introduction: The Problem of John." *The Interpretation of John.* 2nd edition. Edited by John Ashton. Edinburgh: T&T Clark, 1997.

Bauckham, Richard. "Monotheism and Christology in the Gospel of John." *Contours of Christology in the New Testament.* Edited by Richard N. Longenecker. Michigan/UK: Wm B. Eerdmans Publishing Company, 2005, 148-166.

Bennema, Cornelis. "Virtue Ethics in the Gospel of John: The Johannine Characters as Moral agents." *Rediscovering John: Essays on the Fourth Gospel in Honour of Frederic Manns*, edited by L. D. Chrupcała. Milan: Terra Santa, 2013, 167–181.

Borgen, Peder. "God's Agent in the Fourth Gospel." *The Interpretation of John.* 2nd edition. Edited by John Ashton. Edinburgh: T&T Clark, 1997, 83-95.

Burge, Gary M. "Situating John's Gospel in History." *Jesus in Johannine Tradition.* Edited by Robert Tomson Fortna and Tom Thatcher. Louisville and London: Westminster John Knox Press, 2001, 35-46.

Caragounis, Chrys C. "Abide in Me": The New Mode of Relationship between Jesus and His Followers as a Basis for Christian Ethics (John 15)." *Rethinking the Ethics of John: "Implicit Ethics" in the Johannine Writings.* Edited by Jan G. van der Watt and Ruben Zimmermann. Tubingen: Mohr Siebeck, 2012, 250-263.

Charlesworth, James H. "The Gospel of John: Exclusivism Caused by a Social Setting Different from That of Jesus (John 11:54 and 14:6)." *Anti-Judaism and the Fourth Gospel.* Edited by R. Bieringer, D. Pollefeyt, and F. Vandecastelle–Vanneuville. Louisville: Westminster John Knox Press, 2001, 247-278.

Culpepper, R. Alan. "The Christology of the Johannine Writings." *Who Do You Say That I Am? Essays on Christology in Honor of Jack Dean Kingsbury.* 1st edition. Edited by Mark Allan Powell and David R. Baur. Louisville, Kentucky: Westminster John Knox Press, 1999, 66-87.

_______. "Anti-Judaism in the Fourth Gospel as a Theological Problem for Christian Interpreters. " *Anti-Judaism and the Fourth Gospel.* Edited by R. Bieringer, D. Pollefeyt, and F. Vandecastelle-Vanneuville. Louisville: Westminster John Knox Press, 2001, 61-82.

de Boer, M. C. "Narrative Criticism, Historical Criticism, and the Gospel of John." *The Interpretation of John.* 2nd edition. Edited by John Ashton. Edinburgh: T&T Clark, 1997, 301-314.

Dokki, Trond S. "Irony and Sectarianism in the Gospel of John." *New Readings in John*. JSNTS 182. Edited by J. Nissen and S. Pedersen. London: Sheffield Academic Press, 1999, 83-107.

Du Rand, Jan A. "The Creation Motif in the Fourth Gospel: Perspectives on its Narratological Function Within a Judaistic Background." *Theology and Christology in the Fourth Gospel.* Edited by G. Van Belle, J. G. Van Der Watt and P. Maritz. Leuven: Leuven University Press, 2005, 21-46.

Edwards, Ruth B. "The Johannine Epistles." *The Johannine Literature*. Edited by Barnabas Lindars, Ruth B. Edwards & John M. Count. Sheffield: Sheffield Academic Press Ltd., 2000, 110-205.

Glicksman, Andrew T. "Beyond Sophia." *Rethinking the Ethics of John: "Implicit Ethics" in the Johannine Writings*. Edited by Jan G. van der Watt and Ruben Zimmermann. Tubingen: Mohr Siebeck, 2012, 83-101.

Glicksman, Andrew T. "Light, Truth, and Time: Ethical Connections between Old Testament Wisdom Literature and John's Gospel" a paper presented during conference: Ethics in the Johannine Literature (Nijmegen, May 2010).

Hays, Richard B. "Mapping the Field: Approaches to New Testament Ethics." *Identity, Ethics and Ethos in the New Testament.* Edited by Jan G. van der Watt. Berlin: Walter de Gruyter, 2006, 3-22.

Karakolis, Christos. "Semeia Conveying Ethics in the Gospel According to John." *Rethinking the Ethics of John: "Implicit Ethics" in the Johannine Writings.* Edited by Jan G. Van der Watt and Ruben Zimmermann. Tubingen: Mohr Siebeck, 2012, 192-212.

Labaln, Michael "It's Only Love"- Is That All? Limits and Potentials of Johannine "Ethic" – A Critical Evaluation of Research." In *Rethinking the Ethics of John: "Implicit Ethics" in the Johannine Writings.* Edited by Jan G. van der Watt and Ruben Zimmermann. Tubingen: Mohr Siebeck, 2012, 3-43.

Lamarche, Paul. "The Prologue of John." *The Interpretation of John*. 2nd edition. Edited by John Ashton. Edinburgh: T&T Clark, 1997, 47-65,

Lohr, Hermut. "'Εργον as an Element of Moral Language in John." *Rethinking the Ethics of John: "Implicit Ethics" in the Johannine Writings.* Edited by Jan G. van der Watt and Ruben Zimmermann.Tubingen: Mohr Siebeck, 2012, 229-249.

Longenecker, Richard N. "Christological Materials in the Early Christian Communities." *Contours of Christology in the New Testament*. Edited by Richard N. Longenecker. Michigan/UK: Wm. B. Eerdmans Publishing Company, 2005, 47-76.

Lund, Glen. "The Joys and Dangers of Ethics in John's Gospel." *Rethinking the Ethics of John: "Implicit Ethics" in the Johannine Writings.* Edited by Jan G.

van der Watt and Ruben Zimmermann.Tubingen: Mohr Siebeck, 2012, 264-289.

Meeks, Wayne A. "The Ethics of the Fourth Evangelist." *Exploring the Gospel of John: Essays in Honour of Dwight Moody Smith.* Edited by R. Alan Culpepper and C. Clifton Black Louisville: Westminster John Knox Press, 1996, 317-326.

_______. "The Man from Heaven in Johannine Sectarianism." *The Interpretation of John.* 2nd edition. Edited by John Ashton. Edinburgh: T&T Clark, [1986] 1997.

_______. "The Divine Agent and His Counterfeit in Philo and the Fourth Gospel." *Aspects of Religions Propaganda in Judaism and Early Christianity.* Edited by Elizabeth Schussler Fiorenza. Notre Dame: University of Notre Dame Press, 1976, 43-67.

Mulholland, M. Robert. "Sociological Criticism." *Interpreting the New Testament: Essays on Methods and Issues.* Edited by David Alan Black & David S. Dockery. Nashville: Broadmann & Holman Publishers, 2001.

Nissen, Johannes. "Community and Ethics in the Gospel of John." *New Readings in John: Literary and Theological Perspectives.* Edited by Johannes Nissen and Sigfred Pederson. Sheffield: Sheffield Academic Press, 1999, 194-212.

R. G. Loader, William. "The Law and Ethics in John's Gospel." *Rethinking the Ethics of John: "Implicit Ethics" in the Johannine Writings.* Edited by Jan G. Van der Watt and Ruben Zimmermann. Tubingen: Mohr Siebeck, 2012, 143-158.

Rabens, Volker. "Johannine Perspective in Ethical Enabling in the Context of Stoic and Philonic Ethics." *Rethinking the Ethics of John: "Implicit Ethics" in the Johannine Writings.* Edited by Jan G. van der Watt and Reuben Zimmermann. Tubingen: Mohr Sieback, 2012, 114-142.

Smith, D. Moody. "Ethics and the Interpretation of the Fourth Gospel of John." *Word, Theology, and Community in John.* Edited by John Painter, R. Alan Culpepper, and Fernando F. Segovia. St. Louis: Chalice Press, 2002, 109-122.

Smith, Morton. "Palestinian Judaism in the First Century." Reprint in *Essays in Graeco-Roman and Related Talmudic Literature.* New York: n. p., 1977, 195-196.

van der Watt, Jan G. "Ethics alive in Imagery." *Imagery in the Gospel of John: Terms, Forms, Themes, and Theology of Johannine Figurative Language.* Edited by. Jorg Frey, Jan G. van der Watt and Ruben Zimmermann. Tubingen: Mohr Siebeck, 2006, 421-448.

_______. "Ethics Through the Power of Language." *Moral Language in the New Testament.* Edited by Ruben Zimmermann and Jan G. van der Watt. Tubingen: Mohr Siebeck, 2010, 139-167.

_______. "Radical Social Redefinition and Radical Love: Ethics and Ethos in the Gospel According to John." *Identity, Ethics, and Ethos in the New Testament.* Edited by Jan G. van der Watt. Berlin: Walter de Gruyter, 2006, 107-134.

_______. Ethics of/and the Opponents of Jesus in John's Gospel." *Rethinking the Ethics of John: "Implicit Ethics" in the Johannine Writings*. Edited by Jan G. van der Watt and Ruben Zimmermann. Tubingen: Mohr Siebeck, 2012, 175-191.

Weyer-Menkhoff, Karl. "The Response of Jesus: Ethics in John by Considering Scripture as Work of God." *Rethinking the Ethics of John: "Implicit Ethics" in the Johannine Writings.* Edited by Jan G. Van der Watt and Ruben Zimmermann. Tubingen: Mohr Siebeck, 2012, 159-174.

Witherington III, Ben. "Jesus as the Alpha and Omega of New Testament Thought." *Contours of Christology in the New Testament.* Edited by Richard N. Longenecker. Michigan/UK: Wm. B. Eerdmanns Publishing Company, 2005, 25-46.

Zimmermann, Ruben "Is There Ethics in the Gospel of John." *Rethinking the Ethics of John: "Implicit Ethics" in the Johannine Writings.* Edited by Jan G. van der watt and Ruben Zimmermann.Tubingen: Mohr Siebeck, 2012, 44-82.

Commentaries

Barrett, C. K. *The Gospel According to St John: An Introduction with Commentary and Note on the Greek Text.* 2nd edition. Philadelphia: Westminster Press, 1978.

_______. *The Gospel According to St John: An Introduction with Commentary and Notes on the Greek Text*. SPCK: London, 1960.

Beasley-Murray, George R. *WBC*: John vol. 36. Texas: Word Books Publisher, 1987.

Boice, James Montgomery. *An Expositional Commentary: The Gospel of John.* Vol. 4. Michigan: Baker Books, 1999.

Brown, Raymond E. *The Anchor Bible: The Gospel According to John.* Vol. 1. New York: Doubleday & Company, 1966.

_______. *The Anchor Bible: The Gospel According to John.* Vol. 2. New York: Doubleday & Company, 1966.

Bultmann, Rudolf. *The Gospel of John: A Commentary.* Translated by G. R. Beasley-Murray, R. W. N. Hoare and J. K. Riches. Philadelphia: Westminster Press, 1971.

Carson, D. A. *The Gospel According to John*. Michigan/U.K.: Wm. B. Eerdmans Publishing Company, 1991.

Hoskyns, Edwyn Clement. *The Fourth Gospel.* 2nd edition. London: Faber and Faber, 1961.

_______. *The Fourth Gospel.* Edited by Francis Noel Davey. London: Faber and Faber Limited, 1947.

Kanagaraj, Jey J. and Ian S. Kem, *Gospel of John*. Bangalore: Asia Theological Association, 2000.

Kanagaraj, Jey J. *The Gospel of John: A Commentary*. Secunderabad: OM Books, 2005.

Keener, Craig S. *The Gospel of John: A Commentary.* Vol. 1. Peabody, Massachusetts: Hendrickson Publishers, 2003.

_______. *The Gospel of John: A Commentary.* Vol. 2. Peabody, Massachusetts: Hendrickson Publishers, 2003.

Lindars, Barnabas. *The Gospel of John.* Michigan: Wm. B. Eerdmans Publishing Company, [1972] 1987.

Moloney, Francis J. *The Gospel of John.* Edited by Daniel J.Harrington. Minnesota: The Liturgical Press, 1998.

_______. *The Gospel of John: Text and Context.* Leiden: Brill, 2005.

Morris, Leon. *The Gospel According to John: The English Text with Introduction, Exposition and Notes*. Michigan: William B. Eerdmans Publishing Company, 1971.

O'Day, Gail R. "The Gospel of John: Introduction, Commentary, and Reflections." *The New Interpreter's Bible.* Vol. 9. Nashville: Abingdon Press, 1995.

Ridderbos, Herman. *The Gospel of John: A Theological Commentary*. Translated by John Vriend. Michigan/Cambridge: Wm. B. Eerdmans Publishing Company, 1997.

Sanders, J. N. and B. A. Mastin. *The Gospel According to St. John*. Peabody, Massachusetts: Hendrickson Publishers, 1968.

Schnackenburg, Rudolf. *The Gospel According to St. John.* Vol. 1. Translated by Kevin Smyth. Kent: Burns & Oates, 1968.

_______. *The Gospel according to St. John*. Vol. 2. Translated by Cecily Hastings, Francis McDonagh, David Smith & Richard Foley. London: Burns and Oates, 1980.

_______. *The Gospel According to St. John.* Vol. 3. Translated by David Smith and G. A. Kon. London & Kent: Burns & Oates, 1982.

Smith, D. Moody. *ANTC: John*. Nashville: Abington Press, 1999.

Tate, W. Randolph. *Biblical Interpretation: An Integrated Approach*. Third edition. Grand Rapids, Michigan: Baker Academic, 2008.

Classical and Rabbinical Writings

Aristotle. *Nicomacean Ethics. The Basic Works of Aristotle*. Translated by W. D. Ross. Edited by Richard McKeon. New York: Random House, 1941.

Plato. *Gorgias. The Dialogues of Plato*. Translated into English with Analyses and Introductions by B. Jowett. Vol. 2. Oxford: Clarendon Press, 1953.

_______. *Phaedrus. The Dialogues of Plato.*Translated into English with Analyses and Introductions by B. Jowett. Vol. 3. Oxford: Clarendon Press, 1953.

_______. *Republic. The Dialogues of Plato*. Translated into English with Analyses and Introductions by B. Jowett. Vol. 2. Oxford: Clarendon Press, 1953.

The Mishnah. Translated from the Hebrew with Introduction and Brief Explanatory Notes by Herbert Danby. Oxford: Oxford University Press, 1933.

Dictionaries and Encyclopedias

Abelson, Raziel and Kai Nielsen, "History of Ethics." *The Encyclopedia of Philosophy*. Vols. 3 & 4. Edited by Paul Edwards, *et al.* New York/London: Macmillan Publishing Company & The Free Press/Collier Macmillan Publishers, 1967, 81-117.

Barrois, G. A. "Temple." *Interpreter's Dictionary of the Bible, R-Z.* Edited by George Arthur Buttrick *et al.* Nashville: Abington Press, 1962, 560-568.

Blackman, E. C. "Faith." *The Interpreter's Dictionary of the Bible, E-J*. Edited by George Arthur Buttrick *et al.* Nashville: Abington Press, 1962, 222-234.

Borowitz, Eugene B. "Judaism: An Overview." *The Encyclopedia of Religion*, vol. 7. Edited by Mircea Eliade *et al.,* New York/London: Macmillan Publishing Company/Collier Macmillan Publishers, 1987, 127-149.

Bultmann, Rudolf. "πιστεύω, πίστις, πιστός." *TDNT*. Vol. 6. Edited by Gerhard Friedrich. Michigan: Wm. B. Eerdmans Publishing Company, 1968, 174-228.

Buttrick, George Arthur *et al. The Interpreter's Dictionary of the Bible*. Nashville, New York: Abington Press, 1962.

Glasswell, M. E. "ἦθος ους τό." *Exegetical Dictionary of the New Testament*, vol. 1. Edited by Horst Balz and Gerhard Schneider. Michigan: Wm. B. Eerdmans Publishing Company, 1980.

Hare, R. M. "Ethics." *A Dictionary of Christian Ethics*. Edited by John Macquarrie. London: SCM Press, 1967, 114-116.

Hempel, J. "Ethics in the OT." *The Interpreters Dictionary of the Bible*. Edited by George Arthur Buttrick, *et al.* Nashville: Abington Press, 1962, 153-161.

Jessop, T. E. "History of Ethics." *A Dictionary of Christian Ethics*. Edited by John Macquarrie. London: SCM Press, 1967, 116-119.

Klassen, William. "Love in NT and Early Jewish." *The Anchor Bible Dictionary.* Vol. 4. Edited by David Noel Freedman *et al.* New York: Doubleday, 1992, 381-396.

Renstorf, Karl Heinrich. "σημεῖον." *TDNT*. Vol. 2. Edited by Gerhard Friedrich. Michigan: Wm. B. Eerdmans Publishing Company, 1971, 200-269.

Shepherd, M. H. "Foot Washing." *The Interpreter's Dictionary of the Bible, E-J.* Edited by George Arthur Buttrick *et al.* Nashville: Abington Press, 1962, 308.

Sonne, I. "Synagogue." *The Interpreter's Dictionary of the Bible*. Edited by George Arthur Buttrick, *et al.* Nashville: Abington Press, 1962, 476-491.

Waddams, Herbert. "Marriage." *A Dictionary of Christian Ethics*. Edited by John Macquarrie. London: SCM Press, 1967, 206-207.

Journals and Periodicals

Beckwith, Roger T. "The Pre-history and Relationships of Pharisees, Sadducees and Essence: A Tentative Reconstruction." *RevQ* 11 (1982): 27.

Bennema, Cornelis. "Moral Transformation in the Johannine Writings." *In die Skriflig* 51/3 (2017): 1-7.

Bolyki, Janos. "Ethics in the Gospel of John." *Communio Viatorum* 45 (2003): 63-80.

Brown, Raymond E. "The Paraclete in the Fourth Gospel." *NTS 13* (1967): 113-132.

Carapiet, M. "Jesus and Christian Ethics Today." *Jeevadhara* 23 (1993): 437-455.

Collins, Adela Yarbro. "The Origin of the Designation of Jesus as 'Son of Man.'" *HTR* 80 (1987): 391-408.

Harin, Patrick J. "Remain in Me (John 15:15): The Foundation of the Ethical and Its Consequence in the Farewell Discourses." *Neotestamentica* 25/2 (1991): 341-356.

Kaiser, Jr. Walter C. "New Approaches to Old Testament Ethics." *JETS* 35/3 (September, 1992): 289.

Kanagaraj, Jey J. "The Implied Ethics of the Fourth Gospel: A Reinterpretation of the Decalogue." *Tyndale Bulletin* 52/1(2001): 33-60.

Keck, Leander E. "Rethinking "New Testament Ethics."*JBL* 115/1 (1996): 3-16.

Kvalbein, Hans. "The Kingdom of God in the Ethics of Jesus." *Studia Theologia* 51 (1997): 60-84.

Manson, T.W. "The Son of Man in Daniel, Enoch and the Gospels." *Bulletin of the John Rylands Library*. Vol. 32 (1950): 171-193.

McGrath, James F. "Change in Christology: New Testament Models and the Contemporary Task." *Irish Theological Quarterly* 63/1 (1998): 42-49.

Meeks, Wayne A. "The Man from Heaven in Johannine Sectarianism." *JBL* 91 (1972): 42-72.

Moule, C. F. D. "The Individualism of the Fourth Gospel." *Novum Testamentum* 5 (1962): 171-190.

O'Day, Gail R. "Toward a Narrative Study of John." *Interpretation* 49 (1995): 340-346.

O'Grady, J. F. "Johannine Ecclesiology: A Critical Evaluation." *Biblical Theology Bulletin* 7 (1977): 36-44.

Smalley, S. S. "Diversity and Development in John." *NTS* 17 (1970): 276-292.

Spohn, William C. "Jesus and Christian Ethics." *Theological Studies* 56 (1995): 92-107.

van der Watt, Jan G. "Ethics and Ethos in the Gospel according to John." *ZNW* 97 (2006): 147-176.

van der Watt, Jan G. The Gospel of John's Perception of Ethical Behavior." *In die Skriflig* 45 (2011): 431–447.

Reference Books

A Greek- English Lexicon of the New Testament and other Early Christian Literature. 3rd edition. Revised and edited by F. W. Danker based on Walter Baur's. Chicago & London: University of Chicago Press, [1957, 1979] 2000.

Arndt, William F. & F. Wilbur Gingrich. *A Greek- English Lexicon of the New and Other Early Christian Literature*. Fourth revised & augmented edition. Illinois/Cambridge: University of Chicago Press/Cambridge University Press, 1952.

Barton, Stephen C. "The Epistles and Christian Ethics." *The Cambridge Companion to Christian Ethics*. Edited by Robin Gill. Cambridge: University Press, 2001.

Bauer, W., W. F. Arndt, and F. W. Gingrich. *A Greek-English Lexicon of the New Testamernt and Other Early Christian Literature.* 2nd edition. Revise and augmented by F. W. Gingrich and F. W. Danker. Chicago: University of Chicago Press, 1979.

Davies, G. Henton "Tabernacle." *The Interpreter's Bible*. Edited by George Arthur Buttrick *et al.* Nashville: Abington Press, 1962, 498-506.

Herr, Moshe David. "Festivals." *Jewish Values*. Jerusalem: Keter Publishing House, 1974, 287-301.

Jacobs, Rabbi Louis. "Judaism." *Jewish Values.* Jerusalem: Keter Publishing House, 1974, 3-26.

Licht, Jacob and Andre Neher, "Ethics."*Jewish Values*. Jerusalem: Keter Publishing House Jerusalem Ltd., 1974, 132-146.

Spicq, Ceslas. "πίστις." *Theological Lexicon of the New Testament,* παι – ψευ. Vol. 3. Translated and edited by James D. Ernst. Peabody, Massachusetts: Hendrickson Publishers, 1994, 110-116.

Teutsch, David A. "Ethical Theories in the Reconstructionist Movement." *The Oxford Handbook of Jewish Ethics and Morality.* Edited by Elliot N. Dorff and Jonathan K. Crane. Oxford: Oxford University Press, 2013, 259-271.

The Greek New Testament. Fourth Revised Edition. Edited by Kurt aland, *et al.* D-Stuttgart: Deutsche Bibelgesellschaft, 1994.

The Holy Bible. New Revised Standard Version. Michigan: Zondervan Publishing House, 1996.

The Holy Bible. New International Version. Michigan: Zondervan Publishing House [1973, 1978, 1984] 1989.

The New Greek – English Interlinear Testament. Illinois: Tyndale House Publishers, 1990.

Webliography

Catholic-resources.org/John/Vocab-Life.html. Accessed on 24-07-2017.

http://ijs.org.au/The-Ethical-Teachings-of-Judaism/default.aspx. Accessed on 11-08-2017.

https://toriavey.com > what-is-shavuot. Accessed on 30-08-2017.

http://links.myjewishlearning.com. Accessed on 05-10-2017.

www.myjewishlearning.com. Accessed on 30-08-2017.

www.hebrew4christians.com. Accessed on 30-08-2017.